Inequalities of the World

Inequalities of the World

Edited by Göran Therborn

VERSO

London • New York

First published by Verso 2006
© in the collection, Verso 2006
© in the contributions, the individual contributors

All rights reserved
The moral rights of the authors have been asserted

1 3 5 7 9 10 8 6 4 2

Verso
UK: 6 Meard Street, London W1F 0EG
USA: 180 Varick Street, New York, NY 10014–4606
www.versobooks.com

Verso is the imprint of New Left Books

ISBN-13: 978–84467–015–4 (hbk)
ISBN-10: 1–84467–015–5 (hbk)
ISBN-13: 978–84467–519–7 (pbk)
ISBN-10: 1–84467–519–X (pbk)

British Library Cataloguing in Publication Data
A catalogue record for this book is available from the British Library

Library of Congress Cataloging-in-Publication Data
A catalog record for this book is available from the Library of Congress

Typeset in Baskerville by Hewer Text UK Ltd, Edinburgh
Printed in the UK by Bath Press

Contents

List of Tables and Figures   vii

List of Abbreviations and Acronyms   xi

Preface   xiii
Göran Therborn

1 Meaning, Mechanisms, Patterns, and Forces: An Introduction   1
Göran Therborn

Part I   Varieties of Inequality

2 Do Health Inequalities Persist in the New Global Order?
A European Perspective   61
Denny Vågerö

3 How French and American Workers Define Cultural Membership   93
Michèle Lamont

4 Economic Change and Social Mobility   119
Michael Hout

5 Nonstandard Employment Relations and
Labour Market Inequality: Cross-national Patterns   136
Arne L. Kalleberg

6 Knowledge and Inequality   163
Peter Weingart

Part II   Case Studies

7 Inequality in Brazil: Facts and Perceptions   193
   Elisa P. Reis
8 Globalization and Inequality in Rural China   220
   Huang Ping
9 Classes in the Making? The Russian Social Structure in Transition   247
   Markku Kivinen
10 Are Social Classes Really Dead? A French Paradox in
      Class Dynamics   295
   Louis Chauvel

   List of Contributors   319
   Index   323

List of Tables and Figures

Tables

1.1 Inequality Mechanisms and their Interactive Dynamics   14
1.2 Equality Mechanisms   14
1.3 Life Expectancy at Birth, 1965 and 2002   21
1.4 Comparative Life Expectancy, 1900–2002   21
1.5 Landmarks of Twentieth-Century Existential (In)Equality   24
1.6 Countries with Abnormally Low Male–Female Differences
in Life Expectancy, 2000–05   25
1.7 The Least Unequal Countries of the World, and their
Routes: Disposable Income after Taxes and Transfers   27
1.8 The Most Unequal Countries of the World   29
1.9 Mainstream Inequality: The Big Countries   32
1.10 Women's Income as a Percentage of Men's, *c*. 2000   33
1.11 National and International Income Shares around 2000   34
1.12 Vital Inequality in England and Wales, 1910–93   36

4.1. Combinations of Structural Mobility and
Association in a Mobility Table   123

5.1 Characteristics of Standard and Nonstandard Work
Arrangements   138
5.2 Percentage of Part-Time, Fixed-Term Temporary, and
Self-Employed Persons, by Country   143

7.1 Principal Obstacles to Democracy in Brazil According
to the Elites   201
7.2 Principal Domestic Problems in Brazil According to the Elites   202
7.3 Principal Medium-term Domestic Objectives in Brazil According
to the Elites   203
7.4 The Worst Consequences of Poverty in Large Brazilian Cities   206
7.5 Explanations for the Failure of Social Policies in Brazil
According to the Elites   207
7.6 Political Priorities to Combat Inequality in Brazil According
to the Elites   208

8.1 Income Inequality in Rural China and Urban China   228
8.2 Per Capita Annual Income and its Use among Urban
and Rural Households   229
8.3 Regional Disparity: Per Capita Income of Urban Households   230
8.4 Regional Disparity: Per Capita Income of Rural Households   230
8.5 Per Capita Annual Net Income of Rural Households   233

9.1 Class Structure in St Petersburg, the Baltic Countries and
Finland, 1994/96   265
9.2 Scales Estimations of the Middle Class   267
9.3 Selected Features of the Situation of Russian Class Groups, 1996   269
9.4 Social Benefits Provided by the Labour Collective,
1996/Earlier   279
9.5 Participation of Russian Social Classes in Privatization   282
9.6 The Sectoral Composition of Employment: Russia 1990–2000   286
9.7 Alternative Models of Class Relations   287

10.1 Catch-up Time-lag, 1955–2000   304
10.2 Average Share in the Household Budget and *Cadres/Ouvriers*
Gaps, 1995   306

Figures

1.1 World Income Inequality, 1820–2000   37
1.2 US Income Inequality, 1929–2000   40
1.3 Global and Sub-Global Determinants of Global Inequalities   43
2.1 Infant Mortality in Sweden, 1751–1970   63
2.2 Trends in Infant Mortality by Social Class, England and Wales, 1911–71   64

2.3 Whooping Cough: Death Rates for Children Under 15, England and Wales, 1850–1970   66

2.4 Life Expectancy at Birth by Per Capita Total Health Expenditure, 1997   68

2.5 Life Expectancy by Regions in the World, 1950–2000   69

2.6 Dispersion Measure of Mortality for Regions in the World, 1950–2000   74

2.7 Age-Standardized Mortality from All Causes Among Men in Regions of Europe, 1990–91   76

2.8 Life Expectancy at Birth in Russia, Estonia, Finland, and Sweden, 1970–2000, Men and Women Combined   76

2.9 Age-Standardized Mortality from Circulatory Diseases among Men in France, Poland, Russia, and the United Kingdom, 1950–98   77

2.10 Mortality for Non-Manual and Manual Workers in Nine European Countries, Ranked by Absolute Level of Mortality of Manual Workers; Age Groups 45–59   84

2.11 Probability of Dying Between 45th and 65th Birthday: Men in Non-Manual and Manual Classes   85

2.12 East/West Mortality Rates Ratio Compared to Low/High Social Class Mortality Rate Ratio, for 16 Causes of Death   87

4.1. Percentage of American Men Employed in Professional or Managerial Occupation by Father's Occupation and Year   124

4.2. Percentage of African American Men Employed in Professional or Managerial Occupation by Father's Occupation and Year   128

4.3. Percentage of African American Men Who Were Upwardly Mobile Between 1962 and 1973 by Father's Occupation and Occupation in 1962   129

4.4. Percentage Professional or Manager by Father's Occupationand Years: Russia   132

6.1 Adult Illiteracy Rates in Selected Countries   168

6.2 Expected Years of Schooling by Gender   169

6.3 Number of Students per 100,000 Inhabitants   170

6.4 Gross Enrolment Ratios by Gender and Region, 1980 and 1995   170

6.5 Public Expenditure on Education as Percentage of GDP, 1980 and 1995   171

6.6 Public Expenditure on Research and Experimental Development as Percentage of GDP   172

6.7 Scientists and Engineers in Research and Experimental Development per Million People   172

6.8 Research and Experimental Development Personnel by Sector   173

6.9 Scientific Output: Number of Publications per Year in ISI Journals   174

6.10 Number of Publications in ISI Journals per 1,000 Inhabitants, by Year 175
6.11 Share of Citations in International Scientific Literature (ISI),
1996–2000   175
6.12 Number of Book Titles per Year, 1990s   176

7.1 Principal National Problems According to Brazilians   210
7.2 Principal National Problems According to Brazilian Elites   210
7.3 Principal National Problems According to Brazilians with
Different Levels of Education   211
7.4 Distribution of the Perception of Brazilians from Different
Social Classes Regarding the Importance of Luck in Personal
Advancement   212
7.5 Who Is Responsible for Reducing Social Inequalities in the
Opinion of Brazilians   214
7.6 Social Policy Priorities According to Brazilians   215
7.7 Social Policy Priorities According to the Elites   215

8.1 Rural–Urban Population Ratio in the National Census, 1953–2000   230
8.2 Rural Labour in Agriculture vs. Non-agriculture, 1985–2000   231
8.3 Income and Expenditure Structure in Rural Households, 1978–2001   232

9.1 The Structure of Russian Culture: Binary Code and Unsuitable Reality   255
9.2 Poverty Rate Series, 1985–99   272
9.3 Cumulative SOS Contributions of Per Capita Income, Inequality
and Poverty Line Effect, 1985–99   274
9.4 Level of Economic Development and Inequality in Incomes
Distribution   275
9.5 Changes in Income Inequality in Selected Transition Economies   276
9.6 Winners and Losers from Reform   285

10.1 Number of Book Titles in the Catalogue of the Bibliothèque
Nationale de France   297
10.2 Distribution of Occupational Groups in the French Labour
Force, 1969–2000   302
10.3 Annual Average Wage for Full-time Wage-earners, 2000   303
10.4 Income and Wealth Strobiloïd, 2000   308
10.5 Respondents Answering that they belong to a Social Class,
1966–2002   309
10.6 The Historical Social Class Spiral   311

Abbreviations and Acronyms

AIDS	acquired immune deficiency syndrome
CEDAW	Convention on the Elimination of All Forms of Discrimination Against Women
CIS	Commonwealth of Independent States
DC	developing country
FAO	Food and Agriculture Organization (UN)
FDI	foreign direct investment
GDP	gross domestic product
GNP	gross national product
HIV	human immuno-deficiency virus
IC	industrialized country
IK	indigenous knowledge
IMF	International Monetary Fund
ISSP	International Social Survey Program
LDC	less developed country
NATO	North Atlantic Treaty Organization
NGO	non-governmental organization
NIC	newly industrialized country
NIS	national innovation system
ODA	official development assistance
OECD	Organisation for Economic Co-operation and Development
R&D	research and development

SEZ	Special Economic Zone (China)
SOE	State-Owned Enterprise (China)
TVE	Town and Village Enterprise (China)
UN	United Nations
UNAIDS	UN Programme on HIV/AIDS
UNESCO	UN Educational, Scientific, and Cultural Organization
UNFPA	UN Fund for Population Activities
UNICEF	UN Children's Fund
USAID	United States Agency for International Development
WCS	World Conference on Science
WHO	World Health Organization
WIDER	World Institute for Development Economics Research

Preface

Inequality is a familiar feature of social life, and it is a stock in trade of the social sciences, and of sociology in particular. However, familiarity often breeds myopia and lack of serious interest. Academic investigations and conference discussions may easily become unquestioned routine. This volume came about out of two concerns: one moral, the other scholarly. First, inequality is an important phenomenon, currently of mounting importance. Second, the prevailing mainstream sociological treatment of inequality is tending to become uninspiring routine, feeding repetitive, stereotypical public discourse. There are now the well-known, well-established categories of income distribution, class, gender, and race/ethnicity. There are the well-rehearsed arguments about exploitation and inheritance versus achievement or 'status attainment'. And by now, welfare state typologies and wage-dumping globalization seem to have been referred to often enough.

Is inequality really something simple, self-evident, and crude? Amartya Sen (1992) indicated in the early 1990s that it was not – perhaps even a bit too eloquently in elaborating some complications. Aren't there different kinds of inequality? What is the difference between a difference and an inequality? How, through what processes, are inequalities actually produced, increased, or reduced? Wouldn't a serious discussion of the effects of current globalization require some kind of comparative framework, distinguishing between and comparing global and non-global processes?

These and related questions called for a collective effort, but not for a collective answer. Social scholarship is not advanced by collective mobilization and by one common answer. Instead, I invited the views of a set of scholars of world distinction, working on different kinds and aspects of inequality. Variety does exist, but it tends to be strongly segmented. As always, contingent circumstances changed the original composition somewhat, but as editor I am very proud of the width and the depth of expertise gathered here.

The editorial collection apart, nobody is responsible for anything more than her or his chapter. The analytical framework laid out in Chapter 1, then, commits nobody else than its author. This volume is meant to present a range of perspectives on inequality, for public, political debate as well as for scholarly exchange, and for academic teaching.

Most, if not all, the contributions derive from a series of panel discussions at the World Congress of Sociology in Brisbane in 2002, with the aim of highlighting the multidimensionality of inequality. Publishing crises and mishaps have delayed publication, but the actuality of the chapters has not diminished.

Inequality of health and mortality and vital inequality are analysed by the Swedish medical sociologist Denny Vågerö, in 2004 appointed by the WHO to a group of high-level experts on socioeconomic differences of life and health. In the world, Vågerö finds persistent international differences, aggravated by deteriorations in sub-Saharan Africa and in post-communist Eastern Europe. Within Europe, he finds that in 2000 socioeconomic differences were probably bigger than in 1984 in most countries, including Western Europe.

Within-country vital inequality is, of course, no specialty of Europe. From the serious deterioration of health services in rural China, found by Huang Ping in his contribution in this volume, it is clear that vital inequality, like other inequalities, is rising in China. In Africa, for instance, there are huge ethno-social differences of mortality. A Kikuyu baby has almost four times a larger chance of surviving until his/her fifth birthday than non-Kikuyu children of Kenya; a Baganda child a 36 per cent better chance than other children of Uganda; and a (pre-genocide) Tutsi child stood a 20 per cent better chance than a Hutu in Rwanda (Brockerhoff and Hewett 2000, table 2, data referring to 1982–93).

Existential inequality may be seen as cultural distinctions between worthy and unworthy persons. Conflicts around it involve the drawing or lifting of categorical boundaries, and of naming and renaming, such as of Gypsies as Romas, of Untouchables as Dalits, and so on. Michèle Lamont uses this perspective for an exploration of relations of class and race in a comparative interview study of French and American workers. The former tend to draw boundaries of exclusion with regard of Muslim immigrants, and the latter to Afro-Americans and to the poor. The moral motivation for the exclusions differs between American and French workers, Lamont finds.

Existential inequality usually includes inheritance of different life chances. As such it is related to a large branch of methodologically advanced sociology: mobility studies. Michael Hout, a prominent member of that fraternity, sees one of his tasks as communicating findings of mobility research in a non-technical language. He applies this to four cases: American men (generally) in the 1960s and 1970s; African American men in the same period; Irish employees for the last 30 years; and economically active Russians since the last days of communism, with some comparative attention also paid to other Western European countries. Among his results are a wider range of opportunities for Afro-Americans, but mainly for men of middle-class background, and sharply decreased opportunities in Russia, with family origin becoming more important. More generally, Hout emphasizes the importance of educational and other public policies for social mobility.

Forms of social and economic existence also pertain to existential inequality. An important aspect is constituted by conditions of work and employment. Arne Kalleberg focuses on the growth of nonstandard employment relations and their implications of insecurity. Nonstandard employment, deviating from the norm of advanced industrial societies, here refers to 'triangular employment' via a manpower agency, to part-time jobs, temporary employment, and self-employment. Since the crisis of the mid-1970s there has been a strong, though internationally uneven, increase in that kind of employment, the long-term effects of which are still little known.

Kalleberg's is a study of the rich OECD countries. In the rest of the world, where no industrial standard has ever been reached, the corresponding work existence is most frequently referred to as the 'informal sector' of precarious self-employment or micro-enterprise jobs without any social rights. In India informal labour is estimated to account for about 85 per cent of the labour force, about two-thirds of whom are self-employed (Harris-White 2003: 17, 19). The ILO (2001: 39) has estimated that in Kenya in the mid-1990s formal wage employment comprised 18 per cent of the labour force, and in Zimbabwe 25 per cent. In Latin America, informal employment increased its share of non-agricultural employment from 43 to 46 per cent between 1990 and 1998 (ILO 2001: 30).

Current invocations of a knowledge economy and a knowledge society highlight the increasing importance of knowledge as a resource, and of knowledge inequality as a crucial form of resource inequality. Peter Weingart offers a comprehensive global analysis of the contradiction between the global commodification and the global diffusion of knowledge, highlighting the vast differences of educational systems in the world, and, above all, the enormously concentrated production of scientific knowledge. He also submits current theses on the relations between, on one hand, knowledge and knowledge systems of different kinds, and economic and social development, on the other, to a critical discussion. He underlines the cumulative effects of inequality of scientific knowledge production, including the brain drain from poor countries. For instance, of 600 physicians trained in Zambia since independence in 1964, only about fifty are still in the country (according to a USAID report of 2003).

Social structuration, social perception, and economic resource inequality constitute the theme of four major case studies. Elisa Reis found in her studies of Brazilian elite perceptions a general awareness of Brazil being 'the country with the greatest inequality in the world', a widespread recognition of state responsibility to reduce it, and, together with an emphasis on raising levels of education, a priority of agrarian reform as an inequality-reducing measure. But elite endorsement of agrarian reform is interpreted by Reis as largely a way of reducing urban violence and insecurity, and she found little support for policies of redistribution. Brazilian inequality is one of the best documented and most persistent in the world.

The reintroduction of capitalism after communist socialism in China and Russia has meant a drastic increase in inequality. A major difference is, of course, that in China this has been part of rising average income, while most Russians are impoverished. Huang Ping focuses on rural China, home to a good 60 per cent of the country's population in 2001, and its relations to the urban sector. While internal sectoral differences increased, the first phase of Chinese marketization meant a diminishing gap of rural and urban income, with the annual rural household income rising from 39 per cent of the urban income in 1978 to 46 per cent in 1988. Since then urban distantiation has widened again, back to the rural income being the average of only 34 per cent of the urban in 2001. Regional disparities have also grown. Huang underlines in particular the mounting problems of a huge 'surplus' population created by state enterprise lay-offs, agrarian under-employment, and land scarcity. WTO entry is likely to aggravate the problem.

The gigantic task, which Huang Ping underlines, of developing decent forms of employment or other modes of living for the rural poor, looks even more problematic in India, which has a larger agricultural population and a much smaller manufacturing base. Neither the ILO nor the World Bank provides recent data on sectoral employment in China and India. But from Huang Ping's note 6 emerges that by the end of 2001 about 45 per cent of Chinese employment was in rural agriculture, while in the mid-1990s India involved 67 per cent of employment (Harris-White 2003: 19). In terms of production, Indian manufacturing accounted for only 16 per cent of GDP in 2003, as compared to 39 per cent in China (World Bank 2005, table 4.2).

Markku Kivinen analyses both the class restructuration and rising inequality in post-communist Russia. On the whole, he finds Russia currently characterized by a weak bourgeoisie and a weak middle class – with a large marginalized potential middle class of professionals without any autonomy – as well as a weak working class, and he ends by discussing the prospects of future class constellations. The enormous impoverishment of the bulk of the population – 60 per cent poor in 1999 in comparison with 10 per cent in 1985–89 according the same standards – has been caused roughly equally by falling average income and by towering inequality.

France is a country of classical egalitarian rhetoric with persistent resource inequalities, of cultural capital as well as of income and wealth. Louis Chauvel adds to a mainstream analysis of inequality and class structuration an original generational dynamic. After the equalization of the 1970s, the French wage/salary distribution has remained basically stable, in contrast to the increasing inequality of the Anglo-Saxon countries. However, Chauvel stresses, a generation perspective gives a different picture. Among the cohorts born after 1955 there is more young adult poverty, which is likely to prefigure a long future of relative poverty. Another inegalitarian push, according to Chauvel, is the growing importance of capital assets to household wealth and income, and asset inequality is more than twenty times larger than income inequality. He finds a current mismatch between a subjective erosion of class awareness and an emergent new class structuration. Chauvel's dynamic model of class analysis points to the instability of that situation, like that of other configurations of class awareness, class conflict, and inequality.

Whatever the forms they take, the struggles for privilege and the struggles for equality and justice are bound to continue in this century.

Göran Therborn
Edenborg, Sweden, January 2006

References

Brockerhoff, M., and P. Hewett, 2000, 'Inequality of child mortality among ethnicity groups in sub-Saharan Africa', *Bulletin of the World Health Organization*, 78: 30–41.

ILO, 2001, *World Employment Report 2001*, Geneva: ILO.

Harris-White, B., 2003, *India Working*, Cambridge: Cambridge University Press.

Sen, A., 1992, *Inequality Reexamined*, Cambridge, MA: Harvard University Press.

World Bank, 2005, *World Development Indicators*, Washington, DC, World Bank.

Meaning, Mechanisms, Patterns, and Forces: An Introduction

Göran Therborn

Concerns about inequality are usually first of all moral, political, and empirical. We are interested in inequality for moral and political reasons, and then we want to find out, and to show, what it looks like, its tendencies, and its consequences.

However, inequality also raises fundamental theoretical issues. Does inequality differ from difference, and, if so, how? Is it fruitful to distinguish different kinds and different shapes of inequality, as well as different degrees? Is it possible to find a sort of generative social grammar of inequality? If so, what social processes or mechanisms would it involve? Can corresponding processes of equality be identified?

Social theorizing of inequality has moved forwards enormously in the last decade or so, while more and more data are collected on a global scale, and are subjected to ever increasingly sophisticated analyses. Let me just mention a few of the most sterling contributions, from which I have learnt a lot. A new theoretical level was opened up by Amartya Sen's (1992) *Inequality Examined*, raising the basic question 'Inequality of what?' and answering it by focusing on human capability. Charles Tilly (1998) brought the mechanisms of *Durable Inequality* into focus, developing a formidable structural explanation of enduring inequality between categories of people, such as white and black, or male and female.

Inequality of health[1] has become more central to social science through the development of epidemiology and public health, and broad interest has been stimulated by the hypothesis developed by R. G. Wilkinson,[2] that socio-economic inequality has detrimental effects on a wider population than simply on the most disadvantaged. Problems of what I would call existential inequality have entered the theoretical field through the debate on recognition and redistribution between philosophers Nancy Fraser and Axel Honneth, and by Richard Sennett's characteristically perceptive exploration of respect.[3]

The number of eye-opening empirical studies has become too large for a roll-call, and particularly so in a brief introduction such as this, although one cannot avoid a special tribute to Pierre Bourdieu's (1979) *La Distinction*, which brought current intra-ethnic cultural stratification into the limelight. Sociology has also mobilized hard-science rebuttals of anti-egalitarian ideological crusaders.[4] The core of mainstream sociological inequality studies is constituted by investigations of intergenerational mobility, into and through the educational system, and into the labour market and the class structure. Major findings of these efforts were summed up in two excellent works of the early 1990s by Eriksson and Goldthorpe, and by Shavit and Blossfeld, demonstrating persistent inequality of opportunity.[5]

Although there are significant sociological contributions to the study of global income inequality, by Glenn Firebaugh[6] – methodologically well versed and professionally pedagogic – and others, it is strongest among economists who have devoted more energy to global studies and to the contemporary distributional dynamics of the OECD states under competitive pressure. Readers of distribution economics are immensely grateful for the wisdom of Anthony Atkinson, the doyen of the discipline, and an exemplar of sceptical British empiricism at its very best,[7] co-editor of a valuable *Handbook of Income Distribution*.[8] From the huge recent economic literature, at the very least the incisive, wide-ranging collection gathered and edited by Giovanni Andrea Cornea needs to be singled out.[9]

In an introduction by a sociologist to a Verso book – that is to say, a book on the opposite side of the conventional mainstream – a special acknowledgement is due to a group of economists little likely to be read on the Left, unfortunately, and most accessible on the websites of their employers. I am thinking of a minority set of international bank economists, for instance of Miguel Székely, formerly at the Inter-American Development Bank, and of World Bank economists such as François Bourguignon (recently appointed chief economist of the Bank), Elizabeth King, Branko Milanovic, and Martin Ravaillon, who are all using their privileged positions for perceptive analyses of inequality and poverty.

For all the brilliant lights already shining in the field of the study of inequality, this book was conceived from a sense of something missing, and with an ambition to add something of importance, theoretically as well as empirically. The starting point was the idea that inequality should be understood as a plurality, as *inequalities*. It guided the invitation of participants, each one a prominent expert in their topic. A multi-dimensional view of inequality also called forth a theoretical effort, highlighting what I think are the three fundamental dimensions of inequality – vital, existential, and resource inequality – two of which have been largely neglected in the world literature. Even distinguished broad-minded, even if mainly national overviews, such as the *Daedalus* Winter 2002 special issue, Fitoussi and Savidan's work or the book by Barlösius fail to put the whole field into focus.[10]

Furthermore, if one thinks that inequality or equality are important social outcomes, social science should try to systematize the mechanisms of their production. Tilly's aforementioned work was a major contribution, but it confined itself to one particular, even though particularly important, process. A much more general approach, including corresponding mechanisms of equality, will be needed, laying out how inequalities and equalities are socially generated.

Empirically, the object is the globe, although most of our individual contributors are specialists on this or that part of it. The intention is to get a grasp of global multi-dimensionality and of global cum-sub-global causality.

Social Theory: Meaning and Mechanisms

Differences and Inequalities

Human beings are all different in some sense. How do we distinguish an inequality from a difference? Each of us is different from one another. In some sense, then, none of us is equal to others. On the other hand, in some other sense, it is widely believed that 'all men are created equal'. The relationship between difference and inequality has been much discussed in contemporary feminism, but that does not seem to have spread into other theoretical fields.

So, what differences make inequality? Inequalities are differences that we consider unjust. In-equality is a negation of equality. Behind a perception of inequality there is a notion of injustice, a violation of some equality. Discourses on inequality contrast to ones on superiority/inferiority. There is one more aspect of inequality. While equality may be divine – coming from the Creator – inequality is manmade. That is, it is something changeable.

The conception of justice underlying empirical studies of, or even political mobilizations against, inequality is rarely, if ever, reflected upon and discussed. But they are variants of three notions of injustice: a difference may constitute an unjust inequality because

- it is a difference that constitutes a violation of some just equality, of human rights, of citizenship – in brief, of some human qualification held to be equal, whether by humanity, by social membership or by achievement;
- it is too large a difference, limiting the life possibilities of the disadvantaged, either directly materially by concentrating resources among the privileged, or indirectly via social psychological mechanisms of humiliating signals of superiority and inferiority;
- it goes in the wrong direction, giving undeserved, unfair advantages to some – for example, to people born in certain countries or milieux, or to people on the basis of power rather than of contribution.

The question of why there is inequality in the world, then, requires a moral answer before any sociological one. Some of the differentials of the conditions of life are unequal and unjust, because they constitute violations of the most elementary, human rights, of life and of the pursuit of happiness, that is, of a moral conception of fundamental human equality. Other differentials create inequalities in the capabilities of fully participating in the potentials of contemporary social and cultural life in the world.

For this writer, those are the two basic reasons for being concerned with human world inequality. Why shouldn't a newborn child in Congo have the same chance to survive into healthy adulthood as a child in Sweden? Why shouldn't a young Bihari woman have the same autonomy to choose her life pursuits as a young white American male, or an Egyptian college graduate the same as a Canadian? Why shouldn't all Pakistani and Brazilian families have the same access as British or French to good sanitation, air conditioning and/or heating, washing machines, and holiday tickets? Why should many children have to work? Why shouldn't a black HIV-positive person in Southern Africa have the same chance to survive as a white European? Why should a handful of individual 'oligarchs' be able to expropriate most of the natural resources of Russia, while a large part of population have been pushed into pauperism? Why should big-business executives be able to pay themselves hundreds of times more than the workers they are constantly pushing to work harder, more 'flexibly', and at lower cost?

In brief, there is inequality in this world because so many are denied the chance to live their lives at all, to live a life of dignity, to try out their interests in life, to make use of their existing potential. The inequalities of the world prevent hundreds of millions of people from developing their differences.

Inequality of What?

Amartya Sen advanced the frontier of reflections on inequality when he raised and treated the question 'Inequality of What?'[11] But it may be wondered how far his answer of human 'functionings' has reached beyond the high table of high philosophical and economic theory. General public discussion still feeds upon the stale diet of 'inequality of opportunity and inequality of outcome'. True, perceptions of injustice and unfairness are widespread, against which right-wing punditry of 'envy' and 'resentment' carry little weight. However, there is a need to elaborate Sen's question a bit in the direction of a simple social theory, easily understandable for purposes of civic discussion and political change, as well as useful for empirical investigations.

In this vein, inequality may be conceived as having three fundamental dimensions. They refer to human beings as biological organisms, as persons, and as actors.

LIFE AND HEALTH

Most basically, there is inequality of life and death – that is, of differential exposure to fatal risk. We may call this *vital inequality*, and it can be measured by life expectancy, if possible corrected for disability, by mortality and/or morbidity rates, and by the incidence of malnutrition. That the incidence of disease and the age of death are amenable to social change is one of the most important social and medical discoveries of the last two centuries. In this way the issue of vital inequality was established, where before there had been only murders, accidents, and divine punishments.

It may well be argued that vital inequality is the most important of all, given its reference to the ultimate question of life, health, and death. But if so, it plays an astonishingly modest role in public debate and in political controversy. This may have something to do with the remarkable combination involved in vital inequality, on the one hand of personal, bodily intimacy, on the other of statistical abstraction. The rich are more clearly visible at a distance than the long-lived and healthy, not to speak of rates of morbidity or mortality.

The HIV–AIDS catastrophe in Africa is only slowly bringing vital inequality to wider attention.

There is one significant vital differential, which, however, is usually not regarded as an inequality. That is the generally greater longevity of women in comparison with men, a difference that can be very large, and often as large as, or even larger than, the differential between classes or continents. In a country such as Russia it amounts to a likelihood of 13 extra years of life, counted from birth.[12] The female sex is genetically stronger than the male, and therefore human populations give birth to somewhat more boys than girls (105–6 to 100) But life expectancy differentials vary considerably among large (say national) populations.

Why has there been no morally driven counting of the 'missing men' of the former Soviet Union, comparable to Amartya Sen's calculation of the missing women of patriarchal (northern) India, from the excess mortality of young girls? It is presumably because the abnormally shorter lives of men in some countries is perceived not as unjust but as self-inflicted, either by the victims themselves, by alcoholism, violence, and bodily neglect, or by other men. This difference is not perceived as an inequality. The mounting generational conflicts and their actuarial arguments may well change the terms of the debate. And with respect to Russia there is of course a pertinent question: why has male life expectancy been shortened so much with the restoration of capitalism? (below we shall come back to that question).

FREEDOM AND RESPECT

Second, there is the unequal recognition of human individuals as persons. This creates an *existential inequality*, which allocates freedom and unfreedom in the pursuit of personal life projects, rights, and prohibitions to act, and distributes affirmations and denials of recognition and respect. The struggle for, and the denial of, recognition is a classical theme of social philosophy, at least since Hegel,[13] but it has rarely been incorporated into systematic thought on inequality.[14] Stigma is the opposite of recognition, and stigmatization is a basic process of producing and reproducing existential inequality.[15]

Patriarchy, slavery, caste, estates, and racism have been the main, stark, classical forms of institutionalized existential inequality. Religious domination, when it was not bent on outright annihilation, as in Western Europe from the mid-Middle Ages to the Enlightenment, also included limitations on what the, for instance, Jewish or Christian, minority must and must not do.

'Equality of opportunity' is, in one sense, 'existential equality lite'. It is a light version that refers to equality only at one or a few – crucial, it is true – moments of life, that is, to some moment(s) of entry, such as to school or to a job. It is silent on the rest of the life course. However, unequal opportunities, the inheritance of disadvantages, and social immobility are denials of existential freedom.

Existential inequality can be pervasive without being institutionalized and formally inscribed in society at large. Giving or withholding recognition and respect is intrinsic to social action and social relations. But differences of recognition and respect do not *per se* make up an inequality, according to my argument above. When do they? There is little of any quantitative benchmark here, but whenever there is humiliation, there is existential inequality.

When existential inequality is no longer backed up by strong norms of difference and by stark resource inequality, the reaction tends to be explosive. A great deal of contemporary youth violence in the rich countries seems to arise out of perceptions of non-respect. The enormous resentment that the crusades by Bush and Blair are creating among Muslims everywhere, and among young male Muslims in particular, appears to derive from a deep sense of being humiliated, non-recognized, and non-respected. And, in contrast to the damned of the earth of yesterday, these frustrated men have some resources, both cognitive, including lethal knowledge, and communicational. Existential humiliation is not to be played with.

RESOURCES: MATERIAL AND SYMBOLIC

Third, even as healthy organisms and respected persons, human actors can be very unequal in their capability to act. This may be summed up as *resource inequality*. (In contrast to Ronald Dworkin[16], I think resources would be better seen as just one rather than the only dimension of (in)equality.) For many purposes, a study of the distribution of income will give the most pertinent picture of resource inequality, given its easy measurability and its wide-ranging convertibility. But adequate resources to act also include, for example, knowledge or education, social networks, and the right to claim social security in case of need. From the work of Pierre Bourdieu we may divide the inequality of resources into economic, cultural, and social forms of 'capital'.

Resources also take on a symbolic meaning, with differentials creating existential inequality as well. Income, work space, or education credentials may be disrespected or respected, signalling whether you are a 'winner' or a 'loser'. While income is a universally convertible resource currency, symbolic differentiations constitute inequality only to the extent that they have connotations of unfair (dis)advantages. Differences in cultural capital[17] may just refer to cultural differences between different strata, as do different lifestyles.[18]

Experimental economics has illustrated the operation of humiliating resource allocation in its so-called ultimatum games. The experimenter gives one person a sum of money, which she has to allocate between herself and another person. If that person accepts the proposed allocation, the two divide the money accordingly, but if the person rejects the offer, neither gets anything. The results show that a division of 7–3 or lower is rejected by most people, who prefer to get nothing than accept a humiliating offer: it is a reaction of honour, rejecting a purely economic rationality. On the other hand, when the proposals are made non-intentionally, by random procedure (a kind of lottery), even a 9–1 division is accepted by a majority.[19]

Arenas, Interactions, Basic Sources, and Pathways

Inequalities are produced in different social arenas, 'fields' in the nomenclature of Bourdieu, 'social sub-systems' in the eyes of Niklas Luhmann.[20] Vital inequality is mainly produced in the personal life-world (but also at work) and its habitat, existential inequality in adult social interaction, and resource inequality above all in the areas of property and employment. The evolutionary tendency of social differentiation tends to increase these arenas and their autonomy of each other. A plurality of cultural milieux provides a variety of criteria of status, and huge incomes may be generated in very different ways, from media displaying an ample bosom or golf scoring to capitalist entrepreneurship and property ownership.

However, while specific in their meaning and in their dynamics, the three dimensions of inequalities also interrelate and interact.

Vital inequality is determined by natural conditions 'genetic and ecological', by resource inequality (including cognitive), and by cultural differences (of consumption and body care), and it will be reinforced, and occasionally overruled, by existential inequality. In Pakistan, northern India, and until very recently in Bangladesh, female life expectancy is lower than male (see Table 1.6). The HIV–AIDS epidemic in sub-Saharan Africa has become particularly virulent against the background of a witches' cauldron of African sexual inequality, colonial migration, and post-colonial poverty.[21]

Existential inequality is first of all culturally determined by a cultural system, and inscribed in family socialization, often fastened on to natural signs (of sex or skin colour) or stemming directly from the power of one culture (for example a religion) over another. It is reinforced by resource inequality. But it is also possible that the cultural system allocates existential recognition according to a person's command of resources. The amount of income or the knowledge credential a person has may be interpreted as the person's worth.

Resource inequality can follow from natural endowments of territories as well as of individuals, from productivity differentials, and from systemic structuring of opportunities and rewards. Like the ecology of vital inequality, resource inequality is significantly affected by the demography of the population. It is strongly reinforced by categorical existential inequality – between genders, races, ethnic groups[22] – and its reproduction over time is reinforced by vital inequality of childhood. Undernourishment and maltreatment leave enduring handicaps.

Inequalities feed on sources or bases, and are produced and reproduced, or alternatively dismantled, by processes of social interaction. The latter operate along a number of different paths, and not infrequently in opposite directions, making the distributive outcome a net sum of conflicting tendencies (this was a major finding of Bourguignon et al. in their tracing of different distributive paths in East Asia and Latin America[23]).

Summing up, inequalities derive from four basic factors of social differentiation:

- natural endowments (of individuals, groups, territories);
- systemic arrangements of opportunities and rewards;
- the performance or productivity of actors; and
- individual and collective distributive action, including via use of the state.

Class struggle is one form of distributive action. Inequalities among their members are affected by the growth, or other dynamics, of the populations.

The relative importance of these factors provides a major part of the interminable ethical and explanatory controversies about inequality. Each determinant can also operate along an indeterminate number of social pathways.

However, inequalities are outcomes of action. They do not derive just from sources, whatever the argumentation. Inequalities are produced, reproduced, reduced, and dismantled by social interaction. It may therefore be fruitful to try to specify these mechanisms of interaction whereby inequality or equality are produced and sustained. Again, the number four appears the most appropriate.

Four Mechanisms of Inequality:
Distantiation, Hierarchization, Exclusion, and Exploitation

As these mechanisms have very different moral valencies, the reader is now entering a minefield of controversy. Ideologically, the analysis has often been portrayed as divided between '[individual] achievement' and 'exploitation',[24] or between inequality and equality of opportunity. I argue that what is called 'achievement' is in fact largely dependent on systemic game construction and reward structuration, while 'exploitation' is currently much more rare than Marx would have suspected, and, third, that 'equality of opportunity' is no more than a fleeting moment in the overall process of (in)equality.

Inequalities are produced and sustained by distributive action, individual as well as collective, and by social systemic arrangements and processes. It is crucial to pay systematic attention to both. 'Distributive action' is here taken as any social action with direct distributive consequences, be they actions of advance, of retardation, or of allocation/redistribution. Together, distributive action and system dynamics produce and maintain inequalities through four different mechanisms, with different implications for evaluation and for change. The mechanisms refer to the kind of social interaction that yields a certain distributive outcome. They operate among children at school as well as within regions of the world economy.

This interaction is hung between two poles. At one pole we have the distance produced by A running ahead of B, because of A's more helpful parents or other better preconditions, more training, lucky start/course, or harder effort. No interaction between A and B is necessary to produce the distance between them, but A and/or B, as well as their onlookers, may find it important. And, whatever produced the initial distance, social psychological mechanisms of self-confidence, ambition, and dedication often tend to consolidate and to widen it. We may refer to the process at that pole as *distantiation*. In liberal, individualist discourse, this mechanism is often referred to as 'achievement', and held to produce not inequality but legitimate rewards.

Distantiation is an important mechanism of inequality, and should not be subsumed under other processes. But 'achievement' would be a notion with ideological blind spots here. It is blind to everything but the achieving actor, telling us nothing about her relations to others, or about the contexts of opportunities and rewards. Social distance may very well be considered an unjust inequality, albeit not necessarily. Distantiation can be a systemic process, by virtue of game goals (the definition of what constitutes 'winning), the formulation of cultural objectives (such as 'growth' or 'success', or by a value of social distance in general), and by reward patterning, such as the logic of 'winner takes all'[25] or the cumulation of success by increasing returns to scale.

At the other pole, A derives his inequality over B because of the valuable items that B provides him with. At this pole we have inequality by *exploitation*. Exploitation involves a categorical division between some superior and some inferior people, whereby the former unilaterally or asymmetrically extract values from the latter. Once some notion of elementary human equality has been accepted, exploitation is always unjust. It can be denied, or disguised as benevolent exchange, but not defended.

Between distantiation and exploitation we may discern two other kinds of mechanisms producing inequalities. *Exclusion* means barring the advance or access of others, a division into in-groups and out-groups. As an explanatory mechanism, exclusion had better be seen as a variable, rather than as a category, as a set of hurdles being placed in front of some people, a set that includes hindrances, discriminations of various sorts, as well as a closed gate. Exclusion figures in economics as monopolization, land rent and other kinds of 'rent-seeking'.[26] French empirical sociology made it in the 1990s into a major, policy-pertinent social category in France[27] and in the EU, which since its Laeken Council in 2001 has endorsed a set of indictors to measure it.

Stigmatization is a marker of exclusion, bestowing upon those outside never-healing cultural wounds.

We may also have a kind of inequality deriving from some institutionalized ranking of social actors, some high, others low, from some super- and subordination. This is inequality by *hierarchization*, highlighting the importance of formal organization. An interesting modern example, no doubt inspired by ancestral tradition, was the system of civil service ranking set up in communist China in 1953. It was a ladder with 26 ranks, which governed not only your salary, the appearance of your uniform, and the size and amenities of your apartment, but also your access to information and your means of travel when on duty. Only from grade 14 and above could you buy a plane ticket or a comfortable, 'soft' train seat, and only from grade 13 could you book a hotel room with a private toilet.[28]

Hierarchization can also be anchored in an articulated value system. Pre-modern social orders were usually perceived and formulated in terms of hierarchical orders, estates, or castes, with a core division of intellectuals (priests, Brahmins, Mandarins, *ulama*), warriors, traders/craftsmen, and farm-ers. A similar hierarchy survived into contemporary high cultures through aesthetic value systems of 'taste' and 'style'. In contemporary Europe this cultural hierarchization is probably most clear in France. Pierre Bourdieu devoted his perhaps very best work to it.[29] He started from something that is no longer so self-evident, especially not outside France: 'To the socially recog-nized hierarchy of the arts . . . corresponds the social hierarchy of [their] consumers', whereby cultural taste can function as 'privileged markers of "class"'.[30]

These four mechanisms are cumulative. The exclusion mechanism becomes relevant and important to the extent that the excluding barriers or hindering obstacles are put up by those who are in some sense ahead of and more advantaged than others.

For hierarchization to be institutionalized, some barring divide between superiors and inferiors must be in place. Exploitation, finally, presupposes distantiation, exclusion, and institutionalized superiority/inferiority, and then adds on top of all that an extraction of resources from the inferiors.

Exclusion, super-/subordination, and exploitation are all transitive mechanisms of inequality, mechanisms which, in contrast to distantiation, directly disadvantage the disadvantaged.

Table 1.1   Inequality Mechanisms and their Interactive Dynamics

Mechanism	Direct agency	Dynamics Systemic dynamics
Distantation	Running ahead/falling behind	Reward structuration and normation, e.g. 'Winner takes all', 'Matthew effect', 'star' system
	Outcompeting	Returns to scale
	Social psychology of success/failure	Opportunity structuration
Exclusion	Closure, Hindering, Opportunity hoarding	Membership boundaries, entry thresholds Cumulation of advantages
	Discrimination, monopolization	Stigmatization Citizenship/property rights
Hierarchization	Super-subordination	Organizational ladder, status/authority distance
	Patron–client relations	Hierarchy of family roles
	Put-down/deference	Systemic centre and peripheries
		Ethnic/racial/gendered hierarchies
		Generalizations of super-inferiority
Exploitation	Extraction	Polarized power relations
	Utilization	Asymmetric dependence
	Abuse	Tributary systems

To each of these mechanisms of inequality there is also a corresponding kind of opposite mechanism.

Table 1.2   Equality Mechanisms

Catching up	Field-evening, compensatory capacitation, 'affirmative action', new opportunity openings
Inclusion	Entitlement, migration, human rights
Organizational/institutional flattening	Empowerment, democratization, unionization, user rights
Redistribution	Taxation, social policy

Catching up may be due mainly to extra effort, as in individual cases of achievement. On a larger scale it is usually dependent on system changes, which, of course, does not render the question of effort insignificant. Field-evening occurs in several countries, from the Indian quota of public sector jobs to scheduled castes to gender quotas, or special educational efforts targeted at disadvantaged children in the North Atlantic area. It was the core mechanism of classical as well as of 'actually existing' socialism, through the collectivization of property. Catching up may also start from new systemic opportunities – for instance, new technologies or new markets, to which latecomers may be faster to adopt. In economic history, such 'advantages of backwardness' were highlighted by the Harvard economic historian Alexander Gerschenkron,[31] drawing upon the nineteenth-century industrialization of Central and Eastern Europe. East Asian economic development after the Second World War might be seen in a similar perspective.

Inclusion is the most widespread of the equality mechanisms. It is intrinsic to the modern nation-state, which entitles its citizens and normally also its permanent residents to certain rights and public services. For EU membership the new member states each had to provide a National Action Plan on Social Inclusion by 2004. Migration possibilities within and across states opened channels of inclusion. Human rights, including rights to social and economic development, and the diffusion of medicine and medical knowledge, exemplify efforts at global inclusion.

Organizational/institutional flattening has become a significant management doctrine in recent decades, largely inspired by post-First World War Japanese management, and by cultural upheaval following the student rebellions of the 1960s. Movements of organizational democratization were a central part of '1968', following upon a century of working-class struggles for trade union rights. In some parts of the world, especially in north-western Europe, significant empowerment of the propertyless has been achieved by popular movements of land and house tenants. Micro-credits targeted at women, pioneered by the Grameen Bank in Bangladesh, have empowered women in parts of the Third World.

Redistribution has been the main social democratic road to more equality, and, as we shall see below, it has been powerful and comparatively successful.

The relative importance of these mechanisms of inequality and equality is at the centre of scholarly as well as political controversies about world development, although the mechanisms are usually implied in area-specific notions. Did world inequality rise mainly because of distantiation at the time of the Industrial Revolution, with the North Atlantic economies running ahead and away? Or was it also due to hindering exclusive practices, such as the crowding out of Indian manufactures by the British rulers, the violent 'opening' of China, the hierarchization of the whole world into a 'civilized' colonizing part and an 'uncivilized' colonized part? To what extent was Western European prosperity, and its initial industrial advantage, built upon colonial exploitation, of the Americas in particular? Is the recent widening of income differentials in the USA and elsewhere due to technological change and in ensuing demand shifts, or is it significantly an effect of excluding processes of socially and politically disorganizing the popular classes?

Similar questions are being raised with regard to processes with aims of equality. Does affirmative action lead to equal fairness? Is migration a solution to inter-area inequality? Is the human rights discourse effective? Does empowerment of, say, women or ethnic minorities have real equalizing effects? How effective are taxation and social policy? As all these mechanisms may operate simultaneously, fuel for controversy is abundant.

An introduction is not the place to claim to settle such controversial issues. However, the following scan of worldwide variation, in time as well as in space, does indicate that no inequality is a fatality. Alternatives exist, even in this unequal world.

(In)equality Among Whom?

Inequality as a comparison always refers to some, often implicit, population. Inequality arose mainly as a national concern, confined to a population defined as a nation or to nations within an empire. The divine basic human equality included in the two major world religions, Christianity and Islam, had for a long time little this-worldly significance, although it did produce some minimalist protection, *qua* human souls. The Iberian Catholic conqueror states did include the Indians of Ibero-America as human subjects, and Islamic polities did provide some shelter to all 'peoples of the book', that is, to Christians and Jews in the West, and to Hindus in the East. Totalitarian

European Christianity did not reciprocate. But Enlightenment Anglo-Saxon Protestantism and humanism spawned anti-slavery societies.

Only recently has the planetary human population – after the Second World War and after de-colonization – become a relevant 'reference group'. World statistics are being regularly produced, by the UN Development Programme, UNICEF, the World Bank, the ILO, and others, and spread through mass media throughout the world. Environmental perspectives and pension politics have also recently pointed to populations of generations.

Except for the limiting case of the totality of humanity, (in)equality is bounded. For the Founding Fathers of the USA the boundary of equality was that between white adult males and everybody else. For the most generous post-war European welfare states, equality refers to the national territory and its permanent residents (citizens or not).

The sharpness and the surveillance of the boundary may vary negatively with the internal inequality. White North America was more equal than white Ibero-America, but the exclusion and the treatment of non-whites was more vicious in the Anglo-Saxon North. In South Africa, it was the egalitarian Boers who were the most ferocious enemies of the blacks. Indeed, it has been argued by a great US historian that it was precisely exclusivist racism and slavery that bred the Republican ideals of equality and liberty in the 'Virginia gentlemen' who created the USA, Jefferson, Washington, Madison, Monroe et al.[32] As Morgan notes,[33] the link was seen already by an English diplomat to Jefferson's presidency: 'The Virginians can profess an unbounded love of liberty and of democracy in consequence of the mass of the people, who in other countries might become mobs, being there nearly altogether composed of their own Negro slaves.'

This co-variation of internal equality and external inequality is no universal law. Contemporary Sweden, for example, while maintaining a relatively egalitarian socioeconomic orientation, has recently become the most open immigration country of Europe, with about 12 per cent of its population currently foreign-born, similar to the USA.

Third, population is important as the numerical size of units of comparison, such as nations for global inequality, and in the context of differential fertility rates, among classes or ethnic groups. World international inequality looks completely different if you think of the world in UN General Assembly terms, of one nation, one vote. Then inequality has widened continuously in the past 50 years, and continues to do so. But if you give each citizen one vote, and calculate in terms of the population of each nation, then world inequality is going down – basically because of the growth of China, a huge, previously very poor country. Recently, the invigorated economic growth of India has contributed to world economic equality.[34]

Higher fertility among the poorer classes adds substantially to the (already) high inequality of Latin America. If sub-Saharan Africa had had the same fertility rates after independence as China, per capita income would have been about 40 per cent higher.[35]

Populations matter, then, for comparisons, boundaries, and numbers.

Shapes of Inequality: Ladders and Circles

Spontaneously and off the cuff, most of us would probably think of inequality in terms of higher or lower, or perhaps as larger or smaller. But inequality may appear in very different shapes. It can take on two very different basic forms, which are not reducible to quantitative comparisons of more or less, or of polarization or concentration in the middle.

Inequalities may manifest themselves as ladders or as circles. A ladder is an obvious, that is, explicit, vertical ordering of differences, with more than one barrier and step, and an order in which there is an intrinsic possibility of ascending or descending. An income distribution, an organizational chart, an ethnic rank order exemplify a ladder in this sense. The distribution of the population on the ladder may of course be of different shapes, such as a pyramid, an onion, or a slim-waisted Venus.

Circles, on the other hand, order units more horizontally, only implicitly or indirectly vertically into core–periphery, centre–satellites, insiders–outsiders, and so on, by processes of exclusion/inclusion, segregation, or segmentation. The centre–periphery problematic, always significant to urban planning and geography, was developed in Latin American economics by Raúl Prebisch, an Argentinian who made the UN Economic Commission for Latin America and the Caribbean a brilliant centre of regional analysis.[36] Along the Atlantic diagonal of inequality and equality the conceptualization was brought into the Northern mainstream of post-Second World War social science by two great Norwegian scholars, the political scientist Stein Rokkan,[37] on European state and party formation, and the sociologist/peace and conflict researcher Johan Galtung.[38] We find it in the 'modern world system' (as Immanuel Wallerstein[39] has taught us). In labour markets, distinctions are made between core and marginal workers, or insiders and outsiders.[40] The lifestyle segmentation of 'expressive inequality', which has perhaps aroused most academic interest in Germany,[41] is another example, in so far as it constitutes inequalities and not just differences.

Basically there is only one barrier around the circle, separating the insiders from the outsiders, although there may be a constellation of circles. While not necessarily impossible *de facto*, the circle line is supposed to be not climbed, but respected. When there are more ladders than one in a society, however defined, they are inscribed in different circles.

Circles have become increasingly important as forms of world inequality, as they circumscribe national populations, with increasingly unequal life chances. There are circles of citizens and of non-citizens, of legal residents and non-legal residents. Their identification of one of two basic forms of inequality may also contribute to explaining the paradox that, second to Latin America, sub-Saharan Africa is the most unequal continent of the world, for instance in income distribution. This is paradoxical, because in contrast to Latin America, Africa, outside the southernmost parts, has no large-scale landownership, no ex-slave plantations, no preserved colonial racial hierarchy. Nor has it had much early industrial development. Furthermore, in contrast to South Asia, Africa has no caste system, nor, in contrast to most of Asia, any strong patrimonial states. Yet, as we shall see in more detail below, tropical Africa generates Gini coefficients of income inequality not much below the worst countries in Latin America, and well ahead of India and most of Asia.

Sub-Saharan Africa is characterized by the world's highest degree of ethnic fractionalization within nation-states. These ethnic groups may occasionally have a vertical order, such as the Tutsis and Hutus in colonial Rwanda and Burundi, but usually they do not at all correspond to the Latin American hierarchies of white, mestizo, and Indian, or the two dozen rungs of mulattos and blacks of contemporary Haiti. African ethnies are a mosaic of bounded ethnic circles, each in a particular ecological niche – currently favourable or unfavourable, each with a distinctive culture, receptive or not to new knowledge from the outside, differentially located in relation to colonial exploitation and development, and to post-colonial political power, and so on. To the extent that this circular inequality is important, inter-ethnic inequality should be more significant than intra-ethnic, and inter-ethnic inequality should be related to territorial location and/or to distinctive ethnic cultural norms. While available evidence is still scanty, there is clearly some empirical support for this hypothesis.[42]

World Pictures: Yesterday and Today

While reporting a broad range of specialized research on different kinds of inequalities of the world, this book does not hold back from trying to answer the boldest of questions. What does world inequality actually look like? Is it increasing or declining?

Following from the perspective outlined above, we shall look not only at income and other resource inequality, but at inequality before death and disease, and at inequality with regard to freedom and respect. This means, of course, a bird's eye view of inequalities in space and time, which at best may yield a global map before descending into the intriguing thicket of everyday life.

Vital Inequality

At birth the average life of a baby in a high-income country (Japan, Western Europe, North America, Oceania) is 20 years longer than that of an infant unlucky enough to be born in a low-income country, 78 and 58 years, respectively. The bulk of the low-income world is South Asia ($^2/_3$) and sub-Saharan Africa ($^1/_3$), and in Africa current life expectancy at birth is only 46 years.[43] The newborn of the rich countries, 15 per cent of the world population, have a life expectancy about eleven years longer than the average human, and those of poor countries (a good third of humanity) have their lives nine years shorter than the human average, and Africans eleven years shorter. Compared to 1965 this is a polarization.

Table 1.3 Life Expectancy at Birth, 1965 and 2002

	1965	1995	2002
World	56	67	67
High-income countries	71	77	78
Low-income countries	49	63	58
Sub-Saharan Africa	42	52	46
South Asia	46	61	63
East Asia[a]	54	68	69

Note: a. Only low- and middle-income countries, i.e., excluding Japan.
Sources: World Bank, *World Development Report 1997*, and *World Development Report 2005*, table 1.

Africa is falling behind, from 14 to 15 to 21 years below world average. At the high end, the advantage of infants of the rich countries first declined from 15 to 10 years, but then seems to be slightly widening again, to 11 years. The absolute decline of life expectancy in Africa should also be noticed. Africa is not only being out-distanced, it is falling back.

The restoration of capitalism in the former Soviet Union has had similar lethal effects. Even after a certain recent recovery, Russian life expectancy, at 66 in 2003, is still well below that of the USSR in 1985, at 70.[44] The first two years of the destruction of communism caused half a million extra dead.[45]

Table 1.4 Comparative Life Expectancy, 1900–2002

	c. 1900	1930s	*c.* 1950	2002
UK[a]	50[b]	61	67	78
China	–	24–35	44[c]	71
India	25[b]	29–30[d]	37[e]	61
Egypt	–	39	46[f]	67
Brazil	–	37[g]	46	69

Notes: a. 1900–1950: England and Wales; b. 1901–11; c. 1953–64; d. 1921–41; e. 1951–61; f. 1960; g. 1920
Sources: UK 1900–50: R. Fitzpatrick and T. Chandola, 'Health', in A. H. Halsey (ed.), *Twentieth-Century British Social Trends*, Basingstoke: Macmillan, 2000, table 3.1. China 1930–50s: J. Lee and Wang Feng, *One Quarter of Humanity*, Cambridge, MA, Harvard University Press, 1999, tables 4.1–4.2; India 1901–61: P. N. Mari Bhat, 'Mortality and Fertility in India, 1881–1961: A Reassessment', in T. Dyson (ed.), *India's Historical Demography*, London, Curzon Press, 1989, table 4; Egypt and Brazil 1930s: UN, *Statistical Yearbook 1949/50*, table 7; Brazil 1950: E. Berquó, 'Demographic Evolution of the Brazilian Population during the Twentieth Century', in D. J. Hogan (ed.), *Population Change in Brazil: Contemporary Perspectives*, Campinas, Unicamp, 2001, table 4; 2002: WHO, *World Health Report 2004*, Annex table 1.

Over the long haul we have only scattered but significant data of comparison. In the 1930s the difference in life expectancy between India and Great Britain was a good 30 years, but in 2002 it was only 17 years.

In this long-term perspective, there was a clear increase of vital inequality in the first third of the twentieth century, and a clear decline in the second half. In the world, vital inequality seems to have culminated in the inter-war decades of 1920–40. But, as we noticed above, there was a new polarizing tendency around the millennium.

Hunger and under-nutrition are still plaguing the world, at the beginning of the twenty-first century one person of eight. Since 1995 the number of under-nourished people has actually increased by 18 million.[46] The hungry are one-third of all Africans, and one-quarter of all South Asians. Hunger, or under-nourishment, is also the fate of one person in eleven of the new capitalist countries of Eastern Europe and Central Asia. India has more than a quarter of the hungry in the world, 220 million. In Africa, the situation is worst in the east and the south, with 40 per cent under-nourished, in Nigeria on the other hand, nine per cent. The introduction of capitalism into the peripheries of the former Soviet Union has been a social disaster. In 2000–02 under-nourishment was the fate of a quarter of the population of Georgia and Uzbekistan, one-third of Armenia, and a staggering 61 per cent of Tajikistan.[47] At the other end, a good proportion of people in rich countries are indulging in obesity.

HIV–AIDS has added heavily to vital inequality in the world, by hitting the poorest continent hardest. Sub-Saharan Africa has about 11 per cent of the world's population, but two-thirds of those infected by HIV–AIDS and suffering three-quarters of all deaths from AIDS in 2004.[48]

There is also much internal vital inequality in African countries. For instance, in Namibia an Ovambo child has a 23 per cent larger chance of surviving its first five years than other Namibian children, and a Kikuyu child a 73 per cent better chance of survival than other Kenyan children.[49]

Existential Inequality

Existential inequality means above all an unequal distribution of freedom to act and of personal respect. In the past century this has above all involved issues of race/ethnicity and gender, although there is also the Indian phenomenon of caste, as well as outlying areas of slavery or servitude in Africa and America. The class structuration of human existence is a persistent and pervasive theme of social life, which will require a treatment of its own.

Even if sexism and racism have far from disappeared, the last 100 years, and especially the last 50, have brought down many institutionalized forms of male and white existential superiority over women and other races, respectively. Ethnic existential inequality is still practised in many places and ways, but it has become thoroughly discredited as a public explicit discourse. Even that is a great stride in comparison with the days when, for instance, 'Keep Australia White' was the official slogan of the Australian Labour Party.

We may summarize the main world road of existential inequality in the twentieth century by listing the most important landmarks on the way.

The second half of the twentieth century dealt some hard blows against patriarchal superiority over women. But at the beginning of the twenty-first century, patriarchy in the sense of domination by fathers or husbands is still a prevalent institution in large parts of the world. On the whole, it reigns in South Asia, most parts of West Asia and North Africa except urban Turkey and some other urban areas, good parts of Central Asia, and most parts of sub-Saharan Africa, with qualifications for the West Coast and the central areas of Southern Africa, where recent legislative gender equality is beginning to take effect. Patriarchy may also be found in parts of China, in the Balkans – in Kosovo for instance – and in Andean regions of South America. It is also practised by Afro-Asian immigrants to Europe, and among US Mormons. The human population under patriarchy amounts to something between one-third and 40 per cent of the total.[50]

The patriarchal population is larger than the post-patriarchal one, unlikely to be more 30 per cent of humanity, generously counted as including most of Europe, the Americas, Japan, and Oceania, excepting some religious, ethnic, or local enclaves. Post-patriarchal societies are, of course, not gender-equal, but male–female inequality has become mainly one of resources.

China and Southeast Asia make up an intermediary zone, often closer to the post-patriarchal world.[51]

Table 1.5 Landmarks of Twentieth-Century Existential (In)Equality

Baseline 1900
Universal, if differentiated, patriarchy, worldwide Euro-American colonialism, universally reigning institutionalized racism of white supremacy, predominant worldwide conception of hierarchy of human existence
1910s
Dismantling of legal patriarchy in Scandinavia and in Russia
After First World War North Atlantic establishment of civic equality, male only in the Latin regions
1920s
Rise and defeats of anti-racist movements in Asia and Africa; rise of pro-indigenous cultural movement in Latin America
Tightened racist immigration legislation in USA
1930s–1945
Nazi German official racism and genocide
Widespread diffusion and policy application of eugenics
1945–50
Discredit of explicit racism, but victory in South Africa
Asian de-colonization
UN Declaration of Human Rights
Dismantling of legal patriarchy in East Asia and Eastern Europe
Civic rights of women in Latin Europe, and, gradually, in Latin America
1954
Racist school segregation declared unconstitutional in USA
1960s
African de-colonization
Global anti-patriarchal student movement
US civil rights movement, US universal right to vote
UN Convention against Racial Discrimination
Erosion of racist immigration legislation in North America and Oceania
1975–85
Tide of Global Feminism, UN Decade for Women, intercontinental dismantling or delimiting of patriarchy
Legal gender equality in all Western Europe
1995
UN Conference of Women in Beijing
1990s–2000s
Widespread struggles for existential difference and equality, of ethnicity, gender, and sexuality
Beginning recognition of sexual equality, with breakthroughs in Western Europe and South Africa
De-limited patriarchal backlash, Muslim, Jewish, Christian
Mounting anti-immigration racism in Europe

Source: G. Therborn, *Between Sex and Power: Family in the World, 1900–2000*, London: Routledge, 2004.

In South Asia and in sub-Saharan Africa, less so in West Asia/North Africa, the effects of patriarchy include a significant lowering of the natural advantage of women with respect to life expectancy. On a world scale, women have currently four more years of life than men, 5.6 years in North America, eight years in Europe (six in Western Europe, and twelve in Russia). China is on the world average, and the Arab countries somewhat below, at 3.2 years of female advantage.[52]

Table 1.6 Countries with Abnormally Low Male–Female Differences in Life Expectancy, 2000–05

Female advantage in years of life expectancy at birth	
South Asia	
Bangladesh	1.8
India	1.4
Pakistan	−0.3
Africa	
East Africa	1.4
Ethiopia	1.0
West Africa	1.3
Nigeria	0.7
Zambia	−0.4
Zimbabwe	1.1
Memoranda	
North Africa	3.7
Arab States	3.2
World	4.3

Source: UNFPA; *The State of the World's Population 2004,* indicators table.

Economic Resources Inequality

Economic resources are not the only important resources. Knowledge is another one, dealt with below by Peter Weingart. Bourdieu taught us the importance of cultural capital accumulation. In this brief overview, however, we shall stay with the topic of income distribution.[53]

Economic resources are very polarized. The people of the rich countries, which make up a bare 16 per cent of the world population, capture more than three times the average world income – expressed in purchasing power parities. The gap between low-income countries – (a good third of world population) and high-income ones (less than half of the former in population) is 13:1, in local purchasing power. In international exchange dollars the gap is 63:1.[54]

Between 1960 and 1990, the African countries lost economic standing, regressing from 14 to 8 per cent of rich country GDP per capita. The Third World as a whole bent slightly downwards, from 18 to 17 per cent of rich country GDP per capita.[55] Since then the gap has rather widened. In 2003, the purchasing power GNP per capita of 'lower- and middle-income countries' was 15 per cent of that of the high-income countries. The per capita GDP of a rich country resident was 17 times that of the average sub-Saharan African – 25 times if we exclude South Africa – and eleven times that of the average South Asian.[56] Since 1993, the African average of purchasing power has gone further down from 23 per cent of world average in 1993 to 19 per cent in 2003. On the other hand, the Indian proportion of the world average has increased from 23 to 31 per cent.[57]

In three parts of the world, absolute poverty has increased in the past 25 years. In Africa the number of people having to subsist on less than US $1 a day increased by a staggering 150 million between 1981 and 2001. In Latin America the poor, by this minimalist World Bank standard, increased by fourteen million over the same period. By Latin American standards of poverty, the poor grew by 85 million in 1980–2002.[58] In comparison with the period before the 1980s, the impoverishment of the third region is most spectacular. In post-communist Eastern Europe and Central Asia, World Bank-defined poverty rose from one million to eighteen million in 2001.[59]

For the whole period of 1975–2002, per capita GDP in sub-Saharan Africa decreased on average by 0.8 per cent every year. From the fall of communism up till and including 2002, Eastern Europe and Central Asia had their national product sliding backwards on the average 1.5 per cent annually. In the meantime world per capita income grew by 1.3 per cent since 1975, and in the richest countries ('High-income OECD') by 2.1 per cent a year.[60]

THE MOST EQUAL AND THE MOST UNEQUAL PARTS OF THE WORLD
The least unequal part of the world is Europe, east of the British Isles, west of Poland, and north of the Alps. That is, the Nordic countries, the Low

Countries, and Slavic-cum-Germanic Central Europe, Austria (uneasily), the Czech Republic, Germany, and Slovenia, and most probably Belarus, although available data do not have the same reliability as the other ones.[61] France is sitting on the fence, more out than in. Their overall distribution of disposable income (after taxes and transfers) is remarkably similar, with a Gini coefficient of 25 in 1995–2000 (Austria up to 28 and France to 29).[62] Contrary to widespread belief, Scandinavia is not unique in this respect. But it is true that if we also take into account relative poverty, for instance the proportion of people who have an income less than half of the median income, Scandinavia does somewhat better than the rest of Europe.

As late as 1992 Slovakia was the most equal country of the world, with a Gini coefficient of 19. But since then capitalization has meant drastic change, to 24 in 1996[63] and to 31 in 2002, with the largest level of poverty among all the new EU members.[64]

Among the countries in the most reliable and comparable dataset, the Luxemburg Income Study, Russia, Estonia, and the UK are the most unequal European countries, with Gini values *circa* 2000 of 43, 36, and 35, respectively. According to the more uneven World Bank series, also used by the UN, Portugal, with 38.5, would come after Russia.

Table 1.7 The Least Unequal Countries of the World, and their Routes: Disposable Income after Taxes and Transfers

Route Coefficient c. 2000	Average	Gini Coefficient
Scandinavian Social Democracy	25	
Particular communist legacy	25	
Western European Christian and social democracy	26	
Northeast Asian national capitalism	32	

Note: Scandinavia: Denmark, Finland, Norway, Sweden; particular communist legacy: Belarus, Czech Republic, Slovenia; Western Europe: Austria, Belgium, Germany, Netherlands; Northeast Asia: Japan, South Korea, Taiwan.

Sources: Belarus: WIDER, *www.wider.unu.edu*; the two 1999 net income coefficients for Belarus average 25.5; Japan: Japan is not part of the Luxemburg Income Study, and recent World Bank and UNDP publications have no recent Japanese income statistics; the source here is the 1999 *National Survey of Family Income and Expenditure* of the Statistics Bureau of Japan, *www.stat.go.jp/english*. But it does not publish a Gini coefficient, so the figure of 32 is an estimate from the decile incomes provided. Korea: World Bank 2004: table 2; the rest from LIS 2004, key figures, *www.lisproject.org/keyfigures*.

The two non-European countries closest to Northwest-Central Europe in income distribution are Taiwan and Canada (both with a Gini coefficient of 30), and the only major region of the world similar to it is Northeast Asia. We may sum up the examples of relative economic egalitarianism in Table 1.7.

To non-specialists, the Gini language may be abstract and difficult to relate to. We may then add that in the least unequal countries, the most prosperous 10 per cent have on average about six times the disposable income of the poorest tenth. In the UK the same ratio is 14 times, and in the USA 16 times.[65] Furthermore, income and wealth tend to be concentrated at the very top. For instance, about half of the income share of the most prosperous tenth of Americans was captured by the richest 1 per cent.[66]

The operation of these different roads to economic inclusion, and their rather equivalent effects, are still only patchily known, mainly because this comparison has hardly ever been made before. Welfare state redistribution, by taxation as well as by social spending, has been the immediate reason in Northwestern Europe. Market income in Sweden in the second half of the 1990s was even more inegalitarian than the British (with then higher unemployment), in Gini terms at a level of 56–58, as compared with the British of 52–54, the Canadian around 50, and the German at 44–45.[67] Communist regimes practised a system of socio-economic inclusion, through public property, full employment, and compression of financial rewards. They were never uniform, anti-communist diatribes to the contrary, and Czechoslovakia (and within Yugoslavia and the USSR, respectively, probably also Slovenia and Belarus)[68] was the most egalitarian part of European communism. Post-communist paths have diverged, but so far the evidence seems to indicate a threshold effect, and the most firmly rooted egalitarianism has shown a remarkable resilience. In the Czech Republic it survived both the neoliberal stridency of Vaclav Klaus and the haute-bourgeois nonchalance of Vaclav Havel.

In Northeast Asian capitalism after the Second World War we may perhaps discern an 'external shock' form of national inclusion. Nationalism was always intense in modern Japan and Korea, but American pressure after Hiroshima, and the threat and challenge of communism in South Korea and

Taiwan, brought, first, extensive land reform, and then a national project of economic development, which – however capitalistic and hierarchical – always had a strong communitarian aspect, rooted in the private enterprises, where managers and workers flocked together, from the daily canteen to company leisure.

At the other end of the world, we have the most inegalitarian countries. They are almost all located in two regions, also socially, culturally, and politically very different, in sub-Saharan Africa and in Latin America.

But before presenting a tidied-up table, we should be aware of some caveats. Good data on income distributions are difficult to get, particularly at the bottom and, even more, at the top of the scale. Taxation records are of little use for most of the world. You have to rely on household surveys, always subject to problems of non-response, representative accessibility, and inaccurate reporting. And all sample surveys have a margin of statistical error. The questions asked also differ. In the rich OECD world and in Latin America they tend to focus on income; in large, but far from all, parts of Africa and Asia surveyors ask about consumption and expenditure. We know that the latter are less unevenly distributed than income, but how much differs from country to country, or even from one survey to another. Moreover, income data are reported gross and net of taxes, and consumption may be based on a recall of the previous week or the previous month. For the world

Table 1.8   The Most Unequal Countries of the World

Region	Gini Coefficient c. 2000
Latin America (income)	
Argentina (Metro Buenos Aires, 2002)	59
Bolivia 2002	61
Brazil 2001	64
Chile	59
Colombia (urban, 2002)	58
Dominican Republic	54
Ecuador 2002	51
El Salvador	55
Guatemala 2002	54
Honduras 2002	59
Mexico 2002	51
Nicaragua	58

Panama (urban, 2002)	52
Paraguay	57
Peru	53
Venezuela 2002	50
Regional exceptions	
Cuba (urban, 1996–98)	38
Costa Rica 2002	49
Uruguay (urban, 2002)	46

Asia
Papua New Guinea (1996)	51 (expenditure)

Sub-Saharan Africa (consumption or expenditure)
Burkina Faso (1998)	58
Central African Republic (1993)	61
Gambia (1994)	69
Lesotho (1995)	67
Malawi (1993)	50
Mali (1994)	51
Namibia (1993)	71
Niger (1995)	51
Nigeria (1997)	51
Sierra Leone (1989)	63
South Africa (1997)	57 (gross income)
Swaziland (1994)	61 (income)
Zambia	55
Zimbabwe (1995)	70
Regional exceptions	
Burundi	33
Ethiopia	30
Ghana	30
Rwanda (1983/85)	29

Memorandum: world households
World households	1988(a)	62
World households	1993(a)	65
World households	1998(a)	64
World households	1999(b)	68

Note: In Asia there are no data from any of the Gulf states, likely to be among the most unequal countries of the world. Their distribution of manufacturing pay is among the most unequal, together with many African countries, Jamaica, Trinidad, Mongolia, and Paraguay (Galbraith 2002: 19). a: revised and preliminary estimates by B. Milanovic; b: estimate by Y. Dikhanov. The two different estimates do not form a common time series.

Sources: Latin America except Cuba: CEPAL (ECLAC) 2004: table 1.7; Cuba: A. Ferriol, Instituto Nacional de Investigaciones Económicas, Havana, written communication; the rest: WIDER 2004; when later data than in the WIDER database reported, UNDP 2004, table 14; World: Milanovic as cited by Wade 2003: 410n; Dikhanov and Ward 2001.

as a whole, the World Bank is the best single statistics producer in this area, but its publications cannot be fully trusted. This means that any sophisticated mathematical modelling of world inequality is based on moving sand.

However, having said this, we can indeed identify the most inegalitarian countries of the world, although the meter of their descent into inequality should be treated with great caution.

The first point to be stressed here is that the citizens of several African and Latin American countries are virtually as unequal as the inhabitants of the planet. The heroic compilation of income or expenditure surveys throughout the world by Branko Milanovic, and the no less heroic combination of national accounts and household surveys by Yuri Dikhanov and Michael Ward, are, of course, to be read with a substantial margin of error. The estimates of the latter are generally somewhat higher than those of Milanovic, so any conclusion of a rise in world inequality from 1998 to 1999 is unwarranted (see Table 1.8). Below we shall return to developments over time. Compared to national data it might be 5 to 10 Gini points. However, the margins above are large enough for it to be possible to assert that the citizens of early-crisis Zimbabwe were at least as unequal as all humankind, perhaps even more. Brazil and South Africa, with very reliable databases, are at least rather similar to the world as a whole.

Ethnic existential exclusion is clearly at work here, but in very different ways. Namibia and Zimbabwe combine colonial settlements with pronounced indigenous underdevelopment, without much of the late apartheid cross-race industrialization of South Africa. But southern Africa apart, African inequality is more a pattern of exclusive ethnic circles – as well as of urban-rural inequality and state kleptocracy – than the Latin American hierarchies of white–mestizo–Indian and white–mulatto–Black.

However, ethnicity is only part of the story still to be told. The onslaught of neoliberalism has almost wiped out the difference between, say, overwhelmingly white Argentina or (slightly less so) Chile, and ethnically much more complex Mexico and Central America. In fact, ethnically very divided Andean countries such as Bolivia, Ecuador, and Peru report slightly lower inequality than Argentina. This may be within the margins of error, but the point is that small, white-dominated, historically relatively democratic countries such as Uruguay (Gini 46) and Costa Rica (Gini 49) no longer stand out very clearly from the rest of this, the world's most inegalitarian region. Only Cuba is different, but it is still, in its post-Soviet crisis, substantially unequal with respect to monetary income by European standards.

A point to be emphasized about sub-Saharan Africa is the enormous width of variation, much larger than in Latin America. The exceptional countries are by no means ethnically homogenous, and not more so than the inegalitarian countries. With all the wide margins of measurement error, we are still standing in front of a puzzle. Clearly, the colonial mining migration of southern Africa has been a major producer of gross inequality. The exclusive appropriation of natural endowments, diamonds in particular, may account for a great deal of inequality in central Africa and Sierra Leone. But neither constellation has any leverage on the unequal poverty of Sahel such as Mali, Niger, or Burkina Faso (Gini 48). At the other end, what do Ghana, Ethiopia, and Burundi/Rwanda have in common, with their different modern histories, colonial backgrounds, and ethnic-religious set-ups – apart from their relative income equality?

After the extremes, we should take a look at the mainstream.

Table 1.9 Mainstream Inequality: The Big Countries

	Gini coefficient
China (2001)	45
India (1999/2000)	(33)[a]
Indonesia (2002)	(34)[a]
Russia (2000)	43
USA (2000)	37

Note: a: Distribution of consumption expenditure, which is more equal than income, in the order of about six points, but more comparable to the disposable income distribution of Russia and USA.
Sources: China, India, and Indonesia: UNDP 2004, table 14; Russia and USA LIS 2004, key figures.

The largest countries of the world are not the most unequal. After the Russian and the Chinese return to capitalism, the USA is no longer the archetype of capitalist inequality.

The figures above are not quite comparable. The Indian consumption surveys yield consistently lower figures – due to saving and borrowings – than income ones, used in China. The Luxemburg Income Study data on disposable income give a more favourable picture of countries with some mechanisms of public redistribution. In the World Bank/UNDP series, the USA appears with a coefficient of 41, Russia with 46, and Mexico with 55, instead of 37, 43, and 49, respectively. As for China, Chinese specialists estimate that the 2004 Gini is about 50.[69]

World income inequality is not just one of international inequality. Before world issues, there are issues of class, ethnicity, and gender. Let us look at the universal issue of gender income.

Table 1.10   Women's Income as a Percentage of Men's, c. 2000

Western Europe		*Eastern Europe*		*North America*		*Latin America*		*East Asia*	
France	62	Czech Rep.	58	Canada	62	Argentina	36	China	66
Germany	50	Hungary	58	USA	62	Brazil	42	Japan	44
Italy	44	Poland	61	Mexico	38				
Sweden	68	Russia	64						
UK	61								

Note: The income is an estimate from the ratio of the average male/female non-agricultural wage, and of the male/female ratio of economically active population.
Source: Calculated from UNDP 2002, table 22. See further Therborn 2004: 128.

This is an estimate with a substantial margin of error. Nevertheless, the table demonstrates clearly that there is a huge and universal economic gap between men and women. It also shows an enduring legacy of communist gender equalization.

National income distributions can be more polarized than international ones. Sub-Saharan Africa is the poorest region of the world, with one-tenth of the world's population. This does not mean it comprises the poorest tenth of world population. But if we subtract its most prosperous nations, South Africa and some small mineral-rich countries and add Nepal, Tajikistan, and Haiti, we get a good proxy for the poorest tenth of the world populations in terms of nations. At the other end we can put together the countries which make up the richest 10 per cent among national populations.

Table 1.11 National and International Income Shares around 2000

	Richest 10%	Poorest 10%	Richest 10% to Poorest 10%
Brazil	47	0.5	85
China[a]	33	1.8	18
Mexico	33	1	33
Namibia[b]	65	0.5	129
Russia[a]	36	1.8	20
South Africa[a, c]	47	0.7	65
USA	30	1.9	16
Sweden	22	4	6
World: national populations[d]	43[e]	1.4[f]	30
World: households 1993	51	0.8	63.5
World: households[a] 1999	54	0.5	104

Notes: Different roundings make for some discrepancies between column 4 and columns 2–3.
a: expenditure instead of income; b: 1993; c: 1995; d: GDP at purchasing power parities;
e: population of the nations making up the richest ten per cent of world population in 2002: North America, Australia, Japan, Austria, Belgium, Denmark, France, Germany, Ireland, Netherlands, Norway, and Switzerland; f: sub-Saharan Africa excl. South Africa, Botswana, Equatorial Guinea, Gabon, Mauritius, Namibia, and Swaziland, but incl. Haiti, Nepal, and Tajikistan.

Source: Richest 10% in Brazil and Mexico: CEPAL (ECLAC) 2004, table 1.6; other countries: UNDP, *Human Development Report 2004*, tables 5, 13, 14; world households 1993: Milanovic 2002, table 17; 1999: Dikhanov 2001, table 10.

What this means is that, contrary to predominant perceptions, world income inequality is not unique. The inequality among national populations is actually surpassed by the inequality within several nations, such as Brazil and South Africa. Even the income distance between world households is within reach of some nations. The Namibian data from 1993 are extreme, but Brazilian polarization is not far away. Another great estimate of the world income distribution among households[70] yields (for 1992) a ratio of the income of the richest 10 per cent in the world to that of the poorest 20 of 24. Calculating the same ratio for Brazil gives 23. As historical backdrop we may remember that in *ancien régime* France just before the Revolution, the richest tenth of the population appropriated 55–60 per cent of the income.[71]

While it is true, after the Depression and at least since 1950,[72] that the major part of total income inequality in the world is between countries, the similarity of some important nation-states to the whole world highlights the crucial significance of (intra-national) ethnic and class relations. Enduring effects of colonial exploitation and exclusion have been incorporated and reproduced in post-colonial nations, even ones having had a profound social revolution, such as Mexico, or decades of universal democratic suffrage, such as Brazil.

Arrows of Time

The trajectories of world inequality have run different courses over the past two hundred years. Vital inequality has been mainly driven by distantiation, and, later, by the counter-tendency of inclusion into a common pool of sanitation, vaccination, and other public health policies. Within Europe, the Nordic countries had by 1900 run ahead of England, France, and Germany with respect to infant mortality.[73] On a larger scale the divergence gained momentum in the second or third decade of the twentieth century, and then turned around (see Table 1.2 above). In 1900, Jamaica had a lower infant mortality rate than Canada, 174 to 187. By 1925, while Jamaica was still at 173, Canada had got down to 93, but thereafter there was a catching up. In 1950 the difference was 36 per thousand, and it was 8 per thousand in 1975.[74]

The second half of the twentieth century issued a major global wave of vital equalization, mainly through the inclusion of the colonial or ex-colonial world into the world of anti-malaria spraying, vaccination, and sanitation services. At work here was an inclusion of the world into the circle of medical and hygienic knowledge: the more advanced colonial powers, Britain and France, played an important and positive role here, carried on, more vigorously, by the WHO, UNICEF, and other UN organizations.[75] Lately, as we noticed above, Eastern European capitalism and African AIDS have restarted the engines of vital divergence.

England and Wales show a remarkably persistent pattern of vital inequality throughout the twentieth century, which is probably exceptional but also significant because of the industrial tradition of the country and its remaining cultural and economic importance.

This is a trajectory of inequality, of increasing distantiation, very different from most, declining in the first half of the twentieth century and increasing in the second. In the 1990s an unskilled manual worker in England ran a risk of dying before the age of 45 that was almost three times as high as that of a professional.

Table 1.12 Vital Inequality in England and Wales, 1910–93

Risk of dying: ratio of standardized mortality rates for men aged 20–44	1910–12	1949–53	1970–72	1991–93
Unskilled manual to professional	1.61	1.37	1.78	2.86
Semi-skilled manual to professional	1.06	1.21	1.48	1.76

Source: Calculated from Fitzpatrick and Chandola 2004, table 3.8.

Stark existential inequality ruled large parts of the world till the last third or quarter of the century, although it was in some kind of a retreat throughout. While Scandinavian liberalism-cum-social democracy and Russian communism did away with institutionalized patriarchy around 1920, important *de facto* restrictions on women's action persisted even there. Only since about 1975 has gender equality been an actual European norm and at least an official norm globally, but with heavy patriarchal limitations still in south and west Asia, and in Africa. Possibly, there is today more international existential inequality between, say, Western Europe and South Asia than there was a hundred years ago.[76]

Official racism survived the defeat of Nazism: blacks got the right to vote in the USA (south) only from about 1970, and the South African apartheid regime was generally delegitimized only in the 1980s, and fell in the early 1990s. The superior rights of Israeli Jews over Arabs in general and over Palestinians in particular are still part of world hegemony. Transnational inclusive action has been crucial in eroding existential inequality in the forms of racism and sexism.

Existential inequalities operate through mechanisms of exclusion. They become endangered when the capabilities of action of the excluded arise, and/ or when the capability of the gatekeepers declines. On a global scale, de-colonization undermined racism, and post-Second World War higher education of women similarly damaged patriarchy.

With regard to intergenerational social mobility (and equality of opportunity) a secular, oscillating stability seems to be the predominant pattern, from European and North American data, with temporary revolutionary disruptions, and a few exceptions of evolving equality.[77] Here the family is the main mechanism of exclusion, and for all its vicissitudes it has maintained itself as a crucial agency of socialization.

Income Inequality: Global and National Curves

Global economic resource inequality clearly increased continuously through-out the nineteenth and the first half or two-thirds of the twentieth century. That seems to be fairly non-controversial. Controversies tend to concentrate on what happened after then, and, of course on the reasons for the mounting inequality. The latter concern the relative importance of distantiation, exclusion, and exploitation. An introducing editor should abstain from committing himself to one of the rival historical explanations.

But there does seem to be empirical evidence enough for concluding the global curve up to the beginning of the twenty-first century. Over the long haul, then, it appears that the long-term historical tendency of increasing

Figure 1.1   World Income Inequality, 1820–2000

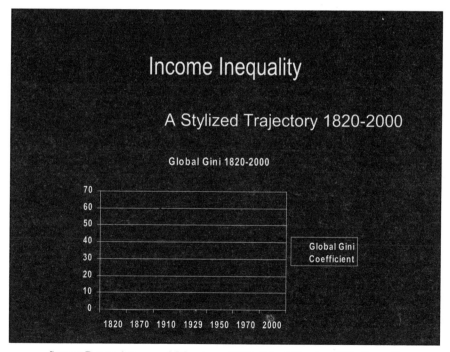

Sources: Bourguignon and Morrisson 2002; Sala-i-Martin 2002, figure 7.

world income inequality has flattened out in the last third of the past century. The main reason is the rise of China, huge and (previously very) poor.

A similar picture, comparing the group of most developed countries with the whole of the Third World, a widening gap until 1950, thereafter basic stability, with a slight decreasing tendency, was drawn by the great economic historian Paul Bairoch.[78]

How the latest decades should be assessed is still subject to debate,[79] but the overall global change seems to be small – in contrast to dramatic changes of some regions and of many nations. Dikhanov and Ward,[80] for instance, estimate a change of the world distribution of personal consumption expenditure between 1970 and 1999 in Gini terms from 0.67 to 0.68. A similar picture of relative stability, when taking the size of national populations and purchasing power into account, emerges also from other studies.[81] Current tendencies have run in opposite directions. The rapid growth of China and the accelerating catch-up of India reduce inequality, but the rise of internal inequality in China and the ex-USSR augment global inequality, like Africa's falling behind.

On the other hand, stability may also be translated as enduring inequality, with Chinese economic growth the main counterweight to a number of current inegalitarian tendencies, national and international.

NATIONAL TRAJECTORIES

Only fragile data and sophisticated but seldom competing estimates are available for long-term national trajectories, and then only for a few countries, of Western Europe and North America. They tend to show that industrialization usually first meant increasing inequality, with soaring capital income, then was often followed by a high plateau of high inequality, occasionally with some slight decline. In France, the inegalitarian thrust from the 1830s did not succeed in undoing the equalizing effects of the Revolution and its aftermath.[82] In non-revolutionary Britain inequality rose from the mid-eighteenth century up to the mid-nineteenth century, then staying at a high plateau until the First World War.[83] The German *Gründerjahre* (years of the foundation of the nation-state and industrial capitalism), the 1870s–1890s, meant more economic inequality, which then began to taper off in the decade before the war.[84] The USA has a long record of rising inequality, from 1774 to 1929, with uncertain spurts of acceleration and periods of slowing down. Nineteenth-century USA also saw a lowering of life expectancy and widening vital inequality until about 1870.[85]

The twentieth century has been a century of national equalization, from the end of the First World War to around 1980.[86] The two world wars, the Russian and the Chinese revolutions, with their international repercussions, the post-Second World War establishment of redistributive welfare states, of East Asian national community capitalism, of Indian (capitalist) 'socialism', and (more unevenly) decolonization have been crucial events. The most dramatic changes occurred at the top, where the super-rich were pulled down somewhat closer to the earth, with reduced capital income. The diminishing gap between agriculture and industry seems to have played only a minor role in Western Europe, whereas organizational flattering and de-hierarchization of remuneration have been significant. Those were the years of the labour movement.

Then what happened? Industrial employment in the developed countries peaked historically around 1970, and the 1970s was the high tide of labour influence. De-industrialization and the economic crises of the mid-1970s and of the early 1980s fatally weakened the forces of labour. Bourgeois *revanchisme* captured the UK and the USA, and from that North Atlantic core set new parameters for the world. In Latin America a similar social historical thrust, albeit under different conditions, pushed popular forces ahead, in the Southern Cone in particular, where they were met and defeated by military Thatcherism *avant la lettre*. In Africa, post-colonial national projects stalled in the 1970s, and in China the paroxysm of the Cultural Revolution was petering out. The financial shock of 1980–81 with ensuing soaring of interest rates threw reckless borrowers into trouble. The Third World debt crisis began, and with it sooner or later the IMF 'structural adjustment' programmes, with strong inegalitarian implications. Then came the post-communist turn to capitalism, in China and Vietnam under political control, in Russia and Eastern Europe as a free-for-all. Whatever route, with only a few small country exceptions, as we noticed above, the result was an enormous increase of inequality.

In brief, a whole, contingent constellation of factors seems to have brought about the historical turn of the twentieth century, from less inequality to more. But the divide was very clearly sociopolitical. Trade unions, popular movements, left-wing and nationalist politicians lost, and right-wing politicians and military, capitalists generally and financial capitalists and consultants in particular won, sometimes with bullets, more often by ballots. There was no economic fatality to it, although the liberalization of financial markets and the electronic revolution opened a field to new fortunes. While the inequality of disposable income increased in the USA from 32 to 37 Gini points between 1975 and 2000, in neighbouring Canada it was oscillating around 29, standing at 29 in 1974 and 30 in 2000.[87] The staying power of the redistributive state has been crucial. As in the previous period of equalization, inegalitarian change was driven by changes ts the top, this time by the highest income-earners increasing their distance from the rest.

However, 25 years of neoliberalism have not undone 50–60 years of twentieth-century equalization. The USA would be the most plausible candidate, but the evidence is clear enough for a negative verdict.

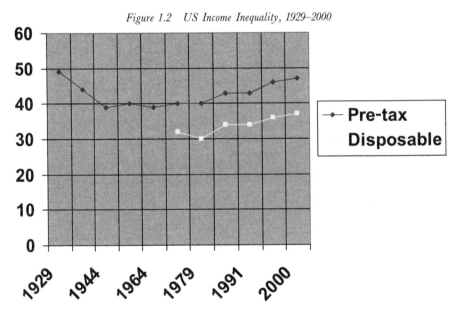

Figure 1.2   US Income Inequality, 1929–2000

Sources: Pre-tax income, 1929–94; Lindert 2000, table 4; 2000: Atkinson 2004, figure 1; disposable income after taxes and transfers: Luxemburg Income Study 2004.

In contrast to Western European countries, inequality in the USA peaked in 1929 on the eve of the Depression. While the distribution of pre-tax income has become rather similar to those days of roaring capitalism, there was then very little of any public redistribution. Disposable income was then not very different from pre-tax income. In the most recent years there has been a tendency in the USA, Mexico, and Western Europe for the inequality surge to flatten out.

Explaining

Explanations of inequalities may focus on mechanisms or on basic sources. Ideally, they should include both.

There are currently two quasi-paradigmatic controversies over how to explain present patterns of income inequality. One pits the politics of power relations and policies against the economics of the supply and demand of different factors. The other contrasts national (or more generally, sub-global) constellations of power and forces to global ones. Most recent debates on economic inequality in the OECD area seem to have concentrated on the relative importance of economics, of productivity differentials above all, and of politics – that is, of power and policies. In the global arena, the main issue is the national versus the global, which is debated in two different ways: in the 'North' mainly with regard to the impact of current economic globalization on national relations and practices, in the 'South' also, and often more frequently, in terms of the weight of the global (imperialist) past upon nations today.

Recent research has strengthened the cases for the prevalence of politics and collective action over technology and economics in the field of income inequality where they have made their strongest claims, and for the importance of national policies and institutions.[88] State redistribution can change the income picture considerably. In the late 1990s, the difference between market income and disposable income after taxes and transfers was 12–13 Gini points in Canada, 16–17 points in Germany, 16–18 points in the UK, and 27–28 points in Sweden.[89]

Put in other words, Swedish inequality was twice as high before taxes and transfers than after. In Latin America, on the other hand, disposable household income is very close to labour market income, with any progressive effect of taxation and social transfers largely counterbalanced by the greater inequality of capital income. In the Brazil of the mid- to late 1990s, the distributive effect of social spending was in fact negative, adding to an already enormously unequal income distribution.[90] Chinese taxes and transfers also add further to inequality.[91]

With regard to existential inequality the evidence of the decisive role played by politics and collective action appears overwhelming. But politics takes place on fields laid out by property, labour, and income.[92]

The picture is more complex with regard to vital inequality, but the current situation clearly includes some crucial sociopolitical forces, as demonstrated by the dramatic health impact of the collapse of communism in Eastern Europe, and from the African geography of AIDS. A major reason for the health catastrophe in capitalist Russia and the deteriorations in other countries of post-communist Europe seems to be the exclusion from control over one's life situation that has been the experience among the unemployed, the impoverished, and the marginalized in the new political economy.[93] Liberal political democracy is apparently no compensation for the loss of everyday social security, sense of control, and meaning for a large part of the population.

One important aim of this book is to contribute to global knowledge and to global research on inequalities. In view of the character of the intense globalization debates of the past ten to fifteen years, a framework for assessing the relative importance of global and non-global factors and mechanisms seems to be called for. We shall end this introduction with a sketch of such an analytical framework.

Explaining Global Outcomes: A Framework

In order to get a handle on so-called globalization, two operations are essential. First, our explanatory framework has to allow explicitly for national (or any other sub-global) determinants as well as global ones, for us to able to assess their relative weight. Second, we should better specify 'globalization' into a set of global, or at least transnational processes.

Nation-states and state-bound societies affect the world pattern of inequalities by their performance – their health policies, their treatment of race/

ethnicity, gender, and other existence-sensitive differences; their economic growth; their internal distribution, of life and health, of freedom and respect, and of resources; and, third, their population and its development, which decide their weight among humankind.

We may distinguish three major sets of global variables, global history, global entanglement, and global flows.

All current nation-states and national economies and societies have been populated, cultured, bounded, and located in the world by extra-national forces and processes. *Global history* is a major global process. Past transnational interactions have placed today's nation-states in a world system, and have provided them with a layered cultural and institutional legacy.

Figure 1.3   Global and Sub-Global Determinants of Global Inequalities

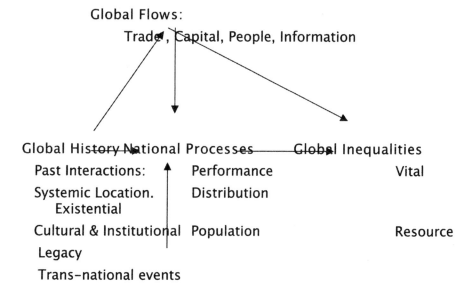

In their current functioning in the world, nations are affected by two ongoing sets of global processes. Most straightforward are global, or at least transnational, flows, of goods and services, of capital, of people, and also, not to be forgotten, flows of information and ideas.

Another current global process we may call global entanglement, referring to the imbrication of institutions, the intertwining of different sets of actors, national and global, local and global. The most tangible form of this entanglement is the emergence of resourceful global organizations affecting and interacting with national and local governments, politicians, and movements. We may lay out the production of global inequality – and of the equality that there is in the world – as in Figure 1.3.

The variety of national development paths, population trajectories, and distributive patterns shows that a global social science that neglects nation-states would be lost. But we have yet to make even a first assessment of the impact of global, or at least transnational processes upon current nations, and upon world inequality. This introduction has no space for a full deployment of the framework outlined above. Here only a few illustrative hints can be given.[94]

GLOBAL HISTORY

Past transnational interactions and their legacy, I think, are by far the most important global processes in determining current inequalities. There are, on one hand, the distant past, still weighing upon us, and, on the other, a fairly recent event, the effects of which are increasingly unfolding.

Current world rankings go far back. For instance, the correlation between the national income of twelve major countries[95] and of the African continent in 1820 and in 1998 is 0.77. In other words, with an 1820 overview almost 60 per cent of income distribution around 2000 between the major countries of the world could be predicted. If one is prepared to trust Angus Maddison's[96] intrepid estimates of life expectancy in 1900 for the same countries, the correlation between 1900 and 1999 would be 0.84. The 'patriarchality' of the world's family systems has seen a few important relative changes, with equality making larger strides in Eastern Europe and in East Asia, but a significant part of the relative differences among family systems going back to the first wave of globalization and the establishment of world religions 14 to 17 centuries ago.[97]

The crucial, recent contingent event is the outcome of the Second World War. The communist revolutions in Eastern Europe and East Asia dealt decisive blows to patriarchy, and so did the US occupation of Japan. However, the decisive outcome of the Second World War was a start of decolonization. I would venture the hypothesis that decolonization and the retrenchment of European imperialism is the major reason for the post-war flattening out of the curve of global inequality. Evidence is gathering that nationally specific institutions[98] and regional contexts[99] are crucial for economic growth. They could only appear after independence, after national empowerment, but only as a possibility.

Three basic problems of post-colonialism had to be mastered, though, before any catch-up with the North Atlantic economies. The potential population explosion following colonial medicine's reduction of mortality had to be met by de-patriachialization and birth control. The colonial elitist abyss between state and society had to be overcome. The anti-elitist revolt had to be prevented from falling into plebeian predation. Large parts of Africa have so far failed to resolve any of them. South Asia have for a long time been burdened with state elitism, even in the case of democratic India, but opportunities are opening. East and Southeast Asia were economically lucky with both their communist and their anti-communist post-colonial rulers, although both authoritarianisms took their heavy human toll.

GLOBAL ENTANGLEMENTS

The entanglement of nation-states and transnational movements and organizations has borne significantly upon inequality, with effects going in opposite directions. The international movement for family planning gradually gathered momentum after the Second World War. The UN Population Conference in 1984 signalled global political victory.[100] Birth control in poor countries has a strong equalizing effect on income inequality.

The erosion of patriarchy and its gender and generation hierarchy owes very much to transnational political entanglements. The social modernism of the international communist movement made the abolition of patriarchal family institutions a central feature of all communist revolutions. A liberal variant of the same modernism made the American occupants push for radical family reform in Japan. The UN soon came to play a key role in rallying feminists and women's movements all over the world in their challenging of male supremacy. The UN Women's Conferences from Mexico in 1975 to Beijing in 1995, the Women's Development Decade 1975–85, and the UN Convention on the Elimination of Forms of All Discrimination Against Women (CEDAW), in effect since 1981, have forced through crucial constitutional and legal changes, as well as providing foci for a worldwide social movement.[101]

By contrast, the states that have had to, or have chosen to, link up with the IMF have taken an anti-egalitarian direction. Domestically, the IMF programmes have meant a massive redistribution from labour to capital, and interstate-wise it appears that these programmes have also had a negative effect on growth. The difficult selection problems in evaluating crisis interventions such as those of the IMF – which are usually resorted to only after the economy has gone badly wrong – seem to have been mastered in recent research.[102] Transnational entanglements, regional as well as global, have become increasingly important. But their distributive effect depends on the kind of the transnational institution or movement.

GLOBAL FLOWS

Global flows – of trade, capital, people, and information – are what most of the globalization debate is about. However, their effects are all ambiguous or contradictory. The complex, largely inconclusive empirical evidence does not support any clear-cut ideological position. Nor, for that matter, do the consequences vindicate the classical theorems of economics, of convergence through free flows.

People

A hundred years ago, migration was a major equalizer among the Atlantic societies, with masses of poor people of Europe moving to the land-abundant, labour-scarce New Worlds.[103] Today's intercontinental migration is just catching up, and its distributive effects still have to be sorted out. Where we have to start is the fact that the swell of Mexican, Caribbean, and Central American emigration into the USA in the last decades of the twentieth century has not (yet) been followed by any decrease of inequality or poverty in this region – on the contrary, the latter have increased.[104] For Mexico and most of the other countries, the interstate national income gap in relation to the USA actually widened in the 1990s.[105] These correlations are, of course, no evidence against the equalizing effects of migration, but show only that so far the latter are overwhelmed by other forces at work.

In rich countries with weak unions, such as the USA, low-skilled immigration tends to depress low wages further, thus increasing national inequality, but the size of the effect is minor even in this case.[106] To poor countries, out-migration may involve a serious brain drain, but it may also mean important monetary inflows of remittances. In 2001 workers' transnational remittances amounted to about $70 billion,[107] which amounted to almost 7 per cent of the total national income of the world's low-income countries (which of course are not the only receivers of remittances, though).

Capital

Capital flows from capital-rich to capital-poor countries reduce interstate inequality, and were important as such a century ago.[108] Today this effect is smaller, because capital flows have become less global and more concentrated among the rich countries themselves, more a process of 'diversification finance' than 'development finance'.[109] Clearly, the spectacular Chinese catch-up has been significantly fuelled by a massive influx of external capital, but there is no robust growth effect of capital account liberalization in evidence.[110] There are also perverse capital movements. Using international trade and finance statistics, it has been estimated that the capital moved out of 25 poor, heavily indebted African countries in 1970–1996 exceeds their stock of foreign debt.[111]

Opening up to transnational capital movements entails risks of exposure to severe shocks from the volatility of short-term capital. East Asian countries from Thailand to Korea were hit heavily by such a shock in 1997, with increasing poverty as a result.[112] People's economic insecurity in Latin America is largely driven by the magnifying effects of volatile capital flows.[113] Opening a nation's capital account is usually associated with power shifts in favour of capital (taxes, labour rights), and is often followed by mounting white to blue-collar differentials. Transnational capital flows therefore tend to increase intra-state inequality by increasing socioeconomic hierarchization, although not intrinsically.[114]

Trade

In spite of their strong free trade instincts, mainstream economists are increasingly recognizing the ambiguous effects of trade. Theoretically, there is now 'no systematic link' between foreign trade and economic growth,[115] and recent trade theory[116] is indeterminate with regard to internal distribution effects of foreign trade. Nor is there any clear empirical relationship between foreign trade and economic growth. The successful East Asian export-oriented growth after the Second World War was for a long time undertaken from very protected home bases, whether in Japan, South Korea and Taiwan or, most recently, China.[117]

Empirical investigations furthermore show no strong or robust net distributive effects in either direction.[118] What is coming out of this fairly intense economic debate might be termed a sociological insight – that trade liberalization as well as protectionism have both losers and winners, and that who falls into which camp does not follow from stylized assumptions of factor endowments, but depends on the country-specific institutions of the trade regime, and on class and power relations.[119]

Looked at more critically, the current global trade system is also a manifest example of hierarchization and exclusion. It is a hierarchy in the sense that the rich and powerful countries, at the top of the international hierarchy, are imposing a trade rule that more or less closes their domestic markets to products in which poor countries have traditionally had a chance to compete, in food and in textiles,[120] while forcing upon the poor financial liberalization and external property rights.

Information

Flows of information may have strong distributive effects, inclusive or exclusive – in what direction depends on the kind of information. Vital inequality in the world has undoubtedly decreased through the diffusion of medical and hygienic information. Most visible was, perhaps, the arrival of pencillin, and of spraying against malaria mosquitoes right after the Second World War, which, for instance, in Ceylon halved the death rate in less than ten years.[121]

Increased inequality, on the other hand, followed from the flow of neoliberalism in the 1980s, institutionally fortified in the Washington Consensus among the US Treasury, the World Bank, and the IMF, and carried by graduates of American economics departments into most corners of the world. While the effects of pure information/ideology flows and of institutional strong-arm methods by the IMF and the World Bank are difficult to sort out, Giovanni Andrea Cornia's[122] argument regarding a global ideological force behind the turn to more inequality in most countries is plausible.

Summing up a first appraisal

An analytical framework and its illustration do not warrant a proper conclusion. But we may end this introduction by summing up a provisional appraisal. National institutions and processes are crucial for global distribution. National rulers have no global alibi for national privileges and inequalities.

Crucial also is global history, weighing heavily upon current institutions, social relations, and human expectations, nationally as well as internationally. What mechanisms of inequality were at work in making the enduring legacies of the past? The shape of the constellation is still very controversial. Historically, there was clearly massive exploitation, from the Spanish robbing of the gold and silver mines of America, via the American invention of plantation slavery, and the British forcing the opium trade upon China, to the plunder of Congo, and the British usage of Indian resources in its two 'world wars'. According to Wallerstein the 'modern world system' has an inherent tendency of what we would here call hierarchization, between the core, the semi-periphery, and the periphery, through a world system of labour.[123] Colonial rule created a modern barrier of exclusion between rulers and ruled, as well as an ethnic/racial hierarchy among the ruled, which post-colonial governance has tended to reproduce, from early nineteenth-century Latin America to late twentieth-century Africa.

But there is also a case for distantiation, and its cumulative effects, through the innovations of late eighteenth- to early nineteenth-century North Atlantic industrialism, and through the post-Second World War dynamics of developed economies. After all, decolonization did not decelerate the European boom.

Global institutional and organizational entanglements have had different effects depending upon the global organization or movement involved and entangled. UN and other global feminisms have opened doors of inclusion to more oppressed women, and transnational entanglements have empowered women all over to attack the exclusions and the hierarchies of patriarchy. IMF involvements with nation-states, on the other hand, have tended to erect or to strengthen the exclusion of workers and of subsistence farmers.

The effects of global flows are contradictory and exceedingly complex. The inclusion of some is simultaneous with the exclusion of others. There may be a catch-up effect, but it tends to decrease the distance to the least privileged among the privileged instead of the most. The flow of people tends to have an equalizing effect, through the inclusion of out-migrants in a richer socio-economic environment, but it can also exclude, or push down on a socio-economic ladder, non-migrants, in societies of emigration as well as of immigration. The flow of capital has the capacity to stimulate a catch-up between two economic environments – be they countries or cities or some other areas – but it may also spiral into increasing distantiation. In practice, concern with capital flows tends to stimulate exclusions of labour, and thereby to increase inequality.

Trade flows appear to be the most unpredictable of all. Trade openings usually mean that new economic opportunities are created, and that some previous economic activities become unsustainable and are destroyed, 'outcompeted'. If everybody could immediately switch to new opportunities, there would be no problem. But if a way of life is connected with destroyed or threatened economic activities, trade opening creates social exclusion. The net balance of trade inclusion and trade exclusion seems to be highly variable. And to what extent can the increased misery of some be justly seen as compensated by the increased welfare of others?

The flow of information, finally, has a power that should not be under-estimated. The direction of its effects derive from the character of the information. The nineteenth-century spread of white racism contributed significantly existential and resource inequality throughout the world. The twentieth-century flow of hygienic and medical information has clearly been conducive to reducing vital inequality.

More rigorous applications of the framework for analysing global and sub-global processes, and more elaborate investigations into the mechanisms of inequality and of equality, may come to different conclusions. But the complexity of the issues may at least in part explain why the protracted struggles for human dignity and equality have so far yielded so modest results. Tools of analysis are also instruments for action.

Inequalities are plural. They have to be understood as operating in multiple ways. The egalitarian struggles against them will have to take various means and various paths. The actual existence of low-inequality societies indicates that a commitment to global equalization, while contro-versial, is not utopian.

Notes

1 Cf. Navarro 2004.
2 Wilkinson 1996, 2000.
3 Fraser and Honneth 2003; and Sennett 2002.
4 E.g. Fisher et al. 1996.
5 Eriksson and Goldthorpe 1992; Shavit and Blossfeld 1993.
6 Firebaugh 2003.
7 See e.g. Atkinson 2004.
8 Atkinson and Bourguignon 2000.
9 Cornea 2004.
10 Fitoussi and Savidan 2003; Barlösius 2004.
11 Sen 1992.
12 WHO 2004.
13 Cf. Honneth 1992.
14 See Fraser and Honneth 2003 and Sennett 2002, however.
15 Cf. Goffman 1963; Elias and Scotson 1992.
16 Dworkin 2000.
17 Bourdieu 1979.
18 Beck 1983.
19 Falk and Fischbacher 2002, 224.

20 Luhmann 1997, Chapter 4.
21 Cf. UNAIDS 2004: 19ff.
22 Cf. Tilly 1998.
23 Bourguignon et al. 2004.
24 Cf. Wright 1994.
25 Cf. Frank and Cook 1995.
26 Cf. Sorensen 1996.
27 Paugam 1996.
28 Chang 1991: 240–1.
29 Bourdieu 1979.
30 Ibid.: I–II.
31 Gerschenkron 1962.
32 Morgan 1975: 375ff.
33 Ibid.: 380.
34 Milanovic 2002, and forthcoming.
35 Therborn 2003.
36 Montecinos and Markoff 2001: 115ff.
37 Rokkan 1967; 1970.
38 Galtung 1971.
39 Wallerstein 1974.
40 Lindbeck and Snower 1988.
41 For example, Lüdtke 1989.
42 Glewwe 1988; Milanovic 2003.
43 World Bank, *World Development Report 2005*, table 1. Life expectancy figures are estimates and in the Third World subject to a certain margin of error. The World Bank figures refer mainly to 2003. A recent UN publication, with estimates for 2000–05, differs somewhat from the World Bank tables. UNFPA, *The State of the World's Population 2004* (2004).
44 World Bank, *World Development Report 1987*, and *World Development Report 2005*, tables 29 and 1, respectively.
45 Calculated from Unicef 1994: 42.
46 FAO 2004, Table 1.
47 Ibid.
48 UNAIDS 2004: 77ff.
49 Data from the early 1990s, Brockerhoff and Hewett 2000, table 2.
50 Therborn 2004.
51 See further Therborn 2004, Chapter 3.
52 UNFPA 2004.
53 For a broader cultural analysis see Therborn 2005.
54 World Bank 2004a, table 1.
55 UNDP 1994, table 7.
56 World Bank 2004, table 1.
57 UNDP 1996, table 1, 2004, table 1.
58 CEPAL 2004, table 1.3.
59 Wolfensohn and Bourguignon 2004, table 1.
60 UNDP 2004, table 13.
61 WIDER 2004.

62 LIS 2004, Key figures. Named after an Italian statistician, the Gini coefficient is the most commonly used summary of income distributions. It ranges from 0 (all being equal) to 100 (or 1, if a decimal version is used), when one person gets everything.
63 Ibid.
64 European Commission 2005, Annex table 8a.
65 UNDP 2004, table 14.
66 Banerjee and Piketty 2003, figure 5.
67 Atkinson 2004, figures 9.2–9.6.
68 WIDER 2004.
69 Professor Li Qiang at the Sociology Department of Tsinghua University, Beijing, personal communication, July 2004.
70 Bourguignon and Morrisson 2002, table 1.
71 Morrisson 2000, table 7b.
72 Bourguignon and Morrisson 2002; table 2.
73 Flora et al. 1987, Chapter 1.
74 Mitchell 1998a, table A7.
75 Melchior et al. 2000.
76 Cf. Therborn 2004, Chapter 3.
77 Eriksson and Goldthorpe 1992.
78 Bairoch 1997: 1037.
79 Cf. Wade 2004; Arrighi et al. 2003.
80 Dikhanov and Ward 2001.
81 Melchior et al. 2000; Milanovic's preliminary 1998 figures.
82 Morrisson 2000: 235ff.
83 Lindert 2000: 174ff.
84 Morrisson 2000: 233–4.
85 Lindert 2000: 186ff.
86 Atkinson 2002; Lindert 2000; Morrisson 2000; Piketty 2000; Banerjee and Piketty 2003; Cornia et al. 2004.
87 Luxemburg Income Study 2004.
88 Atkinson 2004; Piketty 2000.
89 Atkinson 2004, figures 3–8.
90 Inter-American Development Bank 1998, Appendix table 1.2, figure 8.21.
91 Khan and Riskin 2001, table 7.2.
92 On human rights cf. Banton 1996; Steiner and Alston 1996; Glendon 2001; on patriarchy Therborn 2004.
93 Marmot and Bobak 2005.
94 Some others may be found in Therborn 2003a, b.
95 The countries are France, Germany, UK, Spain, Russia, USA, Mexico, Brazil, China, India, Indonesia, Japan, plus the continent of Africa. The correlation was calculated from the data and estimates of Maddison 2001.
96 Maddison 2001, tables 1–5a.
97 Therborn 2004, Chapters 1–2.
98 Rodrik 2001.
99 Milanovic 2002.
100 Therborn 2004, Chapter 8.
101 Ibid., Chapter 2.

102 Przeworski and Vreeland 2000; Vreeland 2002.
103 O'Rourke and Williamson 1999.
104 Székely 2001; Boltvinik 2001.
105 UNDP 2001, table 11.
106 Cooper 2001: 121–2.
107 World Bank 2004b: 305.
108 O'Rourke and Williamson 1999.
109 Obstfeld and Taylor 2002; O'Rourke 2001.
110 Eichengreen 2000, reviewing a number of studies.
111 Boyce and Ndikumana 2001.
112 Stiglitz 2002, Chapter 4.
113 Rodrik 2001.
114 Behrman et al. 2000; Morley 2001.
115 Cooper 2001: 114.
116 Jones 2000.
117 Rodriguez and Rodrik 2001.
118 Behrman et al. 2000; Morley 2001; O'Rourke 2001; Cooper 2001.
119 Milanovic 2004; Ravaillon 2004.
120 Oxfam 2002, Chapter 4.
121 Mitchell 1998b, table A6.
122 Cornia et al. 2004.
123 Wallerstein 1974.

References

Arrighi, G., et al., 2003, 'Industrial convergence, globalization, and the persistence of the North–South divide', *Studies in Comparative International Development*, 38: 3–31.

Atkinson, A., 2002, 'Top incomes in the United Kingdom over the twentieth century', working paper.

— 2004, 'Increased inequality in OECD countries and the redistributive impact of the government budget', in G. A. Cornia (ed.), *Inequality, Growth, and Poverty in an Era of Liberalization and Globalization*, Oxford: Oxford University Press.

Atkinson, A., and F. Bourguignon (eds), 2000, *Handbook of Income Distribution*, Vol. I, Amsterdam: North-Holland.

Bairoch, P., 1997, *Victoires et déboires*, Vol. III, Paris: Gallimard Folio.

Banerjee, A., and T. Piketty, 2003, 'Top Indian incomes, 1956–2000', BREAD Working Paper 046.

Banton, M., 1996, *International Action Against Racial Discrimination*, Oxford: Clarendon Press.

Barlösius, E., 2004, *Kämpfe um soziale Ungleichheit*, Wiesbaden: VS Verlag.

Beck, U., 1983, 'Jenseits von Stand und Klasse? Soziale Ungleichheiten, gesellschaftliche Individualisierungsprozesse und die Entstehung neuer Formationen und Identitäten', in R. Kreckel (ed.), *Soziale Ungleichheiten*, Göttingen: Schwartz.

Boltvinik, J., 2001, 'Welfare, inequality and poverty in Mexico, 1970–2000', paper presented to the 35th Congress of the International Institute of Sociology, Kraków, Poland.

Bourdieu, P., 1979, *La Distinction*, Paris: Ed. de Minuit.

Bourguignon, F., and C. Morrisson, 2002, 'Inequality among world citizens: 1820–1992', *American Economic Review*, 92: 727–44.

Bourguignon et al., eds, *The Microeconomics of Income Distribution Dynamics*, Washington, DC: World Bank.

Boyce, J., and L. Ndikumana, 2001, 'Is Africa a net creditor? Estimates of Capital Flight from severely indebted sub-Saharan African Countries, 1970–96', *Journal of Development Studies*, 38: 27–56.

Brockerhoff, M., and P. Hewett, 2000, 'Inequality of child mortality among ethnicity groups in sub-Saharan Africa', *Bulletin of the World Health Organization*, 78: 30–41.

CEPAL (ECLAC, UN Economic Commission for Latin America and the Caribbean), 2004, *Panorama social 2002–2003*, Santiago de Chile: CEPAL.

Chang, Jung, 1991, *Wild Swans*, London: Flamingo.

Cooper, R., 2001, 'Growth and inequality: the role of foreign trade and investment', in B. Pleskovic and N. Stern, eds, *Annual World Bank Conference on Development Economics 2001/2002*, Washington, DC: World Bank, pp. 107–37.

Cornia, G. A., ed., 2004, *Inequality, Growth, and Poverty in an Era of Liberalization and Globalization*, Oxford: Oxford University Press.

Cornia, G. A. et al., 2004, 'Income distribution changes and their impact in the post Second World War period', in G. A. Cornia, ed., 2004, *Inequality, Growth, and Poverty in an Era of Liberalization and Globalization*, Oxford: Oxford University Press.

Dikhanov, Y. and M. Ward, 2001, 'Evolution of the global distribution of income in 1970–99', *www.eclac.cl/povertystatistics/documentos/dikhanov.pdf*.

Dworkin, R., 2000, *Sovereign Virtue*, Cambridge, MA: Harvard University Press.

Elias, N., and J. Scotson, 1992, *Etablierte und Aussenseiter*, Frankfurt: Suhrkamp.

Eichengreen, B., 2000, 'Capital account liberalization: what do cross-country studies tell us?', *World Bank Economic Review*, 15: 341–65.

European Commission, 2005, *Report on Social Inclusion 2005*, Luxemburg: Office for Official Publications of the European Communities.

Falk, A., and U. Fischbacher, 2002, 'The economics of reciprocity: evidence and theory', in R. Freeman (ed.), *Inequality Around the World*, Basingstoke: Palgrave.

FAO, 2004, *The State of Food Insecurity in the World*, *www.fao.org*.

Firebaugh, G., 2003, *The New Geography of Global Income Inequality*, Cambridge, MA: Harvard University Press.

Fisher, C. et al., 1996, *Inequality by Design*, Princeton, NJ: Princeton University Press.

Fitoussi, J.-P., and P. Savidan, 2003, 'Les inégalités', *Comprendre*, No. 4.

Fitzpatrick., R., and T. Charandola, 2000, 'Health', in A. H. Halsey and J. Webb, eds, *Twentieth-Century British Social Trends*, Basingstoke: Macmillan.

Frank, R., and P. Cook, 1995, *The Winner-Take-All-Society*, New York: The Free Press.

Flora, P. et al., 1987, *State, Economy, and Society in Western Europe 1815–1975*, 2 vols, Vol. II, Frankfurt: Campus.

Fraser, N., and A. Honneth, 2003, *Redistribution or Recognition?*, London: Verso.

Galbraith, J., 2002, 'A perfect crime: inequality in the age of globalization', *Daedalus*, Winter: 11–25.

Galtung, J., 1971, 'A structural theory of imperialism', *Journal of Peace Research*, 2: 307–27.

Gerschenkron, A., 1962, *Economic Backwardness in Historical Perspective*, Cambridge, MA: Belknap/Harvard University Press.

Glendon, M. A., 2001, *A World Made New*, New York: Random House.

Glewwe, P., 1988, 'The distribution of welfare in Côte d'Ivoire in 1985', Washington, DC: World Bank Living Standards Measurement Study Working Paper No. 39.

Goffman, E., 1963, *Stigma*, Englewood Cliffs, NJ: Prentice-Hall.

Harris-White, B., 2003, *India Working*, Cambridge: Cambridge University Press.

Hoff, K., and P. Pandey, 2003, 'Why are social inequalities so durable?', Washington, DC: World Bank Working Paper.

Honneth, A., 1992, *Kampf um Anerkennung*, Frankfurt: Suhrkamp.

ILO, 2001, *World Employment Report 2001*, Geneva: ILO.

Inter-American Development Bank, 1998, *Facing Up to Inequality in Latin America*, Washington, DC: Johns Hopkins University Press.

Khan, A. R., and C. Riskin, 2001, *Inequality and Poverty in China in the Age of Globalization*, Oxford: Oxford University Press.

Lindbeck, A., and D. Snower, 1988, *The Insider–Outsider Theory of Employment and Unemployment*, Cambridge, MA: MIT Press.

Lindert, P., 2000, 'Three centuries of inequality in Britain and America', in A. Atkinson and F. Bourguignon, eds, 2000, *Handbook of Income Distribution*, Vol. I, Amsterdam: North-Holland.

Luhmann, N., 1997, *Die Gesellschaft der Gesellschaft*, 2 vols, Frankfurt: Suhrkamp.

Luxemburg Income Study 2004, *www.lisproject.org/keyfigures*.

Maddison, A., 2001, *The World Economy: A Millennial Perspective*, Paris: OECD.

Marmot, M., and M. Bobak, 2005, 'Social and economic changes and health in Europe East and West', *European Review*, 13(1): 15–31.

Melchior, A. et al., 2000, *Globalisering og ulikhet*, Oslo: Utenriksdepartementet.

Milanovic, B., 2002, 'The world income distribution, 1988 and 1993: first calculation based on household surveys alone', *Economic Journal*, 112: 51–92.

— 2003, 'Is inequality in Africa really different?', Washington, DC: World Bank Working Paper.

— 2004, 'Can we discern the effect of globalization on income distribution?', Washington, DC: Carnegie Endowment for International Peace.

Mitchell, B. R., 1998a, *International Historical Statistics. The Americas 1750–1993*, 4th edn, Basingstoke: Macmillan.

— 1998b, *International Historical Statistics. Africa, Asia, and Oceania 1750–1993*, 3rd edn, Basingstoke: Macmillan.

Montecinos, V., and J. Markoff, 2001, 'From the power of economic ideas to the power of economists', in M.A. Centeno and F. López-Alves, eds., *The Other Mirror*, Princeton, NJ: Princeton University Press, pp. 105–50.

Morgan, W., 1975, *American Slavery American Freedom*, New York: W. W. Norton.

Morrisson, C., 2000, 'Historical perspectives on income distribution: the case of Europe', in A. Atkinson and F. Bourguignon, eds, 2000, *Handbook of Income Distribution*, Vol. I, Amsterdam: North-Holland.

Navarro, V., ed., 2004, *The Political and Social Contexts of Health*, Amityville, NY: Baywood.

Obstfeld, M., and A. Taylor, 2002, 'Globalization and capital markets', Washington, DC: National Bureau of Economic Research Working Paper.

O'Rourke, K., and J. Williamson, 1999, *Globalization and History*, Cambridge, MA: MIT Press.

O'Rourke, K., 2001, 'Globalization and inequality: historical trends', in B. Pleskovic and N. Stern, eds, *Annual World Bank Conference on Development Economics 2001/2002*, Washington, DC: World Bank

Paugam, S., ed., 1996, *L'Exclusion, l'état des savoirs*, Paris: La Découverte.

Piketty, T., 2000, *Les hauts revenus en France au XXe siècle*, Paris: Grasset.

Przeworski, A., and J. Vreeland, 2000, 'The effect of IMF programs on economic growth', *Journal of Development Economics*, 62: 385–421.

Ravaillon, M., 2004, 'Looking beyond averages in the trade and poverty debate', Washington, DC: World Bank Working Paper.

Rodrik, D., 2001, 'Why is there so much economic insecurity in Latin America?', *CEPAL Review*, 73: 7–30.

Rokkan, S., 1967, 'Geography, religion and social class: cross-cutting cleavages in Norwegian politics', in S. M. Lipset and S. Rokkan, eds, *Party Systems and Voter Alignments. Cross-National Perspectives*, New York: Free Press.

— 1970, 'Nation-building, cleavage formation, and the structuring of mass politics', in S. Rokkan et al., *Citizens, Elections, Parties*, Oslo: Universitetsforlaget.

Sen, A., 1992, *Inequality Reexamined*, Cambridge, MA: Harvard University Press.

Sennett, R., 2002, *Respect in a World of Inequality*, New York: W. W. Norton.

Shavit, Y., and H.-P. Blossfeld, 1993, *Persistent Inequality*, Boulder, CO: Westview.

Sorensen, A. B., 1996, 'The structural basis of social inequality', *American Journal of Sociology*, 101: 1333–65.

Steiner, H., and Ph. Alston, eds, 1996, *International Human Rights in Context*, Oxford: Clarendon Press.

Stiglitz, J., 2002, *Globalization and Its Discontents*, London: Allen Lane/Penguin.

Székely, M., and M. Hilgert, 2000, 'What drives differences in inequality across countries?' Washington, DC: Inter-American Development Bank Working Paper.

Therborn, G., 2003, 'Dimensions and processes of global inequalities', in G. Skapska and A. Orla-Bukowska, eds, *The Moral Fabric in Contemporary Societies*, Leiden and Boston: Brill.

— 2004, *Between Sex and Power: Family in the World, 1900–2000*, London: Routledge.

— 2006, 'Europe and Asias: in the global political economy, and in the world as a cultural system', in G. Therborn and H. Khondker, eds, *Asia and Europe in Globalization*, Leiden: Brill.

Tilly, C., 1998, *Durable Inequality*, Berkeley: University of California Press.

UNAIDS, 2004, *AIDS Epidemic Update December 2004, www.unaids.org*.

UNDP, 1994, *Human Development Report 1994*, Geneva: UNDP.

— 1996, *Human Development Report 1996*, Geneva: UNDP.

— 2001, *Human Development Report 2001*, Geneva: UNDP.

— 2002, *Human Development Report 2002*, Geneva: UNDP.

— 2004, *Human Development Report 2004, www.hdr.undp.org*.

UNFPA, 2004, *The State of the World's Population*, New York: UNFPA.

USAID, 2003, 'The health sector human resource crisis in Africa: an issues paper', Washington, DC: USAID.

Vreeland, J. R., 2002, 'The effect of IMF programs on labor', *Word Development*, 30: 121–39.

Wade, R. H., 2004, 'Is globalization reducing inequality?', *International Journal of Health Services*, 34: 381–414.

WHO, 2004, *World Health Report 2004*, Geneva: WHO.

WIDER, 2004, *World Income Inequality Database, www.wider.unu.edu.*

Wilkinson, R. G., 1996, *Unhealthy Societies: The Afflictions of Inequality*, London: Routledge.

— 2000, *Mind the Gap: Hierarchies, Health, and Human Evolution*, London: Weidenfeld and Nicolson.

Wolfensohn, J., and F. Bourguignon, 2004, *Development and Poverty Reduction: Looking, Looking Ahead*, World Bank Report, *www.worldbank.org.*

World Bank, 2005a, *World Development Report 2005*, New York: Oxford University Press.

— 2005b, *World Development Indicators*, Washington, DC: World Bank.

Part I

Varieties of Inequality

2

Do Health Inequalities Persist in the New Global Order? A European Perspective

Denny Vågerö

Introduction

Individuals are not born equal. Health chances already differ systematically at birth, and as individuals move through their life cycles such differences tend to be reinforced. Their health and social careers influence each other mutually at each stage of the life cycle. Often they have common social roots, such as the parents' social, financial, or ethnic position in their country of residence. Thus it is no surprise that large social differences in health are documented in all countries. Even in modern societies, such as the Scandinavian ones, health inequalities are substantial, noticeable also among the newborn. This is the case in spite of a half-century or more of policies and values emphasizing equality.

Cross-national comparisons of countries in Western Europe suggest that the magnitude of health inequalities in these countries is fairly similar. Also, there seems to be no clear relation between the size of health inequalities on the one hand and the size of economic inequalities or the size of the welfare state on the other. However, hardly any study has been able to look at the development of health inequalities and their relation to economic inequalities or the growth of the welfare state from a longer perspective. If health and survival chances in mid-life are dependent on decades of accumulated social experience, data collected at one point in time may not be sufficient to predict either the level of health and survival in a population or its social distribution.

A comparison of Eastern and Western European countries is revealing: the present health gap has developed over a four-decade-long period, although the 1990s saw a particularly sharp increase. Obviously, problems of mass poverty play a role (especially in the former Soviet Union), but it is equally the case that history imposes a health burden on these countries. Even when they advance they might not easily manage to close the gap with Western European countries.

Global health levels can be influenced today by, for instance, reducing infant and child mortality. There are many examples of how levels of health can be improved even in the poorest of countries. However, reducing inequalities in infant, child, and adult mortality in such countries may be more difficult. The policy agenda needs to be long-term, certainly more than one generation. Reducing global health inequalities so that the health chances of a newborn child are not dependent on which country and social class she is born in is a truly formidable task.

Long-term Health Trends

During the last one hundred years, life expectancy has increased by two to three decades in what is now called the developed world. At the end of the nineteenth century, my city, Stockholm, had the same level of infant mortality as have some of the most overcrowded cities in the Third World today. One in five babies died before age one (Burström and Bernhardt 2002). In 2000, in contrast, three babies per one thousand born alive die before the age of one in Sweden (0.032 per cent).

Changes such as these do indeed represent fundamental social change. They are closely linked to the social transformation and modernization of a country. A long-term series of infant mortality for boys and girls born in Sweden from 1750 onwards illustrates this change well (Figure 2.1).

Child mortality displays a similar picture, mainly due to the successive reduction of mortality from childhood infections. It goes without saying that

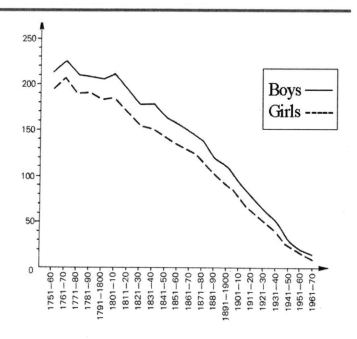

Figure 2.1   Infant Mortality in Sweden, 1751–1970

Source: Statistics Sweden.

parents' attitudes to and expectations for their children change alongside this fall in infant and child mortality. Birth rates came to fall, partly as a result of this improved survival. This phenomenon is known as the demographic transition.

There was also an epidemiological transition. This term was coined by Abdel Omran (1971). By this he refers to the fact that the cause-of-death structure changes radically during the demographic transition. Infectious diseases, which were by far the most common cause of death in the nineteenth and early twentieth centuries, were replaced by chronic illnesses, such as circulatory disease and cancer. In Sweden today one in two deaths are due to circulatory disease (mainly heart disease or stroke), and one in three deaths are due to cancer. In contrast, infectious diseases are a small part of the cause-of-death panorama. The beginning of a process to control chronic disease mortality, which manifests itself as a decline in chronic disease mortality rates

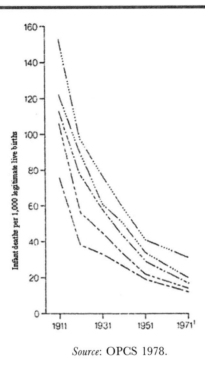

Source: OPCS 1978.

in Western countries, has taken place since about the 1970s. This has been referred to as the fourth stage of the epidemiological transition (Caselli et al. 2002). Western Europe, but not Russia, has entered this stage.

These two processes, the demographic and epidemiological transitions, are linked to each other, intertwined and non-separable. Together they represent a truly revolutionary change in people's life chances, taken literally as chances to survive into adult and old age. These transitions contribute to economic and political change by reducing the disease burden of a population and by allowing human potential to develop more freely (Sen 1999).

Looking instead at the social pattern of mortality is revealing. There is no corresponding sociological transition. British mortality statistics allow us to follow social class differences in mortality from 1911 up to today (OPCS 1978; Drever and Whitehead 1997). Figure 2.2 shows how infant mortality in different social classes falls with the demographic transition, but also how remarkably stable the social class pattern is. We can see that the lines converge somewhat, meaning that differences in infant mortality rates become smaller. Comparing babies born to unskilled workers and babies born to professional households we can note the following: for babies born to unskilled workers, the number of excess deaths (per 1,000 births) during infancy is smaller at the end of the century than at the beginning of it. Absolute differences between social classes have been reduced. But at the same time the relative mortality ratio is almost the same. It is more than twice as dangerous to be born into a family of unskilled workers compared to a professional household both at the beginning and at the end of the century. Thus the old social class pattern seems to be repeated in each new generation. The same is true when looking at adult mortality (OPCS 1978). This social 'inertia' is quite remarkable. The social pattern of death is remarkably resistant to change, even when the most common causes of death have changed and overall mortality falls sharply.

Why? This question is one of the reasons why the study of health inequalities must lead into the study of fundamental social processes.

What Drives Long-term Health Changes?

Long-term determinants of health are usually studied by looking at mortality data. Perhaps the answer to the question depends on which specific time period we are talking about. For instance, it is likely that the importance of medical knowledge increases over time, so that it is more important today than it was a hundred years ago. Stating the importance of medical knowledge is not the same as stating the importance of medical care. Medical knowledge may be important both because it changes medical care and because it changes people's perceptions of what health risks are and how to cope with them – for instance, how to live healthily and how to avoid health risks by individual and collective efforts. Collective efforts to change health risks often enter into local and national politics.

Thomas McKeown, in his famous work on the role of medicine, concluded that medical care was *not* the driving force behind the mortality reduction between 1850 and 1970 (McKeown 1979). He substantiated his controversial claim by looking into trends of mortality reductions, cause by cause. According to his reading of the evidence, the fall of mortality from common causes of death – for instance, child mortality from whooping cough – started long before antibiotics and vaccines were known or became generally available. The introduction of these medications resulted in only minor oscillations around a very steady downward trend in mortality (Figure 2.3). His conclusion was that economic development, leading to better sanitation and public hygiene, and above all to better nutrition, were the driving forces behind the fall in mortality, rather than the introduction of new medical treatments.

In a critique of McKeown, Simon Szreter, a Cambridge historian, took the view that economic development in itself did not guarantee better health for the population. More important was how resources were used. The politics

Figure 2.3 Whooping Cough: Death Rates for Children Under 15, England and Wales 1850–1970

Source: McKeown 1979

concerning these were important. Medical knowledge may have worked not only through the improvement of medical care, but also, and more importantly, by encouraging public health action against known health risks, before any remedies were known. Szreter's formulation is that 'a battling public health ideology' was the crucial influence that shaped the way local communities came to deal with commonly perceived health risks (Szreter 1984).

The first comprehensive public health act in Britain, the Liverpool Sanitary Act, was passed in 1846 under the ominous shadow of growing political radicalism in the urban lower and middle classes. The publication of statistics on mortality became common at this time. It was a pan-European phenomenon, which also included North America. Statistics comparing poor and rich, occupations, regions, or countries were published in Britain, Germany, France, Belgium, Russia, Sweden, the USA, and Canada. Moral statistics became a genre in its own right. Suicide mortality was of particular concern. These published statistics were often used as arguments for social reform. Medical knowledge thus played a role in that social reform process, which culminated in the 1848 European revolutions (Vågerö 1983).

An example can illustrate this: Rudolf Virchow, one of the founding fathers of social medicine, published his study of the causes of the typhus epidemic in Silesia in the 1840s. His conclusion was a question. Is there not an infinite need for reform of housing, clothing, and nutrition to avoid new epidemics? The doctor was the natural ally of the poor, and medicine was a social science and had to be reformed, wrote Virchow. This reform movement inside medicine reached all over Europe. It was linked to the larger social movement of the 1840s. Virchow became a member of the revolutionary Frankfurt Parliament in 1848. When the political tide turned, many of its ideas were nevertheless carried forward and later made imprints in health legislation (Boenheim 1957). Later this ideology influenced government policy in many countries.

Thus the early fall of mortality, based on emerging control of infectious disease, may have been due in large part to public health politics informed by new medical knowledge, and facilitated, but not driven by, growing economic resources.

Today, the situation is more complex. Medicine is more powerful, more often evidence-based, and less influenced by traditional ideas about disease causation; it is more focused on medical treatment and therefore more effective in treating patients and improving survival. Nevertheless, the same argument as earlier could be made. Medical care is not driving the fall in mortality. This does not mean that it is unimportant. Medical care today may be more important for the survival of infants and for the very old than for the survival of young and middle-aged men and women.

Per capita expenditure on medical care is important for life expectancy in poor countries where infant mortality is high, but not very much so among the rich countries (Figure 2.4). So which circumstances do determine health risks in the richer and poorer parts of the world? Sharp differences between social classes, occupational groups, ethnic categories, and countries point to social, economic, and political factors, often referred to as 'the causes behind the causes'.

Figure 2.4   Life Expectancy at Birth in 1999 By Per Capita Total Health Expenditure, 1997

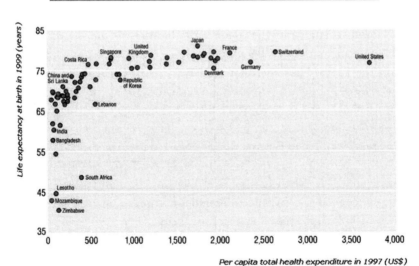

Source: Leon et al. 2001.

Circulatory diseases (or cardiovascular disease, i.e. heart disease and stroke) are a case in point. Their development after 1945 has been referred to as 'the rise and fall of Western disease' (Barker 1989). Immediately after the Second World War they became more common, and mortality due to circulatory disease rose sharply among adult men. However, in the last 20–30 years, incidence of, and mortality from, circulatory diseases fell in Western developed countries (Figure 2.9). Is the present decline in Western Europe and North America due to medication, lifestyle changes, improved nutrition, or higher incomes? And why do we see an increase in social class differences in this group of diseases during the last three decades in rich countries?

It is likely that medical knowledge has played an important role in bringing death rates down – for instance, through lifestyle change. Lifestyle changes were influenced by new medical knowledge about the health hazards of

Figure 2.5   Life Expectancy by Regions in the World, 1950–2000

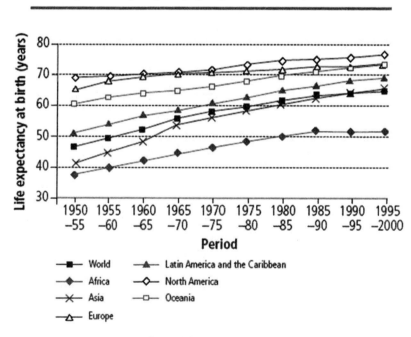

Source: Moser et al. 2005

tobacco smoking, and by the health benefits of exercise and of eating fruit and vegetables, and so on. Government policies were also influenced; we see this most clearly from the ever-increasing taxes on tobacco products. This again illustrates how the role of medical knowledge is much wider than that of medical care. New medical knowledge about health risks can become a tool for politics. When such knowledge is grasped by the population at large it represents an empowering of individuals. In contrast, medical knowledge that does not enhance the understanding of health risks, but is primarily focused on new medical treatments, may create dependency on the medical profession.

The grasp of empowering medical knowledge is certainly unevenly distributed in society, following traditional fault lines. Campaigns to stop tobacco smoking (for instance) have been more successful among the upper than among the lower classes. In this way the upper classes distance themselves from the lower ones in terms of health. Such inequality hardly harms the lower classes, at least not in the short term, but in the long run it probably reinforces social divisions in general. Health education is indeed believed to have contributed to increasing social differences in circulatory and general mortality in many countries in, or around, the 1980s (Wing 1988).

Work-related circulatory disease may be an example of the opposite. Empowering knowledge and collective action to change work-related risks may be more common among blue-collar than white-collar workers, due to the stronger tradition of collective action and unionization among the former. Risks for circulatory disease and accidents have both been linked to the individual worker's influence and control over his/her work. Stress medicine teaches that greater control is linked to lower blood pressure, a more adequate biological response to stress, less heart disease and fewer accidents (Marmot et al. 1997). In Scandinavia, such medical knowledge became a tool used by trade unions to push for work environment reform. One of the most influential Swedish trade unions (Metall), heavily influenced by theories of stress medicine, adopted a programme for the 'good work' in 1989 (Svenska Metallindustriarbetarförbundet 1989). By this they mean a job that allows one to control one's own immediate work process and allows personal development on the job. It should therefore also reduce health risks and protect individual health. Work environment change, and the empowering of workers, represent a substantial potential for reducing chronic disease mortality, such as mortality from cancer, but in particular mortality from circulatory disease. Non-fatal disease such as disorders of the musculo-skeletal system would also be reduced.

Medical knowledge knows no national borders. But changes in circulatory disease mortality in developed countries (from generally rising trends after 1945 to falling trends three or four decades later) did not seem to follow the diffusion of medical knowledge across countries. Finnish circulatory mortality (for males) peaked in the mid-1970s, then fell, presumably under the influence of new and more healthy habits, but in Sweden this turn took place almost ten years later (Baker et al. 1993). Circulatory disease mortality in Finland was higher than in Sweden, thus the new knowledge may have fallen on more fertile soil in Finland and therefore had an earlier impact. In the communist part of Europe this knowledge had little impact: it hardly penetrated down to the common man or woman and had little influence on national policies for health. Russia (like Ukraine, Belarus, and Moldavia) has not yet (in 2003) reached that stage of the epidemiological transition where circulatory disease mortality is beginning to be controlled.[1] Such mortality is still on the increase, while life expectancy is again falling (Goskomstat 2004). Control of circulatory disease mortality is most likely to take place when individuals act to change their behaviour and governments simultaneously act to change policies.

In conclusion, medical and health knowledge could be expected to be increasingly important over time, but there is no one-to-one relationship between the diffusion of new knowledge and improved health. The translation of knowledge into individual and/or collective action seems crucial. This takes place in a cultural/political setting. So far the arena for collective action has usually been local community politics or national politics, but there are also concerns that have become global policy issues. Again, global anti-tobacco politics may be a model for what might happen in other areas later. The global health agenda, as developed by the WHO and similar actors, also influences national governments. For instance, its focus on Health for All and emphasis on health inequalities within and between countries have had a big impact. Rightly so, since the reduction of such inequalities represents one of the major potentials for health improvements (Vågerö 1995). In 2005 this insight lead the WHO to appoint a Commission for Social Determinants of

Health, charged with the task of changing the global health policy agenda towards the 'causes of the causes', in other words towards fundamental social, political, and economic circumstances determining health.

Global Economic Growth and Health

The growth of world GDP is, for reasons stated above, not necessarily linked to an improvement in the health of the world population. If world production is used for military build-up rather than to improve conditions for the world majority it is unlikely to lead to improved global health. The Cold War coincided with an unprecedented arms build-up across the globe. State military expenditures in this era correlated positively with infant mortality; the higher the proportion of state budgets used for military purposes, the higher the infant mortality (Woolhandler and Himmelstein 1995). The military build-up of the Soviet Union, especially after 1970, is believed to have contributed to its long period of stagnation, its rise in infant mortality in the early 1970s and its falling life expectancy from 1970 onwards (Field 1986; Demine 2000). At the end of the 1980s, as the Cold War and its arms race appeared to come to an end, many commentators predicted that this would result in positive economic and social developments, including health, the so-called 'peace dividend'. If there were such a dividend, it fell into the hands of the few.

In addition, many observers have worried about the environmental impact of economic growth. Each national effort to produce wealth leaves a 'footprint' on our common physical and social environment. Is economic growth sustainable? If the world population (presently at 6.2 billion individuals) grows and consumption per capita grows at the same time, perhaps by approaching present US levels, we may exhaust mankind's capacity to sustain itself (McMichael 2000). Global life expectancy today is about 66 years and increasing, but not as rapidly as earlier. McMichael and Butler (2002) suggested that the slowing down of the rate of increase may in fact be a sign that we are approaching such an exhaustion. Living on the margin of our resources could manifest itself either as falling global life expectancy or by falling populations, or both, they suggest. By multiplying the present figure for global life expectancy with the size of the present world population McMichael and Butler created a measure called Global Years of Life Expectancy (GYLE; thus 66 years x 6.2 billion = 410 billion GYLE). This is meant to be a simple measure of our civilization's 'human carrying capacity'.

What is the limit of that capacity? It is certainly dynamic and can be extended by living more carefully, with more regard for nature and basic human needs, and with the help of superior technology. It is predicted that in 2050 the world population will stabilize at around 9 billion individuals (Lutz et al. 2001). The proportion of the world population aged 60 + is estimated by the same authors at being 22 per cent in 2050, as against 10 per cent today, and rising to 34 per cent by the end of the twentieth century. A stabilized world population, with one in three persons aged 60 +, seems a very different situation from the present demographic dynamics.

What will be the state of global health inequalities in such a world? Falling mortality rates across the world will very likely lead to reduced inequalities in an absolute sense (difference in number of deaths per 100,000 population). But, judging from national time trends, this may not stop relative mortality differences (ratio of mortality rate per 100,000 population between two groups of countries) from remaining the same, or even widen. The predictions by Lutz et al. (see also United Nations 1999) are explicitly based on the optimistic view of steadily falling mortality rates accompanied by falling fertility worldwide. Are there any grounds for doubting such a scenario?

Moser et al. (2005) show that country differences in life expectancy grew smaller from 1950 to around 1990 (Figure 2.5). During the 1990s, however, this trend was broken and convergence was replaced by divergence. Figure 2.6 shows the so-called 'dispersion measure of mortality' from 1950–2000. Its increase is mostly explained by 24 countries in the world, which experienced falling life expectancies in the 1990s. Sixteen of those were in sub-Saharan Africa and six in the former Soviet Union; the remaining two were North Korea and Iraq.

New health threats give cause for concern. These include the recent rise in infectious disease including AIDS, and a parallel fall in life expectancy in parts of sub-Saharan Africa. Old unsolved health problems, such as the rise of chronic disease and the resulting fall of life expectancy in parts of the former Soviet Union, should also concern us. These could be seen as inherent shortcomings of a world system characterized by uneven economic growth

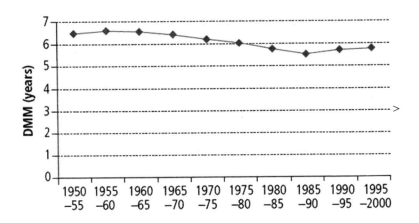

Figure 2.6   Dispersion measure of mortality for regions in the world,
1950–2000

Source: Moser et al. 2005.

without sufficient concern for its environmental and human impacts. The question is whether these recent health setbacks are temporary phenomena, or whether they do indeed represent a more long-term problem of the emerging global order. Cornia cautioned that health improvements have decelerated perceptibly, especially so during the 1990s, under the influence of a new global order of increasing market deregulation, economic shocks, and recurrent social upheavals (Cornia 2001).

If we are getting closer to the margins of present earth resources, differences between countries are no longer a question of certain countries distancing themselves from others, without harming the latter, but rather a cause of conflict. Conflicts about water rights in the Middle East are a simple illustration of this. Another illustration is the depletion of fish stocks on the coast of West Africa, by large European trawling fleets to the detriment of local fishing communities.

In the developing world today, almost one in three children may suffer from malnutrition, a proportion that has remained static during the 1990s. The mortality rate ratio when comparing children of poor and rich families in the developing world is increasing, indicating a persistent, perhaps increasing, social gap. In sub-Saharan Africa twenty countries have a lower income per capita in real terms today than they had in the late 1970s. In five out of seven sub-Saharan countries studied by Demographic and Health Surveys, the proportion of underweight children increased from the 1980s to the 1990s (Minujin and Delamonica 2002). Other parts of the world outside the global market arena also suffer from starvation, in particular North Korea. Starvation is by no means a problem of the past. It is above all caused by war between countries and armed conflicts within countries (Nussbaumer 2003). It seems that the present world system is careless in looking after its human potential. It leaves important segments of the world population behind. Therefore, it is not sufficient to look at the effect of economic growth on average levels of health in the world, nor in countries (Gwatkin 2000). The rapid increase in life expectancy during the twentieth century is indeed encouraging. But the enormous and increasing gap in life chances across the globe after 1990 is alarming.

The East–West Health Divide in Europe

Over the last decades a huge health gap has developed in Europe (WHO 1997; Figure 2.7). Consider two similar countries, very near each other and with related populations, cultures and languages: Estonia and Finland. At the turn of the millennium they differed in life expectancy by more than seven years, in spite of now having (superficially at least) similar social systems (Figure 2.8). It is clear that the 'European Health Divide' of today is in large part an effect of history. It is related to the closely linked histories of the two antagonistic political/economic blocs that stood against each other in Europe for a large part of the twentieth century; and in particular to the way the Soviet system collapsed after 1989. However, the divide goes back further. In 1910 infant mortality rates in those countries that were eventually to become the communist bloc were distinctly lower than in the countries of Western Europe (Caselli 1994).

In the aftermath of the Second World War, up to around 1968, a clear

Figure 2.7   Age-Standardized Mortality from All Causes Among Men in Regions of Europe, 1990–1991

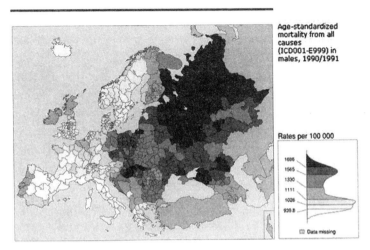

Source: WHO 1997.

Figure 2.8   Life Expectancy at Birth in Russia, Estonia, Finland, and Sweden, 1970–2000, Men and Women combined.

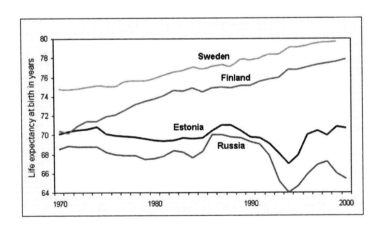

Source: WHO Health for All Data Base, Estonian Statistical Office.

convergence of health trends was at hand across Europe, measuring health as life expectancy. Thus in 1969 Central and Eastern Europe was only around two years behind Western Europe in life expectancy. Russia, which in 1895 had a ten-year lower life expectancy than France, had almost caught up with France at this time (Meslé et al. 1996; Patterson 1995). One important factor behind this convergence was a successful reduction of child mortality from infectious disease all over Europe. The knowledge of how to prevent such disease was shared and could be translated into political and social action in both systems. In contrast, the knowledge of how to prevent circulatory and other chronic disease was not applied in the East, causing sharply diverging mortality trends in Europe. The graph shows this for male circulatory mortality (Meslé 2002; Figure 2.9).

The stagnation of the Soviet system, from 1970 onwards, was visible in health trends. One could talk about a stagnation crisis, with slowly increasing

Figure 2.9   Age-Standardized Mortality from Circulatory Diseases among Men in France, Poland, Russia, and United Kingdom, 1950–98.

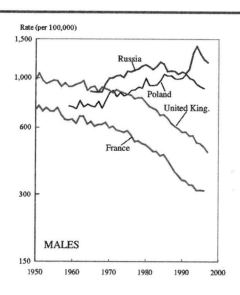

Source: Mesle et al. 2002.

mortality (men) or a stand-still (women) over the 1970–84 period for almost all the communist-led countries in Europe and for each of the republics in the Soviet Union. It was a system-inherent problem, tied to the way the system was managed. Perestroika, the first sign of a vitalization of the system, resulted in a rapid improvement in life expectancy during 1984–87, but the collapse of the system in 1989–91 was followed by an almost unprecedented fall in life expectancy, by seven years between 1987 and 1994 for men in Russia. Walberg demonstrated that those regions (*oblasts*) that had the highest labour turnover during the first years of the new system also had the sharpest fall in life expectancy in 1990–94 (Walberg et al. 1998). Mass poverty in all the ex-Soviet Union republics was certainly one of the driving forces in this development. All the ex-communist countries experienced a shorter or longer crisis in population health as the old system was replaced by the new; least so in the Czech Republic and worst in the ex-Soviet Union republics (Meslé 2002).

The immediate causes behind the East European health crises of the 1990s are being debated lively in specialist journals for the moment. Sometimes the question is put differently: what are the underlying causes that create the difference between East and West? Clearly the high mortality and low life expectancy in the East is primarily driven by shortcomings in their old and new social systems. In the communist countries, unlike in Western Europe, governments had failed to begin to control the rise of chronic disease, and the new governments after 1989–91 all had other priorities than the health of their populations.

But perhaps there is also an element of a 'systemic effect' on health from the 'East/West system' in Europe? The existence of a 'divide' will in itself give rise to a number of social, economic, and political processes. This could be witnessed at any border between countries. These processes could be largely integrative, or alternatively create something like a vicious circle of mutual exclusion and distance. Perhaps it is the awareness of this that has created the irresistible pull towards the European Union on a large number of countries in Central and Eastern Europe, which all prefer to be 'inside' rather than 'outside', excluded. I assume that present social, economic, and political divisions could reinforce each other mutually. Political, economic, and social divisions between different parts of Europe are to some extent driven by the EU and Russia as the main two poles. This includes health divisions – a

Europe divided in health may result from European social, economic, and political divisions, but at the same time reinforce the latter.

A few examples illustrate how this may work, for instance through asymmetric economic relations. The protectionist European agricultural policy means that export opportunities for countries outside the EU are blocked. Economic opportunities in the West attract skilled and unskilled workers from the East. For Russia, the brain drain to the USA and Europe is in fact a big problem. In the spring of 2002 I visited the Academic City (Akademgorodok) outside Novosibirsk, where a hundred research institutes were once concentrated. I was told how a large number of their best scientists had been headhunted by Western companies and had left for Europe, the USA or Israel. Microsoft has bought up a large part of Russia's best computer scientists. In this way the economic divisions perpetuate themselves, with indirect consequences for health.

More directly health-related 'asymmetries' also exist. As Western tobacco companies have become increasingly regulated inside Europe and North America, they have established new markets by going East. Going East was accompanied by the slogan 'Go West', the name of a new brand of cigarettes, heavily advertised in the emerging and unregulated markets of Central and Eastern Europe. A similar practice, of exporting occupational or industrial hazards (most commonly to developing countries), is well documented (La Dou 1992).

Today it is clear that countries in Central and Eastern Europe are moving forward along different paths. Those countries that are already in the EU have seen a more favourable health development than countries such as Russia, Ukraine, Belarus, and Moldavia. It seems that realignment from one sphere of influence to another has already paid off also in terms of health. Of particular interest are Estonia, Latvia, and Lithuania. For decades they have followed mortality trends in Russia closely. This was true during the stagnation crisis in the 1970s during perestroika, when health improved rapidly, and during the shock therapy crisis of the first year of the new social system. In terms of life expectancy 1994 was the worst years for Russia, as well as for Estonia, Latvia, and Lithuania. From 1994 mortality trends in all the Baltic Republics and in Russia, for both men and women, became more favourable. Life expectancy improved from that year until 1998. This was taken as a sign of a positive adjustment to new circumstances (Figure 2.8).

But in August 1998 the 'Asian Flu'', spreading from Thailand and the Asian 'tiger economies', hit Russia, and the rouble collapsed. The rouble crisis in Russia led to immediate loss of income, savings, and employment for many. Life expectancy in Russia again fell in 1999, in 2000, in 2001, in 2002, and 2003, largely driven by a new rise in circulatory disease, this time in spite of the economic upturn from 2000. In sharp contrast, all three Baltic Republics have continued to improve their life expectancy (although modestly) since 1998. The Asian flu hit their economies too, but its impact was less, and health improvements continued. This break between the close paths of Russia and the Baltic republics is quite significant. It shows the vulnerability of the Russian population to externally imposed economic shocks, while it seems that all three Baltic republics have now managed to build up a minimum of control against such impact.

Whether or not the East – West health divide in Europe is going to persist, perhaps reinforced, or disappear gradually, is an open question. The dividing line certainly seems to shift eastwards. The outcome will depend on the larger political and economical developments inside and outside Europe. Of specific importance is the ability of governments in Russia, Ukraine, Belarus, and Moldavia to grasp the causes of their long-standing public health problems and to respond with adequate policies. So far they have been quite passive. The Russian government, for instance, is very concerned about the present population decline in Russia. In spite of a relatively large immigration (7 million persons after 1991 from former Soviet republics) the population is falling slowly (by 2 million from 1990 to 2002). The political response has mainly focused on the fall in fertility. The mortality rise, in contrast, has more or less been ignored. Some observers have seen this as a legacy from the past, where the loss of individual lives was of minor concern for the (Czarist or communist) state. It was in Putin's speech to the nation in May 2003 that the health crisis was for the first time addressed at the highest level (although in vague terms). Here the focus was on drug abuse and infectious diseases such as HIV, numbers one and two concerns of Russia's neighbours and of many international organizations. Russia's biggest health problems, the uncontrolled epidemic of cardiovascular disease and the many deaths from violent causes (such as accidents and suicides), were not addressed.

The present health divide in Europe has historical causes but has at the same time been strongly aggravated by the immediate effect of the social transformation of Eastern Europe. During its first decade this transformation distanced (in health terms) in particular Russia, Belarus, Ukraine, and Moldavia from the rest of Europe. Its most obvious contribution to poor health is mass poverty; more heavy alcohol consumption is another. The rise of alcohol drinking in adverse circumstances, however, is also an example of how 'long waves' of cultural patterns, most clearly in Russia, contribute. Of the historical causes the Second World War experience is probably very important.

Social Inequalities in Health within European Countries

Social differences in health and mortality within countries have been known and documented for more than a century. The last two decades have seen an unprecedented rise of scholarly work in this field. This work has clarified beyond doubt the fact that health and survival are strongly influenced by our social circumstances, the position we have in society, and what kind of society we live in. There are of course also individual health differences between people that are not much affected by such social factors. For someone with a specific gene, a disease such as Huntington's chorea can be virtually unavoidable in whatever social circumstances he/she lives. This is rare, however. Normally the latter kind of difference has not been referred to as a health inequality. Health inequality has been a term by which most researchers have referred to differences by education, occupation, income, ethnicity, region or perhaps country. Gender differences also, in spite of their genetic component, have been described by this term.

The term health inequalities, or the target of 'health equity' as formulated by the WHO, also signals a moral concern; we talk about group differences that are probably morally unjustifiable and therefore likely to appear on the political agenda in one way or another. In 1984 they appeared on the WHO agenda, their reduction being stated as WHO target number one (WHO 1985). The fact that disadvantaged occupations, regions, or ethnic groups find out about their relative health position provides in itself an impetus to reduce that disadvantage. Presumably this was one of the reasons for the urgent call for the documentation of such differences that was also made by WHO.[2]

The targets set by the WHO in 1984 suggested that health inequalities should be reduced by 25 per cent before 2000. This referred above all to differences between social groups within countries, but also to differences between countries. Today we can see, with reference to Europe, that none of these targets has been met. In fact, socioeconomic differences in 2000 were probably bigger than in 1984 in most European countries. Country differences in Europe are also larger, especially along the East–West dimension.

Unfortunately, from the point of view of reaching these targets, their implementation coincided with a wave of neoliberal policies across Europe and elsewhere. Income differences increased; social infrastructure, such as resources for schools and health services, was cut back; state policies of disease prevention came under attack as illegitimate interventions in people's private lives (especially in the East). Thus, the regulation of alcohol production and consumption was dropped in all ex-communist countries and relaxed in Scandinavia; tobacco advertising found a new life in Eastern Europe and health was defined increasingly as a personal, non-collective, responsibility. The new social order in the East was also formed under the influence of neoliberal ideas, where issues of health protection were not important. Thus the failure to live up to WHO targets is perhaps not unexpected. This does not mean that the targets as such were wrong, but rather that the means of achieving them were not thought through properly and/or were not embraced by governments, in spite of their rhetorical commitment to reducing health inequalities.

Countries such as Sweden, which has a long-standing political commitment to equality in general, are nevertheless plagued by health differences by occupation, social class, education, income, and ethnicity. Even among those born recently (in the last two decades) this is evident; thus in 1985 infants born to parents in manual occupations had on average a 200g lower birth weight than children born to parents in professional occupations (Vågerö et al. 1999). Infant mortality also differed, for instance in that babies of women with low education were 1.6 times more likely than babies of women of university education to die during their first year of life (Gisselman 2005)

Part of the explanation for such persisting inequalities has to do with intergenerational, non-genetic, transmission of health disadvantage. Women who have had a poor childhood themselves are more likely to give birth to smaller children, to babies who develop hypertension, and to boys and girls who are more likely to get heart disease and diabetes as adults. This has little to do with genes. Early social factors give a biological 'imprint' as well as an influence on later life, including health. Health risks at adult age are the result of social disadvantage accumulated over the entire life course and in part transmitted from the previous generation(s). Such a life course perspective on human health is a recent development in medicine (Kuh and Ben-Shlomo 1997). In part it has arisen as a critique of the one-sided focus on adult lifestyle factors, such as smoking and exercise, as the main determinants of adult disease. With this perspective it is not surprising that health inequalities persist even in the most modern welfare states and in spite of the will to reduce them. The time perspective necessary for such an achievement must be several decades and span over more than one generation.

The European Concerted Action to study health inequalities in Europe, led by Johan Mackenbach in Rotterdam, is so far the most thorough exercise in comparing the size of health differences by social class in European countries. Great care was taken about problems of comparability, both in data collection (health survey data and mortality data) and in analysing data. One of its most striking results is that similar health inequalities exist in all parts of Europe; the magnitude is also fairly similar, with some variation (Kunst 1997). The ranking of countries differs depending on whether one looks at absolute or relative mortality difference. Sweden and Norway, for instance, have small health inequalities among middle-aged men if an absolute measure is used, but rank high with a relative measure (Vågerö and Erikson 1997; Figure 2.10). Clearly, ranking based on relative difference does not correlate well with the size or comprehensiveness of the welfare state or with income inequalities measured at the same point in time. Ranking based on absolute differences is somewhat closer to such aspects.

A related discussion has dealt with the importance of income inequalities, first for health in general and second for health inequalities. The early reports that countries with large income inequalities also had a shorter life expectancy (Wilkinson 1992) have largely been vindicated, but the interpretation that it was the psychological atmosphere (or social cohesion) in such countries that mediated the effect of income inequalities on life expectancy (Brunner and Marmot 1999) has been strongly challenged. Wilkinson (1996) has advanced

*Figure 2.10   Mortality for Non-Manual and Manual Workers in Nine European
Countries, ranked by Absolute Level of Mortality of Manual
Workers, Age Groups 45–59*

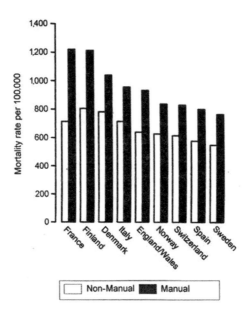

Source: Vågerö and Erikson 1994.

this notion by introducing the concept of 'cultures of inequality'. Such cultures allow inequality in many spheres of life, and subsequently, according to Wilkinson, they will also allow health inequalities to rise. An alternative explanation has focused on the social infrastructure, such as schools, health services, housing, and unemployment benefits, which tend to be more generous in countries with small income inequalities (Davey Smith et al. 1996; Lynch et al. 2002). Mackenbach, in a recent editorial for the *British Medical Journal*, concluded that most of the effect of income inequalities on health was due to individual poverty; there were more people in poverty in countries with large income differentials and thus individual experience of poverty, rather than (aggregate) societal characteristics, was the most likely explanation of the observed association between life expectancy and income inequality. The strongest evidence for an independent (higher-level) effect of income inequalities comes from regional US data, but there is little such evidence from European or Canadian data (Mackenbach 2002).

Regardless of which of these alternative explanations is more correct in explaining country differences in life expectancy, countries with large income inequalities do not necessarily seem to have large health inequalities. According to the same group of studies, health inequalities in the USA were more or less of the same magnitude as in Western Europe, in spite of the much larger income inequalities in that country. Furthermore, even before 1990, mortality differences by education or manual/non-manual class seemed larger in those countries in Eastern Europe for which comparable data were available, for instance Hungary and the Czech Republic, than they were in Western Europe, in spite of the more narrow income distribution in the former group of countries

Figure 2.11   Probability of Dying Between 45th and 65th Birthday:
Men in Non-Manual and Manual Classes

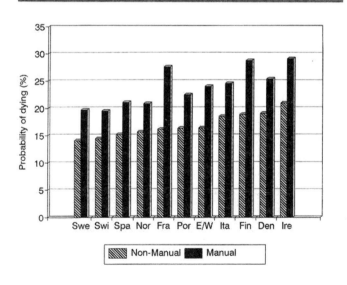

Source: Kunst 1997.

(Kunst 1997). As income distributions became more unequal in Eastern Europe in the 1990s, health inequalities there seem to have widened also. Data from Russia and Estonia on mortality differences by education give evidence for this. In those two countries educational differences in mortality widened sharply during the 1990s (Shkolnikov et al. 1998; Leinsalu et al. 2003).

Unexpectedly, therefore, large income inequalities are not necessarily accompanied by large health inequalities. Neither do small income differences guarantee small health inequalities. The explanation for this may have to do with the fact that health risks are accumulated over decades of social experience, and that health inequalities therefore express social conditions in the past as much as present social conditions. Theoretically, in general we would expect differences in lifetime income careers to be more closely linked to health inequalities than income differences in the present.

Conclusions

From the above we can conclude that 1) the level of economic wealth in a country, 2) its income distribution, 3) the level of health of its population, and 4) its social differences in health are related in a fairly complex way.

Looking at the whole global system of countries we may ask what determines country differences in health. Health differences between countries must be determined in an even more complex way than those within countries. One may assume that they are related to world GDP, world income, and power distribution, and to nationally driven determinants of health.

But again, if health risks are accumulated over a lifetime and across generations, other factors must also be considered. One of them is history. The burden of history is an underestimated issue. Present health inequalities both within and between countries have roots in the past. This is so both because individual health risks are accumulated over the entire life course and because groups of people everywhere have their own deep cultural and political traditions, transmitted across generations, of protecting themselves from health risks. This makes it clear why these relations are so difficult to disentangle on the basis of individual information from the present only, and why studies seem to contradict each other. It also explains why the targeting of health inequalities within and between countries has been relatively unsuccessful. A better theoretical understanding of both kinds of health inequalities and their relationship is called for, together with a much more long-term policy commitment.

An attempt to look systematically at how differences within and between countries are related was made by Leon (Leon 2000). He examined how social class differences in mortality within a country (Britain) were related to country differences in mortality within Europe for each of a number of common causes of death. Figure 2.12 shows the divide between professionals and unskilled workers on the one axis and the East/West difference on the other axis. Each dot represents a cause of death. From the graph it is clear that those causes of death for which there is a large social class difference also tend to be those with a large East/West difference. Presumably this is so because both kinds of difference have some common determinant.

Stomach cancer, for instance, is probably determined largely by poverty in

Figure 2.12   *East/West Mortality Rate Ratio Compared to Low/HIgh Social Class Mortality Rate Ratio, for 16 Causes of Death*

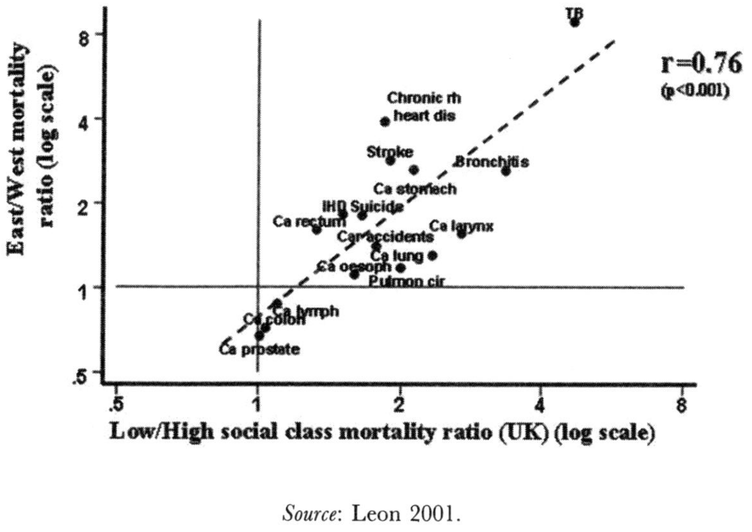

Source: Leon 2001.

childhood. It demonstrates high relative mortality in manual workers compared to non-manual workers and in Eastern Europe compared to Western Europe. This is entirely consistent and logical. This example shows that it is possible to develop a common frame of explanation for both intra- and inter-country differences. Explanations that deal with specific causes of death are more likely to be successful than general explanations that deal with all-cause mortality. Leon's suggestion would therefore seem to be one way of unlocking the present impasse.

Looking more closely at Europe we have seen that the targets once set by the WHO for the region and aiming at the reduction of health inequalities have not been met. Country differences in mortality/life expectancy have increased, especially after the collapse of the Soviet system. Socioeconomic mortality differences within countries have also increased in general, in both western and eastern regions of Europe.

Global economic growth during the last two decades has contributed to improved global health, but there are important world regions where this is not the case, such as sub-Saharan Africa and the former Soviet Union. A pertinent question is whether the problems we see there are temporary phenomena or represent long-term problems. Are they inherent in the present world system of global political and economic developments, with its global redistribution of income and wealth and its insufficient concern for the environment and for the health of populations?

Policies aiming at the reduction of inequalities within countries, between countries in regions of the world and finally globally between North and South, need to be very long-term. The UN Millennium Goals on health do not really address explicitly inequalities in health. It seems much more difficult to change the social pattern of health (within as well as between countries) than to increase life expectancy in general. The aim of the WHO to create health for all in the twenty-first century is therefore a formidable task. The target of giving each child born in a country the same opportunity of surviving the first two years of life is a more modest demand, yet still far-reaching. The latter is now one of the criteria by which health systems in the world have been ranked by the WHO (WHO 2000). National governments as a whole, not only the health ministries, are important for achieving goals such as these.

Medical knowledge is probably one of the most dynamic elements in changing the health risks that people are exposed to. The importance of medical knowledge lies not only in that it improves medical treatment, but more importantly in that it can contribute to the empowering of those individuals, communities, and countries that understand how to protect themselves from avoidable health risks. Reducing the disease burden in a community, a social group, or a country is likely to contribute to its economic progress and social standing in general. Reducing differences between groups and countries across the globe may be much more difficult than reducing its average level of disease; part of the problem is our insufficient understanding of how health inequalities are maintained and produced. The other part of the problem is the tendency to expect the medical profession or the health ministry to solve a problem that is fundamentally social.

Acknowledgements

This work was supported by the Swedish Council for Work Life and Social Research and the Baltic Sea Foundation. I am grateful to Dave Leon for allowing me to use two of his graphs.

Notes

1 One shouldn't give the impression that the epidemiological transition is a series of stages that follow each other in the same way in all countries. Critics have pointed out that the replacement of a traditional cause-of-death structure may show considerable variation in different parts of the world (Caselli et al. 2002)

2 The WHO is now tempted to redefine health inequalities by creating a measure that calculates differences between individuals without regard to their social standing, perhaps inspired by the popularity and simplicity of the Gini coefficient, used to calculate income differences. Measuring of 'individual health inequalities' rather than inequalities between social groups has been advocated and applied, for instance in the evaluation of the performance of health care systems in the world (WHO 2000). Such a practice unfortunately risks obscuring the fact that health and mortality everywhere is socially patterned. To be able to use such a measure one would immediately need to decompose it into socially based variation and other individual variation. A pure 'individual' measure would hardly have the same mobilizing power. It would be further removed from actual social conflict, and thus difficult to link to formulation and implementation of policies. This proposal is quite unexpected given the good track

record of the WHO, which pioneered the targeting of health inequalities as an important policy goal. It would seem that evaluation of the success in meeting those targets once set by the WHO would also be more difficult. The problem is highlighted by the result of the exercise. Thus Chile was estimated to have the highest equality in child survival in the world, followed by the United Kingdom (WHO 2000: 177).

References

Baker, D., D. Vågerö and R. llsley, 1993, 'Today or in the past – the origins of ischaemic heart disease', *Journal of Public Health Medicine*, 15 (3): 243–8, September.

Barker, D., 1989, 'Rise and fall of Western disease', *Nature*, 338: 3–372.

Boenheim, F., 1957, *Virchow: Werk und Wirkung*, Berlin: Rütten and Loening.

Brunner, E., and 'M.Marmot, 1999; 'Social organisation, stress and health', in M. Marmot and R. Wilkinson, eds, *Social Determinants of Health*, Oxford: Oxford University Press.

Burström, B., and E. Bernhardt, 2002, 'The changing cause-of-death pattern among infants, Stockholm 1878–1925', in J. Carling, ed., 'Nordic demography: trends and differentials', *Scandinavian Population Studies*, Vol. 13: 55–64.

Caselli, G., 1994, 'Long-term trends in European mortality', *Studies on Medical and Population Subjects*, No. 56, London: OPCS.

Caselli, G., F. Meslé and J. Vallin, 2002, 'Epidemiologic transition theory exceptions', paper presented at IUSSP seminar 'Determinants of Diverging Trends in Mortality', Rostock, 19–21 June.

Cornia, A., 2001, 'Globalisation and health: results and options', *Bulletin of the World Health Organization*, 79: 834–41.

Davey Smith, G., 1996, 'Income inequality and mortality: why are they related? Income inequality goes hand in hand with underinvestment in human resources', *British Medical Journal*, 312: 987–8.

Demine, A., 2000, 'Public health in Eastern Europe', *Lancet*, 356 (suppl.): 49.

Drever, F., and M. Whitehead, 1997; '*Health Inequalities. Decennial Supplement*, London: Office for National Statistics.

Field, M., 1986, 'Soviet infant mortality: a mystery story', in D. Jeliffe and E. Jeliffe, eds, *Advances in International and Maternal and Child Health*, Vol. 6, Oxford: Clarendon Press, pp. 25–65.

Gisselman M., 2005, 'Education, low birth weight and infant mortality in Sweden 1973–1990: emergence of the low birth weight paradox', *Scandinavian Journal of Public Health*, 33 (1): 65–71.

Goskomstat of Russia, 2004, *The Demographic Yearbook of Russia*, Moscow.

—— 2000, *Regions of Russia CD-ROM*, Moscow.

Gwatkin, D. R., 2000; 'Health inequalities and the health of the poor: what do we know? What can we do? *Bulletin of the World Health Organization*, 78: 3–18.

Kuh, D., and Y. Ben-Shlomo, eds, 1997, *A Life Course Perspective on Chronic Disease Epidemiology*, Oxford: Oxford University Press.

Kunst, A., 1997, '*Cross-national comparisons of socio-economic differences in mortality*', thesis, Erasmus University of Rotterdam.

La Dou, J., 1992, 'The export of hazards to developing countries', in J. Jeyaratnam, ed., *Occupational Health in Developing Countries*, Oxford: Oxford University Press, pp. 340–60.

Leon, D., 2000, 'Common threads: underlying components of inequalities in mortality between and within countries', in D. E. Leon and G. Walt, eds, *Poverty, Inequality and Health: An International Perspective*, Oxford: Oxford University Press, pp. 88–124.

Leon, D., G. Walt, and L. Gilson, 2001, 'International perspectives on health inequalities and policy' *British Medical Journal*, 322: 591–4.

Leinsalu, M., D. Vågerö and A. Kunst, 2003, 'Estonia 1989–2000: enormous increase in mortality differences by education', *International Journal of Epidemiology*, 32.

Lutz, W., W. Sanderson and S. Scherbov, 2001, 'The end of world population growth', *Nature*, 412: 543–5.

Lynch, J., G. Davey Smith, M. Hillemeier, M. Shaw, T. Raghunathan and G. Kaplan, 2000, 'Income inequality, the psychosocial environment and health: comparisons of wealthy nations', *Lancet*, 358: 194–200.

McKeown, T., 1979, 'The role of medicine: dream, mirage or nemesis?', Oxford: Basil Blackwell.

McMichael, T., 2001, *Human Frontiers, Environments and Disease: Past Patterns, Uncertain Futures*, Cambridge: Cambridge University Press.

McMichael, T., and C. Butler, 2002, 'Global health trends: evidence for and against sustainable progress', paper presented at IUSSP seminar 'Determinants of Diverging Trends in Mortality', Rostock, 19–21 June.

Mackenbach, J., 2002, 'Income inequality and population health', *British Medical Journal*, 324: 1–2.

Marmot, M., H. Bosma, H. Hemingway, et al. 1997, 'Contribution of job control and other risk factors to social variation in coronary heart disease incidence', *Lancet* 350: 235–9.

Meslé, F., 2002, 'Mortality in Eastern Europe and the former Soviet Union: long-term trends and recent upturns', paper presented at IUSSP seminar 'Determinants of Diverging Trends in Mortality', Rostock, 19–21 June.

Meslé, F., V. Shkolnikov, V. Hertrich and J. Vallin, 1996, 'Tendances récentes de la mortalité par cause en Russie 1965–1994', *Données Statistiques*, 2.

Minujin, A., E. Delamonica, 2002, *Socio-economic Inequalities in Mortality and Health in the Developing World*, New York: UNICEF.

Moser, K., D. Leon and V. Shkolnikov, 2005, 'World mortality 1950–2000: divergence replaces convergence from the late 1980s', *Bulletin of the World Health Organization*, 83: 202–9.

Nussbaumer, J., 2003, *Macht. Gewalt. Hunger. Schwere Hungerkatastrofen seit 1845*, Vienna: Studienverlag.

Omran, A., 1971, 'The epidemiological transition: a theory of the epidemiology of population change', *Milbank Memorial Fund Quarterly*, 49: 509–38.

OPCS (Office of Population Censuses and Surveys), *Occupational Mortality. The Registrar-General's Decennial Supplement for England and Wales*, London: HMSO.

Patterson, D., 1995, 'Mortality in late czarist Russia: a reconnaissance', *Social History of Medicine*, 8: 179–210.

Sen, A., 1999, *Development as Freedom*, Oxford: Oxford University Press.

Shkolnikov, V., G. Cornia, D. Leon and F. Meslé, 1998, 'Causes of the Russian mortality crisis: evidence and interpretations', *World Development*, 26: 1995–2011.

Shkolnikov, V., D. Leon, S. Adamets, E. Andreev and A. Deev, 'Educational level and adult mortality in Russia: an analysis of routine data 1979–1994', *Social Science and Medicine*, 47: 357–69.

Svenska metallindustriarbetarförbundet, 1989, *Solidarisk arbetspolitik för det goda arbetet. Programkommitteens rapport till kongressen 3–9 sept 1989* (Solidaristic Policies for the Good Work. Report to the 1989 Congress of Swedish Metal Manufacturing Industry Workers), Stockholm: Gotab.

Szreter, S., 1984, 'The importance of social intervention in Britain's mortality decline 1850–1914: a reinterpretation of the role of public health', *Society for the Social History of Medicine*, Vol. X: 1–37.

United Nations, 1999, *Long Range World Population Projections: Based on the 1998 Revision*, New York: United Nations ESA/P/WP.153.

Vågerö, D., 1983, 'The evolution of health care systems in England, France and Germany in the light of 1848 European Revolutions', *Acta Sociologica*, 26: 83–8.

—— 1995, 'Health inequalities as policy issues – reflections on ethics, policy and public health', *Sociology of Health and Illness*, 17: 1–19.

Vågerö, D., and R. Erikson, 1997, 'Socioeconomic inequalities in morbidity and mortality in western Europe', *Lancet*, 350: 516–17.

Vågerö, D., I. Koupilová D. Leon and U. B. Lithell, 1999, 'Social determinants of birth weight, ponderal index and gestational age in Sweden in the 1920s and the 1980s', *Acta Paediatrica*, 88: 445–54.

Vallin, J., F. Meslé and T. Valkonen, 2001, 'Trends in mortality and differential mortality', *Population Studies*, 36 Strasbourg: Council of Europe Publishing.

Walberg, P., M. McKee, V. Shkolnikov, L. Chenet and D. Leon, 'Economic change, crime and mortality in Russia: regional analysis', *British Medical Journal*, 317: 312–18.

Wilkinson R., 1992, 'Income distribution and life expectancy', *British Medical Journal*, 304: 165–8.

—— 1996, *Unhealthy Societies: The Afflictions of Inequality*, London and New York: Routledge.

3

How French and American Workers Define Cultural Membership

Michèle Lamont

This chapter focuses on the place that ordinary citizens give to immigrants in their society. More specifically, drawing on in-depth interviews, it contrasts how French and American workers evaluate immigrants in moral and cultural terms, and whether they include them in their 'imagined communities' of 'people like us'.[1] I also compare the place they give to immigrants with those they give to blacks and the poor. For French workers, 'us' includes all the French, but with some frequency, '*les Français de souche*' only (that is, those who have been French for several generations (*souche*: Fr. 'origin'). A portion of the men I talked to view immigrants – reduced here to Muslim immigrants – as unable to assimilate to a universalistic French culture. They still include the poor and blacks in their definition of the French 'us', as their understanding of the social bond structuring French society downplays internal national divisions and emphasizes humanitarianism, collective responsibility toward indigent fellow citizens, and a universalistic republicanism. In the USA, workers I talked to often draw moral boundaries against the poor and African-Americans in the name of work ethic and responsibility, and the majority is indifferent towards immigrants (implicitly defined as non-black). A few take immigrants 'in' as 'part of us', if they are good neighbours and pursue the American dream. Yet others are critical of immigrants to the extent that they perceive them as refusing to learn English: in doing so, they are viewed as 'bringing down' the country as a whole, thus threatening one of the most precious statuses of workers, that of being American.

In his review of the European research on immigrant integration, Favell criticizes the state-centred character of this literature.[2] Complementing this body of knowledge, my chapter addresses immigrant integration by focusing on popular definitions of cultural citizenship – that is, on how ordinary people define the values that bring people together and evaluate the cultural 'fit' of immigrants in their community. In approaching immigrant integration thus, this chapter differs slightly from other contributions to this volume, which capture immigration integration through state policies or immigrant practices and identities.[3]

My analysis reveals the persistence of strongly contrasted national patterns of symbolic incorporation in how American and French workers think about immigrants. This is at odds with globalization movements in the economy,[4] among immigrants[5] and at the cultural level.[6] My analysis also reveals that if the post-national model at the centre of this volume adequately describes how international organizations and immigrant associations frame immigrant integration by focusing on human rights,[7] it does not apply to the workers I have interviewed: the defence of national culture is important to them – especially in the French case – far more, it appears, than an abstract and remote discourse on human rights. Their imagined communities are primarily framed in moral and cultural, as opposed to political, terms: in defining 'people like us', workers refer to basic moral qualities that allow them to meet the challenges of their own lives – for instance, a strong work ethic and a sense of responsibility. Central to workers' own concept of self, these very traits are mobilized by them to judge negatively other classes, ethnic or racial groups whom they perceive as falling short. Hence workers draw moral, racial, class, and national boundaries simultaneously.

In the conclusion, I will compare briefly the 'official state models' of immigrant incorporation found in France and in the USA, with how workers think about the place of immigrants in their imagined communities. Just as the French republican ideology draws a strong boundary between those who share this sacred political culture and those who do not, a number of French workers draw a strong boundary between those who can assimilate and those who cannot. In the USA, we do not find an 'official' American model of immigrant integration. Instead, we have a loosely defined political culture of pluralism that favours a variable mix of cultural assimilation and multi-culturalism.[8] The absence of a clearly defined official model of immigrant integration in the USA resonates with the fact that immigrants are not particularly salient in American workers' definitions of their imagined community.

By focusing on the place of symbolic boundaries in intergroup relations, this chapter builds on an important sociological tradition that goes back to the writings of Emile Durkheim and Marcel Mauss on classification systems, Georg Simmel on the symbolic status of the 'stranger', Herbert Blumer on racism and the defence of group positioning, and Fredrik Barth on the relational dimension of ethnic and racial identity.[9] In recent years, there has been growing interest in analysing how racial and ethnic groups define their identity and/or imagined community by drawing boundaries towards one another.[10] My work contributes to this line of work by identifying inductively the most salient principles of classification and identification that operate behind workers' evaluations of worth. This method allows me to generate, in a larger study, a comparative sociology of boundaries and ordinary models of definition of community. This sociology documents patterns of inclusion/exclusion based on morality, race, class, and citizenship across groups.[11] This chapter presents partial results from this broader project, as they pertain precisely to the question of immigrant integration.

The study draws on 150 in-depth interviews with low-status white-collar workers and blue-collar workers residing in the suburbs of New York and Paris to reconstruct the symbolic boundaries or mental maps through which individuals define *us* and *them*. I asked people I interviewed to describe their friends and foes, role models and heroes, and likes and dislikes. I also asked them to describe the types of people, abstract and concrete, towards whom they felt superior and inferior, and similar and different. From there, I identified the differences that are at the centre of individual maps of perception as well as the differences that are not salient in the way people discuss worth, status, and, indirectly, community membership. Thereby I revealed the natural order through which workers hierarchize others when, for example, they declare that, of course, it is more important to be honest than refined or that money is not a good indicator of a person's value.

Respondents were randomly selected from phone books of working-class communities. Each interview lasted approximately two hours and was conducted by me at a time and place of their choosing. To be eligible for the study, workers had to have a high school degree (or the French equivalent), but no college degree, and to have been employed full-time for at least five years in a blue-collar or low-status white-collar occupation (for more details, see Methodological Appendix). I interviewed men only, with the goal of comparing workers with college-educated male professionals and managers whom I had interviewed for a previous study.[12] Although for the larger project I interviewed native American and French white workers as well as native African-American workers and North-African immigrants working in France, for this chapter, I describe results from interviews with white respondents only (30 blue-collar workers and 15 white-collar workers in each country). Due to space constraints, I neglect intra-national and intra-group variations to focus on national differences only. I also largely confine myself to describing boundary patterns and refer readers interested in a fuller analysis of causal processes to the larger study.[13]

It should be noted that I compare France and the USA because these two countries have defined themselves as redeemers of the world, as the privileged carriers of the universal ideals of freedom, equality, and liberty, although their respective histories have, until recently, included segregation and colonialism. Today, 28 per cent of the French population has voted for the openly racist and anti-Semitic Front National at least once,[14] while in the USA, symbolic racism has replaced blatant racism within large segments of the population.[15] These paradoxical situations make the comparison particularly enticing.

French Cultures of Solidarity

In a Durkheimian vein, Jeffrey Alexander argues that 'members of national communities often believe that "the world", and this notably includes their own nation, is filled with people who either do not deserve freedom and communal support or are not capable of sustaining them (in part because they are immoral egoists).[16] Members of national communities do not want to "save" such persons. They do not wish to include them, protect them, or offer them rights because they conceive them as being unworthy, amoral, and in some sense "uncivilized".' In contemporary France, these unworthy people are primarily the growing number of Muslim immigrants originating from North Africa, as 'Islam marks the frontier of what is foreign'.[17]

Between 1960 and 1974, the majority of immigrants to France came from North Africa (Morocco, Algeria, Tunisia), and arrived often under temporary permits directing them into the worst-paid, least-desirable jobs in manufacturing, mining, and public work. These immigrants were a visible minority who, after 1974, could establish their families on French soil. Their numbers grew rapidly and they now represent 34 per cent of the immigrant population, and 5 per cent of the population living on French soil.[18] They are concentrated on the outskirts of major cities, where they encounter a variety of problems – crime, drug and alcohol abuse, alienation – associated with poverty and poor housing. Many French citizens have come to blame social problems and unemployment on foreigners, by which they generally mean North Africans. A sense of competition and the breakdown of traditional working-class culture eventually translated into xenophobia and calls for the repatriation of non-Europeans.[19] This movement amplified and resulted in a major breakthrough when, in the 1984 European parliamentary election, the Front National, whose main programme was to oppose immigration, received more than 11 per cent of the vote. This party, which has regularly garnered 15 per cent of the French electorate, laments the disappearance of the old white and culturally homogeneous France, one where neighbourhoods were safe and truly French, where popular culture and collective identity coexisted in an organic way, undisturbed by the mores, smells, and bizarre clothing of non-European immigrants.[20]

During the course of the interviews I conducted with white native French workers, half of the blue-collar workers and a few white-collar workers drew strong boundaries towards North Africans.[21] In doing so, they used three primary types of arguments, which can be sketched thus:[22]

1. Immigrants are lacking in work ethic and sense of responsibility, and have access to a larger share of the collective wealth than they are entitled to. In the name of fighting their social exclusion, the French state favours them, which violates workers' sense of group position[23] and is perceived by workers as unfair, given that the quality of life and education are in steady decline in working class neighborhoods.[24]

2. The French political culture of Republicanism does not recognize particularistic claims based on religion, race, and birth and posits that anyone can join in the polity as long as they assimilate and come to share a same political culture. Unlike other immigrant groups, North Africans are perceived as being unable to, or as refusing to, assimilate, which invalidates their right to reside in France.[25]

3. Muslims are fundamentally culturally different from, and even incompatible with, the French. They lack civility: they spit in front of people, never apologize, are rude, and lack respect for others. They also have barbarous mores (for instance, they kill goats on their balconies at Ramadan). They destroy the French quality of life and should go home. These fundamental differences are described by a railway technician thus:

> We have to be honest: the problem is that they don't have the same education, the same values as we do. We have a general Christian education, most of the French do not believe in God but they all have a Christian education that regulates our relationship. But in the Muslim world, the Koran doesn't have the same values at all. They send children to get killed in the minefields of Iraq. But in France, if you kill children, it is really a scandal. But in those countries, social things are not as important. The mother is happy to send her child to go get killed in the mines. She will cry, it is true, she will have the same pain as a European mother, but it is not the same thing. . . And there is also the respect of the value of life itself. Women in the Muslim world have no place. Whereas here in France, I have washed dishes . . . at some point, my wife had a depression, and I stayed with my children. Their education is different.

Undoubtedly, the rejection of Muslims is linked to the defence of a 'true French culture' that is threatened not only from the inside by foreigners but also from the outside by Americanization. Moreover, colonial notions of France's *'mission civilisatrice'* and of French superiority remain present in the minds of many workers, especially when it comes to barbaric former African colonies.[26] The 'otherness' of Muslims is emphasized as differences in the degree of religious involvement among Muslims are downplayed by respondents. *'Beurs'* (second-generation children of immigrants) who have French citizenship are widely perceived to be immigrants, suggesting again the perceived incompatibility between French culture and Islam.

The importance of immigrants in the boundaries that the French interviewees draw is particularly remarkable when compared with the place that workers give to alternative bases of community segmentation in their discourse on 'the other', and particularly to the place they give to racial others (mostly blacks) and to the poor.

Interviews strongly indicate that race is not an important basis of exclusion among French workers. Indeed, very few workers mention race when drawing boundaries, suggesting a decoupling between racism and blackness that is surprising from an American perspective. Two interviewees pointed to the laziness of blacks, and one brought to my attention the absence of racism in France, offering as a piece of evidence the fact that as French citizens, black Martiniquais and Guadeloupains are by right and *de facto* fully and equally included in the national collectivity on the basis of republican ideals. A recent survey showed that when asked which category of immigrants poses the greatest difficulty for integration, 50 per cent of the French respondents identified North Africans, far more than the 19 per cent who pointed to black Africans or the 15 per cent who named Asians.[27] Less recent survey data consistently provide evidence that negative feelings toward North African immigrants are much stronger than negative feelings towards blacks, towards European immigrants, or towards other racial minorities.[28]

A number of factors combine with the culture of republicanism to create weak boundaries against blacks, as compared to North Africans:

1. Most North Africans are first- or second-generation immigrants. Blacks are more heterogeneous: while some are recent immigrants from sub-Saharan Africa, those from the *Dom-Toms* have been French for several generations. This works against defining 'us' in opposition to 'blacks', and partly trumps the low status of blacks as formerly colonized people.
2. Blacks living in France are more heterogenous religiously than North Africans – for instance, the Senegalese are predominantly Muslims while the Congolese are Catholic[29] – which also works against institutionalizing a clear distinction between 'us' and 'blacks'. While North Africans include a small Jewish population, they are often presumed to be homogenously Muslims.
3. Muslims are more salient to French workers because they constitute a larger group than blacks (again, they make up almost 5 per cent of the French population as compared to less than 2 per cent for blacks).[30]
4. The process of decolonization was much more peaceful in French sub-Saharan Africa than in North Africa, which sustained less negative stereotypes of blacks than of North Africans.
5. Historically, a sizable proportion of black African immigrants came to France to be educated.[31] This population was of a more elite background and was more assimilated than many North African low-skilled workers. Their presence worked against negative views of blacks, at a time when low-skilled black Africans had less easy access to French shores than their North African counterparts due to geographical distance.[32]

The arrival of a rapidly increasing number of West African immigrants might be the undoing of this relative dissociation between blackness and racism. In particular, the policy of family reunification that was put in place after 1974 brought in large numbers of African families, which made Muslim African migration more visible in part by focusing public attention on polygamy and traditional female genital mutilation.[33] Nevertheless, overall, the combined characteristics of blacks living in France work against a clear polarization between 'Frenchness' and 'blackness' in a manner unparalleled for North Africans. Racial 'others', such as Asians, have had a very successful assimilation. They contribute to the playing down of racial differences as a basis for internal differentiation within French society.

French workers also downplay the internal segmentation of their society by including among 'people like us' individuals located in the lower echelons of society. Indeed, they rarely express feelings of superiority towards the poor. These categories of individuals are often simply absent from their descriptions of boundaries. A detailed analysis of the interviews suggests that the majority of the French respondents are indifferent towards or silent about the poor, while this is the case for only a quarter of the American workers (half of them draw boundaries against the poor). Also, a number of French workers explicitly express solidarity towards people below them in the social structure, drawing on a vocabulary of class struggle and class solidarity to point that 'we are all wage-earners, we are all exploited'. References to welfare recipients and the unemployed are often accompanied by critique of the capitalist system. For instance, a bank clerk says, 'I think it is unacceptable that some people are unemployed while others can work as much as they want.' A wood salesman concurs when he says that market mechanisms should not determine salaries, and he concludes, 'All workers should be reasonably well paid.' Like many others, this salesman opposes classical liberalism and its invisible hand because it is inhuman and penalizes the weakest. Social welfare is not in question: the undue protection of foreigners who are not truly part of the collective 'us' is.

Republicanism, Catholicism, and socialism all provide elements of cultural repertoires that favour such weak boundaries by stressing the importance of social solidarity among citizens (independently of race), among the poor, and among workers, respectively.[34] Along these lines, when asked to choose, from a list of traits, five qualities that they find particularly important in others, a third of the French workers chose *solidaire* or *égalitaire*, in contrast to less than a fifth of their American counterparts; also, while none of the French chose 'successful', again a fifth of their American counterparts did. French workers often reject social climbing in the name of personal integrity; to it are opposed notions of togetherness, '*partage*', and egalitarianism. They frequently have negative attitudes towards money and power, which they most often experience as something that is coercive, repressive, and disempowering. They often describe the upper half as exploitative and dehumanizing, suggesting that class, and the discourse of class struggle, remain salient in their world view.[35]

Collectivity American-Style

In the mind of many American workers, social and cultural membership remain largely equated with being white and being at least lower-middle or working-class. Indeed, while the French workers I talked to did not draw strong boundaries against the poor, the opposite is true in the USA. As compared to the French, American workers more often evaluate people on the basis of their 'success' and more readily draw boundaries against individuals below themselves on the socioeconomic ladder. They often resort to arguments having to do with work ethic and ambition in doing so. For instance, Frank Thompson, from Hempstead, Long Island, says that if he had to draw a line to distinguish superior and inferior people, he would draw it against 'some people out there I think that could do better and don't try. There's nothing wrong if you don't want to become something, but don't blame somebody else for it.' Also, a worker from Linden who does not have a college degree says that he feels superior to 'people who have no control over their lives. If a person just does nothing to help themselves, I'm very hard on these people.'

The interviews suggest a close association between moral and class boundaries in the USA. While the literature has clearly documented the association between poverty and irresponsibility, laziness, and lack of self-sufficiency,[36] my interviews reveal similar constructs. For instance, after declaring proudly that he is a diehard Republican, one of the men I talked to explained that being Republican means 'Don't give anything for nothing. Incentive . . . Go get a job . . . [We should not] make it so easy to stay on unemployment, on welfare.' Another explained that he is a conservative Republican because he does not 'like people who try to take advantage of things and take, take, and give nothing back'. These men are angry that they have to pay so much in taxes to support the poor who 'don't work at all and get everything for free'.

They more often stress traditional aspects of morality (such as the Ten Commandments and the defence of traditional work ethic) than the French.[37]

When asked to whom they feel superior and inferior, the majority of American interviewees constantly and subtly shift from moral to racial boundaries, drawing on both at once, and justify racist attitudes via moral arguments.[38] The rhetoric they use to draw boundaries against blacks resembles that they use to reject the poor: they stress their alleged lack of work ethic and sense of responsibility. They also point to their inability to educate their children properly, particularly in moral matters. Again, they accuse blacks of 'getting away with murder . . . with things that I wouldn't even think of doing' (civil servant). They view African-Americans as 'having a tendency to . . . try to get off doing less, the least . . . possible as long as they still maintain being able to keep the job, where whites will put in that extra oomph' (electronics technician). Another electronics technician summarizes the way many perceive the situation when he says:

I work side by side constantly with blacks, and I have no problem with it . . . I am prejudiced to a point . . . What is a nice way to say it . . . I know this is a generality and it does not go for all, it goes for a portion. It's this whole unemployment and welfare gig. What you see mostly on there is blacks. I see it from working with some of them and the conversations I hear . . . A lot of the blacks on welfare have no desire to get off it. Why should they? It's free money. I can't stand to see my hard-earned money going to pay for someone who wants to sit on his or her ass all day long and get free money. That's bullshit, and it may be white thinking, but, hey, I feel it is true to a point . . . You hear it on TV all the time: 'We don't have to do this because we were slaves 400 years ago. You owe it to us.' I don't owe you shit, period. I had nothing to do with that and I'm not going to pay for it . . . Also, I don't like the deal where a black person can say anything about a white, and that's not considered prejudice. But let a white person say even the tiniest little thing about a black person, and bang, get up in front of Reverend Al Sharpton and all the other schmucks. That's bullshit. That's double standard all the way along the line.

This passage illustrates how, for some American workers, class, racial, and moral boundaries work hand-in-hand in such a way that the community of 'people like us' is defined very narrowly and certainly excludes blacks, who are largely constructed as living off working people.[39] That boundaries against the poor and blacks in the USA are so strong is undoubtedly related to the fact that these two groups are associated with one another (in contrast, in the French context, the long-term unemployed are mostly white French workers who are victims of economic restructuring). Hence, in the USA, blackness and poverty trace the limits of social membership, and this trend is likely to become more accentuated as we move towards an opposition between all non-blacks and blacks, despite the centrality of egalitarianism in American political culture.[40]

Survey research shows that while Americans have negative feelings towards immigrants, these feelings are not strongly held.[41] Also, attitudes towards immigrant policies are inconsistent, lack intensity, are not well organized, and are ineffectively articulated.[42] Immigration ranks lower than 'don't know' in surveys when respondents are asked about the 'most important problems' facing the nation today: 'don't know' is chosen five times as frequently as 'immigrants'.[43] Moreover, while many Americans are concerned with the growing number of immigrants, opinion polls report that controlling immigration ranks well below controlling taxes, crime and health costs in public priorities.[44]

This indifference towards immigrants contrasts sharply with the situation in France and is in line with the results from my interviews: when describing their mental maps, few US workers point to immigrants. When they do, it is rarely to single out their moral failures. Some point to failure to assimilate, and are slighted by what they perceive to be a lack of desire to learn English on the part of immigrants. However, workers tend to be more concerned with the dangers this represents for the decline of the relative status of the nation, than for immigrants' moral character.[45] Others have a positive view of immigrants, especially if they are perceived as pursuing the American dream. This is not to say that immigrants are integrated to the workers' definition of their 'imagined community'; their situation is more adequately described as one of non-salience.

Stronger boundaries towards immigrants might be found in states with larger immigrant population (although New Jersey and New York are among the five states with the most immigrants). Also, recent debates about Latino immigration may suggest that we have entered a new phase of xenophobia, which is confirmed by increases in the percentage of the population that expresses negative attitudes towards immigrants.[46]

Conclusion

This brief sketch of the boundary patterns that prevail in France and the USA still needs qualification and raises a number of questions. However, evidence suggests that French and American workers understand differently the place, and integration, of immigrants in their imagined communities: in France, boundaries are erected towards Muslim immigrants whose culture is viewed as fundamentally incompatible with a universalistic French culture that, in the past, successfully assimilated immigrants. Simultaneously, boundaries against blacks and the poor are downplayed in the name of a view of morality that stresses universalism, humanitarianism, and solidarity, and is influenced by Republicanism, Catholicism, and socialism. In contrast, in the USA, we find strong moral boundaries drawn against the poor and African-Americans on the basis of responsibility and work ethic. Also, immigrants are much less salient for American than for French workers. To the extent that workers discuss immigrants, they describe them in a positive light if they partake in the American dream, or criticize their reluctance to learn English, which brings down the status of the country as a whole. As suggested in the introduction, the presence of such contrasted ways of conceiving the place of immigrants in an imagined community contradicts globalization perspectives, which would predict greater similarity between the views of French and American workers.

Again, this chapter complements research on immigrant integration by focusing not on policies or immigrants' identities, but on how ordinary citizens perceive immigrants and their place among 'people like us'. While the model of post-national citizenship emphasizes the diffusion of universalistic and human rights discourse at the political level and among immigrants' associations, this shift is not found among workers, and particularly French workers: their discussions of the place of immigrants in their community focuses not on human rights, but on the moral and cultural characteristics of the immigrant population. They appear to be particularly wedded to the defence of their national community against those who refuse to assimilate.

In line with the central tenets of liberalism, French republicanism posits citizens who have equal political rights and enter voluntarily and explicitly into a covenant by which they delegate their political sovereignty directly to the state, whose role is to define and promote the common good.[47] The state stands above particular interests as a neutral agent embodying universal reason and acting for the benefit of an undifferentiated mass of equal citizens. In the USA, although individuals are at the foundation of the political system, a pluralistic logic prevails, and groups make claims based in part on their cultural identity.[48] For the French, this is the path to be avoided at all costs, in part because it has led to the destruction of the American social fabric – as exemplified by the Los Angeles riots, pervasive poverty, ethnic conflicts, and identity politics.[49] Hence, in France, 1) intermediary bodies are not recognized; 2) citizens participate in the public sphere as individuals, not as group members; and 3) individuals are considered to be equal citizens, independently of their cultural, natural, or social characteristics. This means that ethnic, racial, religious, regional, and corporate groups cannot use their distinctive identities as bases for making claims in the public sphere. They also face pressure to assimilate in the name of a universalistic polity[50] and do not get the benefit of American-style pluralism. Hence, officially, France does not have a North African minority, but it shelters 'aliens' who are defined in reference not to their cultural identity, but to their economic status.[51] It does not have a category of 'blacks', as a 1978 law prohibits the collection of ethic and religious statistics.[52] Finally, it has weak anti-discrimination laws, as the logic of republicanism is taken to be a powerful warranty against discrimination.[53]

Historically, centralized institutions such as the army and the school system have played important roles in turning republican principles into reality: they turned peasants, immigrants, and everyone else into French people by teaching them the rules of cultural membership, including the downplaying of particularistic identities.[54] The goal is to produce a national community with largely overlapping cultural and political boundaries, such that political culture acts as the line separating the national in-group and the out-groups.[55] Although republicanism is now in crisis, it still constitutes the official model of immigrant integration, and it is in line with the model promoted by the workers I have interviewed, who, as we have seen, criticize immigrants for their reluctance to abide by the general social contract.[56] In contrast, in the USA, the relative non-salience of or loose tolerance for immigrants found among workers is in line with the absence of an 'official' American model of immigrant integration and with a political culture of pluralism that promotes a variable mix of cultural assimilation and multiculturalism.[57]

We have seen that French and American workers define their 'imagined community' of 'people like us' differently, drawing boundaries that exclude different categories of people. These 'folk models' of communities appear to be in line with the models promoted by national political cultures and institutions. A closer look at the causal process by which boundaries become taken for granted and institutionalized will be necessary before we can fully understand the dynamic between these two levels of definitions of imagined communities.

Methodological Appendix

In the USA, I talked with 60 stable blue-collar workers who have a high school degree but not a college degree.[58] This includes 30 self-identified African-Americans and 30 self-identified Euro-Americans, who were, when possible, matched in terms of occupation and age.[59] I also talked with 15 Euro-American low-status white-collar workers. They were randomly selected from phone books of working-class towns located in the New York suburbs, such as Elizabeth and Linden, in New Jersey, and in Hempstead on Long Island.

In France, I talked with 30 white native-born blue-collar workers and 15 white-collar workers. I also talked with 30 North African immigrants. The criteria of selection for the French workers were parallel to those used for American workers. As for North Africans, the criterion of level of education was not applied because most members of this group had attended school for only a few years. Both groups of interviewees were found in the working-class suburbs of Paris such as Aubervilliers, Stains, and Ivry-sur-Seine.

This random selection and the relatively large number of respondents aimed not at building a representative sample, but at tapping a wide range of perspectives within a community of workers. Although produced in specifically structured interactional contexts, interviews can get at relatively stable aspects of identity by focusing on the respondents' taken for granted perceptions.[61]

Acknowledgements

This research is supported by grants and fellowships from the National Science Foundation, the German Marshall Funds of the United States, the John Simon Guggenheim Memorial Foundation, and the Russell Sage Foundation. I thank Christian Joppke and Ewa Morawska for their useful comments.

Notes

1 The concept of 'imagined community' is borrowed from Benedict Anderson (*Imagined Communities: Reflections on the Origin and Spread of Nationalism*, revised and extended, 2nd edn, London: Verso, 1991, pp. 6–7), who argued that most communities are imagined because community members never know most of their fellow members. He also characterizes communities as involving deep horizontal comradeship and as limited – meaning that they have external boundaries and are not coterminous with mankind.

2 Adrian Favell, *Philosophies of Integration: Immigration and the Idea of Citizenship in France and Britain*, London: Macmillan, 1997.

3 See introduction by Christian Joppke and Ewa Morawska in Michèle Lamont, 'North African immigrants respond to French racism: demonstrating equivalence through universalism', in Abdellah Hammoudi, *Universalizing from Particulars*, London: I.B. Tauris, forthcoming, I analyse how immigrants understand their similarities with the host group – an important aspect of immigrant integration. I focus on the specific case of North African immigrants to France.

4 John Naisbitt, *Global Paradox*, New York: William Morrow, 1994.

5 Alejandro Portes, 'La mondialisation par le bas: l'émergence des communautés transnationales', *Actes de la recherche en sciences sociales*, Vol. 129, 1999: 15–25.

6 Mike Featherstone, *Global Culture: Nationalism, Globalization and Modernity*, Newbury Park: Sage, 1990.

7 Yasemin Nuhoglu Soysal, *Limits of Citizenship: Migrants and Postnational Membership in Europe*, Chicago: University of Chicago Press, 1994.

8 Gary Gerstle, 'Liberty, coercion, and the making of Americans', *Journal of American History*, 84(2), 1997: 524–58; Donald L. Horowitz, 'Immigration and group relations in France and the United States', in *Immigrants in Two Democracies: French and American Experience*, New York: New York University Press, 1992, pp. 3–35; Christian Joppke, 'Multiculturalism and immigration: a comparison of the United States, Germany, and Great Britain', *Theory and Society*, Vol. 25, 1996: 449–550.

9 Fredrik Barth, 'Introduction', in Fredrik Barth, ed., *Ethnic Groups and Boundaries: The Social Organization of Culture Difference*, London: George Allen and Unwin, 1969, pp. 9–38; Herbert Blumer, 'Race prejudice as a sense of group position', *Pacific Sociological Review*, Vol. 1, 1958: 3–7; Emile Durkheim and Marcel Mauss, *Primitive Classification* (translated and with an introduction by Rodney Needham), Chicago: University of Chicago Press, 1963; Georg Simmel, 'The stranger', in Kurt W. Wolff, ed., *The Sociology of Georg Simmel*, New York: Free Press, 1950, pp. 402–408.

10 Michèle Lamont, ed., *The Cultural Territories of Race: Black and White Boundaries*, Chicago: University of Chicago Press and New York: Russell Sage Foundation 1999; Katherine Verdery, 'Ethnicity, nationalism, and state-making, ethnic groups and boundaries: past and future', in Hans Vermeulen and Cora Govers, eds, *The Anthropology of Ethnicity: Beyond 'Ethnic Groups and Boundaries'*, Amsterdam: Het Spinhuis, 1994, pp. 33–58; Mary Waters, *Black Identities: West Indian Immigrant Dreams and American Realities*, New York: Russell Sage Foundation and Cambridge, MA: Harvard University Press, 1999; Aristide R. Zolberg and Long Litt Woon, 'Why Islam is like Spanish: cultural incorporation in Europe and the United States', *Politics and Society*, 17(1); 1999.

11 Michèle Lamont, *The Dignity of Working Men: Morality and the Boundaries of Race, Class, and Immigration*, Cambridge, MA: Harvard University Press and New York: Russell Sage Foundation, forthcoming. I share the usual reservations concerning the notion of national 'model': that it downplays the importance of international influences, variations internal to specific societies, and the impact of reform on traditions. For a critique of this concept, see Riva Kastoryano, *La France, l'Allemagne et leurs immigrés: négocier l'identité*, Paris: Armand Colin, 1996.

12 Michèle Lamont, *Money, Morals, and Manners: The Culture of the French and American Upper-Middle Class*, Chicago: University of Chicago Press, 1992.

13 Michèle Lamont, *The Dignity of Working Men: Morality and the Boundaries of Race, Class, and Immigration*, forthcoming.

14 Personal communication with Professor Martin Schain, expert on the French far-right party, the Front National.

15 David O. Sears, 'Symbolic Racism', in Phyllis A. Katz and Dalmas A. Taylor, eds, *Eliminating Racism: Profiles in Controversy*, New York and London: Plenum Press, 1988, pp. 53–84.

16 Jeffrey Alexander, 'Citizen and enemy as symbolic classification: on the polarizing discourse of civil society', in Michèle Lamont and Marcel Fournier, eds, *Cultivating Differences: Symbolic Boundaries and the Making of Inequality*, Chicago: University of Chicago Press, 1992, p. 291.

17 Kastoryano, *La France, l'Allemagne et leurs immigrés*.

18 In 1990, European immigrants made up 40 per cent of the 3,607,590 foreigners living in France, while Africans made up 46 per cent of foreigners, and 6.4 per cent of the French population. Thirty-four per cent of these Africans originated in Algeria,

Tunisia, and Morocco, with only 5 per cent coming from the sub-Saharan franco-phone countries (Institut national de la statistique et des études économiques, *Recensement de la Population de 1990. Les Populations des DOM-TOM, nées et originaires, résidant en France*, Paris: Documentation Française 1993, p. 16). This last figure is increasing very rapidly: in 1975, sub-Saharan Africans made up only 2 per cent of foreigners residing in France (*ibid*).

19 Michel Wieviorka, *La France raciste*, Paris: Points, 1992.

20 Pascal Perrineau, 'Le Front national: du désert à l'enracinement', in Pierre-Andre Taguieff, ed., *Face au racisme, Vol. 2. Analyses, hypothèses, perspectives*, Paris: La Découverte 1991; Nonna Mayer and Pascal Perrineau, *Le Front national à découvert*, Paris: Presses de la Fondation nationale de science politique, 1989.

21 Respectively 15 out of 30 blue-collar workers and three out of 15 low-status white-collar workers (or 20 per cent of this latter group) made statements that created a hierarchy between the French and North Africans. In contrast, in the USA, respectively 63 per cent and 60 per cent of the Euro-American blue-collar and white-collar workers made such statements (i.e., 18 out of 30 and 8 out of 15 individuals respectively). Conversely, the anti-racist rhetoric, which defends equality between groups, is less widely spread in the USA than in France: while respectively 13 per cent and 20 per cent of Euro-American blue- and white-collar respondents make anti-racist statements of the types described below (respectively five and six respondents), it is the case for 23 per cent and 73 per cent of the French blue- and white-collar workers (respectively seven and ten individuals). More Americans have neutral positions or do not discuss racial inequality. It is the case for 30 per cent of the American white-collar workers and 20 per cent of the American blue-collar workers compared to respectively 26 per cent and 6 per cent of their French counterparts. The percentages have to be interpreted with caution given that they are based on a small sample. Drawing on David Goldberg (*Racist Culture: Philosophy and the Politics of Meaning*, New York: Blackwell 1993, p. 98), I define racism as a rhetoric aimed at promoting exclusion based on racial membership and produced by a dominant group against a dominated group. Following Herbert Aptheker (*Anti-Racism in U.S. History*, New York: Greenwood, 1992), I define anti-racism as a rhetoric aimed at disproving racial inferiority.

22 See Lamont, *The Dignity of Working Men*, chapter 5, for a more detailed account.

23 Blumer, 'Race prejudice as a sense of group position'.

24 Ibid.

25 Gérard Noiriel, *The French Melting Pot: Immigration, Citizenship, and National Identity*, trans. Geoffrey de Laforcade, Minneapolis: University of Minnesota Press, 1996.

26 Alice L. Conklin, *A Mission to Civilize: The Republican Idea of Empire in France and West Africa, 1895–1930*, Stanford, CA: Stanford University Press, 1998; Herman Lebovics, 'Where and how did the French get the idea that they were the trustees of western civilization, 1513–1959?', paper presented at the New York Area French History Seminar, 1996.

27 Horowitz, 'Immigration and group relations in France and the United States', p. 19.

28 Already in 1966, a survey showed that ten negative attributes were viewed as applying primarily to Algerians by 129 respondents, while only 39 believed that these attributes applied primarily to black Africans and 13 to Portuguese (Michel Hannoun, L'homme est l'espérance de l'homme. Rapport sur le racisme et les discriminations en France, *Paris: La Documentation Française*, Collection des rapports

officiels 1987). A national survey conducted in 1973–74 also found that 34 per cent and 21 per cent had a rather bad or a bad opinion of North Africans compared to only 15 per cent and 8 per cent for black Africans – the figures for European immigrants hover around 5 per cent (Alain Girard, Yves Charbit, and Marie-Laurence Lamy, 'Attitudes des français a l'égard de l'immigration étrangère: nouvelle enquête d'opinion', *Population*, Vol. 6, 1974: 1028).

29 Michèle Tribalat (*Faire France. Une enquête sur les immigrés et leurs enfants*, Paris: La Découverte, 1995) finds that 40 per cent of the black Africans she surveyed were from Muslim countries, and 14 per cent are from exclusively Christian or animist areas (p. 21). Nearly half of the black African immigrants are from religiously hetero-geneous regions.

30 See note 5.

31 Robert Delerm ('La population noire en France', *Population*, 19(3), 1964) estimated that the black African population in France in 1964 was composed of 10,000 to 12,000 students; 4,000 to 5,000 former students who stayed; 5,000 interns (*'stagiaires au titre de la coopération'*); and 40,000 to 50,000 workers, of whom 28,000 inhabited the Parisian metropolitan area (pp. 522–3).

32 Hélène Bergues ('L'immigration de travailleurs noirs en France et particulièrement dans la région parisienne', *Population*, 28(1), 1973) discusses a 1965 survey that revealed favourable views held by the French about black Africans. She wrote: 'They are considered pleasant, polite, hardworking, quite childish, but of good disposition'; 'The general opinion is that the coming of African workers is a good thing, if we need workers and they take on jobs that the French do not want. ('L'immigration de travailleurs Africains noirs en France et particulièrement dans la région parisienne', p. 73.) Bergues also remarked elsewhere that 'Good relations are generally established between black Africans and French workers or other Europeans. Only the relations with the North African groups appear difficult' (p. 74).

33 Jacques Barou, 'Les immigrations africaines', in David Assouline and Mehdi Lallaui, eds, *Un Siècle d'immigration en France: 1945 à nos jours: du chantier à la citoyenneté?* Paris: Diffusion Syros, 1996, pp. 31–46.

34 The inclusion of the poor within the collective definitions of community produced by French workers resonates with France's institutional policy towards the poor. The Socialist party gave priority to unemployment (i.e., to 'solidarity' and 'fighting exclusion' from the early eighties on. It created the *'revenu minimum d'insertion' (RMI)* to facilitate the inclusion of the unemployed and of part-time workers. This is part of a well-established national tradition of solidaristic social insurance policy that favours the poor and the self-employed (for a history, see Serge Paugam, *La Société française et ses pauvres*, Paris: Presses universitaires de France, 1993, and Peter Baldwin, *The Politics of Social Solidarity: Class Bases of European Welfare State*, New York: Cambridge University Press, 1990; for a comparison of pension, private health care, poor relief, and other social benefits programmes in France, Canada, and the USA, see Gosta Esping-Anderson, *Three Worlds of Welfare Capitalism*, London: Polity Press, 1990, pp. 70–1.) For a broader discussion of issues of exclusion in France, see Robert Castel, *Les Métamorphoses de la question sociale*, Paris: Fayard, 1995.

35 Sociologists suggest that the boundary between the working class and the bourgeoisie was more salient in public debates prior to 1980 than it is now. Its importance has diminished with the downfall of the French Communist Party and the decline in the rate

of unionization in the late 1970s (René Mouriaux, 'Stratégies syndicales face au chomage et à l'intervention industrielle de l'état dans la période 1962–87', in James F. Hollifield and George Ross, eds, *Searching from the New France*, New York and London: Routledge, 1991). This boundary and the boundary drawn against immigrants were not very salient in the interviews that I conducted with professionals and managers. For an explanation for these trends, see Lamont, *Money, Morals, and Manners*, chapter 3.

36 E.g. Michael Katz, *The Underserving Poor: From the War on Poverty to the War on Welfare*, New York: Pantheon, 1989. As many have argued, Americans take poverty to reflect personal deficiency, and they often blame the victim for structural inequality. To illustrate this argument, Lomax Cook (*Who Should be Helped: Public Support for Social Services*, Beverly Hills: Sage, 1979) has found that American adults are less likely to want to help poor adults than any other segments of the needy population, including children and the disabled, blaming them for their own fate.

37 An excellent comparison of French and American policies and approaches to poverty is available in Hilary Silver, 'National conceptions of the new urban poverty: social structural change in Britain, France, and the United States', *International Journal of Urban and Regional Research*, 17 (3), 1993: 336–54.

38 For the comparative distribution of French and American interviewees, see note 6.

39 The racist views of the men I talked to are not exceptional. In their extensive study of change in racial attitudes in the USA, Schuman, Steeh, and Bobo (*Racial Attitudes in America: Trends and Interpretation*, Cambridge, MA: Harvard University Press, 1985) have found that while more educated respondents show higher levels of support to integration, they also tend to oppose placing whites in settings in which they are no longer in the majority (p. 199). More generally, these authors find that, for both blacks and whites, questions that pertain to the implementation of policies 'always reveal a much lower level of support than for the principles themselves' (p. 197). They also observe that 'by 1983, the approval of integrated marriage had reached only the same level that approval of integrated transportation had reached in the early 1940s [i.e., 40 per cent]' (p. 195).

40 Herbert Gans, 'The possibility of a new racial hierarchy in the 21st century United States', in Michèle Lamont, ed., *The Cultural Territories of Race: Black and White Boundaries*, Chicago and New York: University of Chicago Press and Russell Sage Foundation, 1999, pp. 371–90; Seymour Martin Lipset, *The First New Nation: the United States in Historical and Comparative Perspective*, New York: Norton, 1979; Alexis de Tocqueville, *Democracy in America*, New York: Vintage, 1945. My interviews bring support to authors who have suggested that for Americans moral obligations apply to an increasingly limited number of people defined by common blood, ethnicity, and religion, or by physical proximity that translates into a similar income level (Constance Perin, *Belonging in America*, Madison: University of Wisconsin Press, 1988; Jim Sleeper, *The Closest of Strangers: Liberalism and the Politics of Race in New York*, New York: Norton, 1991; Hervé Varenne, *Americans Together: Structured Diversity in a Midwestern Town*, New York: Teachers College Press, 1977; Alan Wolfe, *Whose Keeper? Social Science and Moral Obligation*, Berkeley and Los Angeles: University of California Press, 1989).

41 Thomas J. Espenshade and Maryann Belanger, 'Immigration and public opinion', in Marcelo Suarez-Orozco, ed., *Crossings: Mexican Immigration in Interdisciplinary Perspectives*, Cambridge, MA: Harvard University Press, 1998.

42 Edwin Harwood, 'American public opinion and U.S. immigration policy', in Rita J. Simon, ed., 'Immigration and American public policy,' *Annals of the American Academy of Political and Social Science*, Vol. 487, Beverly Hills: Sage, 1986, p. 205, cited by Espenshade and Belanger, 1998, p. 21.

43 Espenshade and Belanger, 'Immigration and public opinion', p. 19.

44 Philip Martin, 'The United States: benign neglect toward immigration', in Wayne A. Cornelius, Philip L. Martin, and James F. Hollifield, eds, *Controlling Immigration: A Global Perspective*, Stanford, CA: Stanford University Press 1994, p. 87.

45 National surveys show that in the early 1980s, the percentage of Americans who did not perceive immigrants as 'basically good, honest people' was only around 20 per cent, and the percentage who did not consider them as hardworking was only 18 per cent (John S. Lapniski, Pia Peltola, Greg Shaw, and Alan Yang, 'The pools-trends. Immigrants and immigration', *Public Opinion Quarterly*, Vol. 61, 1997: 367).

46 See Espenshade and Belanger, 'Immigration and public opinion', and Lapniski, Peltola, Shaw, and Yang, 'The pools-trends. Immigrants and immigration'.

47 Claude Nicolet, 'Le passage à l'universel', in Claude Nicolet, ed., *La République en France. Etat des lieux*, Paris: Le Seuil, 1992, pp. 122–68. These republican principles, including the symbolically crucial notion of secular education, have gained a sacred status since the Third Republic. At the end of the nineteenth century, Republicans won over the Royalists who had been fighting a counter-revolution with the support of the Catholic Church since 1789, contesting in particular the principle of the separation of state and Church.

48 On the impact of pluralism on American society as compared to French society, see Denis Lacorne, *La Crise de l'identité américaine. Du melting-pot au multiculturalisme*, Paris: Fayard 1997; Kastoryano, *La France, l'Allemagne et leurs immigrés: négocier l'identité*, 1996; Laurent Thévenot and Michèle Lamont, 'Exploring the French and the American polity', in Michèle Lamont and Laurent Thévenot, eds, *Rethinking Comparative Cultural Sociology: Repertoires of Evaluation in France and the United States*, Cambridge: Cambridge University Press, 2000.

49 Eric Fassin, 'The politics of difference in the American mirror: immigration and ethnicity in France', paper presented at the conference 'Multiculturalism, Minorities, and Citizenship', European University Institute, Florence, 1996. On this issue, see also Adrian Favell, *Philosophies of Integration*, p. 183. Republicanism presumes that the assimilation of minority groups is a requirement for the reproduction of the polity, and for the defence of majority interest (Noiriel, *Population, immigration et identité nationale en France, XIXième et XXième siècles*, Paris: Hachette, 1992, chapter 3). Rogers Brubaker (*Citizenship and Nationhood in France and Germany*, Cambridge, MA: Harvard University Press, 1992) proposes that this assimilationist approach constitutes the distinctively French cultural idiom of nationhood that characterizes French political culture.

50 William Safran, 'State, nation, national identity, and citizenship: France as a test case', *International Political Science Review*, 12 (3), 1991, 219–38.

51 Sophie Body-Gendrot, 'Migration and the racialization of the postmodern city in France', in Malcolm Cross and Michael Keith, eds, *Racism, the City and the State*, London: Routledge, 1992, pp. 77–92.

52 This law was based on the understanding that such information would eventually

lead to quotas and social balkanization, and would represent a danger to individual liberty. In fact, the prohibition to count the population based on race goes back to 1848, when slavery was abolished in the French Caribbeans (personal communication with Emmanuelle Saada). The collaboration of the Vichy government with the Nazis feeds into concerns for the protection of citizens' privacy from the state. One of the unintended consequences of this law, however, is that it is difficult to establish access discrimination in the absence of ethnic statistics. See Erik Bleich, 'Ideas and race policies in Britain and France', paper presented at the Eleventh International Conference of Europeanists, Baltimore, 26–28 February 1998, p. 18.

53 A law against discrimination in employment, housing, provision of services, and incitement to racial hatred was passed in 1972 but is rarely enforced. The country was relatively slow to pass it (in contrast to other Western nations) because French decision-makers believed that all citizens were equally protected by French law, the latter *de facto* embodying republican principles (Gary Freeman, *Immigrant Labor and Racial Conflict in Industrial Societies: The French and British Experience 1945–75*, Princeton, NJ: Princeton University Press, 1979, p. 156). Simultaneously, in order to give it more bite, this law was included under criminal law, with the result that relatively few cases are brought to justice because criminal standards of proof are difficult to establish. Indeed, while in 1991 British civil procedures led to 1,471 cases of employment-related discrimination, in France only four cases were brought to justice (cited by Bleitch, 1998, p. 4.)

54 Noiriel, *The French Melting Pot*. Also Eugen Weber, *Peasants into Frenchmen: The Modernization of Rural France, 1870–1914*, Stanford, CA: Stanford University Press, 1976.

55 Favell, *Philosophies of Integration*; Miriam Feldblum, *Reconstructing Citizenship: The Politics of Nationality Reform and Immigration in Contemporary France*, New York: State University of New York Press, forthcoming; George Fredrickson, 'America's diversity in comparative perspective', Presidential Address, Organization of American Historians, Indianapolis, 1998; Lamont, *The Dignity of Working Men*.

56 See Lamont, *The Dignity of Working Men*, chapter 5.

57 Gary Gerstle, 'Liberty, coercion, and the making of Americans', *Journal of American History*, 84 (2), 1997: 524–58.

58 These workers have been working full-time and steadily for at least five years. They do not supervise more than ten workers. I explicitly do not use income as a criterion of selection of respondents in order to include in the sample workers of various economic status. I consider the fact of not having a college degree as most determinant of workers' life chances and privilege this criterion in creating the sample. Respectively 30 per cent and 50 per cent of white and black respondents have completed some college courses, while the remaining individuals have a high school degree or GED.

59 Hundreds of letters were sent to potential respondents living in working-class suburbs in the New York area. In a follow-up phone interview, these men were asked to self-identify themselves racially and we chose interviewees who categorized themselves as black and white and who meet other criteria of selection pertaining to occupation, age, nationality, and level of education. I take the terms 'black' and 'white' to be moving categories that are the object of intersubjective negotiation within determined parameters.

60 The methodology described in this Appendix refers to the larger study, M. Lamont (2000), *The Dignity of Working Men*, Cambridge, MA: Harvard University Press.

References

Alexander, Jeffrey, 'Citizen and enemy as symbolic classification: on the polarizing discourse of civil society', in Michèle Lamont and Marcel Fournier, eds, *Cultivating Differences: Symbolic Boundaries and the Making of Inequality*, Chicago: University of Chicago Press, 1992, pp. 289–308.

Anderson, Benedict, *Imagined Communities: Reflections on the Origin and Spread of Nationalism*, revised and extended, 2nd edn, London: Verso, 1991.

Aptheker, Herbert, *Anti-Racism in U.S. History*, New York: Greenwood, 1992.

Baldwin, Peter, *The Politics of Social Solidarity: Class Bases of European Welfare State*, New York: Cambridge University Press, 1990.

Barou, Jacques, 'Les Immigrations africaines', in David Assouline and Mehdi Lallaoui, eds, *Un Siècle d'immigration en France: 1945 à nos jours du chantier à la citoyenneté?* Paris: Diffusion Syros, 1996, pp. 31–46.

Barth, Fredrik, 'Introduction', in Fredrik Barth, ed., *Ethnic Groups and Boundaries: The Social Organization of Culture Difference*, London: George Allen and Unwin, 1969, pp. 9–38.

Bergues, Hélène, 'L' immigration de travailleurs noirs en France et particulièrement dans la région parisienne', *Population*, 28 (1), 1973: 59–79.

Bleitch, Erik, 'Ideas and race policies in Britain and France', Paper presented at the Eleventh International Conference of Europeanists, Baltimore, MD, 26–28 February 1998.

Blumer, Herbert, 'Race prejudice as a sense of group position', *Pacific Sociological Review*, Vol. 1, 1958: 3–7.

Bobo, Lawrence, and Ryan A. Smith, 'Antipoverty policy, affirmative action, and racial attitudes', in Sheldon H. Danziger, Gary D. Sandefur, and Daniel H. Weinberg, eds, *Confronting Poverty: Prescriptions for Change*, New York: Russell Sage Foundation, 1994, pp. 365–95.

Body-Gendrot, Sophie, 'Migration and the racialization of the postmodern city in France', in Malcolm Cross and Michael Keith, eds, *Racism, the City and the State*, London: Routledge, 1992, pp. 77–92.

Brubaker, Rogers, *Citizenship and Nationhood in France and Germany*, Cambridge, MA: Harvard University Press, 1992.

Castel, Robert, *Les Métamorphoses de la question sociale*, Paris: Fayard, 1995.

Conklin, Alice L., *A Mission to Civilize: The Republican Idea of Empire in France and West Africa, 1895–1930*, Stanford, CA: Stanford University Press, 1998.

Delerm, Robert, 'La population noire en France', *Population*, 19 (3), 1964: 515–28.

Durkheim, Emile, and Marcel Mauss, *Primitive Classification* (translated and with an introduction by Rodney Needham), Chicago, IL: University of Chicago Press, 1963.

Espenshade, Thomas J., and Maryann Belanger, 'Immigration and public opinion', in Marcelo Suarez-Orozco, ed., *Crossings: Mexican Immigration in Interdisciplinary Perspectives*, Cambridge, MA: Harvard University Press, 1998.

Esping-Anderson, Gosta, *Three Worlds of Welfare Capitalism*, London: Polity Press, 1990.

Fassin, Eric, 'The politics of difference in the American mirror: immigration and ethnicity in France', paper presented at the Conference 'Multiculturalism, Minorities, and Citizenship', European University Institute, Florence, 1996.

Favell, Adrian, 'Integration policy and integration research: a critique of current cross-national and comparative approaches', report prepared for the Carnegie Endowment Comparative Citizenship Project, 1999.

— *Philosophies of Integration: Immigration and the Idea of Citizenship in France and Britain*, London: Macmillan, 1997.

Featherstone, Mike, *Global Culture: Nationalism, Globalization and Modernity*, Newbury Park: Sage, 1990.

Feldblum, Miriam, *Reconstructing Citizenship: The Politics of Nationality Reform and Immigration in Contemporary France*, New York: State University of New York Press, forthcoming.

Fredrickson, George, 'America's diversity in comparative perspective', Presidential Address, Organization of American Historians, Indianapolis, 1998.

Freeman, Gary, *Immigrant Labor and Racial Conflict in Industrial Societies: The French and British Experience 1945–75*, Princeton, NJ: Princeton University Press, 1979.

Gans, Herbert, 'The possibility of a new racial hierarchy in the 21st century United States', in Michèle Lamont, ed., *The Cultural Territories of Race: Black and White Boundaries*, Chicago and New York: University of Chicago Press and Russell Sage Foundation, 1999, pp. 371–90.

Gerstle, Gary, 'Liberty, coercion, and the making of Americans', *Journal of American History*, 84 (2), 1997: 524–58.

Girard, Alain, Yves Charbit and Marie-Laurence Lamy, 'Attitudes des français a l'égard de l'immigration étrangère: nouvelle enquête d'opinion', *Population*, Vol. 6, 1974: 1015–69.

Goldberg, David, *Racist Culture: Philosophy and the Politics of Meaning*, New York: Blackwell, 1993.

Hannoun, Michel, *L'Homme est l'espérance de l'homme: rapport sur le racisme et les discriminations en France*, Paris: La Documentation Française, Collection des rapports officiels, 1987.

Harwood, Edwin, 'American public opinion and U.S. immigration policy', in Rita J. Simon, ed., 'Immigration and American public policy', *Annals of the American Academy of Political and Social Science*, Vol. 487, Beverly Hills, CA: Sage, 1986, pp. 201–12.

Horowitz, Donald L., 'Immigration and group relations in France and the United States', in *Immigrants in Two Democracies: French and American Experience*, New York: New York University Press, 1992, pp. 3–35.

Institut National de Statistique et Etudes Economiques, *Recensement de la population de 1990: les populations des DOM-TOM, nées et originaires, résidant en France*, Paris: Documentation Française, 1993.

Joppke, Christian, 'Multiculturalism and immigration: a comparison of the United States, Germany, and Great Britain', *Theory and Society*, Vol. 25, 1996: 449–550.

Kastoryano, Riva, *La France, l'Allemagne et leurs immigrés: négocier l'identité*, Paris: Armand Colin, 1996.

Katz, Michael, *The Undeserving Poor: From the War on Poverty to the War on Welfare*, New York: Pantheon, 1989.

Lacorne, Denis, *La Crise de l'identité américaine: du melting-pot au multiculturalisme*, Paris: Fayard, 1997.

Lamont, Michèle, 'North African immigrants respond to French racism: demonstrating equivalence through universalism', in Abdellah Hammoudi, *Universalizing from Particulars*, London: I.B.Tauris, forthcoming.
— *The Dignity of Working Men: Morality and the Boundaries of Race, Class, and Immigration*, Cambridge, MA: Harvard University Press and New York: Russell Sage Foundation, forthcoming.
— ed., *The Cultural Territories of Race: Black and White Boundaries*, Chicago, IL: University of Chicago Press and New York: Russell Sage Foundation, 1999.
— *Money, Morals, and Manners: The Culture of the French and American Upper-Middle Class*, Chicago, IL: University of Chicago Press, 1992.
Lapniski, John S., Pia Peltola, Greg Shaw and Alan Yang, 'The pools-trends: immigrants and immigration', *Public Opinion Quarterly*, Vol. 61, 1997: 356–83.
Lebovics, Herman, 'Where and how did the French get the idea that they were the trustees of western civilization, 1513–1959?', paper presented at the New York Area French History Seminar, 1996.
Lipset, Seymour Martin, *The First New Nation: The United States in Historical and Comparative Perspective*, New York: Norton, 1979.
Lomax Cook, Fay, *Who Should Be Helped: Public Support for Social Services*, Beverly Hills, CA: Sage, 1979.
Malkki, Lisa H., *Purity and Exile: Violence, Memory and National Cosmology among Hutu Refugees in Tanzania*, Chicago IL: University of Chicago Press, 1995.
Martin, Philip, 'The United States: benign neglect toward immigration', in Wayne A. Cornelius, Philip L. Martin and James F. Hollifield, eds, *Controlling Immigration: A Global Perspective*, Stanford, CA: Stanford University Press, 1994, pp. 83–99.
Mayer, Nonna, and Pascal Perrineau, *Le Front national à découvert*, Paris: Presses de la Fondation nationale de science politique, 1989.
Mouriaux, René, 'Stratégies syndicales face au chomage et à l'intervention industrielle de l'état dans la période 1962–87', in James F. Hollifield and George Ross, eds, *Searching from the New France*, New York and London: Routledge, 1991.
Naisbitt, John, *Global Paradox*, New York: William Morrow, 1994.
Nicolet, Claude, 'Le passage à l'universel', in Claude Nicolet, ed., *La République en France: état des lieux*, Paris: Le Seuil, 1992, pp. 122–68.
Noiriel, Gérard, *The French Melting Pot: Immigration, Citizenship, and National Identity*, trans. Geoffrey de Laforcade, Minneapolis: University of Minnesota Press, 1996.
— *Population, immigration et identité nationale en France, XIXième et XXième siècles*, Paris: Hachette, 1992.
Paugam, Serge, *La Société française et ses pauvres*, Paris: Presses universitaires de France, 1993.
Perin, Constance, *Belonging in America*, Madison: University of Wisconsin Press, 1988.
Perrineau, Pascal, 'Le Front National: du désert à l'enracinement', in Pierre-Andre Taguieff, ed., *Face au racisme, Vol 2. Analyses, hypothèses, perspectives*, Paris: La Découverte, 1991.
Portes, Alejandro, 'La mondialisation par le bas: l'émergence des communautés transnationales', *Actes de la recherche en sciences sociales*, Vol. 129, 1999: 15–25.
Safran, William, 'State, nation, national identity, and citizenship: France as a test case', *International Political Science Review*, 12(3), 1991: 219–38.
Schuman, Howard, Charlotte Steeh and Lawrence Bobo, *Racial Attitudes in America: Trends and Interpretation*, Cambridge, MA: Harvard University Press, 1985.

Sears, David O., 'Symbolic racism', in Phyllis A. Katz and Dalmas A. Taylor, eds, *Eliminating Racism: Profiles in Controversy*, New York and London: Plenum Press, 1988, pp. 53–84.

Silver, Hilary, 'National conceptions of the new urban poverty: social structural change in Britain, France, and the United States', *International Journal of Urban and Regional Research*, 17 (3), 1993: 336–54.

Simmel, Georg, 'The stranger', in Kurt W. Wolff, ed., *The Sociology of Georg Simmel*, New York: Free Press, 1950, pp. 402–8.

Sleeper, Jim, *The Closest of Strangers: Liberalism and the Politics of Race in New York*, New York: Norton, 1991.

Soysal, Yasemin Nuhoglu, *Limits of Citizenship: Migrants and Postnational Membership in Europe*, Chicago, IL: University of Chicago Press, 1994.

Thévenot, Laurent, and Michèle Lamont, 'Exploring the French and the American polity', in Michèle Lamont and Laurent Thévenot, eds, *Rethinking Comparative Cultural Sociology: Repertoires of Evaluation in France and the United States*, Cambridge: Cambridge University Press, 2000.

Tocqueville, Alexis de, *Democracy in America*, New York: Vintage, 1945.

Tribalat, Michèle, *Faire France: une enquête sur les immigrés et leurs enfants*, Paris: La Découverte, 1995.

Varenne, Hervé, *Americans Together: Structured Diversity in a Midwestern Town*, New York: Teachers College Press, 1977.

Verdery, Katherine, 'Ethnicity, nationalism, and state-making. Ethnic groups and boundaries: past and future', in Hans Vermeulen and Cora Govers, eds, *The Anthropology of Ethnicity: Beyond 'Ethnic Groups and Boundaries'*, Amsterdam: Het Spinhuis, 1994, pp. 33–58.

Waters, Mary, *Black Identities: West Indian Immigrant Dreams and American Realities*, New York: Russell Sage Foundation and Cambridge, MA: Harvard University Press, 1999.

Weber, Eugen, *Peasants into Frenchmen: The Modernization of Rural France, 1870–1914*, Stanford, CA: Stanford University Press, 1976.

Wieviorka, Michel, *La France raciste*, Paris: Points, 1992.

Wolfe, Alan, *Whose Keeper? Social Science and Moral Obligation*, Berkeley and Los Angeles: University of California Press, 1989.

Zolberg, Aristide R., and Long Litt Woon, 'Why Islam is like Spanish: cultural incorporation in Europe and the United States', *Politics and Society*, 17(1), 1999.

4

Economic Change
and Social Mobility

Michael Hout

The run-up in social inequality in many nations over the last 20 years has led to a variety of social and economic problems. Yet when social scientists point out the difficulties that can be traced to inequality, conservatives frequently counter their arguments with claims that cross-sectional inequalities overstate the problems because today's inequalities are undone by tomorrow's social mobility.[1] Research over the last 30 years shows that the conservatives' optimism is misplaced. For while it is true that social mobility does occur, it is far from perfect, even in the most open societies of Western Europe.[2] On average, a person's place in society maintains a strong, positive correlation with social origins – between 0.25 and 0.40 in rich countries.[3] Furthermore, most mobility that occurs reflects occupational upgrading and economic growth that affects everyone, regardless of their social origins. While this may mask some of the social consequences of inheritable privilege, it does not negate them.[4]

Expressing change across generations succinctly has proved to be a formidable task. The mathematical conventions of modern statistical analysis have aided researchers enormously. All too often, though, the research community has contented itself with exchanges within the group, making little effort to keep the broader sociological community a breast of developments. This has led to a triumph of mathematical expressions over verbal ones within the group, and a suspicion among some other sociologists that there was more mathematics than sociology going on. In an 'age of extremes' (to borrow Massey's[5] phrase), the work of mobility researchers is very important. Communicating it deserves higher priority.

With that in mind, I have two goals in this chapter. The first and more important goal is to link what we know about social mobility to social inequality as more broadly conceived. My secondary goal is to translate some of the recent research on social mobility into terms that might be more transparent for non-specialists – both researchers in other fields and persons who have an interest in comprehending current events. To that end I am going to step away from the generalizing approach so typical of social scientific writing and focus instead on how economic growth, occupational change, inequality, and social mobility played out in four specific cases of changing social mobility: American men during the 1960s and 1970s, African American men in the USA during the Civil Rights struggles of the same period, Irish employees during the last 30 years, and economically active Russians from the last days of communism to the present time. First, however, I will define some terms and describe the intellectual project that underlies the research into the four case studies.

Structural and Exchange Mobility

Social mobility is the change in people's social positions over time. Academic interest in the topic goes back about 125 years. Already by 1927 the sociologist Pitrim Sorokin had documented 17 studies.[6] Popular interest undoubtedly goes back further. Academics and others alike are fascinated by the contrast between the closed and static feudal social order and the dynamic, mobile industrial order that replaced it in much of Europe. Quantifying social mobility gives a measure to the qualitative difference between the social orders. Over time, as the feudal order has receded into history, social mobility has become a standard measure for comparing the openness of one industrial (or post-industrial) society *vis-à a-vis* another. By definition, the further a society gets from an exact reproduction of one generation's social order in the next, the more open its social structure.

Early studies took the measure of openness by making a gross calculation of how many individuals' current class position differed from the class position of the family they grew up in. Over time, attention has shifted to the strength of the statistical association between those social origins and destinations – for reasons I hope will become clear in the next few paragraphs.

The most fundamental distinction that mobility researchers routinely make is the distinction between what they call 'structural' and 'exchange' mobility. Structural mobility refers to the differences between peoples' social origins and their current positions. However, only a subset of differences qualify as 'structural mobility'. The differences that reflect social changes that affect everyone, regardless of their social origins, count; differences arising from changes in specific origins do not. For example, in most European and American nations, manufacturing employment grew while agricultural employment shrank throughout the twentieth century. To some extent this important change in the distribution of economic opportunity affected everyone who looked for work, regardless of their social origins. Similarly, the post-industrial shift to services – both simple and professional – affect every job-seeker's opportunities for employment by supplying more of both the most desirable and least desirable occupations. Those kinds of universal influences are what mobility researchers have in mind when they talk about structural mobility.

Formally, researchers define structural mobility as the sum of all the factors that make the distribution of destinations different from the distribution of origins without affecting the statistical association between them. The first scholars to be concerned with structural mobility applied a straightforward logic to the mobility table itself. If there were absolutely no mobility in society, everyone would work in an occupation in the same class that they grew up in. Therefore, if we observe that some occupation or class is more frequently a social destination than a social origin, then someone must have moved into it from some other origin; conversely, if some occupation or class is less frequent as a social destination than as a social origin, then someone must have moved out of it to some other social destination. Much of the statistical work on mobility tables over the years from 1949 to 1985 was directed towards getting structural mobility right. Important early contributors include Natalie Rogoff and David Glass.[7] The main contributor in the 1960s and 1970s was Leo Goodman.[8] The formulation that most researchers use now was an adaptation of Goodman's work by Sobel, Hout, and Duncan.[9]

Exchange mobility refers to moves between particular origins and destinations. Again, the eclipse of agricultural employment makes a clear example. As farms offered ever fewer employment opportunities, farmers' sons and daughters felt the effects more than people with urban origins did. This occasioned an 'exchange' between farming and some other occupations, especially low-skilled, blue-collar occupations. Mobility that is selective in this sense – that is, mobility that pertains particularly to a specific combination of social origins and destinations – is what mobility researchers have in mind when they talk about exchange mobility.

Another useful way to think about these issues is to focus on the statistical association between persons' current positions (destinations) and their origins. Structural mobility is completely unrelated to this correlation; it is mobility that does not select one kind of origin over another. Exchange mobility reduces the correlation by moving some people from selected origins to other destinations. In a perfectly complementary way, a high correlation between origins and destinations impedes exchange mobility while a low correlation implies a lot of exchange.

Sobel, Hout, and Duncan[10] worked out all these relationships in a mathematically general way. Readers who are interested in the fully general specification can look there. The key issues can be seen, though, in the more familiar simple regression model:

$$y = a + bX + e \qquad\qquad [1]$$

where y is destination (occupational status score or wage or some other numerical representation of outcome), X is origin (scored identically), e is an error term, and a and b are coefficients. Mobility, in this framework, is just the difference between destination and origin:

$$M = y-X = a + (b-1) X + e . \qquad\qquad [2]$$

Whether we use equation 1 or 2, structural mobility – the amount of change from generation to generation that everyone can expect to experience – is reflected in the coefficient a, and exchange mobility is captured by b because it is sensitive to origins. In every study I know of, b (or the equivalent) is between 0 and 1. When b is close to zero, (b–1) is close to – 1. Substantively it means that people from lower origins move up a lot, those with average origins hardly move at all, and those with advantaged origins move down a lot. On the other hand, when b is close to one, (b–1) is close to zero and mobility is too (unless a or e is large). When b is large, origins determine destinations.

Social stratification changes when either structural mobility or the association between origins and destinations changes (and, of course, when both change). There are actually 8 possible combinations of these two elements that result in social change, since a change can come about from either an increase or a decrease in either or both types of mobility. Table 4.1 maps out the possibilities with illustrative cases named in some of the cells. Some combinations, especially those involving negative or no structural mobility, are rarely observed – positive structural mobility being the norm in most complex societies in the last 125 years. In the following pages I will consider four cases studies, representing four different combinations of structural mobility and association. The mobility of American men in the USA between 1962 and 1973 is a case of structural mobility increasing while the association between origins and destinations decreased; the mobility of African American men during the same period is a case of increasing structural mobility and association; the mobility of Russians between 1988 and 2001 is a rare case of *decreasing* structural mobility and increasing association; and the mobility of Irish employees, 1973–97, is a case of positive structural mobility and constant association. Nearly all of the studies reviewed above would fall into the first two cells of the last row.

Table 4.1. Combinations of Structural Mobility and Association in a Mobility Table

| Structural Mobility | *Association Between Origins and Destinations* | | |
	Decreasing	Constant	Increasing
Decreasing	Not observed	Not observed	**Russia**
Neutral	Not observed	Not observed	Not observed
Increasing	**USA**, France, Sweden, Netherlands	**Ireland**, UK	**African Americans (1962-1973)**

Note: Boldface type indicates a case that is discussed in detail.

American Mobility, 1962–73

The economic expansion in the USA in the immediate post-war decades vastly expanded opportunities for employment, prosperity, and, it turns out, social mobility. Affluent professionals and managers increased their annual earnings, but the lowest-paid manual and clerical employees increased theirs even more.[11] We lack national estimates of mobility rates before the expansion started, but the Occupational Changes in a Generation study of 1962[12] and its sequel in 1973[13] document men's mobility trends at the peak of the expansion. Good data on women's mobility do not exist prior to 1973, and inequality had started to rise by that point.

Statistical analyses of the two mobility studies, first by Featherman and Hauser[14] and later by Hout[15] and Biblarz and Raftery[16] confirm that structural mobility increased and the association between origins and destinations decreased. Figure 4.1 provides a simple illustration of the implications of these more sophisticated analyses by arraying the percentage of men in professional and managerial occupations by origins and year. Note first that

Figure 4.1   Percentage of American Men Employed in Professional or Managerial Occupation by Father's Occupation and Year

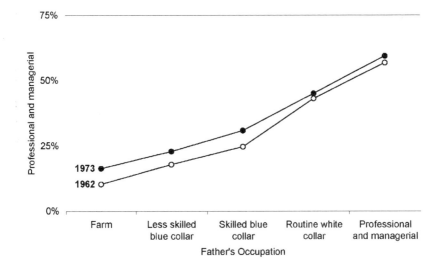

the 1973 line is clearly above the 1962 line. This is the trace of structural mobility – the sum of the factors that raise occupational status for all origins. Note, too, that the slope of the 1973 line appears to be less steep than that of the 1962 line. That is the evidence that the association between origins and destinations was weaker in 1973 than in 1962.

The American case is very close to the British and French cases for the early 1970s, so it warrants some close inspection. Structural mobility expanded the supply of professional and managerial positions from about one-quarter (24 per cent) of men in 1962 to about one-third (31 per cent) in 1973. A majority of men whose fathers had a professional or managerial occupation achieved one (57 per cent in 1962 and 59 per cent in 1973). Minorities ranging from 11 per cent up to 45 per cent of men with lower origins achieved professional or managerial status in their current occupations. If there was no mobility, these proportions would be 100 per cent for those with professional and managerial occupations and zero otherwise. So the mobility is substantial. Nevertheless, the association between origins and destinations is strong relative to other social science correlations – about the same as the correlation between education and wages in 1962 and about 80 per cent as strong as that benchmark in 1973.

The association between origins and destinations fell between 1962 and 1973, mainly because men from disadvantaged backgrounds had significantly better prospects in 1973 than a decade earlier, while men from privileged backgrounds did only slightly better than a decade earlier. Detailed analyses indicate that university education was the main vehicle for long-distance upward mobility of men from farm and less-skilled manual backgrounds.[17] Most American states expanded their public universities in the 1950s and 1960s. Millions of young men and women had the opportunity to be the first members of their families to earn a university credential. In the labour market, university credentials proved to be doubly important. Not only did a diploma improve chances relative to people with less education, but it also cancelled the effect of social origins: among college graduates, origins had no effect. Thus, as education expanded, more and more American workers were free of the influence of their background, and the overall association became weaker. This pattern – think of it as a 'baccalaureate bonus' – was not unique to the USA. Recent research has shown that a university education wiped out the effect of origins in France and Sweden as well.[18]

Men with working-class backgrounds benefited in another way as well. University education, the key to occupational achievement, was itself less selective than secondary education. That is, although origins had a large effect on the probability of successfully completing academic secondary education, lower-origin youths who survived that trial were on a nearly-equal footing with their counterparts from privileged backgrounds.[19] This pattern, known as the 'Mare effect', is even more general than the baccalaureate bonus, evident in all 15 countries for which good data were available.[20]

The Mare effect is known to most stratification researchers and the baccalaureate bonus is becoming more familiar in the research community, but no one has remarked on the important theoretical implications of these two empirical regularities. In *Distinction, Homo Academicus*, and *State Nobility*,[21] Bourdieu discussed how the cultural capital of privileged youth increases their competitive advantages in the higher reaches of the emerging academic system. In particular he theorized that expanding higher education had shifted the locus of the competition for credentials from the secondary schools to the universities and would soon shift it further upward into graduate education. This research record shows quite the opposite. Not only did the expansion of higher education open opportunities for first-generation matriculants, but the premium on their credentials in the labour force compounded those opportunities. Of course circumstances in higher education can change at any time and Bourdieu's derivations, always so reasonable in their articulation, even if not always borne out by data, may yet prove accurate in the long run. For now, however, the key proposition that selection works by thwarting those who get closest to the prize rather than by reserving early exits to the least privileged is overturned by the case under study and by many other cases as well.

The positive lesson of this case study concerns the efficacy of public action. We live in an age when conservatives and 'third-way' advocates tout market incentives over direct governmental actions any time the state is called upon to act. Here is a case in point in which government intervention improved opportunities in the way it was intended and in other ways as well. The intended and the unintended consequences were all positive. By expanding low-cost higher educational facilities, the governments of many US states gave working-class youth the opportunity of a lifetime. They got the chance to earn credentials that their parents had not been able to try for, then they found that the returns on that degree exceeded their expectations.

African American Mobility: The Increasing Significance of Class

The Civil Rights movement arose during that very same time of soaring economic opportunities in the USA. The shameful exclusion and segregation of African Americans imposed, in varying degrees, between the 1880s and 1920, was still in place in much of America in 1962. A strategy of civil disobedience, landmark court cases, and, finally, legislation in the form of voting rights and equal employment opportunity laws in 1964 and 1965 raised optimism. The OCG-I and OCG-II studies gave researchers an opportunity to measure the first consequences of these changes.

Analysing the 1962 data, Blau and Duncan found that the pattern of African American men's social mobility was dramatically different from that of other American men.[22] Black men's social origins had almost no effect on their destinations. While a weak association between origins and destinations is usually a welcome sign of social openness, African Americans faced such a limited set of opportunities that this openness was pernicious. My analysis of the 1962 data found that two-thirds of black men had unskilled blue-collar occupations regardless of whether their father worked in a professional, white-collar, skilled, or unskilled occupation.[23] Exclusion and discrimination meant that even the rare African American family that beat the formidable odds of American apartheid could not pass the entitlements of that privileged class position on to the next generation. The sons of professionals were as likely to be porters as the sons of porters were, because so many employers saw a black applicant and thought 'porter'. In his influential essay 'Inheritance of poverty or inheritance of race?' Duncan went beyond the mobility table results to show how educated African American men were also denied the pay-off to their educational credentials.[24]

The 1973 OCG-II study revealed a much more typical pattern of intergenerational mobility for African American men just eleven years later.[25] While the sons of unskilled blue-collar fathers could still expect unskilled blue-collar employment at rates approaching the 1962 figure (60 per cent), only half of the sons of skilled blue-collar fathers faced that limit, 45 per cent of the sons of white-collar fathers did, and only 35 per cent of the sons of professionals and managers did. Origins now stratified life chances for African American men the way they did for other Americans. In a complementary way the chance of achieving a professional or managerial outcome rose dramatically for men from middle-class backgrounds, as I show in Figure 4.2. The most dramatic change was the much higher rate of professional and managerial employment for men whose fathers were professionals and managers. They still trailed other men. The burdens of discrimination were lightened but not eliminated. It was evidence like Figure 4.2 that led William Julius Wilson to announce the declining significance of race.[26]

Some part of the emerging stratification of the African American population was due to the treatment that 1970s school-leavers were receiving. New labour force entrants were far more stratified (and far more educated) than any previous generation of black men. But the career mobility of men already

Figure 4.2 Percentage of African American Men Employed in Professional or Managerial Occupation by Father's Occupation and Year

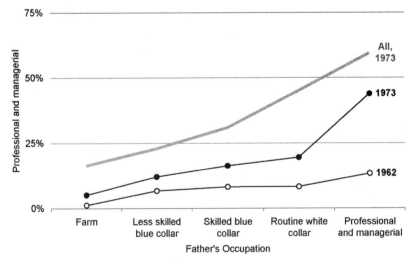

employed in 1962 was the key to the emerging stratification. As Figure 4.3 shows, African American men from higher-status origins were more likely to be upwardly mobile between 1962 and 1973 than their lower-status counterparts were. The most discriminated against – the men whose fathers were professionals and managers who found themselves in unskilled jobs in 1962 – were the most upwardly mobile. Nearly half of these men moved up between 1962 and 1973. As I wrote in 1984, 'the new opportunities that opened up for blacks during the 1962–73 period benefited men with relatively advantaged backgrounds more than other men'.[27]

The general lesson is, once again, that government action can indeed affect social mobility patterns. In formulating policies to reverse the consequences of racial exclusion and discrimination, the government altered social mobility. Here the results were, on balance, salutary, but progressively minded scholars must give them two cheers not one. If class privileges are going to exist, it is best that they work the same for socially out-of-favour groups as they do for favoured ones. So changes that enable African American men to exercise the same class privileges that their white counterparts routinely exercise is progress. Rarely, though, is an increase in the association between social origins and destinations a mark of progress.

Figure 4.3   Percentage of African American Men Who Were Upwardly Mobile Between 1962 and 1973 by Father's Occupation and Occupation in 1962

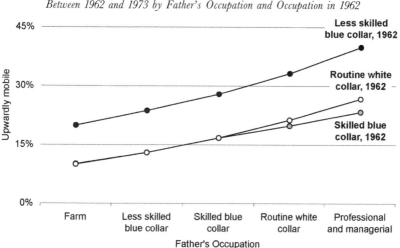

These two cases of changing American social mobility are old news. I brought them up because more contemporary discussions of the relationship between class and society[28] lead me to suspect that their importance for understanding social stratification has been lost on people outside the limited sphere of mobility research.[29] To avoid giving the impression that the most interesting results are old, however, I now turn to two emerging cases: Ireland and Russia in the 1990s.

Irish Mobility, 1973–97

Ireland emerged in the 1990s as the Emerald Tiger – a European nation whose economic performance rivaled that of the Asian Tigers (Singapore, Hong Kong, Taiwan, and Korea). Ireland's 'bust-to-boom' performance was built on three pillars: a huge national investment in higher education, the judicious investment of funds provided by the European Union, and a national wage agreement that traded short-term restraint for long-term gains.[30] The social mobility picture is one of massive structural mobility but a stable association between origins and destinations.[31]

The expansion of higher education is the most relevant aspect for understanding the link between Ireland's economic boom and the attendant pattern of social mobility. As in the American case, the expansion of universities and the emergence of other post-secondary institutions created unprecedented opportunities for educational advancement for working-class and farm-origin youth. This weakened the association between origins and educational credentials. This would normally result in a weaker association between origins and destinations in a mobility table. As Blau and Duncan showed, the association in the mobility table is the sum of two parts: the direct connection between origins and destinations and the part that is indirect through the educational system. The indirect path through education is the product of the effect of origins on educational attainment and the subsequent effect of educational credentials on occupational attainment. Ireland's dramatic expansion of higher education did its part by weakening the association between origins and education. But the labour market returns to those credentials also rose rapidly, offsetting the decreased educational stratification. The product of the two paths did not change.

What set off the rising return to educational credentials in Ireland? The pattern is new and the evidence is spotty. But in my research on an earlier generation's mobility experiences, I noted that Ireland's high proportion of family-owned businesses held down the returns to education.[32] The particularism of family employers constrained and encouraged them to hire family members over better-qualified non-relatives. The labour market was so informal that most of this familial exclusion was hidden from view. Vacancies were created and filled in a family context. Outsiders had no opportunity to compete, and employers never confronted the exclusionary and unfair consequences of their practices. Enter modern, high-tech, large-scale global employers. Suddenly the new generation of university-educated Irish techies applies for jobs and competes on credentials, and the correlation between education and occupation rises. It appears to be just a coincidence that the increase in the association between education and occupation is just big enough to perfectly balance the decrease in the association between origins and education, netting out to no change in the overall association between origins and destinations.

Structural mobility, meanwhile, reached unprecedented levels. The array of destinations contains far more desirable occupations than did the array of origins. Thus the average Irish worker in 1997 was upwardly mobile. Structural mobility also increased the supply of undesirable jobs, though. Overall the distributions of destinations is more unequal than the array of origins. Thus there is also somewhat more downward mobility of a sort.[33]

Russian Mobility, 1988–2001

At the end of the Soviet era, Russia had a mobility pattern that resembled Britain's, at least to a first approximation.[34] The economic collapse that followed the liberalization of prices and other 'shock therapies', which began in 1992 and continue dramatically, altered the occupational structure of Russia. New research shows its implications for social mobility.[35]

A decade of economic crisis in Russia reduced the number of desirable jobs and displaced millions of workers. When the displaced found work again, they were mostly in occupations closer to their social origins than before. This was no hardship for the majority from relatively privileged origins, but, for most Russians, their new positions were less desirable than the jobs they had under the old regime. In this sense, market transition in Russia has made social origins more relevant for how occupational opportunities get apportioned. To understand these changes of fortune, Gerber and I speculate somewhat on the reasons why post-Soviet stratification emerged this way.[36] One thing we know is that the new Russian state abandoned both the rhetoric and actions that the Soviet state took to promote opportunity for people with working-class and peasant origins. Meanwhile, competition for high-status occupations increased because there were fewer of them and the pay gap between them and lower-status occupations got wider. Apparently elites used whatever advantages they had to secure better outcomes for members of their families.

Figure 4.4 illustrates the Russian mobility experience. In a formal sense it complements the case of African American men's upward mobility: outcomes

Figure 4.4   Percentage Professional or Manager by Father's Occupationand Years: Russia

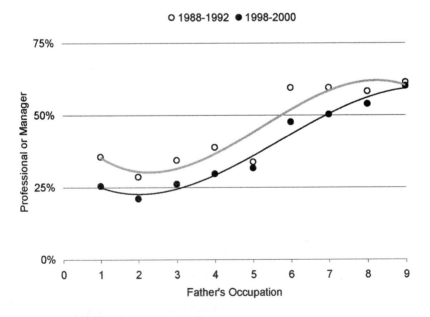

are better for people from privileged backgrounds in both cases. But the Russian experience is depression. Structural mobility was downward in Russia in the 1990s. Privilege did not so much apportion opportunities as shield the more privileged from some of the most deleterious consequences of economic failure. Russia's declining fortunes illustrate the dark side of the link between economic performance and social mobility. When the economy fails, the disadvantaged lose more – it is part of the disadvantage.

Conclusion

Four cases have illustrated aspects of the relationship between economic performance and social mobility. The preponderance of economic progress over the last hundred years means that we have far more cases of positive structural mobility to pore over and learn from. The one well-studied economic collapse – Russia in the 1990s – is yielding new insights. In every case under consideration – from America and Ireland at their heights to Russia at its depths – the role of the state underscores the point that social mobility reflects a nation's *political* economy. Government controls the supply of college-educated workers. This is hugely important for social mobility. It also sets the rules and enforces the fairness of employment practices. These have even more direct consequences for mobility chances. Cross-national variation in mobility outcomes reflect political choices. One hundred years of research have produced a clear record that politics and public policy shape the opportunity structure. Empirical regularities give social scientists some leverage in predicting what mobility will look like. But there is ample evidence of political consequences to support the proposition that nations can take a number of actions to affect the extent to which opportunities are openly distributed or restricted on the basis of class origins.

Notes

1 W. Michael Cox and Richard Alm, *Myths about Rich and Poor*, New York: Basic Books, 1999.
2 For reviews see: Ronald Breiger, 'Social structure and the phenomenology of attainment', *Annual Review of Sociology*, Vol. 21, 1995: 115–36; Samuel Bowles and

Herbert Gintis, 'The inheritance of inequality', *Journal of Economic Perspectives*, Vol. 16, 2002: 3–30; Michael Hout, 'How inequality might affect social mobility', in Kathryn Neckerman, ed., *Social Inequality*, New York: Russell Sage Foundation, 2004, pp. 969–93; Michael Hout and Thomas A. DiPrete, 'What have we learned? RC28's contributions to knowledge', *Research in Social Stratification and Mobility*, Vol. 25, 2006, forthcoming.

3 Bowles and Gintis, 'The inheritance of inequality'; Michael Hout, 'How inequality might affect social mobility'.

4 John H. Goldthorpe, *Social Mobility and Class Structure in Modern Britain*, Oxford: Clarendon Press, 1980.

5 Douglas Massey, 'The age of extremes', *Demography*, Vol. 33, 1996: 395–412.

6 Pitrim A. Sorokin, *Social and Cultural Mobility*, New York: Harper and Brothers, 1927.

7 Natalie Rogoff, *Recent Trends in Occupational Mobility*, Glencoe: Free Press, 1953.

8 Leo A. Goodman, 'On the statistical analysis of mobility tables', *American Journal of Sociology*, Vol. 70, 1965: pp. 564–85; 'How to ransack mobility tables,' *American Journal of Sociology*, Vol. 75, 1969: 1–39; 'Multivariate analysis of qualitative data', *Journal of the American Statistical Association*, Vol. 65, 1970: 226–56; 'Simple models for the analysis of association in cross-classifications', *Journal of the American Statistical Association*, Vol. 74, 1979: 537–52.

9 Michael E. Sobel, Michael Hout and Otis Dudley Duncan, 'Exchange, structure, and symmetry in occupational mobility', *American Journal of Sociology*, Vol. 91, 1985: 359–72.

10 Ibid.

11 Michael Hout, Richard Arum and Kim Voss, 'The political economy of inequality in the age of extremes', *Demography*, Vol. 33, 1996: 421–5.

12 Peter M. Blau and Otis Dudley Duncan, *The American Occupational Structure*, New York: Wiley, 1967.

13 David L. Featherman and Robert M. Hauser, *Opportunity and Change*, New York: Academic Press, 1978.

14 Ibid.

15 Michael Hout, 'Status, autonomy, and training in occupational mobility', *American Journal of Sociology*, Vol. 89, 1984: 1379–409.

16 Timothy Biblarz and Adrian E. Raftery, 'The effects of family disruption on social mobility', *American Sociological Review*, Vol. 58, 1993: 97–109.

17 Hout, 'Status, autonomy and training'.

18 Louis-André Vallet, 'Change in intergenerational class mobility in France from the 1970s to the 1990s and its explanation', paper presented to the ISA Research Committee on Stratification and Social Mobility (RC28), Tokyo, 1 March 2003; Richard Breen and Jon O. Jonsson, 'Period and cohort change in social fluidity: Sweden, 1976–1999', paper presented to the ISA Research Committee on Stratification and Mobility (RC28), Mannheim, April 2001, revised May 2003.

19 Robert D. Mare, 'Social background and school continuation decisions', *Journal of the American Statistical Association*, Vol. 75, 1980: pp. 295–305; Adrian E. Raftery and Michael Hout, 'Maximally maintained inequality: educational stratification in Ireland', *Sociology of Education*, Vol. 65, 1993: 41–62; Samuel R. Lucas, 'Effectively maintained inequality', *American Journal of Sociology*, Vol. 106, 2001: 1642–90; Michael Hout, 'Maximally maintained inequality revisited: Irish educational mo-

bility in comparative perspective', in Maire NicGhiolla Phadraig and Elizabeth Hilliard, eds, *Changing Ireland, 1989–2006*, forthcoming, 2006.

20 Yossi Shavit and Hans-Peter Blossfeld, 'Introduction', in Yossi Shavit and Hans-Peter Blossfeld, eds, *Persisting Inequality: Educational Stratification in 13 Nations*, Boulder, CO: Westview, 1993, pp. 3–24; Robert M. Hauser and Megan Andrew, 'Another look at the stratification of educational transitions,' paper presented to the Research Committee on Social Stratification and Mobility (RC28), Oslo, 7 May 2005.

21 Pierre Bourdieu, *Distinction: A Social Critique of the Judgment of Taste*, Cambridge, MA: Harvard University Press, 1984; *Homo Academicus*, Stanford, CA: Stanford University Press, 1988; *The State Nobility*, Stanford, CA: Stanford University Press, 1996.

22 Blau and Duncan, *The American Occupational Structure*.

23 Michael Hout, 'The occupational mobility of black men in the United States, 1962–1973', *American Sociological Review*, Vol. 49, 1984: 308–22.

24 Otis Dudley Duncan, 'Inheritance of poverty or inheritance of race?', in Daniel Patrick Moynihan, ed., *On Inequality*, New York: Basic Books, 1969, pp. 85–110.

25 David L. Featherman and Robert M. Hauser, 'Changes in the socioeconomic stratification of the races', *American Journal of Sociology*, Vol. 82, 1976: 621–51; David L. Featherman and Robert M. Hauser, *Opportunity and Change*, table 6.5.

26 William Julius Wilson, *The Declining Significance of Race*, Chicago, IL: University of Chicago Press, 1978.

27 Hout, 'The occupational mobility of black men', p. 318.

28 For example, Jan Pakulski and Malcolm Waters, 'The reshaping and dissolution of social class in advanced society', *Theory and Society*, Vol. 25, 1996: 667–91.

29 See John H. Goldthorpe, 'Globalisation and social class', *West European Politics*, Vol. 25, 2002: 1–28, for a full critique and Michael Hout, Clem Brooks, and Jeff Manza, 'The persistence of classes in postindustrial societies', *International Sociology*, Vol. 8, 1993: 259–77.

30 Brian Nolan, Phillip O'Connell and Christopher J. Whelan, 'Conclusion: The Irish experience of growth and inequality', in Brian Nolan, Phillip O'Connell and Christopher J. Whelan, eds, *Bust to Boom: The Irish Experience of Growth and Inequality*, Dublin: Institutes of Public Administration, 2001, pp. 340–54.

31 Richard Layte and Christopher J. Whelan, 'The rising tide and equality of opportunity', in Brian Nolan, Phillip O'Connell and Christopher J. Whelan, eds, *Bust to Boom: The Irish Experience of Growth and Inequality*, Dublin: Institutes of Public Administration, 2001, pp. 90–108.

32 Michael Hout, *Following in Father's Footsteps: Social Mobility in Ireland*, Cambridge, MA: Harvard University Press, 1989.

33 Richard Layte and Christopher J. Whelan, 'The rising tide and equality of opportunity'.

34 Gordon Marshall, Svetlana Sydorenko and Stephen Roberts, 'Intergenerational social mobility in communist Russia', *Work, Employment, and Society*, Vol. 9, 1997: 1–27.

35 Theodore P. Gerber and Michael Hout, 'Tightening up: declining class mobility during Russia's market transition', *American Sociological Review*, Vol. 69, 2004: 677–703.

36 Ibid., p. 696.

5

Nonstandard Employment Relations and Labour Market Inequality: Cross-national Patterns

Arne L. Kalleberg

Introduction

In the past quarter-century, many industrial nations have witnessed a shift away from the standard work arrangement as the normative basis of the employment relationship and an increase in nonstandard work arrangements. This change in the nature of employment relations has made labour markets and organizations more flexible, and has enabled some people and their families to obtain greater flexibility to accomplish their goals. At the same time, this enhanced flexibility often has a 'dark side', sometimes leading to greater labour market inequality and excluding some workers from the social protections previously available to them through the standard employment relationship.

Cross-national research is essential for understanding these changes in the nature of employment relations and their impacts on labour markets and workers. For example, comparative research permits an assessment of the role of the state and economic and social institutions (such as laws and regulations governing trade union influence), as well as societal values, norms, and beliefs in shaping patterns of labour market inequality and exclusion.

This chapter discusses some important correlates and consequences associated with these changes occurring in the nature of employment relations in industrial societies. I first summarize some of the main cross-national patterns in the use of the various types of nonstandard work arrangements, and suggest some of the reasons that nations and organizations have for using them. I then provide an overview of some issues related to labour market inequality associated with the use of these nonstandard employment arrangements in industrial societies; these issues constitute important components of a research agenda needed to understand cross-national differences in employment relations and patterns of labour market inequality and exclusion.

Standard and Nonstandard Work Arrangements

During the 'long boom' of the post-war period, many sociologists argued that an evolutionary process governed by a logic of industrialism would lead to a convergence among industrial societies towards a model of 'pluralistic industrialism'. This model predicted a long-term historical shift towards the dominance of one standard pattern of production relationships,[1] despite a 'wide and persisting degree of cross-national variation'.[2] The standard employment relationship (or *emploi total*[3]) had three main characteristics (see Table 5.1): (1) a personal relationship between a dominant master or employer and subordinate worker; (2) the work is done full-time; and (3) the employment relationship is generally assumed to continue for a substantial period or indefinitely.[4] In addition, the work is generally done at the employer's place of business and usually under the employer's direction.

Standard work arrangements were the norm in many industrial nations for much of the twentieth century and were the normative basis of the framework within which labour law, collective bargaining, and social security systems developed.[5]

Changes beginning in the mid-1970s created conditions that led countries, organizations, and workers to adopt nonstandard employment relations that depart from one or more of the essential features of the standard work

Table 5.1 Characteristics of Standard and Nonstandard Work Arrangements

Type of work arrangement	Who is the *de jure* employer?	Who is the *de facto* employer?	Dimension of work arrangements			
			Assumption of continued employment by *de jure* employer?	Assumption of continued employment by *de facto* employer?	Who directs work?	Hours of Work
Standard	Organization A	Organization A	Yes	Yes	Organization A	Full-time
Part-time	Organization A	Organization A	Sometimes	Sometimes	Organization A	Part-time
On-call/day labour	Organization A	Organization A	No	No	Organization A	FT or PT
Short-term temporary	Organization A	Organization A	Sometimes	No	Organization A	FT or PT
Temporary help agency	THA agency	Organization A	Yes	No	Organization A	FT or PT
Contract company[a]	Contract company	Organization A	Yes	No	Contract company	FT or PT
Independent contracting, self-employment	Self	Client(s)	Yes	No	Self	FT or PT

[a] Contract company employees may have a standard work arrangement with their *de jure* employer (the contract company), but from the point of view of Organization A their work arrangements are nonstandard.

arrangement (see Table 5.1). First, some employment relations do not involve a direct relationship between an employer and employee. This occurs when administrative control and responsibility for the employee is 'externalized',[6] creating 'detached' workers[7] or 'triangular' employment relations where a worker establishes connections with several employers.[8] Examples of such nonstandard employment relations include temporary help agency employment (in which the client organization directs the work of the temporary help agency's employee) and contract company employment (in which employees are directed by their contract company employers but often work at the client's site). In these cases, the workers' *de jure* employers differ from the *de facto* employers who use their labour most directly, and the meanings of the terms 'employer' and 'employee' become ambiguous. These terms are socially constructed products of negotiations: for example, the designation of temporary help agencies as employers rather than as employment agencies in the USA was the result of a campaign carried out over four decades by the temporary help agencies and their corporate backers.[9]

Second, some work deviates from the norm of full-time employment. The most common form of such nonstandard work is *regular part-time* employment, which is usually defined as regular wage employment in which the hours of work are less than 'normal'.[10] The definition of what is considered to be part-time work varies across countries (see below).

Third, some work does not involve the assumption of continued employment. In standard employment relations, the expectation still exists that employment is permanent or at least non-temporary for an indefinite period (even if in reality it is not 'permanent'). By contrast, short-term temporary employment is usually designated as such, as is the case with temporaries who are directly hired by the organization for a short term or on an on-call basis. Fixed-term contracts have been particularly important in countries where employers have a difficult time terminating contracts of indefinite duration, such as France, Germany, Italy, and Spain.[11]

Finally, some work arrangements do not involve an employer at all, as in the case of self-employment or independent contracting. In these situations, workers direct their own activities and are 'employed' by clients who pay them for services performed or goods provided, not for their labour power.

Nonstandard employment relations are not new. Employers have a choice between organizing work in markets or hierarchies,[12] and there have always been work arrangements that did not fit the model of full-time work: history is replete with examples of peripheral labour forces and flexible labour markets in which work is unstable and temporary.[13] For instance, in the inside contracting system that existed in the USA in the nineteenth century, management provided machinery and space in the factory, supplied raw material and capital, and arranged for the sale of the product while contractors were responsible for production and hired the workers and paid and supervised them.[14] Indeed, the efficiencies associated with organizing work in standard, hierarchical employment relations and internal labour markets in the post-Second World War period may have been more of an historical irregularity than is the use of nonstandard employment relations.

There are several major reasons why nonstandard work arrangements became attractive to industrial societies and organizations in the past quarter-century, although the causes of the growth of nonstandard work arrangements differ by type of nonstandard work arrangement (e.g., part-time vs. temporary work) as well as by country.

First, the growth in nonstandard work arrangements was due in part to the need for greater labour market flexibility as a result of the economic crises of the post-1975 period. Sluggish economic growth triggered high unemployment that made it clear, especially in Europe, that economies were incapable of generating enough jobs to provide full-time wage employment for all workers.[15] These nations sought greater flexibility to cope with unemployment and labour market rigidities that impeded efficiency in periods of reduced economic growth and lowered productivity rates. Global economic changes increased competition and uncertainty among firms and put pressure on them to push for greater profits and be more flexible in contracting with their employees and responding to consumers. These pressures encouraged them to seek greater flexibility to redeploy labour among tasks or to adjust the size of their workforces through the use of part-time (e.g., the Netherlands) or fixed-term (e.g., Spain) work arrangements.

This type of response to the economic crises of the mid-1970s may be termed dualism,[16] a strategy adopted in countries such as Britain, West

Germany, and France. This contrasts with the other major response, which was corporatism, a strategy adopted in countries such as Austria, Sweden, and Norway. Here, the high degree of union power led to institutional arrangements designed to be 'inclusionary' and to involve the interests of major economic groups (especially unions) in the development and carrying out of economic policy. The key actors here are unions and their members, who represent the interests of the working class as a whole.

The growth of nonstandard work arrangements in countries such as Britain, West Germany, and France represented an attempt to exclude groups of people from the protections afforded by the standard employment relationship and to expose them to market forces. This was accomplished by encouraging immigration, as migrant workers were employed to serve as a form of 'industrial reserve army', at least until reliance on immigrants entailed social costs that may outweigh the economic costs; and enlarging the portion of the indigenous population who is subjected to market forces and excluded from the protections of the standard employment relation. Employers and their managements are the key actors in this decentralized response to economic crisis.

A second reason for the adoption of nonstandard work arrangements was the shift – in all industrial societies – from a manufacturing to a service economy. The expansion of part-time work, in particular, accompanied the process of de-industrialization and the expansion of the service economy, which began in most OECD countries during the period 1965–70. In the Scandinavian, and especially the Swedish, case, the expansion of the welfare state, from the late 1960s and on, was accompanied by the growth in female part-time employment.

Third, the growth of nonstandard work arrangements was related to demographic changes in the composition of the labour force, such as the increase in married women workers and older workers, who often preferred the flexibility available through nonstandard work arrangements[17] in order to balance work with family and other non-work activities. The increase in part-time and short-term temporary work arrangements also served to draw into the labour force those workers (such as young and older persons) who might not have otherwise sought standard employment.

The adoption of nonstandard work was facilitated by technological improvements in communication and information systems that made it easier for organizations to specialize their production, assemble temporary workers quickly for projects, and rely more on outside suppliers. Labour laws designed to protect permanent employees also fuelled the growth in nonstandard work by encouraging employers to avoid the mandates and costs associated with these laws.[18]

Cross-national Patterns in Nonstandard Employment Relations

There has been a general tendency for all industrial countries to expand their use of one or more types of nonstandard work arrangements and to shift away from the standard employment relationship as the *normative* model of employment that is the basis for labour law and other employment protections.[19] Within this general tendency, however, countries differ in the extent to which they use the various types of nonstandard work arrangements. This suggests that employers' strategies depend on institutional contexts such as worker control, institutional conditions related to skills and trust, and legal and regulatory systems that affect the relative costs of using standard employment relations, as well as different forms of flexibility such as part-time or temporary work. The extent to which a country uses nonstandard work arrangements and who and how many persons are excluded from the standard employment relationship depends on the institutional features of the society as well as its unique cultural and social characteristics.

Table 5.2 presents information on country differences in the use of part-time work, temporary (short-term) contracts, and self-employment. It should be noted that these comparisons are often hampered by imprecise measures and sometimes inconsistent definitions of nonstandard work arrangements across countries.

Part-time Work

The definition of what constitutes part-time work varies among countries. In the USA, part-time work is generally defined as less than 35 hours a week,

Table 5.2 **Percentage of Part-Time, Fixed-Term Temporary, and Self-Employed Persons, by Country**

Country	Percent part-time[a] 1973	1998	Percent fixed-term temporary[b] 1983	1998	Percent self-employed[c] 1973	1993
USA	15.6	18	–	3.2	6.7	7.7
Australia	11.9	25.9	15.6	26.4	9.5	12.9
Canada	9.7	18.7	7.5	8.3	6.2	8.6
Japan	13.9	23.6	10.3	10.8	14	10.3
Austria	6.4	11.5	–	7.8	11.7	6.3
Belgium	3.8	16.3	5.4	7.8	11.2	13.3
Denmark	22.7	17	12.5	10.1	9.3	7
Finland	6.7	9.7	11.3	17.7	6.5	9.5
France	5.9	14.8	3.3	13.9	11.4	8.8
Germany	10.1	16.6	10	12.3	9.1	7.9
Greece	–	–	16.2	13	–	–
Ireland	5.1	15.2	6.1	7.7	10.1	13
Italy	6.4	11.8	6.6	8.5	23.1	24.2
Luxembourg	–	–	3.2	2.9	–	–
Netherlands	16.6	30	5.8	12.7	9.2	8.7
Norway	23	21	–	–	7.8	6.2
Portugal	7.8	7.7	14.4	17.4	12.7	18.2
Spain	–	13.5	15.7	32.9	16.3	18.7
Sweden	23.6	24.2	12	12.9	4.8	8.7
United Kingdom	16	23	5.5	7.1	7.3	11.9

[a] Percentage of total employment: 1973 (ILO and OECD) estimates from Standing (1997), table 3; 1998 estimates from *OECD Employment Outlook 1999*, table E; US estimates from Bureau of Labor Statistics.

[b] Percentage of total employment: 1983 (ILO and OECD) estimates from Standing (1997), table 3; and Campbell and Burgess (2001), table 1; 1998 estimates from Campbell and Burgess (2001), table 1.

[c] Percentage of non-agricultural employees: 1973 and 1993 estimates from Standing (1997), table 3.

while Canada and the United Kingdom normally use 30 hours as the cut-off for part-time.[20] In France, part-time is defined as at least 20 per cent below the statutory level of working hours (which became 35 hours on 1 January 2000), while in Germany it is less than 36 hours of work per week.[21] By contrast, part-time employment in Japan is explicitly related to status within the firm and not to hours worked; indeed, recent Japanese surveys indicate that 20–30 per cent of those classified by their employers as 'part-time' actually work as many hours as 'full-time' workers.[22] Other examples of less-than-full-time employment are various forms of short-time work such as zero-hours contracts in Britain or relay contracts in France, Italy, and Spain, where workers are hired to work a few hours a day to perform work previously done by older workers nearing retirement.[23]

Nearly one in five workers in the USA currently works part-time, making it by far the most widely used form of nonstandard work in that country. Part-time work in Europe is slightly lower than in the USA, with an average of about 16 per cent of the European Union's total labour force working part-time in 1996.[24] There is, however, wide variation among countries (see Table 5.2). In the Netherlands, about a third of the labour force – and over half of women – work part-time, leading a prominent economist[25] to characterize it as the 'only part-time economy of the world, with a finger in the dike of unemployment'. The Netherlands illustrates a case where part-time employment was used to combat (successfully) high levels of unemployment.

Part-time employment is also relatively high in Scandinavia (with the exception of Finland), with about 20 per cent of the labour force working part-time. By contrast, part-time work constitutes relatively small proportions of the labour force in Portugal[26] and Finland. Unlike in the USA, part-time employment is increasing relatively rapidly in a number of countries in Europe, where it has often been used as a way to alleviate unemployment and is the major source of employment growth since the 1980s.[27] Again, there is wide variation among countries: part-time employment has increased particularly rapidly in the Netherlands, Belgium, France, and Ireland.

In all industrial countries, most part-time workers are women.[28] This reflects in part women's greater responsibilities for housework and raising children. Women's share of part-time employment in the USA (about 65 per cent) is much lower than in Germany and France (about 90 per cent) and in the UK and Japan (about 80 per cent). The lower proportion of women part-timers in the USA may reflect the greater incidence of part-time work among students, both male and female.

The growth in part-time work in the USA since 1979 appears to have been due to the expansion of industries that typically employ many part-timers (services, retail trade, finance, insurance, real estate) rather than to the substitution of part-time for full-time workers within industries, which occurred mainly in the 1970s.[29] Similarly, the growth of part-time employment has accompanied the expansion of the service sector in other industrial countries.[30]

Short-term Employment

The number of people on fixed-term temporary contracts has increased in the European Union by some 25 per cent in the past decade, though this still represents only about 12 per cent of employees and there is significant country variation in this (see Table 5.2).[31] Temporary work in Europe has generally grown less than part-time work and plays a lesser role in the overall labour market. Unlike part-time work, temporary employment does not seem to mitigate unemployment, being rather an indicator of weak worker labour market position (especially among youth) in periods of high unemployment.[32]

Fixed-term contracts have been particularly important in countries where employers have difficulty terminating contracts of indefinite duration, suggesting that labour market rigidities can lead to the greater use of temporary workers. For example, the proportion of fixed-term contracts more than doubled between 1983 and 1998 in Spain and France (which had 33 and 14 per cent fixed-term contracts in 1998, respectively), two countries that have strong restrictions on dismissals of regular workers;[33] these highly protective labour laws may have made employers more adept at getting around them by using short-term hires. While the easing of restrictions on the use of fixed-term contracts has encouraged their utilization in some cases, this varies among countries. For example, in the mid-1980s Spain and Germany significantly eased restrictions on the use of fixed-term contracts, but with very different impacts. In Spain, the use of fixed-term contracts increased sharply, going from about 16 per cent to a third of dependent employment; in Germany, by contrast, fixed-term employment grew slowly and still accounts for only about 12 per cent of employment (if apprentices are included).

Holmlund and Storrie[34] maintain that there has been a 'remarkable' increase in fixed-term employment in Sweden in the 1990s, from 10 per cent in early 1990s to 16 per cent at the end of the century. This increase in fixed-term employment was accompanied by a large increase in unemployment.

They argue that the growth in fixed-term employment in Sweden reflects mainly the greater incentives that employers have to offer temporary rather than permanent contracts during recessions, and the generally greater willingness of workers to accept temporary jobs when the labour market is depressed. They show that labour demand was a more valid explanation of the rise in temporary employment in Sweden during the 1990s than were accounts based on changes in regulation or the preferences of workers.

On the other hand, some countries (such as Greece and Luxembourg) experienced a decrease in fixed-term employment during the 1983–98 period (see Table 5.2). There is a lack of good data on the incidence and trends in short-term employment in the USA. A rough estimate is that 3.3 million workers (a little more than 3 per cent of the employed) were direct-hire temporaries in 1995.[35]

The interpretation of the relatively high proportion of temporary jobs in Australia has been the subject of some debate.[36] Campbell and Burgess' indicator of temporary work is the proportion of the labour force in 'casual' employment, which they equate with 'non-permanent' waged work. Fixed-term temporary employment as measured in Europe is not the same as casual employment in Australia, although both concepts refer to workers who are not entitled to the usual array of job-related benefits, such as paid leave. Casual workers are not necessarily employed on a fixed-term basis: Wooden estimates that only about 4.9 per cent of Australian workers have fixed-term contracts, considerably less than the 26 per cent who are estimated to have casual employment. This disagreement illustrates the difficulties in comparing categories of nonstandard workers across countries.

Temporary Help Agencies

Employment in the temporary help services industry in the USA has experienced explosive growth since the early 1970s, increasing at an annual rate of over 11 per cent, and its share of total US employment rose from under 0.3 per cent in 1972 to nearly 2.5 per cent in 1998. By contrast, total non-farm employment grew at an annual rate of 2 per cent during this period.[37] Changes in temporary work exhibit much greater variance than other forms of employment and are very sensitive to the business cycle, rising and falling with the state of the economy.[38]

Temporary help agencies are also growing rapidly in Europe,[39] although there is considerable variation among countries. Some nations feel that temporary help agencies are useful as employment intermediaries, while others object to them for reasons such as the principle that job placement should be done by public, not profit-making, agencies. In the mid-1980s, temporary help agencies were authorized (subject to some restrictions) in Argentina, Belgium, Brazil, Denmark, France, Germany, Ireland, Japan, the Netherlands, Norway, Portugal, and Switzerland, among other countries. They were banned in Algeria, Costa Rica, Gabon, Greece, Italy, the Libyan Arab Jamahiriya, Madagascar, Mauritania, Senegal, Spain, Sweden, and Zaire.[40] In general, though, the restrictions on the use of temporary help agencies have tended to be eased in most countries.[41] The growth of temporary help agency employment in both the USA and Europe has been generally driven by employers' needs,[42] as well as the entrepreneurial efforts of temporary help agencies themselves.[43] Moreover, it is likely that temporary staffing agencies will increasingly replace the direct hire of temporaries (especially for low-skilled work[44]).

Contracting Out

Contract companies, in contrast to temporary help agencies, supervise their employees' work, although this distinction may not always be clear-cut. Until the mid-1980s or so, subcontractors were independent businesses that provided a product or service; since then, subcontractors increasingly provide employees as well.[45] While contract work has always existed in some industries, such as construction, there has been an increase in the purchase of services (especially business services and engineering and management services) by US firms since the 1970s.[46] As firms began to contract out services that were previously done in house, they gained a greater appreciation of the variety of services (such as advertising, consumer credit reporting and collection, mailing and stenography, maintenance and cleaning, personnel supply, computer and data processing, protection, research and development) that could be contracted and realized that business service organizations could often supply these services more cheaply and efficiently.[47]

The trend towards greater subcontracting also characterizes all major west European countries.[48] France and Italy are two countries in which there are strong traditions of small-scale enterprise, and in which there are lots of opportunities for subcontracting.[49] In the United Kingdom, outsourcing grew substantially in the 1990s after agencies in the public sector were required in the 1980s to go through a process of competitive tendering for catering, laundering and domestic services.[50] Benson and Ieronimo[51] compared the outsourcing of maintenance work between Australian-owned firms and Japanese manufacturing firms operating in Australia. They found that the Australian-owned firms sought to improve their flexibility via externalization (subcontracting), while Japanese firms sought to enhance flexibility via internalization strategies. Industrial relations issues such as labour rigidity, restrictive work practices, and demarcation disputes were central to these firms' outsourcing decisions.

Independent Contractors

Independent contractors are self-employed in that they have neither an employer nor a wage contract and are responsible for their own tax arrangements. However, not all self-employed persons consider themselves to be independent contractors, and this makes it difficult to draw empirical conclusions as to trends in this form of nonstandard work. For example, small shopkeepers who work at a fixed location are not likely to call themselves independent contractors. Nevertheless, information on self-employment is the best indicator of the presence of independent contractors. These data suggest that there has been relatively little change in the proportion of the US labour force that is self-employed since 1973.[52] Self-employment growth also correlates only modestly with aggregate employment growth.[53]

The trends in self-employment in Europe are diverse. There has been a decline in self-employment in some countries (for example, Austria, Denmark, France, Germany and Norway). In other countries (such as Finland,

Ireland, Portugal, Sweden, and the United Kingdom), there has been an increase in self-employment.

Consequences of Nonstandard Work Arrangements for Labour Market Outcomes

The use of nonstandard work arrangements in industrial societies has important implications for labour market phenomena such as the degree of employment security, the quality of jobs, and opportunities for training and mobility. In this section, I provide an overview of some of the implications of the growth of nonstandard work arrangements for labour market patterns of inequality and exclusion.

Increase in Job Insecurity?

The shift away from the standard employment relation has led to a general increase in job insecurity with the employer. Almost all workers – those in standard as well as nonstandard employment relations – face greater job insecurity than in the past, due to increases in the practice of downsizing, layoffs, and other expressions of employers' willingness to treat labour as a variable cost of production. This increase in insecurity characterizes all industrial societies, and there is a convergence among nations in a shift away from a 'full employment' society characterized by standard employment toward a 'risk society' in which workers are increasingly called upon to bear the risks of their own employment.[54]

The media as well as some social scientists often exaggerate the view that the standard employment relationship has given way to nonstandard work. For example, objective measures of job stability such as job tenure show little overall change over time. An analysis of European countries (as well as Japan and the USA)[55] found little if any decline in job stability (as measured by average job tenure) in the last two decades: there was little change for men and an improvement for women in average job tenure, resulting in a general stability or slight increase of average tenure in almost all countries examined (except for Ireland). At the same time, Auer and Cazes found that there was an increase in perceived job insecurity on the part of workers, along with the clear increase in perception of this by the media and many observers, accompanying the small (if any) decline of job stability. They suggest that this paradox of objective stability and perceived insecurity might reflect the continuation of labour market segmentation: that is, the standard employment relationship still constitutes the core of the employment relationship, although the periphery has grown, creating the perception of greater insecurity for all.

The consequences of this greater insecurity for workers may differ from one country to another, depending on factors such as the welfare regimes available to provide workers with 'safety nets' to reduce the impacts of unemployment, underemployment, and unstable employment.

Growth of Bad Jobs?

The growth of nonstandard work arrangements has increased the number of people who are excluded from social protections and, in some countries, who earn relatively low wages from their jobs. Unfortunately, studies of the consequences of employment in standard as opposed to nonstandard work arrangements are relatively scarce.

In the USA, every nonstandard work arrangement is more likely to be associated with lower fringe benefits than standard work arrangements, and sometimes with lower wages. In particular, male and female temporary help agency employees, on-call workers and day labourers, and part-time workers, are consistently more likely than workers in the other nonstandard arrangements to have low pay and to lack insurance and pension benefits (an exception is some women who are self-employed, who are the most likely group of women to have jobs with low wages). Moreover, most workers in these arrangements (especially temporary help agency employees, on-call workers, and day labourers) prefer standard, full-time employment.[56] In view of these findings, the explosive growth of the temporary help industry, in particular, makes the strong negative effect of employment in temporary help agencies on job quality a matter of concern.

Part-time work in particular is generally low-paid and low-status (such as sales, catering, and cleaning) in the USA. This is also true in Europe, although there is also some growth of higher-level part-time jobs in some countries. An analysis by the OECD[57] found that the median hourly earnings of part-time workers were lower than those of full-timers for all countries for which data were available. Differences among countries in labour law and employment regulations such as job security entitlements affect the extent to which part-time work is of significantly lower quality than full-time employment. Thus, countries differ in whether the use of part-timers represents a marginalization strategy that provides employers with a source of cheap labour or an integration strategy used to retain valued workers. In some countries (such as Sweden, France, Belgium, the Netherlands, Spain), labour law enforces equal treatment between full-time and part-time workers,[58] preventing the use of part-time workers as a cheap labour source. By contrast, in the UK, Germany, and Japan, part-time employees' hours or income generally fall below thresholds that exclude them from coverage under certain laws.[59]

Cebrián et al.[60] find that temporary and part-time workers in Spain and Italy do not earn less per hour than those on full-time contracts (and part-timers earn more when controlling for the duration of their contract). The distance between temporary and permanent workers is higher in Italy than Spain. Self-employed persons are in a clearly worse position than permanent employees in both countries.

An important question when assessing the consequences of nonstandard work arrangements is the extent to which fringe benefits are tied to employment status. Fringe benefits such as health insurance and pensions are distributed on the basis of employment in the USA, and part-time workers are much less likely to receive benefits such as health insurance and retirement benefits, in addition to being paid low wages.[61] By contrast, these benefits are given out as rights of citizenship in many other countries. So, while working in nonstandard work arrangements might be a source of insecurity, one has a sense that one's needs for health insurance and retirement are taken care of and any disadvantage of part-time work is much less salient.

The growth in nonstandard work arrangements, particularly part-time and short-term temporary jobs, has increased the number of people who are excluded from social protections and subject to low-wage employment. The latter trend coincides with the movement in countries such as the USA, UK, and others towards workfare policies that tie receipt of welfare benefits to employment. In most cases, this means employment in low-wage, 'contingent', nonstandard jobs, since workfare recipients are often low-skilled workers without a history of stable employment. While their underlying causes may be different, then, the expansion of contingent work is thus consistent with, and mutually reinforcing of, the growth of workfare.[62]

Whether a job is considered 'bad' depends to some extent on the expectations of workers. Thus, new immigrants to a country may be very willing to take jobs that citizens of that country do not want, and to be happy with these jobs. Similarly, workers who have jobs in the informal economy may be relatively satisfied with them: these jobs may be the best forms of work available to these workers, despite the lack of rewards and legal protections.

Polarization of Job Quality and Increased Inequality?

Nonstandard jobs are not all bad: there are also high-quality, high-skilled nonstandard jobs. In the USA, some nonstandard workers – particularly self-employed men and contract-company employees – earn higher wages than regular full-time workers in standard jobs (although the contract company workers are less likely to receive health insurance and retirement benefits). Moreover, relatively few workers in these particular nonstandard arrangements express a preference for standard jobs.[63] Over time, the tasks for which temporary workers are used have changed, and there has been an increase in their use in high-skilled as well as low-skilled jobs.[64] For example, the wages of temporary help agency employees differ considerably: temporary help agency nurses earn wages that are typically higher than those of nurses who are regular employees of a hospital, while auto supply workers who are employees of temporary agencies typically earn less than regular employees.[65]

There are also occupational differences in wages as well as fringe benefits within type of work arrangement. In the USA, Kalleberg, Reskin, and Hudson[66] found that women operatives, sales workers, and service workers – nearly one-third of all women – experience significantly more bad job characteristics than female managers do. Men and women in more complex (and thus more highly skilled and autonomous) occupations are less likely to obtain low wages, and more likely to obtain health insurance and pension benefits from their jobs. Moreover, within part-time workers, men and women in low-skilled occupations (and low-end service and sales occupations in particular) earn less, and receive fewer health and fringe benefits, than members of other occupations, which supports the idea of a duality within part-time employment.[67]

Careers and Mobility

An important indicator of whether nonstandard jobs are 'good' or 'bad' is the extent to which they are 'dead-end traps' or 'bridges' to more permanent jobs. Moreover, as discussed above, nonstandard work arrangements might be viewed as less problematic than otherwise if they are populated mainly by the young, women, and immigrants, who are likely to have relatively low levels of work commitment and/or low expectations with regard to work.

Mobility opportunities from nonstandard to standard employment are likely to vary both by type of nonstandard work arrangement as well as by country. Countries differ in the extent to which they have inter-firm institutions that are created by unions or occupational associations that enable skill development/training and processes of inclusion between firms; hence, workers who have been excluded from their firms may be included via processes of social closure in inter-firm institutions. An example of these inter-firm institutions is the industrial apprenticeship system found in Germany, which requires high-trust relations such as those maintained through occupational communities.[68] These occupational institutions provide workers with portable skills that make them employable in a variety of organizations.

The presence of such inter-firm institutions may help explain the results of an OECD study, which showed that fixed-term jobs in Germany are concentrated among first-time job seekers, while in Spain they are spread across a much broader range of workers and firms. A higher proportion of fixed-term workers in Germany obtain permanent positions compared to Spain, where only about 10 per cent do so. These differences may be due to several things:

the tradition of social partnership in Germany (but not in Spain) may encourage employers to regard standard employment relations as a positive asset and see fixed-term contracts as a way of screening workers for permanent positions, while in Spain employers see fixed-term employment as a way of obtaining numerical flexibility. Also, the greater availability of apprenticeship contracts in Germany may lead employers to see them as preferable alternatives to fixed-term contracts. It may also be the case that the potential firing costs of permanent employees remain higher in Spain, though it is unclear if this is as true today as in the late 1980s.[69]

This also suggests that employers in different countries may use temporaries for different reasons, as Casey et al.[70] showed in their study of temporary workers in Britain and the (then) Federal Republic of Germany. British employers were more likely to use temporaries to obtain numerical flexibility, in order to increase or decrease their workforce size. German employers sought instead to obtain functional flexibility (the ability of employees to do a variety of tasks) by giving temporaries permanent contracts once they acquired the needed skills.

In Italy, fixed-term, temporary workers tend to be concentrated in relatively less-skilled occupations, and people who hold them are relatively young. This suggests that temporary work has been concentrated in segments of the labour force that might prefer transitory employment anyway.[71]

An analysis by the OECD found that the rate of transition out of part-time work into full-time work is much higher for men than women, and more frequent for younger, more highly educated and more highly skilled workers. For France and the Netherlands, part-time workers working very short hours are less likely to move into full-time jobs than other part-timers.[72]

Moreover, the OECD study showed that part-timers received less job-related training than full-timers. Nonstandard workers are generally less likely to receive job-related training than standard workers, as showed by Hoque and Kirkpatrick's[73] analysis of data from the United Kingdom. They found that managers and professionals on nonstandard (part-time and/or short-term) contracts had less access to training opportunities and were less often consulted about workplace practices than full-time permanent managers and professionals. This suggests that nonstandard employees are treated differently regardless of their occupational level, and that there is not a dualism with regard to training between high and low occupations on nonstandard contracts.

Triangular Employment Relations

Nonstandard work arrangements such as temporary help agencies, leasing companies, and contract companies alter the power dynamics between employers and employees. The separation of the legal (*de jure*) employer from the actual (*de facto*) employer creates a triangular employment relationship or network among organizations. These networks develop differently from one country to another, depending on its economic factors, customs, norms, and regulations. In the USA, the temporary help and contract company industry developed in response to market forces. In other countries (such as many countries in Europe), these triangular relations have been influenced considerably by institutional factors such as union organization and regulations governing these market-mediating institutions.[74]

LABOUR LAW AND EMPLOYMENT REGULATIONS/PROTECTIONS

Triangular employment relations raise complex legal issues as to which employer is responsible for complying with governmental regulations (such as unemployment insurance or social security payments) and especially who is liable for accidents and other aspects of the employment relationship. A classic example of liability is the case in the USA of accidents in the petrochemical industry.[75] Client organizations in this industry used contract and temporary help agency employees to do much of the 'dirty' work, yet client companies sought to maintain a distance from the contract workers to avoid being considered their employers and thereby assuming some liability for their actions. Since often neither the client nor the contract company provided training for these workers, these untrained workers had higher accident rates than non-contract workers.

The difficulty of identifying the 'true' employer in order to enforce compliance with legal obligations occurs in all industrial countries, and labour laws around the world need to be modified to take into account the movement away from the standard employment relationship.[76] In particular, there is considerable debate and controversy concerning the principles that should be used to regulate temporary help agencies and fixed-term contracts.[77]

The rise of nonstandard work arrangements (both those who are hired directly as part-time and short-term temporaries, and those hired through employment intermediaries such as temporary help agencies and contract companies) has also led to a concern with regulations to protect nonstandard workers. This is needed since most social protections were designed on the basis of the standard employment relationship. Changing ILO standards and conventions regulating nonstandard employment do not provide protections for contract and temporary workers that are comparable to those they enjoyed under the standard employment relationship, raising the question of whether the triangular employment relationship necessarily implies greater insecurity for workers.[78]

UNIONS AND COLLECTIVE BARGAINING

The growth of triangular employment relations has often had a negative impact on the power of unions. In the USA, triangular employment relations have contributed to a decline in union membership by limiting workers' ability to reduce the power imbalance with either employer through collective bargaining.[79] For example, temporary workers do not have the sustained contact with their *de jure* co-workers necessary to organize collectively to demand better benefits from the temporary agencies that nominally employ them. Moreover, their transient status and the fact that their *de facto* co-workers do not share their marginal status prevent collective action with their *de facto* co-workers.

These problems affecting unionization and collective labour relations are not restricted to the USA. For example, in Portugal and the Netherlands, membership in workers' committees and works councils are restricted to permanent employees; and in Norway and Sweden, part-time employees who work less than a certain number of hours per week are not allowed to vote in elections for workers' representatives to the firm's governing boards.[80]

Conclusions

The growth in nonstandard work arrangements constitutes an important shift in employment relations that has pervasive consequences for societies, organizations, and workers. While there appears to be a convergence among industrial nations in the use of nonstandard work arrangements, the consequences of these arrangements for labour market outcomes depend on the institutional context within each country. In this Chapter, I have sought to provide an overview of the kinds of nonstandard work arrangements that are increasingly being used in industrial societies, and to indicate some of their implications for patterns of labour market inequality and exclusion.

The use of nonstandard employment relations is consistent with a 'new *laissez-faire*' policy of shifting the responsibility for economic outcomes to the market and giving employers wide freedom of action to seek flexibility. This appears to be the case even in 'corporatist' countries such as Sweden as they face troubled economic conditions. The growing availability of nonstandard work arrangements and the greater institutionalization of mechanisms of providing them (such as through temporary help agencies and contract companies) have created more opportunities for societies and employers to use these arrangements.

The expansion of nonstandard work arrangements has had many benefits. It has helped some nations to combat unemployment and has enabled many employers and employees to obtain greater flexibility in their relations with each other. At the same time, there has been a 'dark side' to many of these nonstandard work arrangements in some countries, as these employment relations have helped to generate greater labour market inequality and led to the greater exclusion of some workers from social protections.

The different kinds of nonstandard work arrangements point to different kinds of problems and solutions. For example, part-time work is very different from short-term temporary work, which is different from temporary help agency work, which is different from contract work. Moreover, the distributional consequences of the growth of nonstandard work arrangements and their impacts on class structuration depend on various things. For temporary jobs, for example, it depends on whether people are trapped in them, or can move out of them when they want more permanent jobs. Answering these questions and testing hypotheses about the nature of careers associated with nonstandard employment relations requires longitudinal ('flow') data (as opposed to 'stock' data), which unfortunately, are scarce.

There is much we do not know about the consequences of nonstandard work arrangements, and there is as yet relatively little cross-national research on the consequences for organizations and workers of their use. This is unfortunate, since the study of how institutional and macro-level factors influence the consequences of changes in employment relations is a great opportunity for comparative research. These gaps in our information about these processes and outcomes represent important components on the agenda for future research on social stratification and labour markets.

Notes

1 Clark Kerr, John T. Dunlop, Frederick H. Harbison and Charles A. Meyers, *Industrialism and Industrial Man*, Cambridge, MA: Harvard University Press, 1960.
2 John H. Goldthorpe, 'The end of convergence: corporatist and dualist tendencies in modern Western societies', in John H. Goldthorpe, ed., *Order and Conflict in Contemporary Capitalism*, Oxford: Oxford University Press, 1984, pp. 315–43 (quote from p. 332).
3 Efrén Córdova, 'From full-time wage employment to atypical employment: a major shift in the evolution of labour relations?', *International Labour Review*, Vol. 125, No. 6, 1986, pp. 641–57.
4 Clyde W. Summers, 'Contingent employment in the United States', *Comparative Labour Law Journal*, Vol. 18, No. 4, 1997, pp. 503–22.
5 Alain Supiot, *Beyond Employment: Changes in Work and the Future of Labour Law in Europe*, Oxford: Oxford University Press, 2001.
6 Jeffrey Pfeffer and James N. Baron, 'Taking the workers back out: recent trends in the structuring of employment', *Research in Organizational Behavior*, Vol. 10, 1988, pp. 257–303.
7 Summers, 'Contingent employment in the United States'.
8 Córdova, 'From full-time wage employment to atypical employment'; A. S. Bronstein, 'Temporary work in Western Europe: threat or complement to permanent employment?', *International Labour Review*, Vol. 130, No. 3, 1991, pp. 291–310.
9 George Gonos, 'The contest over "employer" status in the postwar United States: the case of temporary help firms', *Law and Society Review*, Vol. 31, No. 1, 1997, pp. 81–110.
10 J. E. Thurman and G. Trah, 'Part-time work in international perspective', *International Labour Review*, Vol. 129, No. 1, 1990, pp. 23–40.
11 Córdova, 'From full-time wage employment to atypical employment'.
12 Oliver E. Williamson, 'The organization of work: a comparative institutional assessment', *Journal of Economic Behavior and Organization*, Vol. 1, No. 1, 1980, pp. 5–38.

13 For examples from the USA, see Summers, 'Contingent employment in the United States'.

14 John Buttrick, 'The inside contracting system', *Journal of Economic History*, Vol. 12, No. 3, 1952, pp. 205–21.

15 Córdova, 'From full-time wage employment to atypical employment'.

16 Goldthorpe, 'The end of convergence'.

17 Pfeffer and Baron, 'Taking the workers back out'.

18 Peter Cappelli, Laurie Bassi, Harry Katz, David Knoke, Paul Osterman and Michael Useem, *Change at Work*, New York: Oxford University Press, 1997.

19 Leah F. Vosko, 'Legitimizing the triangular employment relationship: emerging international labour standards from a comparative perspective', *Comparative Labor Law Journal*, Vol. 19, No. 1, 1997, pp. 43–84.

20 Hilda Kahne, 'Part-time work: a hope and a peril', in B. D. Warme, K. P. Lundy and L. A. Lundy, eds, *Working Part-time: Risks and Opportunities*, New York Praeger, 1992, pp. 295–309.

21 Susan N. Houseman, 'Part-time employment in Europe and Japan', *Journal of Labor Research*, Vol. 16, No. 3, 1995, pp. 249–62.

22 Susan N. Houseman and Machiko Osawa, 'What is the nature of part-time work in the United States and Japan?', in J. O'Reilly and Colette Fagan, eds, *Part-Time Prospects: An International Comparison of Part-Time Work in Europe, North America and the Pacific Rim*, New York: Routledge, 1998, pp. 232–51.

23 Córdova, 'From full-time wage employment to atypical employment'.

24 Colette Fagan, 'Non-standard work arrangements: the UK in European perspective', unpublished paper, Department of Sociology, University of Manchester, 1999.

25 Richard Freeman, 'War of the models: which labour market institutions for the 21st century?', *Labour Economics*, Vol. 5, No. 1, 1998, pp. 1–24.

26 Andries de Grip, Jeroen Hoevenberg and Ed Willems, 'Atypical employment in the European Union', *International Labour Review*, Vol. 136, No. 1, 1997, pp. 49–71; Olga Tregaskis, Chris Brewster, Lesley Mayne and Ariane Hegewisch, 'Flexible working in Europe: the evidence and the implications', *European Journal of Work and Organizational Psychology*, Vol. 7, No. 1, 1998, pp. 61–78.

27 Chris Brewster, Lesley Mayne and Olga Tregaskis, 'Flexible staffing in Europe', *Journal of World Business*, Vol. 32, No. 2, 1997, pp. 133–51.

28 Hans-Peter Blossfeld and Catherine Hakim, eds, *Between Equalization and Marginalization: Women Working Part-Time in Europe and the United States of America*, New York: Oxford University Press, 1997; Colette Fagan and J. O'Reilly, 'Conceptualizing part-time work: the value of an integrated comparative perspective', in J. O'Reilly and Colette Fagan, eds, *Part-Time Prospects: An International Comparison of Part-Time Work in Europe, North America and the Pacific Rim*, New York: Routledge 1998, pp. 1–31.

29 Thomas Nardone, 'Part-time employment: reasons, demographics, and trends', *Journal of Labor Research*, Vol. 16, No. 3, 1995, pp. 275–92.

30 Houseman, 'Part-time employment in Europe and Japan'.

31 De Grip et al., 'Atypical employment in the European Union'; Klaus Schömann, R. Rogowski and T. Kruppe, *Labour Market Efficiency in the European Union: Employment Protection and Fixed-Term Contracts*, New York: Routledge, 1998.

32 DeGrip et al., 'Atypical employment in the European Union'.

33 Fagan, 'Non-standard work arrangements'.

34 Bertil Holmlund and Donald Storrie, 'Temporary work in turbulent times: the Swedish experience', Munich: Center for Economic Studies and Institute for Economic Research Working Paper No. 671(4), www.CESifo.de, 2002.

35 Anne E. Polivka, 'Are temporary help agency workers substitutes for direct hire temps? Searching for an alternative explanation of growth in the temporary help industry', paper presented at the Society of Labor Economist Conference, 3–4 May, Chicago, 1996.

36 See, for example, the exchange between Iain Campbell and John Burgess, 'Casual employment in Australia and temporary employment in Europe: developing a cross-national comparison', *Work, Employment and Society*, Vol. 15, No. 1, 2001, pp. 171–84 and Mark Wooden, 'How temporary are Australia's casual jobs?', *Work, Employment and Society*, Vol. 15, No. 4, 2001, pp. 875–83.

37 Lewis M. Segal and Daniel G. Sullivan, 'The growth of temporary services work', *Journal of Economic Perspectives*, Vol. 11, No. 2, 1997, pp. 117–36.

38 Lonnie Golden and Eileen Appelbaum, 'What was driving the 1982–88 boom in temporary employment? Preference of workers or decisions and power of employers', *American Journal of Economics and Sociology*, Vol. 51, No. 4, 1992, pp. 473–93; Lewis M. Segal, 'Flexible employment: composition and trends', *Journal of Labor Research*, Vol. 17, No. 4, 1996, pp. 525–42.

39 Bronstein, 'Temporary work in Western Europe'.

40 Córdova, 'From full-time wage employment to atypical employment': 657, note 16.

41 *OECD Employment Outlook*, Paris: Organisation for Economic Co-operation and Development, June 1999.

42 De Grip et al., 'Atypical employment in the European Union'.

43 C. M. Ofstead, 'Temporary help firms as entrepreneurial actors', *Sociological Forum*, Vol. 14, No. 2, 1999, pp. 273–94.

44 See Alan Burton-Jones, *Knowledge Capitalism: Business, Work, and Learning in the New Economy*, Oxford: Oxford University Press, 1999.

45 Jonathan G. Axelrod, 'Who's the boss? Employer leasing and the joint employer relationship', *Labor Lawyer*, Vol. 3, No. 4, 1988, pp. 853–72.

46 Angela Clinton, 'Flexible labor: restructuring the American work force', *Monthly Labor Review*, Vol. 120, No. 8, 1997, pp. 3–17.

47 Katharine G. Abraham and Susan K. Taylor, 'Firms' use of outside contractors: theory and evidence', *Journal of Labor Economics*, Vol. 14, No. 3, 1996, pp. 394–424.

48 Brewster et al., 'Flexible staffing in Europe'; Tregaskis et al., 'Flexible working in Europe'.

49 Goldthorpe, 'The end of convergence'.

50 Gareth Rees and Sarah Fielder, 'The services economy, subcontracting and the new employment relations: contract catering and cleaning', *Work, Employment and Society*, Vol. 6, No. 3, 1992, pp. 347–68.

51 John Benson and Nick Ieronimo, 'Outsourcing decisions: evidence from Australian enterprises', *International Labour Review*, Vol. 135, No. 1, 1996, pp. 59–73.

52 John E. Bregger, 'Measuring self-employment in the United States', *Monthly Labor Review*, Vol. 119, Nos. 1 and 2, 1996, pp. 3–9.

53 Segal, 'Flexible employment'.

54 Ulrich Beck, *The Brave New World of Work* (translated from German by Patrick Camiller), Oxford: Polity Press, 2000.

55 Peter Auer and Sandrine Cazes, 'Stable or unstable jobs: untangling and interpreting the evidence in industrialized countries', paper presented at Conference on Nonstandard Work Arrangements in Japan, Europe, and the United States, W. E. Upjohn Institute for Employment Research, Kalamazoo, MI, 25–26 August.

56 Arne L. Kalleberg, Edith Rasell, Naomi Cassirer, Barbara F. Reskin, Ken Hudson, David Webster and Eileen Appelbaum, *Nonstandard Work, Substandard Jobs: Flexible Work Arrangements in the U.S.*, Washington, DC: Economic Policy Institute and Women's Research and Education Institute, 1997.

57 OECE, 'Employment outlook 1999'.

58 Thurman and Trah, 'Part-time work in international perspective'.

59 Houseman, 'Part-time employment in Europe and Japan'; Fagan and O'Reilly, 'Conceptualizing part-time work.'

60 Immaculada Cebrián, Gloria Moreno, Manuela Samek, Renata Semenza and Luis Toharia, 'Atypical work in Italy and Spain: the quest for flexibility at the margin in two supposedly rigid labour markets', paper presented at Conference on Nonstandard Work Arrangements in Japan, Europe, and the United States, W. E. Upjohn Institute for Employment Research, Kalamazoo, MI, 25–26 August 2000.

61 See Arne L. Kalleberg, Barbara F. Reskin, and Ken Hudson, 'Bad jobs in America: standard and nonstandard employment relations and job quality in the United States', *American Sociological Review*, Vol. 65, No. 2, 2000, pp. 256–78.

62 Jamie Peck, *Workfare States*, London: Guilford Press, 2001.

63 See Kalleberg et al., 'Nonstandard work, substandard jobs'.

64 Bronstein, 'Temporary work in Western Europe.'

65 See Susan N. Houseman, Arne L. Kalleberg, and George Erickcek, 'The role of temporary agency employment in tight labor markets', *Industrial and Labor Relations Review*, Vol. 57, No. 1, 2003, pp. 105–27.

66 Kalleberg, Reskin and Hudson, 'Bad jobs in America'.

67 Chris Tilly, *Half a Job: Bad and Good Part-Time Jobs in a Changing Labor Market*, Philadelphia: Temple University Press, 1996.

68 David Marsden, *A Theory of Employment Systems: Micro-Foundations of Societal Diversity*, Oxford: Oxford University Press, 1999.

69 OECD, 'Employment outlook 1999'.

70 Bernard Casey, Rudiger Dragendorf, Walter Heering and Gunnar John, 'Temporary employment in Great Britain and the Federal Republic of Germany', *International Labour Review*, Vol. 128, No. 4, 1989, pp. 449–66.

71 Cebrián et al., 'Atypical work in Italy and Spain'.

72 OECD, 'Employment outlook 1999'.

73 Kim Hoque and Ian Kirkpatrick, 'Dualism in nonstandard employment? Evidence from the 1998 WERS employee questionnaire', paper presented at 17th EGOS Colloquium, Lyon, France, 5–7 July, 2001.

74 See OECD, 'Employment outlook 1999', for a discussion of country differences in the regulation of market-mediating organizations and other forms of nonstandard work.

75 See, for example, James Rebitzer, 'Job safety and contract workers in the petro-chemical industry', *Industrial Relations*, Vol. 34, No. 1, 1995, pp. 40–57.

76 See, for example, Supiot, *Beyond Employment*.

77 Córdova, 'From full-time wage employment to atypical employment'.

78 Vosko, 'Legitimizing the triangular employment relationship'.
79 H. L. Dennard, 'Governmental impediments to the employment of contingent workers', *Journal of Labor Research*, Vol. 17, 1996, pp. 595–612.
80 Córdova, 'From full-time wage employment to atypical employment'.

6

Knowledge and Inequality

Peter Weingart

Introduction

Knowledge is like light. Weightless and intangible, it can easily travel
the world, enlightening the lives of people everywhere. Yet billions of
people still live in the darkness of poverty – unnecessarily. Knowledge
about how to treat such a simple ailment as diarrhea has existed for
centuries – but millions of children continue to die from it because their
parents do not know how to save them.[1]

This opening sentence of the World Bank's *World Development Report 1998–99:
Knowledge for Development* frames the problem in very simple terms. It seems
easy to diffuse knowledge throughout the world, and yet its uneven distribution has dire consequences for those whom it does not reach. In a similar vein
the UNESCO World Science Declaration stated:

Most of the benefits of science are unevenly distributed, as a result of
structural asymmetries among countries, regions and social groups, and
between the sexes. As scientific knowledge has become a crucial factor in
the production of wealth, so its distribution has become more inequi-
table. What distinguishes the poor (be it people or countries) from the
rich is not only that they have fewer assets, but also that they are largely
excluded from the creation and the benefits of scientific knowledge'.[2]

Lack of knowledge puts people at a grave disadvantage. Who suffers from this lack of knowledge? Why is knowledge unevenly distributed throughout the world? What are the obstacles to the seemingly easy diffusion of knowledge? Does knowledge have the same meaning to different people?

When the World Bank links knowledge and development, two assumptions appear as givens: the knowledge referred to is scientific and technical knowledge, and it is believed to be the crucial factor responsible for development – that is, economic well-being and thus quality of life. More precisely, the World Bank speaks about two kinds of knowledge: knowledge about technology or technical knowledge (know-how) and knowledge about attributes, for example about the quality of goods. With respect to the former, knowledge gaps reflect the unequal distribution across and within countries; with respect to the latter, the incomplete knowledge of attributes is termed information problems. Due to the neo-classical credo of the Bank it holds market formation to be the crucial mechanism in development. This perspective is in line with and enhances the secular trend towards globalization. Globalization provides the backdrop against which knowledge gaps and the uneven distribution of knowledge in the world become apparent. It suggests that there is a standard against which all countries can be measured. It may be said that today, inequality in the distribution of knowledge is equivalent to inequality of development.

Ever since the early 1950s and the creation of UNESCO it was recognized that science and technology may have a role in fighting 'underdevelopment'. Some developing countries (DC), notably South Korea, were highly successful in following that strategy. Others made initial progress in investing in science and setting up national research systems. However, their success could not be sustained. Economic crisis and in some cases political turmoil neutralized the early progress. Thus, despite some success stories in recent years, the grim news comes from other parts of the world: especially with respect to sub-Saharan Africa the gap of knowledge inequality is widening. (Within 15 years median Africa lost 25 per cent of its share of world publications[3].) The rate of investment in R&D sustained by the industrialized countries (ICs), being manifold that of the less developed countries (LDCs), already gives them an accumulative advantage that borders on a virtual monopoly in scientific and technological knowledge. Meanwhile, the importance of knowledge is steadily growing as modern economies are becoming increasingly knowledge-based. The role model and the reference of successful development for the DCs are the industrialized countries that by now have shifted to knowledge-based industries and hold a commanding position in the global economy.[4]

Thus, once again, development (and the issue of inequality) are tied to knowledge. The evidence in support of this position is impressive, indeed. Command of scientific knowledge, and a strong role in the production of this knowledge, correlates highly with the economic strength of a country. The G5 nations – USA, UK, Canada, Japan, and Germany – are the strongest contributors to the stock of scientific knowledge, and are also the strongest economies. Together with some smaller countries such as Switzerland, Sweden, Holland, and Belgium, which are also highly productive relative to their populations, they also have the highest standard of living. At the opposite end of the spectrum are the poorest countries, most of them on the African continent, some in Asia. Their contribution to world scientific knowledge is minuscule or nonexistent, and so is their capacity to participate in scientific communication and, thus, to control technological development. Their economic income is low, and their health systems are appalling.

The issue of knowledge and inequality is exacerbated by two concepts dominating public discourses, at least in the industrialized countries, and has an impact on political institution building as well as on the leading economies: *globalization* and the emergence of the *knowledge society*. The process of globalization means, among other things, the worldwide communication of knowledge, information, standards, and so on, which implies that singular societies with particular cultures are increasingly unable to shield themselves from outside influence. With respect to knowledge standards, benchmarks and rankings emerge that are global in extent and, in principle, provide a common frame of reference. This has profound effects where the knowledge in question is linked to economic productivity and value. In a global order of knowledge in which knowledge is being more and more commodified it is a major issue if local, or culturally specific, knowledge provides a sufficient basis to offset disadvantages in the competition for new knowledge.

In the following, I shall first look at a number of macro-indicators. Of course, macro-indicators do not sufficiently reflect the historical, cultural, and contextual differences between countries that have to be addressed when development policies are implemented. Their function is to give a first impression of the dimensions of inequality of knowledge in the world, of magnitudes, differences in scale, and thus the gravity of the problem. The crucial question, which makes the diffusion and transfer of (scientific) knowledge so difficult, will be approached with the differentiation between capacities of knowledge use and of knowledge production. Thus, I shall discuss the model underlying these indicators and their order. While this may not be a terribly new insight, a look at different models of development, including the more recent focus on and debate over the role of indigenous knowledge, reveals, surprisingly, that the diffusion of scientific and technical knowledge is more the object of ideological controversy than of justifiable development strategies. In conclusion I shall suggest that in order to achieve a more equitable distribution of knowledge there is no alternative to 'capacity building from below'.

Indicators of Inequality of Knowledge

The macro-indicators of the inequality of knowledge presented below carry one fundamental implication, which, as will be discussed, is controversial to some extent. This is that the knowledge in question is Western, universal knowledge, and that the education and science and technology (S&T) system in Western ICs is the yardstick for the assessment of the inequality of knowledge. The global extension of that knowledge system was prepared by the global institutionalization of mass education, first through colonization and the spread of the nation-state, and in an enhanced fashion since the Second World War in the framework of a global model of modernization.[5] By now knowledge of Western origin is the basis of global scientific and technological development and among the crucial resources for any society.

Another implication of the indicators and the way they are compared is that knowledge, in so far as it is considered an important determinant of inequality (particularly material inequality), must be evenly distributed in any society if such inequality is to be avoided. Societies with a high proportion of scientists and engineers are considered to have an economic advantage over societies with a lower proportion of such highly qualified manpower. This ignores the experience of some countries in which a small but highly educated elite may be more successful in absorbing (and possibly creating) knowledge. This 'colonial' situation reflects, for example, the Indonesian case.[6]

If the indicators are to be useful to 'indicate' knowledge inequalities with a perspective on how they could be rectified they should fit *some theoretical model* of how knowledge is produced, diffused and used in a society, and how different societies come to differ with respect to such an *order of knowledge*.[7] The capacity to benefit from scientific and technical knowledge has two basic elements: the *ability to acquire and to apply knowledge* that already exists, and the *ability to produce new knowledge*. This is obvious from experience with technology transfer. It is not enough to transfer knowledge, e.g. knowledge embedded in a particular technology, from one country/society to another. Instead, in order to achieve a sustained development it is necessary for the knowledge-importing country/society to be able to acquire it, to absorb the knowledge, to understand it, to interpret and to adapt it to local needs, and subsequently to produce knowledge endogenously along the same line.[8] The transfer of new knowledge, e.g. from academia to industry, is already a non-trivial problem in the ICs. How much more difficult must it be in societies that have only a weak tradition of higher education, scientific or technical training, to transfer knowledge from a different country! It will therefore be sensible to distinguish between the *scientific-technological potential* of a country, which here is taken to indicate the capacity to take part in scientific and technical communication and to receive and develop imported knowledge (1), and the actual *participation in and production of scientific and technical knowledge* (2). But before discussing these issues I present the indicators in an order that reflects the above distinction.

These are highly simplified indicators falling far behind various approaches attempting to capture the much more complex interrelation between structural, economic, and cultural factors. As the data are very incomplete (and their reliability questionable especially but not only in the DCs), figures are given only for selected countries. To highlight differences, i.e. inequalities, I give the highest and lowest figures of respective countries within the same region:

- Scientific-technological potential is measured by a) adult illiteracy rate, b) years of schooling of the relevant age cohort, c) public expenditure on education as a percentage of GNP, d) public expenditure on R&D as percentage of GNP, e) scientists and engineers in R&D per million population.
- Participation in the production of scientific and technical knowledge is measured by a) share of papers in percentage of world scientific output, b) number of scientific publications (journal articles) per 1000 people, c) number of book titles, d) percentage of internet users.

Some obvious indicators of education represent the very basis of the engagement with knowledge. First, the most fundamental condition of taking part in the world of knowledge is literacy. Even the illiteracy of part of the population will seriously impair the opportunities to involve fully every new generation in the communication and production of knowledge. The illiteracy rate indicates the future prospects of a society with respect to becoming part of the modern world of knowledge.

Figure 6.1   Adult Illiteracy Rates in Selected Countries

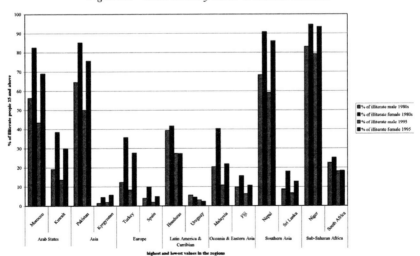

As is evident from the figures, the African countries are in a particularly critical situation. In countries such as Burkina Faso, Niger, and Sierra Leone, between eight to nine out of ten women are illiterate. This situation contrasts most sharply with that of the NICs such as Korea, where it is virtually no longer an issue. But even India still has a surprisingly high rate, especially among women (62 per cent).[9]

The second indicator is the years of schooling an age cohort receives, as this is the precondition for further involvement in knowledge acquisition and production. Figure 6.2 gives the numbers for some selected countries. The data are incomplete, and even some ICs do not report. The picture is well known and clear: in the ICs members of an age cohort can expect to attend school for 13–15 years and have an enrolment ratio of 100 per cent of the relevant age group. In the poorest DCs, such as Mali or Burkina Faso, less than a third of the relevant age group attended primary school, and the expected years of schooling hover around 2–3.

Figure 6.2   Expected Years of Schooling by Gender

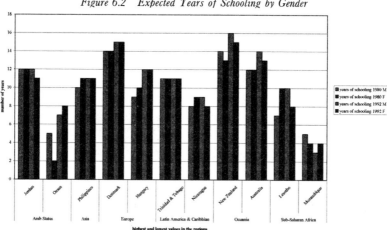

Accordingly, the number of students (per 100,000 inhabitants) is bound to be a fraction of the number enrolled in primary and secondary schools. The students indicate the next generation of those who are supposed to carry on the torch of knowledge. Note countries where the number is dropping and those where it is rising steadily (Korea).

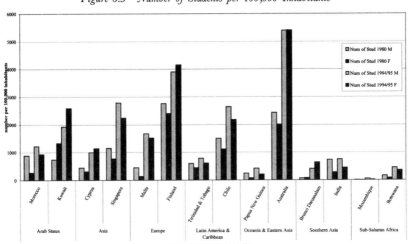

Figure 6.3   Number of Students per 100,000 Inhabitants

A similar impression may be gained from a graph showing the gross enrolment ratio (GER) in tertiary education (see Figure 6.4).

Figure 6.4   Gross Enrolment Ratios by Gender and Region, 1980 and 1995

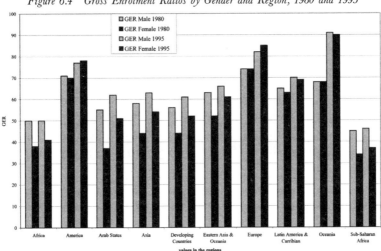

The ability and willingness of a country to promote education is best reflected in its expenditures in education as percentage of its GDP. Here the somewhat surprising picture is that some DCs are spending as much or more than the ICs (Lesotho, Namibia!, Zimbabwe), while others are trailing far behind (Burundi, Mali, Niger). The effect of this expenditure must obviously be seen before the background of the actual GDP.

Figure 6.5   Public Expenditure on Education as Percentage of GDP, 1980 and 1995

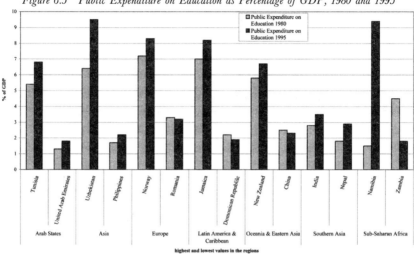

While expenditures on education provide the support for the educational base, i.e. formal schooling and higher education, governments' expenditure on R&D indicates the direct support of knowledge production and of its application in the productive sector. Worldwide R&D expenditures amounted to an estimated US $470 billion in 1994, the greatest share of which was spent in the USA (37.9 per cent), in Western Europe (28 per cent), and in Japan and the NICs (18.6 per cent). The remaining 25.5 per cent is spent by the rest of the world.

The ICs have converged on spending on average slightly more than 2 per cent of their GDP on R&D. Most DCs are far from that mark spending as little as 0.2 per cent (Arab states) to 0.3 per cent (sub-Saharan Africa). It would be unrealistic to expect them to develop the capacity to participate in the global science and technology game any time soon.

A further indicator in this category is the number of scientists and engineers relative to the population as a whole. This is the central human resources indicator that signals a country's ability to acquire and implement knowledge

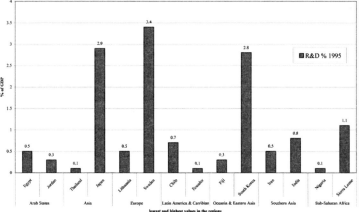

from outside, as well as to produce new knowledge within its own realm. It is evident that the larger that number the greater the variety of competencies and, thus, the probability that new knowledge can be absorbed and developed further. Again, the picture does not hold any surprises except, perhaps, the differences *among* the ICs. But the distance to the DCs is so large that one cannot very well imagine how the situation could be reversed. Japan has not only nearly twice as many scientists and engineers per million people than Germany, but contrasts with countries such as Benin (177), Madagascar (22),

Figure 6.7   Scientists and Engineers in Research and Experimental Development per Million People

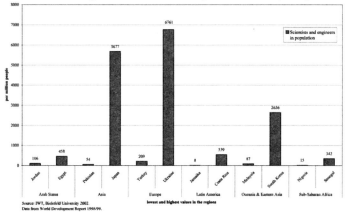

and Rwanda (12). The difference between a country that has roughly 3,000–5,000 scientists and engineers per million people and countries that have fewer than 100 sets them worlds apart. In the latter there is not enough critical mass to even sustain an internal intellectual community, let alone a differentiated one.

These numbers may be complemented by some additional data, i.e. the distribution of R&D personnel between the productive sector and higher education. It may be assumed that in order to have a smooth and efficient transfer of knowledge from the institutions of higher education and research into industry (and vice versa!) it is necessary to have the appropriate competence at both ends (and preferably mobility of the personnel between them). This is an important part of the 'absorptive capacity'. In the ICs the pattern seems to have evolved that roughly 50–60 per cent of the R&D personnel is employed in the productive sector, 25–30 per cent in higher education and the remainder in general service.

Figure 6.8   Research and Experimental Development Personnel by Sector

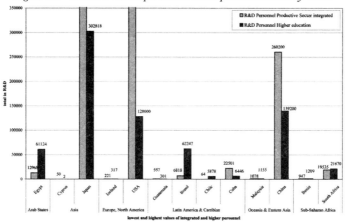

Next we turn to indicators of the actual participation in the communication and production of knowledge. The most common measure of scientific activity is the production of publications. This is a problematic simplification because the communication and production of knowledge assumes other forms as well, be it the training of students or the transfer of knowledge to people in the production process or the services. When focusing on scientific publications, additional problems emerge with the available data sets. The databanks used to compile scientific production focus on the Anglo-Saxon world, primarily the USA, and discriminate against publications in the DCs. Another concern is that the scientific paper is a type of knowledge production not necessarily adequate or relevant for DCs. These problems will be discussed later. First I shall present the picture as it is reflected in the databanks at hand (SCI and Compumath). Again, it is apparent that the relevant scientific activity takes place in the USA, Western Europe, and Japan, together with the newly industrialized countries (NICs). Since 1990 some relevant changes have taken place. Japan and the NICs gained 19 per cent until 1995, the USA has lost slightly (–4 per cent), Western Europe has improved its position by 9 per cent, and the dramatic changes in Eastern and Central Europe since the breakup of the Soviet Union are reflected in the CIS's share dropping by 44 per cent and the CEE countries by 17 per cent. Without the political changes as an explanation sub-Saharan Africa has dropped by 19 per cent.[10]

Figure 6.9   Scientific Output: Number of Publications per Year in ISI Journals

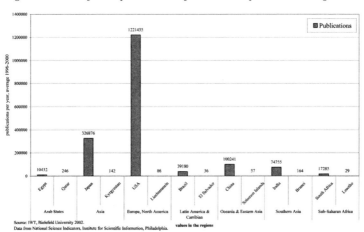

Again, to just give a rough idea about the place that knowledge production has in a particular country one may take as a measure the number of scientific papers per 1,000 inhabitants. It does not come as a surprise that very populous nations come out on a lower rank than smaller nations. Relatively small countries, namely Sweden and Switzerland, are at the top of the list. If one were to ask which countries are the most active and efficient knowledge producers they are the ones.

One stable pattern is that none of the DCs has a ratio higher than 1:0 whereas all the ICs do.

Figure 6.10 Number of Publications in ISI Journals per 1,000 Inhabitants, by Year

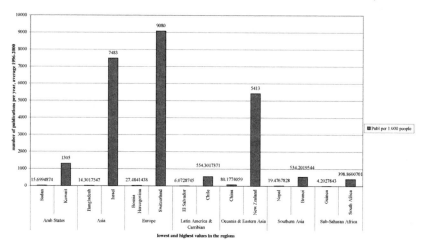

Figure 6.11 Share of Citations in International Scientific Literature (ISI), 1996–2000

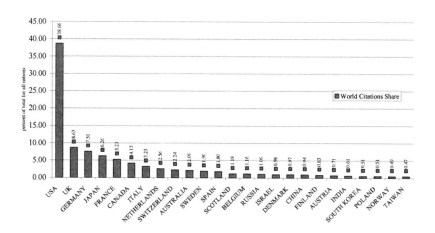

Another indicator of knowledge production compiled by UNESCO is the number of book titles published in a country. The figures very likely reflect the level of intellectual activity and the culture of reading, i.e. dealing with knowledge much more broadly than does the production of scientific papers.

In some cases the figures have to be treated with caution. Notably, those of the UK and the Netherlands may also reflect the concentration of international publishers in these countries.

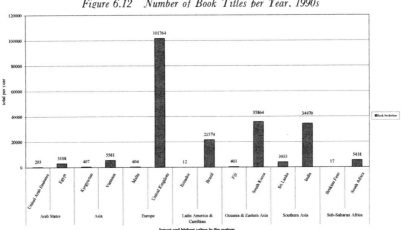

Figure 6.12   Number of Book Titles per Year, 1990s

Next to book titles UNESCO lists a series of other indicators as presumably reflecting the state of cultural development and the intensity of communication, among them the number and volume of daily newspapers, the number of radio receivers, and the production of films. In recent years another medium has assumed much greater importance with respect to information gathering: the Internet. The Internet has become a source of information not only for the acquisition of goods and services, but also for research. In addition, it provides a new communication technology with email. Manuel Castells has pointed to the connection between the development of information technology and the growing inequality emanating from unequal access to information and availability of the respective technology.[21] It is generally recognized and accepted that the ability to use the Internet and access information at any time is rapidly becoming a key qualification, and only those economies will be competitive, those societies will have a high standard of living, whose production elites know how to use the new information and communication technology. In fact, as Castells shows, the inequalities of IT distribution applies no longer to countries but even within countries, where dramatic inequities emerge between urban conglomerates and the rural hinterland.

Consequently, the number of Internet hosts by country is an important indicator of the development of that capacity. The only caveat: the numbers are changing rapidly from year to year especially in the ICs. The gap between them and the DCs, foremost those in Africa, is obvious, however. The deficits with respect to access to information and computer power are judged to be as wide as ever. For September 2002 the Internet statistics compiler Nua.com reported that Europe had passed the USA and Canada in the number of Internet users for the first time and accounted for 32 per cent of global Internet users, while only 6 per cent were based in Latin America, and just 2 per cent in the Middle East and Africa.[12]

Determinants and Dynamics of Knowledge Inequalities

The indicators presented above show the familiar fact that there is a great imbalance with respect to *knowledge production*. The great share of new scientific knowledge in the world (*c.* 80 per cent) is produced by very few countries (USA, Canada, EU, Switzerland, and Japan). As long as knowledge is functionally specific to the exigencies of particular regions or countries imbalances in knowledge production may not be a pressing problem. Knowledge about agriculture is not crucial where seafaring is of geographical importance; knowledge about mining is of little help in low-lying marshlands, and so on. However, this idealized situation no longer exists, if it ever did. The emergence of a common, though structured global system of knowledge has begun with the emergence of modern science, i.e. with the establishment of networks of corresponding scholars across political and language boundaries promoted by the academies in the seventeenth and eighteenth centuries. With the appearance of the nation-state in the eighteenth and nineteenth centuries one can observe a 'nationalization' of science, i.e. a limitation of scientific communication, but by the end of the nineteenth century internationalization of science was again well under way. Since then this process has continued, slowed only by the world wars, and accelerated once more since the 1980s.[13]

This process of internationalization and now globalization of science communication is very uneven, resulting in a polarization into a centre and a periphery that is even more extreme than that in terms of economic wealth.[14] In a global economy where the production of technologies shifts from one country to another following cheap labour and, to a lesser extent, market demand, a country's privilege of commanding a particular field of knowledge becomes less and less likely.

Instead, the strong knowledge producers gain a cumulative advantage: the stronger their knowledge base the more new knowledge they are likely to produce. The crucial mechanism is the link between knowledge and economics and has to do with an important characteristic of knowledge: new scientific knowledge is produced only once. Once it is known (and not forgotten) it is no longer new, and it does not make sense to invest in a 'second discovery', as it is easier to copy. From then on it may be shared with others, but whenever it is useful for practical purposes and in demand by others it may become a commodity. This economic mechanism favours the leading knowledge producers and exacerbates the inequality among them as the demand for new knowledge is focused on the small group of 'front-runners' who find it increasingly tempting to protect their knowledge against free diffusion and turn it into commercial profit instead. The drive to protect intellectual property rights is getting stronger, and it already functions as an obstacle to the free diffusion of knowledge.

A recent illustration of this was the warning by the secretary-general of NATO, who indicated that the technological gap between the USA and all the other member states had reached such dimensions that they could no longer take part in the same kind of war and risked being relegated to doing the 'dirty work'. In other words, in the area of advanced military technology, which is admittedly the extreme end of the spectrum, the inequality of knowledge production is caused by secrecy, and it already affects the ICs themselves.

Another example may also serve to illustrate this point. Therborn lists information and ideas (thus knowledge) among the determinants of global (in)equality. Knowledge, it appears at first sight, is among those resources that contribute most to the balancing of inequalities, not least because of its apparent fluidity. He makes the case for medical knowledge, which has 'played an outstanding role . . . in bringing about the most important process of equalization of the world'.[15] Proof of this is given in terms of life expectancy figures across the globe.

Medical knowledge may, indeed, be an example of a comparatively easy diffusion of knowledge, driven by humanitarian motives. The quandary of the AIDS epidemic in southern and eastern Africa, however, raises some doubts even about this case. AIDS has effected a dramatic downturn of life expectancy in the countries concerned, and the protection of intellectual property rights and, thus, the financial interests of the pharmaceutical industry, is at least one reason among others restricting the free flow of knowledge.

The inequality with respect to *knowledge use* is almost as extreme. The spread of mass education is another global diffusion process of knowledge but, as the figures above show, it is also very uneven. If primary and secondary education are regarded as the crucial condition for the acquisition and use of knowledge the uneven distribution of this capacity follows the same pattern of a North/South division. The provision of education is primarily a function of the wealth of a society. Here again, the self-reinforcing dynamic between economic poverty and lack of knowledge capacity prevails. The poor nations cannot provide primary and secondary education of the same breadth and quality as the rich ones, so they continuously lose ground in the game of knowledge production and absorption.

As the world grows into an order of universal scientific and technical knowledge the differentiation between knowledge producers and knowledge users becomes a *global* distinction. The distinction between knowledge producers and knowledge users, although it is not a fixed and unequivocal one, draws attention to the fact that knowledge production may be increasingly concentrated, relegating some countries that used to be knowledge producers to the role of primarily being knowledge users. The best way to illustrate this growing dependency of some countries relative to others is to look at patent statistics.[16]

Perhaps even more compelling is the movement of scientists and engineers from all over the world to the leading knowledge-producing countries. The country attracting most successfully highly trained personnel and thereby profiting from and relying on a sizable 'brain gain' is the USA. The NSF/NSB reports that 'an increasing number (nearly 30 percent) of PhD-level scientists and engineers at U.S. universities and colleges are foreign born' and that 'participation by foreign-born doctorate-holders in U.S. academic S&E increased continuously during at least the past two decades'. In civil engineering the percentage of foreign-born doctorate holders is highest with 51.5 per cent.[17] The growing concentration of researchers in the highly developed part of the world is reflected to some extent by the increase between 1993 and 1997 at a 5.3 per cent rate annually to roughly 3 million in OECD member states (to 1.11 million in the USA alone). Yet even within the OECD there are those that gain brains and those that lose them. Of the immigrant nationals holding high S&E degrees in the USA 8 per cent come from India, 7 per cent from China, but 4 per cent come from Germany. Japan is another country attracting highly skilled workers, attracting 40 per cent the number of its annual university graduates, roughly 241,000 workers in 1999, that is estimated at 'nearly double the number of entries to the U.S. in . . . similar categories'.[18] The full effect of this mobility of highly trained personnel to the few knowledge-producing countries on those affected by 'brain drain' remains unaccounted.

Among the potential knowledge users some countries even remain virtually excluded from the use of scientific and technical knowledge because they lack the capacity to absorb and use new knowledge produced elsewhere. The dynamics governing the distribution of knowledge throughout the world are such that the gap between knowledge producers and knowledge users is widening, and even within these categories the differences are more likely to grow.

Strategies to Overcome Inequalities of Knowledge

The sequence of indicators presented above was governed by an implicit but obvious model: the development of a 'culture' conducive to scientific knowledge starts with basic and secondary education as the base, it grows if the capacity to absorb knowledge is developed on a substantial scale, and it can lead to a sustained indigenous production of new knowledge if this capacity is developed to such an extent that a critical mass of people are provided with sufficient means to pursue exclusively that goal. The major problem is the self-reinforcing nature of this process and its dependence on an economic, political, and social environment that allows it to start in the first place. This appears almost self-evident and is in line with development strategies that have been proposed already several decades ago. Nevertheless, debates continue over the question of what it is in the nature of scientific knowledge that makes transfer difficult, and what are the adequate strategies to initiate development in the knowledge sector. The development models reflect these debates.

Already at the end of the 1960s modernization theorists had responded to this question. They were confronted with the intriguing research findings that the transfer of knowledge as embodied in technology required an economic infrastructure, i.e. labour and capital, as well as a sound primary and secondary education base if it were to have a positive effect on national economic development.[19] Thus, although knowledge can be easily copied and diffused (at least those parts that can be formalized and written down), to absorb it and use it effectively is another matter. The conclusion was that development could only be achieved by developing an 'absorptive capacity', i.e. creating an indigenous base of knowledge production. The Advisory Committee on the Application of Science and Technology to Development of the UN Economic and Social Council stated in its 'World Plan': 'It is difficult for a developing country without a science and technology capacity of its own, and particularly without the trained people involved, to know what useful technology exists elsewhere, to understand it, to select it, to adapt, to absorb, to repair and maintain, to operate.' The report therefore saw it as essential 'to build up indigenous scientific capability in the developing countries'.[20] Thus the priority of development aid shifted to cooperation rather than short-term transfer, to strengthening 'endogenous scientific and technological capabilities that are in harmony with the social and cultural traditions and the conditions specific to each DC all the while emphasizing the importance of satisfying basic needs'.[21]

These shifts in policy reflect a better understanding of the *systemic character* of knowledge management in the broadest sense, and students of science, technology, and the innovation process in general attempt to catch this with the notion of National Innovation Systems (NIS).[22] 'World systems theory'[23] and institutionalists[24] have denounced such a strategy although for slightly different reasons. The target of their criticism was the assumption that capacity building, as it is called today, would entail the establishment of higher education institutions oriented to basic research and, thus, costly support for speciality-driven science that had no relevance in the respective DCs. In the dependency model (which world systems theory is) the 'Western' science model was depicted as ideological and non-transferable to DCs.

The neo-institutionalists claim that the development model ascribing a central role to Western science is based not on demonstrated effect but on belief. More specifically, they question the implicit hierarchical model which presupposes a linear relationship between science, technology, and economic development. It is now generally recognized that the original optimistic (or naive?) view of a linear relationship between investment in basic research, applied research, technological development, and economic growth cannot be upheld. Evidently the connection is more complex. The establishment of universities and research laboratories does not guarantee scientific advance or development.[25] Thus the correlation between scientific and technological capacity and economic well-being reflecting past developments in ICs and NICs may be hiding different causalities.

Instead, the critics advance a so-called symmetrical model, which argues that both science and technology affect economic development in unique ways. Science transmits values of development and modernization, technology offers ' "solutions" for the connection between resources and local economic needs.' Thus Drori, on the basis of an analysis of 54 DCs, comes to the conclusion that the symmetrical model is more applicable to them.[26] This finding contrasts sharply with experience in the West, where the correlation between science, technology, and economic wealth is high.

However, probably no one would seriously advocate any more that an unmitigated transfer of Western-style basic research institutions would be a viable development strategy. 'Backwash effects' of such a strategy were identified more than three decades ago. Elite higher education institutions with their basic research orientation are operating in an enclave when set up in DCs. Their relevant references are in the specialty communities abroad. They get their research topics as well as the reputation for performed research from them. The result is knowledge production that is irrelevant to the local needs of the country and the brain drain of their highly educated citizens, internally to other sectors, or externally to Western knowledge-producing countries. It does not help much to denounce the universalist mode of Western science as ideology in order to realize that it presents a Catch-22 for the DCs. Earlier attempts to find a solution implied the reorganization of the science and technology systems in the West so as to block 'backwash effects', but that amounted to restating the problem.[27]

In this chapter the focus is on knowledge inequality as such. Thus the economic side of the issue is not treated. However, the obvious should at least be mentioned, namely that the absorption of knowledge depends not only on the knowledge infrastructure but on the economic potential as well. Without firms that provide a demand for the educated and an opportunity for them to put their knowledge to work, there will be little motivation to acquire that knowledge or to stay in the country. In this connection it is important to note that both development aid (ODA) and private foreign investments (FDA) that alone could create such a demand, are declining or non-existent in sub-Saharan Africa. The lack of an academic labour market in these countries may be the greatest long-term obstacle to a more equitable distribution of knowledge.

All these findings remain contradictory, in part based on conceptual decisions embedded in the indicators by which different configurations are measured. The only safe conclusions that may be drawn from various studies are that generalizations are hard to come by and that all cases seem to be different and have to be judged on their own merits.

'Indigenous Knowledge' as the New Paradigm of Development

It is no accident that in view of the dimensions of the knowledge gap between the ICs and DCs, the fact that it is widening for many of them, and the apparent failure of policies, the notion of 'indigenous knowledge' has captured the attention of DC governments, political activists, and NGOs. The debate over 'indigenous knowledge' was clearly initiated and is still driven by a guilt complex among Western countries in response to their role as colonial powers. The UN declared the years 1995–2004 as the International Decade of the World's Indigenous People to 'strengthen international co-operation for the solution of problems faced by indigenous people in such areas as human rights, the environment, development, education and health'.[28] UNESCO is trying to establish new development paradigms that will support the active participation of indigenous communities in sustainable development strategies. The World Conference on Science (WCS) declaration stated, *inter alia*, 'that traditional and local knowledge systems, as dynamic expressions of perceiving and understanding the world, can make, and historically have made, a valuable contribution to science and technology, and that there is a need to preserve and protect, research and promote this cultural heritage and empirical knowledge'.[29] Along a similar line the South African government, through its National Research Foundation, has established as a new research focus the interface of indigenous knowledge (IK) and Western science. It considers indigenous knowledge systems as having hitherto been suppressed and having to be brought 'into the mainstream of knowledge'.[30] The focus on IK is, in effect, a new approach in development policy and represents a major change in development paradigms as it places *knowledge* at the centre of development strategies, and recognizes, for the first time, the importance of *local knowledge* and participation in decision-making. By highlighting the significance of local cultural contexts and knowledges and, thus, the conditions of adaptation for the transfer of knowledge from outside, development strategies avoid the appearance of benign colonialism and pay respect to cultural identities.

As the whole arena of development policy is ideologically highly charged it is not surprising that the term 'indigenous knowledge' means different things to different parties.[31] Two strategies may be distinguished. One is pragmatically oriented and seeks to integrate IK into Western knowledge. The other is more radical and claims an autonomous status for IK as an alternative route to development, thereby repeating some of the previous controversies between modernization and dependency theorists.

Proponents of the second view see a major flaw in the pragmatic position's underlying assumption that Western science, i.e. the 'international knowledge system', remains the frame of reference against which all IKs are judged. The (hierarchical) distinction between IK and Western science 'seeks to separate and fix in time and space . . . systems that can never be separated or so fixed', and the proposed strategies of storing and exploiting IK will only once again 'benefit the richer, more powerful constituencies . . . thus undermining the major stated objectives . . . to benefit the poor, the oppressed, and the disadvantaged'.[32] Support of this argument is supposedly provided by five decades of development policies that have failed mainly because they have ignored the 'social, political and cultural contexts in which they were implemented'.[33] The conclusion drawn from this argument either implicitly or explicitly is that the support of IK can serve as an alternative to being involved in the Western system of (scientific) knowledge and as a sufficient base of development.

However, several caveats have to be mentioned with respect to IK as a development scheme.

First, to take IK as an alternative knowledge system to build up a research capacity appears to be highly risky. IK is primarily bound to a rural and agrarian lifestyle. It pertains to local flora and fauna, to their sustainable use as food or for medicinal purposes. It may make good sense to take this knowledge into account and to resurrect it where it was lost when empowering farmers, not least to protect them against Western knowledge that comes with a price tag or proves to be useless or, worse, harmful. However, several much advertised cases of bio-prospecting and bio-piracy that are supposed to prove the wisdom and utility of IK do not give support to IK as an alternative knowledge system. As in the example of the Hoodia cactus, the isolation of the respective compound that is the precondition of its utility requires scientific knowledge, and so do the clinical trials before it can be marketed.[34] In other words, the pragmatic strategy to use IK in conjunction with science may smack of exploitation, but it may at least return some profits to the countries where that knowledge exists if that knowledge is properly protected. In no case is it a solution to the problem of knowledge inequality.

Second, although it is true that development strategies in the past have underestimated the role of context in the transfer of knowledge and technology, it is equally exaggerated to claim that Western science is so context-bound that it defies transfer to African or Asian culture altogether. Korea has embraced Western science with great success, and its economy has grown tremendously during the last three decades along with it. China, with its very different knowledge culture, has, with help from the West, transferred know-how and research capacity in biotechnology, among other areas, and aims to rival leaders in the field with its own version of Silicon Valley in and around Shanghai. South Africa has a long-established science system in place that before the end of apartheid primarily served the military and modern industry controlled by the ruling white minority. However, the new government 'takes great care not to weaken this apparatus' but rather tries to 'realign research, better to serve basic needs and industrial competitiveness; and to give the chance to Black South Africans to get a hold on the system'.[35]

Third, there is reason to be cautious of a misplaced romanticization of IK. To take the example of South Africa again, in the debate over HIV/AIDS President Thabo Mbeki gave undue support to the questionable practices of healers by doubting that the virus causes the syndrome, calling for 'African solutions to an African problem' while at the same time blocking distribution of recognized medication to those affected. While the 'African' version of the problem, according to virologists, is indeed different (HIV-C type) the reference to 'African' solutions has given abusive healers the undeserved legitimacy of IK. The case demonstrates that a delineation between sound IK and quackery may be the greatest challenge.

Conclusion

As has often been noticed, globalization is a contradictory process. We still cannot be sure that we fully understand its dynamics and its ultimate outcome. On the one hand, the polarization of the global into a relatively small centre of knowledge-producing countries and a periphery of countries whose capacity to use that knowledge varies widely. This points towards a hegemony of knowledge producers whose power is additionally augmented by the fact that knowledge becomes the most crucial commodity in what is now termed the 'knowledge society'. With respect to the economic benefits derived from knowledge production in its present form many countries, especially in sub-Saharan Africa, are truly excluded. They cannot even use knowledge that is on the market and turn it into useful technology and products for their own needs, for lack of the indigenous capacity to deal with it.

On the other hand, there may be a reverse process under way. By virtue of the very process of globalization the ensuing diffusion of mutual awareness first of all directs attention to the growing imbalances of knowledge and their consequences. The above-mentioned activities of the UN and UNESCO are testimony to that. Alongside the shift of global attention to indigenous people who are to be included in the global community a host of programmes has been established that are designed to create a global perspective on specific issues, coordinate research among member states both in ICs and DCs, thereby gathering information in world-wide networks, and at the same time contribute to capacity building in participating countries that are in need of it. Anthropogenic climate change, the maintenance and sustainable management of biodiversity, problems of global environmental change, and the threats of desertification have become crystallizing issues around which large supranational research programmes have been established that engage researchers, NGOs, and governments around the globe. While it may not be surprising that these programmes reproduce to some extent the North/South division of labour, i.e. data collection in the DCs and interpretation of the data in the ICs, they are nevertheless a starting point in involving the DCs in the global process of scientific communication on behalf of their own concerns.

Of course, there are also troubling developments that may counteract the beneficial effects of the global science projects. Analyses of the African science systems and the status of researchers seem to indicate that there is a change in the mode of production of scientific knowledge. World-wide, international demand for research replaces national demand and determines programmes and objectives. The system is regulated no longer by peer assessment but by the market, where researchers are out 'for hire'.[36] If this observation proves stable the long-term consequences for the weaker countries would be similar to those of the brain drain but perhaps more drastic, as it would prevent the sustained development of indigenous capacities of knowledge use and production.

Whatever the longer term consequences of these contradictory developments are, one fact seems to stand out as unchallenged: inequalities of knowledge can only be erased from the bottom up, i.e. by setting up functioning systems of primary and secondary education. Wherever education systems are in place they have provided the basis for further development and, ultimately, for the stability of the respective social systems and for securing an acceptable standard of living.

Notes

1 World Bank 1999: 3.
2 UNESCO 1999.
3 Waast 2001: 6.
4 World Bank 1999: 8.
5 Meyer, Ramirez and Soysal 1992.
6 Cf. H. D. Evers, 'Transition towards a knowledge society: Malaysia and Indonesia in comparative perspective', *Comparative Sociology*, in print.
7 I take the 'order of knowledge' in any society to be the given ensemble of social arrangements regulating the production and diffusion of knowledge.
8 Cohen, and Levinthal 1990.
9 World Bank 1999.
10 UNESCO 1998: 22.
11 Castells 2000: 375–85.
12 *www.usabilitynews.com/news/article637.asp*, 5/28/2003.
13 Schott 1991.
14 Frame, Narin and Carpenter 1977: 502–4.
15 Therborn Ms. 2002: 28.
16 Chapter 5.
17 Ibid.
18 Ibid.
19 Shrum and Shenhav 1995: 62; Meyer, Hannan, Robinson and Thomas 1979.
20 UN Economic and Social Council 1969: 102.
21 Gaillard 1990: 352.
22 The concept of NIS recognizes that innovation (which may here be taken as equivalent to economic development) is a process that is highly contingent and complex, involving many institutions and their respective configuration. The secondary and higher education system, the organizational structure of the research system, the system of science funding and science policy-making, the taxation system promoting or preventing private investment in knowledge production, and others are in some way responsible for the capacity of a country to participate in the global

process of communicating and producing new knowledge and developing new technology either for a domestic or an international market (Nelson 1993). The causal relationship between these factors is not always clear, nor are there simple models into which the many different configurations they assume in different countries can be moulded. Also, we do not have satisfactory indicators for every factor, and often the appropriate data to substantiate them are lacking. But raw descriptions are better than none, and nothing more than a raw description is attempted here.

23 Wallerstein 1974.

24 Meyer and Ramirez 2003.

25 Gaillard 1990: 348.

26 Drori 1993: 211.

27 Cf. UN Economic and Social Council 1969: 114.

28 *www.unesco.org/culture/indigenous/*.

29 UNESCO 1999.

30 *www.nrf.ac.za/focusareas/iks/*. South Africa's Medical Research Council also seeks to support models that integrate 'Western' and indigenous knowledge systems. Iowa State University-based Centre for Indigenous Knowledge for Agriculture and Rural Development (CIKARD), one of the key global players in the IK network, operates on the assumption that indigenous knowledge are central to participatory approaches to rural development. Thus it documents IK for dissemination to development experts and scientists to arrive at beneficial synergies with 'the international knowledge systems' (Warren and McKiernan 1995: 426–33, cited in Ravjee 2002: 56).

31 Cf. *www.nuffic.nl/ik-pages/about-ik.html* for a description of IK characteristics. On the relation between local and indigenous knowledge see Antweiler 1998.

32 Agrawal 1995: 434.

33 Ibid., 425.

34 Ravjee 2002: 21. The South African CSIR had patented the appetite-suppressing compound of the Hoodia cactus (p.57) in mid-1990 after it had been isolated in 1983. The original utility and thus the origin of the knowledge about it, namely to stave off hunger for the San people on their long hunting trips, has become obsolete as the remaining San have given up their tradition. It is now replaced by a different utility in the form of a multi-million dollar demand for slimming aids to fight obesity among the overfed in Western countries. The issue if CSIR hands down a share of its royalties to the San who protested CSIR's deal with a British pharmaceutical company selling them the rights is another issue. The irony of this and similar cases is that the IK may even have lost its significance in its original context and may only regain it in a new one.

35 Waast 2001: 11.

36 Ibid.: 5.

References

Agrawal, A., 'Dismantling the divide between indigenous and scientific knowledge', *Development and Change*, 26, 1995: 413–39.

Antweiler, C., 'Local knowledge and local knowing', *Anthropos*, 93, 1998: 469–4.

Castells, M., *The Rise of Network Society*, 2nd edn, Oxford: Blackwell, 2000.

Cohen, D. A. Levinthal, 'Innovation and learning: the two faces of R&D', *Economic Journal*, 99, 1990: 569–96.

David, P. A., and D. Foray, 'An introduction to the economy of the knowledge society', *International Social Science Journal*, 171, 2002, pdf version.

Drori, G. S., 'The relationship between science, technology and the economy in lesser developed countries', *Social Studies of Science*, 23, 1993: 201–15.

Drori, G. S., J. Meyer, F.O. Ramirez and E. Schofer, *Science in the Modern World Polity: Institutionalization and Globalization*, Stanford, CA: Stanford University Press, 2003.

Epstein, H., 'The mystery of AIDS in South Africa', *New York Review of Books*, 20 July 2000, *www.nybooks.com/articles/9*.

Evers, H. D., 'Transition towards a knowledge society: Malaysia and Indonesia in comparative perspective', *Comparative Sociology*, 2 (2), 2003

Frame, D. J., F. Narin and M. P. Carpenter, 'The distribution of world science', *Social Studies of Science*, 7, 1977: 501–16.

Gaillard, J., 'Science in the developing world: foreign aid and national policies at a crossroads', *AMBIO*, 19, 8 December 1990: 348–53.

Meyer, J. W., F. O. Ramirez and Y. N. Soysal, 'World expansion of mass education, 1870–1980, *Sociology of Education*, 65, 1992: 128–49.

National Science Board (NSB), *Science and Engineering Indicators – 2000*, Vol. 1, Arlington, VA: National Science Foundation.

Ravjee, N., 'Beyond the "indigenous" versus "Western" knowledge dichotomy', Ms., 2002.

Schott, T., 'The world scientific community: globality and globalization', *Minerva*, 29, 1991: 440–62.

Shrum, W., and Y. Shenav, 'Science and technology in less developed countries', in S. Jasanoff et al., eds, *Handbook of Science and Technology Studies*, Newbury Park: Sage, 1995, pp. 627–51.

Therborn, G., 'Globalization and inequality: issues of conceptualization and of explanation', *Sociologias*, 6, July/December 2001.

UN Economic and Social Council, Science in Underdeveloped Countries, 1969.

UNESCO, *World Science Report 1998*, Paris: UNESCO.

— 'Declaration on science and the use of scientific knowledge', World Conference on Science, 1999, *www.unesco.org/science/wcs/end/declaratione.htm*

Waast, R., 'Science in Africa: a survey', Ms., 2001.

Wallerstein, I., *The Modern World System*, New York: Academic Press, 1974.

World Bank, *World Development Report 1998–99*, Washington, DC, 1999.

Part II

Case Studies

7

Inequality in Brazil: Facts and Perceptions

Elisa P. Reis

Introduction

The scope of this chapter is twofold. First, it seeks to draw attention to the importance of incorporating values and norms when discussing social inequality from a theoretical or a practical perspective. Second, it comments on how the Brazilian population in general and its elites see poverty and inequality in both cognitive and normative terms. Do they perceive poverty and inequality as pressing issues? How do they explain it? What are their preferences in terms of policies for meeting social needs? Are there significant differences between the perceptions of the elite sectors and those of the general population?

In what follows, I begin by commenting on the importance of introducing perceptions in research into poverty. I then proceed to describe briefly the magnitude of the problem of poverty and the scope and profile of inequality in Brazil. The third and fourth sections touch on the way first the elites and then Brazilians in general see poverty and inequality based on a research survey and in-depth interviews. Finally, I conclude with a few words of speculation about the prospects for significant change in the prevailing patterns of redistribution.

Social Inequality

The idea of social inequality presupposes its opposite, namely social equality. In other words, these are relational notions: to understand the one we need to comprehend the other. This draws attention to the fact that it is in the realm of culture that we must locate ideas about equality and inequality. It also sheds light on the fact that for the social sciences the contrast of 'equal versus unequal' expresses something quite different from the mathematical notion that what is not 'equal' is 'different'. Social equality (or social inequality) presupposes reference to a unit, a collective within which moral judgments about criteria and patterns of distribution are valid.

Society defines what is acceptable or unacceptable in terms of the distribution of goods and resources by reference to a shared moral code.[1] In this sense, the centrality of the cultural aspect when approaching the inequality issue is unavoidable. Yet, in practice, the cultural dimension has not received enough attention in studies into inequality. Apart from Oscar Lewis' controversial studies about the culture of poverty, we have not seen much effort in this direction.[2] To be sure, political culture studies frequently inquire into prevailing notions of justice, but seldom do they explicitly explore perceptions of poverty and social inequality among the non-poor.[3]

The very tendency to associate the notions of poverty and inequality in some fashion has to be understood as a historical and cultural phenomenon. As convincingly argued by Dumont, equality is a modern value.[4] The idea of equality as something valued positively is absent in the pre-modern, hierarchical world. Thus, even when the poor rebelled and revolts occurred, the objects of moral indignation were 'bad' lords and rulers, without ever contesting the legitimacy of the prevailing social hierarchy. It is true that the remote origins of equality as a positive value are much older. We can trace the idea of equality back to ancient Greece and early Christianity, but their transformation into a ruling concept has its historical symbol in the French Revolution. From then on, the idea of inequality as the opposite to equality began to replace the assumption that differences between people are 'natural' and that, therefore, they are 'naturally' placed side by side in social hierarchies that express adscriptive characteristics.

Against the natural order of a fixed hierarchy, the modern normative order sees equality as a universal value. Moreover, the value of equality has progressive features, that is to say, it involves an expansive process that aims at abolishing successive sources of 'usurpation'. The expansion of citizenship is the clearest manifestation of the modern notion of equality. Not only are individuals equated as citizens of a nation-state, but also their rights progress to the extent that new sources of privileges are identified and abolished.[5]

Whatever the circumstances, to say that equality came to constitute a key value, an ideal or an ethos for contemporary society is merely to confirm the historical status of the concept. But how do we define what is equal or unequal? Individuals and groups in a society share a generic notion of equality to some extent. Usually, we all know, to some extent, what others are talking about when they refer to social equality/inequality. It is part of a contemporary cultural consensus that we all think of equality as something good, desirable and virtuous. Even those who seek moral justification for some forms of inequality do it in the name of other forms of equality – most frequently, equality of freedom.[6]

Yet this concept we all value suddenly becomes controversial when we attempt to define it precisely. As universal as the recognition of equality as a positive value is, the matter of agreeing on a single definition for it is equally elusive. The voluminous controversies leave no doubt as to the disputes over the issue. Philosophy, legal studies, political and social theory provide us with abundant proof of this. Furthermore, no consensus exists with respect to the principles that orient policies to counteract inequality in practice. As Douglas Rae points out pertinently, it is only when we get into concrete policies that we succeed in making explicit our understanding of what equality is, since such policies must necessarily indicate just what concept of equality is being pursued.[7]

Being a value and a normative ideal, equality is, by definition, an incomplete, dynamic, and unattainable concept.

In spite of this, the social sciences make it possible to find answers to specific aspects such as: how is existing inequality understood, justified, or denied? How to measure inequality? What are possible causal explanations for it? How to influence social distribution through policy measures? Questions such as these make inequality a legitimate subject for the social sciences.

In this context, what specifically interests me is to comment on the way Brazilians in general and the elites in particular see the inequality issue in both cognitive and normative terms. In order to achieve this, I use information gathered through sample surveys, complemented in the case of the elites by in-depth interviews, which I take as useful approximations to shared perceptions of equality and inequality. The identification of shared values, beliefs, and opinions constitutes the best way to approach the concepts of equality and inequality prevailing in a particular context. This is what converts the focus on political culture into something directly relevant to studies on social inequality. Specific concepts of justice and equality are key dimensions of a political culture that intervene in social policy-making and implementation.

While studies about the profile and magnitude of inequality and poverty are legion, investigation into how societies and groups perceive and define such phenomena is almost non-existent. The very disputes involving social policy evaluation are usually treated as purely technical debates. In fact, it is possible to confine such disputes to technical grounds, just as it is possible to evaluate policy results only in terms of specific interests, without resorting to moral arguments. However, what has been widely neglected is the fact that even interest-based justifications have to take into account prevailing social definitions of what is socially acceptable or unacceptable in the distribution of goods, resources and services. In other words, even if we adopt models of analysis based upon the interested behaviour of individuals, norms and values constitute parameters that circumscribe rational choices.

We all tend to converge towards definitional criteria that centre upon the material conditions of life as the appropriate parameters for evaluating distribution patterns. However, beyond this minimal common denominator there is a whole universe of cultural patterns that give meaning to measures and provide the basis for moral judgments. To emphasize that Brazil's inequality is 'n' times greater than in country 'C' is very relevant if our concern is to look at Brazil's relative position in the international system. However, if Brazil's inequality ranking in the world is to become meaningful to the internal discussion about patterns of distribution, it has to be placed in its own context, and the notions of justice and equity prevailing there have to be incorporated.

While recognizing the great relevance of international comparisons regarding levels and degrees of inequality, I also draw attention to the need to compare normative definitions and evaluative perceptions about such questions across nations, groups, classes and social sectors. My central argument here is that the political-cultural dimension provides us with keys to capture the meaning socially attributed to inequality, and to the way in which it is experienced, justified or denied. In turn, such understandings contribute to identify efficacious ways to alter distribution patterns.

Facts about Brazilian Inequality

As mentioned above, even technical definitions of poverty and inequality point to a certain way of looking at such issues. Yet what I call 'facts' here are standard ways of assessing and measuring distribution in a given context. 'Facts' therefore correspond here to objective measures, as opposed to one's knowledge and evaluation of the state of affairs that the measures and technical assessments describe. Universal ways of assessing facts about inequality make it possible to compare existing patterns of distribution, and to evaluate the results of policies aimed at reducing inequality. In this sense, even though measurements and indicators of inequality are no more than an expression of conventional agreement among specialists, it is right to treat them as objective facts.

The fact that Brazil disputes the unenviable position of most unequal country in the world with a couple of African countries is frequently mentioned in the local media. People refer to it as a shameful and humiliating record and contrast it to Brazil's potential affluence, which could provide for better distribution. They call attention to idle fertile lands, an abundant water supply, and mineral resources as unexplored wealth, as things that should make life easier for everybody. Such reasoning constitutes a good illustration of the tendency of Brazilians to conflate poverty and inequality: reacting to current levels of inequality, their immediate answer is to search for potential sources of additional wealth to distribute to the poor, instead of considering alternatives to redistribute current resources. Elites and people in general share to some extent the tendency to conflate poverty and inequality.

The reaction mentioned above is certainly not peculiar to Brazilians. People everywhere tend to reveal a preference for solutions to social problems that involve fewer sacrifices. What is particularly interesting in this case, though, is the fact that knowledge of existing inequality levels is not matched by an accurate assessment of Brazil's actual, as opposed to potential, wealth. There seems to be little awareness that official statistics do not rank Brazil among poor countries. With 170 million people and a GDP of US$610.1 billion in 2000, Brazil is the ninth largest economy in the world, and belongs to the group of medium income countries. Per capita income per annum is US$3,580, and the purchasing power parity of its per capita income is US$7,300, figures that are close to those of Botswana and Costa Rica, which ranks the three countries around the upper seventies/low eighties in terms of per capita income (World Bank data, 2000). While Botswana has income inequalities similar to those in Brazil, Costa Rica has a far less unequal income distribution pattern.

However, although Brazil as a nation cannot be considered to be poor, there is indeed severe poverty affecting a large number of its population. Official data estimate that 33.6 per cent of the Brazilian population lived below the poverty line, and 14.6 per cent below the extreme poverty line in 2001.[8] The evidence for income concentration is appalling: the share of the poorest 40 per cent of the Brazilian population in national income is close to 8 per cent, while the top 10 per cent gets nearly 50 per cent. In fact, these figures express a consistent pattern, as observed by Barros and his colleagues, who showed that these shares have been stable from the late seventies to the present, while the Gini coefficient has remained around 0.60.[9]

Unequal distribution is not only constant, but also pervasive. It runs along the rural/urban axis and across regions. Though the large majority of the poor live in urban areas, poverty is more acute in the countryside. By way of illustration, data for 1997 indicate that the average per capita monthly income was three times higher for the urban population than that resident in the countryside. Similarly, in the same year, the wealthiest Brazilian state of São Paulo, located in the south-eastern region, had an average income almost three times greater than the average income for the impoverished north-eastern region.[10]

Skin colour and gender are also crucial variables to grasp the pervasiveness of the unequal patterns of distribution prevailing in Brazil, as evidenced by income and education differentials for whites and non-whites pointed out by Henriques.[11] To summarize, it has been estimated that if you are a black female living in the rural north-east you have a 95% chance of falling below the extreme poverty line.

Notwithstanding the predictive power of the rural/urban divide or of the region inhabited, the degrees of inequality one finds along these variables are present within every region and within every big town. The levels of income inequality we find, for example, between rural and urban dwellers, or between the north-east and the south-east, we also find within a Brazilian metropolis, suggesting that acute inequality is indeed a national feature. While income is the clearest evidence one has for unequal distribution, it is easy to observe that access to public services and goods is also very unequally distributed. Public education, health facilities, sanitation, retirement benefits, and other 'citizenship goods' are notoriously biased against those at the bottom of the social ladder. All in all, the consistent evidence leaves no margin of doubt as to the deep and persistent social inequality prevailing in Brazil.

How the Brazilian Elites Perceive Inequality

If, as I stressed before, we use a cultural code to legitimize or de-legitimize a given pattern of social equality/inequality, the cognitions and norms regarding what is acceptable and unacceptable in the ways resources are distributed in a society are central to the study of inequality. This premise has guided my concern with the understanding of the perception of Brazilian elites regarding poverty and inequality. From the start it should be clear that choosing to consider perceptions regarding poverty and inequality together is due to the fact that the elites themselves tend to group the two topics. Even when urged to differentiate them or order them according to political priorities, they tend to confuse the two issues. If this confusion can obscure understanding of the problems and their solutions, it is also true that it is important to consider them in order to understand the political culture of the elites.

Bearing in mind that the elites occupy strategic positions, control resources, and exert a central role in the choice of public policies, it seemed necessary to me to investigate what notion of equality they have, how they justify it, what distribution pattern they consider fair or acceptable, etc. The importance of this type of analysis derives most of all from the fact that such perceptions, whether cognitive or normative, tell us about the limits and possibilities of social policy in a given society. Such an analytical perspective is often erroneously identified as a negation of the capacity for initiative on the part of the people. However, my argument here is simply that, whether as a response to pressures coming from below or an effort to prevent them, elites everywhere have a crucial role in the shaping of distribution policies.

In an attempt to comprehend the view Brazilian elites have of poverty and inequality, I began with a research survey conducted in 1993/94, involving a sample of 320 interviewees, namely representatives, at the federal level, of the business, political, techno-bureaucratic and union sectors.[12] Subsequently, with the idea of comparing the perception of the Brazilian elite and those of five other countries, I decided to conduct semi-structured interviews with eighty members of diverse segments of the elite.[13] In addition to the four privileged sectors in the research survey, intellectuals and opinion makers, religious leaders, the military, and representatives of the judicial branch and non-governmental organizations were also included. In both cases an 'institutional' definition of the elite was adopted. i.e., instead of adopting, for example, 'reputation-based' criteria for selecting individual representatives of this segment, the option was to interview those holding positions of leadership in prominent national institutions.

Naturally, a comparison of the survey information and the in-depth interviews can only be impressionistic, but, in general, it was possible to establish an impressive convergence of results in the two studies. In addition, the conducting of in-depth interviews permitted further verification and confirmation of perceptions already outlined in the survey. A third source of investigation used was a broad cross-section of written material penned by representatives of the elite that was published over a five-year period in eight major-circulation newspapers in four Brazilian capitals, two in the mid-south region and two in the north-east, precisely where the in-depth interviews were conducted (São Paulo, Rio de Janeiro, Salvador and Fortaleza).

In this context, what interests me most is comparing the perceptions of the Brazilian elite with those of society as a whole. To do so, one needs to know, for example, if the cognitive and normative views of the elite regarding inequality coincide with those of the population in general. This will enable us to examine the degree of congruity or incongruity between the cultural policies of the elite and the population in general. The identification of potential areas of consensus could contribute to shed light on the possible bases for a broad coalition aimed at implementing distribution policies. Alternatively, mere identification of the different cultural codes between the elites and the people in general regarding what is legitimate in terms of distribution would, in itself, provide relevant information concerning Brazilian society.

In the next paragraphs, I will present a brief summary of the principal conclusions drawn regarding the view of the elites, followed by a comparison with the findings of the survey regarding Brazilian society's perception of inequality.

To start with, I should point out that the Brazilian elites perceive poverty and inequality as problems of great relevance and magnitude. Both the replies to the survey and what was said in the in-depth interviews reflected this clearly. Thus, as indicated in Table 7.1, where we asked what the main

Table 7.1 Principal Obstacles to Democracy in Brazil According to the Elites

Obstacles	%
Low educational level of the population	24.1
High indices of poverty and social inequality	23.4
Absence of party tradition	15.8
Corporatism of groups and sectors in society	10.4
Incompetence of those in power	6.0
Lack of popular political organization	5.4
Egotism of the elites	4.7
Political cronyism	3.8
Concentration of power in the executive branch	3.2
High inflation rates	1.3
Impoverishment of the middle class	1.3
Prolonged economic recession	0.6
Threat of military intervention	0.0
Total	**100 (n = 316)**

obstacles to democracy in Brazil were, poverty and inequality were among the problems considered as a priority by 23.4 per cent of the elite, very close to the percentage that considered the low educational level of the population as the greatest threat to democracy in Brazil.

Similarly, when the question no longer focused on democratic stability but simply asked what the main domestic problems were or what the government's priorities should be, the issues of poverty and inequality remained among those most often cited, as illustrated in Tables 7.2 and 7.3. Thus, one can see in Table 7.2 that poverty and inequality rank third in the number of replies, surpassed only by inflation and questions related to education and health.

Table 7.2   Principal Domestic Problems in Brazil According to the Elites

Obstacles	%
Inflation	17.5
Education and health	15.9
Poverty and inequality	14.3
Governability	11.5
Income distribution	8.3
Other political factors	8.3
Other economic factors	5.4
Corruption	4.8
Recession and unemployment	4.1
Behaviour of the elites	3.5
External dependence	3.2
Moral crisis	2.2
Other social factors	1.0
Total	**100 (n = 314)**

In Table 7.3, which indicates what the principal domestic objectives ought to be, one can once again see that a significant part of the elite perceives eradication of poverty and inequality as being the overriding objective. Only the improvement of education levels and reduction of the size of the state also scored higher in the survey.

As can be seen, if we add to the specific references to poverty and inequality in any of the three above-mentioned tables, other replies related to deficiencies in the provision of public goods and services, classically associated with

Table 7.3 Principal Medium-term Domestic Objectives in Brazil According to the Elites

Obstacles	%
Improve educational levels	23.0
Reduce the size of the state	18.2
Eradicate poverty and reduce inequality	17.6
Increase popular participation in political decisions	16.4
Preserve the democratic regime	11.3
Guarantee economic growth	9.7
Integrate the economy with the international market	2.3
Ensure domestic tranquillity	0.9
Greater integration with Mercosul	0.3
Protect the environment	0.3
Total	**100 (n = 318)**

the notion of social rights, we can conclude that the elites consider social questions to be a major problem in the country. Thus one sees that low educational levels together with poverty and inequality account for approximately half of the replies in the first table, almost a third in the second and 40 per cent in the third. Similarly, in the responses to the in-depth interviews, the social question was always brought up spontaneously. The reference to Brazil as 'the country with the greatest inequality in the world' arose in all of the interviews, without exception.

Among the social dimensions highlighted by the Brazilian elites, education in particular was prominent. It is invoked as the key element in explaining the high levels of inequality in the country and, even more prominently, in identifying the pressing priorities for public policy intervention. This is clearly apparent in what all sectors of the elite say, both in the mid-south and the north-east. The elites put their faith in education as the favoured resource for assuring equality of opportunity, which is clearly the way they define equality. In the normative code of the elites, as obvious as acceptance of the value of equal opportunities is the repudiation of equal results and even equal conditions. In line with this perspective, there is among those interviewed an explicit rejection of the adoption of affirmative action measures. Thus, although there is a broad consensus regarding the existence of racial and sexual prejudice in Brazil, there is also agreement among the elites that exercising positive discrimination to compensate those social segments discriminated against does not constitute an appropriate solution. When asked to justify this point of view, those interviewed systematically expressed their preference for equal opportunity and criticized quota policies that, according to them, validate the principal of inequality because they manipulate and distort opportunity.

Furthermore, the very emphasis placed on education as an instrument for correcting inequalities is perfectly coherent with the view of the elite, which considers distributive reforms to be unnecessary and undesirable. As revealed in the in-depth interviews, the broad offering of educational opportunities is perceived as a strategy that does not penalize more privileged sectors or classes. They contend that raising the educational level of the population in general is all that is needed for everyone to be better off. In other words, education is perceived as a strategy that does not involve redistribution, i.e. that it is not a zero sum game. In the view of the elites, if poor people improve their educational level they will succeed in progressing individually and still contribute to enhance the country as a whole, without placing a burden on the more privileged.

Highlighting the emphasis on the value of equal opportunity, it is also worth noting the belief in the instrumental value of education, which is predominantly perceived as a tool for entering the market, namely as a means of social mobility through job occupation. Unlike other national elites, ours do not highlight the role of education as a means to political awareness or of 'empowerment' that would render those excluded more capable of demanding their inclusion in the system.[14] Education is seen as a resource for individual mobility and the formation of human capital. In this respect, many of those interviewed pointed out that there is a convergence of interests here between the rich and the poor, capitalists and workers. All parties would benefit from the educational improvement of society; the poor would receive better salaries and the rich would have access to more qualified labour. Despite perceiving educational improvements as a resource for increasing productivity, the elites tend to attribute responsibility for investing in this area exclusively to the government. There are clear indications that they believe that the government can do much more and make much better use of the resources that it already has for that purpose. And as many point out, the government could be more efficient, without further burdening those that already pay excessive taxes.

The perceptions mentioned above point to a curious situation, whereby the elites spontaneously emphasize the problem of inequality and consider it to be problematic for society as a whole, but tend to reject the idea of the restructuring of distribution. As a resource for changing the pattern of accentuated inequality, they commend measures sponsored by the government aimed at providing better conditions of life for all. In other words, the elites favour a political orientation that favours overcoming poverty but not inequality.[15]

In fact, even though the elites are aware of the high levels of inequality prevalent in the country and indicate in a variety of ways that inequality foments violence and insecurity, they tend to reject the idea of the restructuring of distribution. The more open discourse of the in-depth interviews made it clear that their preferred solution, namely economic growth, ought to be the strategy for dealing with the enormous shortfalls faced by Brazilian society, without penalizing the rich. While recognizing that the trickle-down effect of growth has not reduced inequality, the elites continue to back this option.

All this information clearly points to the fact that the elites feel they are affected by social problems in general, and by inequality in particular. There is a very sharp perception of social interdependency, i.e., inequality is seen as something that does not only penalize those located at the bottom of the social pyramid. There is a general consensus regarding the negative external aspects of poverty. The elites systematically emphasize that poverty and, above all, inequality breed insecurity, violence, pressure on public services, and a deterioration of public places.

The results of the research survey are also revealing about how the elites perceive the consequences of poverty on the non-poor. Thus, in Table 7.1 we see that they consider social problems to be the principal threat to democracy. Similarly, as can be seen in Table 7.4, more than half of those interviewed pointed to crime, violence and insecurity as the main negative effects of poverty, constituting a general menace to life in the large urban centres, affecting the quality of life of the population as a whole.

Table 7.4   The Worst Consequences of Poverty in Large Brazilian Cities

Consequences	%
Violence/crime/insecurity	51.6
Dehumanization/social Apartheid	10.2
Risk of social conflict/chaos	8.4
Declining quality of life	5.5
Social misery	5.1
Unemployment	4.4
Vicious cycle of poverty	4.0
Barriers to development	2.8
Lack of housing/slumification	2.1
Threat to democratic stability	1.5
Encourages political opportunism	1.1
Others	3.3
Total	**(n = 275)**

Although far less pronounced, there is also a marked perception that the social situation is a barrier to economic development. As pointed out earlier, the perception that a better educated population would contribute to increased productivity is mentioned with some frequency. The possibility of organized political mobilization and violence, however, is not perceived as a real threat by the elites. Contrary to the concept of social interdependency that led its European counterparts in the past to adopt social welfare programmes, ours do not fear the risks of epidemic contagion, population exodus or political upheaval.[16] What they essentially fear is the threat to their persons and their wealth, as well as the deterioration of public places in large urban centres.

Faced with the above-mentioned risks, do the elites feel they are responsible for finding solutions to poverty and inequality? Are they prepared to bear the costs inherent in solving such problems? The two forms of interview and the newspaper material researched do not suggest that a sense of commitment is widespread among the elites. They, including those in government, clearly assert that the state, the government or politicians are responsible and demand solutions from them. In their normative view, it is the government that has to deal with this issue.

Similarly, when they evaluate the performance and assess the role of NGOs and philanthropic players, in general they demonstrate many reservations concerning their relevance and efficiency, always adding that the state is primarily responsible for combating poverty and inequality.

Another indirect way to shed light on the question of responsibility is to verify what players are blamed for the failure of social policies designed to deal with poverty and inequality. Corroborating the idea that the elites tend to see public power as primarily responsible, Table 7.5 shows that technical administrative explanations, those that depend on the state apparatus, appear prominently in the perception of the elites, featuring in nearly a third of the responses. On the other hand, the proportion of responses centred on the low involvement of civil society or the private sector is among those at the bottom of the table.

In addition to attributing responsibility, the in-depth interviews also revealed that the elite sees an imponderable historical heritage as the central cause of extreme inequality. 'Our colonial heritage' and 'our history of slavery' appear as consensual causal explanations in the discourse of the elites. Blaming 'genetics' appears as a constant that to a certain extent exonerates current players from responsibility.

Table 7.5   Explanations for the Failure of Social Policies in Brazil According to the Elites

Reasons	%
Bad planning and execution	29.3
Lack of political will/low priority	18.8
Political and/or personal use of these policies	12.7
Corruption	8.6
Characteristics of the elites*	5.4
Paternalism and/or the palliative nature of the policies	5.7
Priority attributed by the state to other areas**	5.4
Lack of resources***	4.5
Lack of participation of civil society	3.8
Structural problems in the economy	2.2
Lack of private participation in the execution of policies	1.4
Others	2.2
Total	**100 (n = 314)**

* Egotism, lack of vision, authoritarianism, etc.

** In other words, the state is considered to be extremely large and too involved in economic activities, which drains human and capital resources from social areas.

*** This item does not concern criticisms regarding the state's activities, but rather the perception that resources are scarce to carry out the social policy agenda.

Curiously, when asked what the priority measures to combat poverty should entail, the majority of replies cited agrarian reform, as can be seen in Table 7.6. In the in-depth interviews, it was clear that the underlying idea was, almost always, to export from large urban centres social problems that, in the perception of the respondents, stimulate violence, and increase insecurity. It should be observed, however, that the option for agrarian reform is typical of the non-business sectors of the elites. It is, by and large, the technocrats, liberal professionals, public opinion-makers, government employees, and union leaders who point to agrarian reform as the priority solution.

Table 7.6 Political Priorities to Combat Inequality in Brazil According to the Elites

Initiatives	%
Promote agrarian reform	31.1
Increase efficiency of public services	16.4
Control population growth	13.4
Deregulate the economy	10.2
Make income taxes more progressive	9.5
Expand social expenditure	8.5
Implement worker profit-sharing	8.3
Institute a wealth tax	2.6
Total	**100 (n = 305)**

In the research survey, the second largest concentration of replies regarding measures to fight poverty, summarized in Table 7.6, emphasizes the government's need to improve the efficiency of public services, while an effective increase in social expenditure is mentioned far less by the elites. Birth control, a measure that is equally the responsibility of the state, ranks third in the preference of the respondents. Redistribution through more progressive taxation is accepted only by approximately 10 per cent of the elites. This ordering of priorities tallies with that of the in-depth interviews: both highlight with equal intensity that the government is responsible for combating poverty and reducing inequality. We now turn to an examination of the convergences and divergences between the perceptions of the elites and those of Brazilian society as a whole.

Inequality as Perceived by Brazilians

Does the perception of the Brazilian elites regarding the social question and, in particular, inequality, correspond to the perception of Brazilians in general? In what follows, I seek to answer this question using the national survey on 'Perceptions of Inequality' conducted in 2001 as my source.[17] It should be pointed out, however, that the comparison here is derived from a variety of criteria. In a few cases, it is drawn from the answers to identical questions formulated in the two surveys involving Brazilians in general and the elite. At other times, the comparison is far more impressionistic, confronting the responses to the national questionnaire with the statements of members of the elite in the in-depth interviews. In this regard, the analysis that follows is of a merely exploratory nature, geared to proposing options for future investigation.

If we start from the observation in Figure 7.1, which shows what Brazilians consider the country's main problems to be, we will see that, although answers differ, there is some correlation between their opinion and that of the elites. In order of importance, violence, unemployment and the public health situation are the problems that affect the largest number of Brazilians. Figure 7.2 summarizes the responses to this same question that were obtained from the elites: inflation, education and health, and poverty. The differences encountered are, in part, related to the immediate context. In this regard, it seems natural that concern with inflation, still in the recent memory of the elites at the time of the survey, had disappeared in 2001, to be replaced by the major threat of unemployment. However, there are similarities and differences worthy of note between the perceptions of the elites and those of the populace in general. Thus, while the former excessively emphasize issues of education and health, for the people at large, health figures most prominently, with education being listed by less than 5 per cent of those interviewed as a central problem. However, the proportion of those who include poverty among the country's main problems is surprisingly consistent between people in general and the elite.

Might one find greater consistency between the view of the elite and that of those segments of the population that are ranked higher on the social ladder?

Figure 7.1   Principal National Problems According to Brazilians (%)

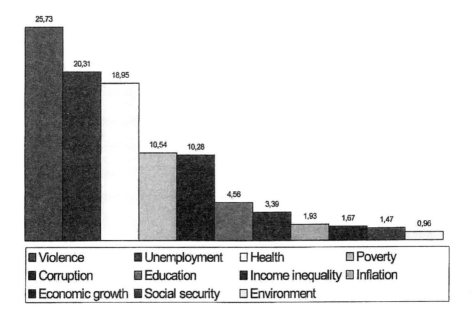

Figure 7.2   Principal National Problems According to Brazilian Elites (%)

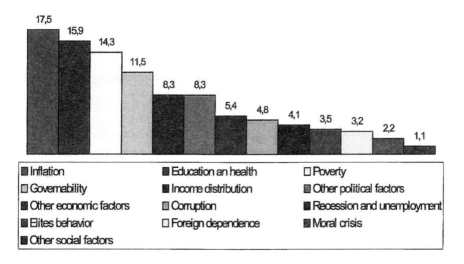

Using the education level of the respondents as a proxy for the latter, what conclusions can we draw? Figure 7.3 gives us an idea of how the response patterns are distributed with respect to the main national problems according to the education level of the individuals. It is interesting to note that, although they all stress the issue of violence, unemployment appears more prominently among those with no schooling. Another group that deviates from the norm consists of those individuals who have not completed university education (probably students), among whom the issue of corruption features high on the list of responses. Note also that the priority attributed by the elites to the problem of education is not so popular among Brazilians in general. And it is precisely among those with less schooling that education is less perceived as a priority problem.

There are other clear indications that the Brazilian population does not have as much faith in education as a strategy to assure equality of opportunity

Figure 7.3   Principal National Problems According to Brazilians with Different Levels of Education (%)

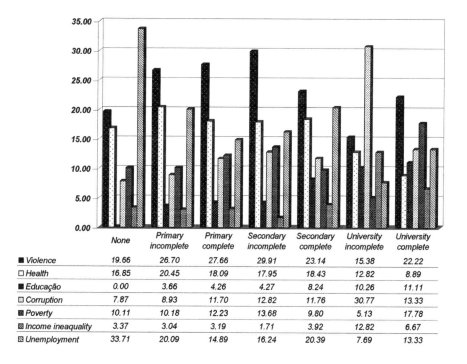

	None	Primary incomplete	Primary complete	Secondary incomplete	Secondary complete	University incomplete	University complete
■ Violence	19.66	26.70	27.66	29.91	23.14	15.38	22.22
☐ Health	16.85	20.45	18.09	17.95	18.43	12.82	8.89
■ Educação	0.00	3.66	4.26	4.27	8.24	10.26	11.11
☐ Corruption	7.87	8.93	11.70	12.82	11.76	30.77	13.33
■ Poverty	10.11	10.18	12.23	13.68	9.80	5.13	17.78
▨ Income ineaquality	3.37	3.04	3.19	1.71	3.92	12.82	6.67
▨ Unemployment	33.71	20.09	14.89	16.24	20.39	7.69	13.33

as the elites do. Observe, for example, that the belief in the luck factor as an element of social improvement and upward mobility is clearly more popular than belief in personal effort or even personal intelligence and ability. While this kind of fatalism is common to the various social classes, it is curious to observe that, contrary to what one would expect, it is particularly accentuated among those that identify themselves as members of the upper or upper middle class, as indicated in Figure 7.4.

Can we see the above opinion patterns as effective indications that Brazilians differ from their elites regarding faith in the principle of equal opportunity? The response to this question will certainly require more detailed investigation. For the time being, I would merely point out that there are indications according to which, while the elite believes in equal opportunity as a principle of distribution to be maximized, especially through adequate access to education, the population in general tends to believe that

Figure 7.4   Distribution of the Perception of Brazilians from
Different Social Classes Regarding the Importance of Luck in Personal Advancement (%)

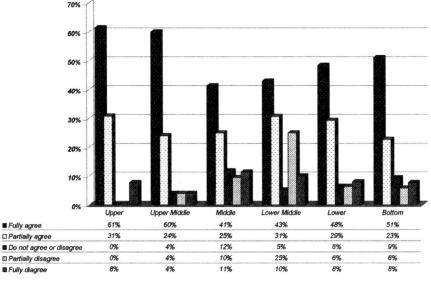

	Upper	Upper Middle	Middle	Lower Middle	Lower	Bottom
■ Fully agree	61%	60%	41%	43%	48%	51%
☐ Partially agree	31%	24%	25%	31%	29%	23%
■ Do not agree or disagree	0%	4%	12%	5%	6%	9%
▨ Partially disagree	0%	4%	10%	25%	6%	6%
■ Fully diagree	8%	4%	11%	10%	8%	8%

Note: Individuals were asked to express their evaluation of the statement:
'One must have luck to move up the social ladder'.

luck and random chance have greater weight in shaping opportunities for individual advancement. In addition, it must also be borne in mind that the attitude of the elite in this case is clearly normative. What it contends is that, with equal opportunities for education, anyone who makes the effort will have a chance to get ahead. On the other hand, the view of the people would seem to reflect a more cognitive stance.

Another question to be examined more fully is understanding how this 'fatalistic' view of life comes to be even more prevalent among those who define themselves as belonging to the most prosperous segments of society. It is common knowledge that this attitude is traditionally characterized in literature as being typical of the very poor or less enlightened who are, for that reason, less inclined to believe in volition and personal effort. Based on other responses collected in the survey, my theory is that the preference for an explanation based on luck would be an attempt to attribute the inequalities, which are so accentuated in this country, to random factors, thereby exonerating specific social players from any responsibility. In other words, the invocation of luck as an explanatory factor is an attempt to legitimize a pattern of distribution that runs counter to current social notions of justice and equity. In this context, it is interesting to see that the same class sectors that put more faith in luck are those that most tend to agree with the concept that to get ahead in life one has to be corrupt.

Even though luck is invoked to explain why some have so much and others nothing at all, a separate question concerns the attribution of responsibility for who should tackle the problem of inequality and poverty. Which players, for example, should be responsible for intervening to correct serious social needs? Here the Brazilian viewpoint coincides in large measure with that of its elites. For both, the state is undoubtedly the player responsible for finding solutions to the problem of inequality. The responses obtained in the national survey presented in Figure 7.5 tally closely with the opinions expressed by the elites in the interviews.

How should we interpret this common perception of the elite and the people, who predominantly attribute responsibility to the government when assessing the current situation and recommending which player should combat inequality? Since we lack the input to examine this question in

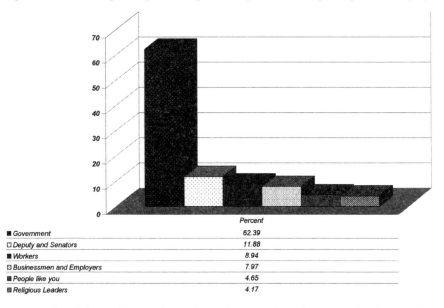

Figure 7.5   Who Is Responsible for Reducing Social Inequalities in the Opinion of Brazilians (%)

	Percent
■ Government	62.39
□ Deputy and Senators	11.88
■ Workers	8.94
▨ Businessmen and Employers	7.97
■ People like you	4.65
▨ Religious Leaders	4.17

greater detail here, I would merely point out that there are similar studies relating to other countries that enable me to characterize the view shared by the elite and the people in Brazil as 'state-oriented'.[18]

There is also a convergence of perceptions between the elite and the people regarding identification of what the priority social policies should be. Thus, improved public services and agrarian reform appear as the two main priorities for both, as can be seen in Figures 7.6 and 7.7. Note, however, that the order is different for the elite and the people. Improvement in public services is priority number one for the population, while agrarian reform takes the lead among the elites. It is also important to observe the weighting of these two priorities for the two categories. Thus, while approximately 70 per cent of the general populace selects them, this figure is less than 50 per cent among the elites.

Other factors restrict the attainment of such a margin of consensus between the elite and the people even further. In this regard, note, for example, that worker participation in company profits – which was the third priority chosen by Brazilians, with a weighting of 16 per cent – such a measure is seen less sympathetically by the elites (8.2 per cent)

Figure 7.6   Social Policy Priorities According to Brazilians (%)

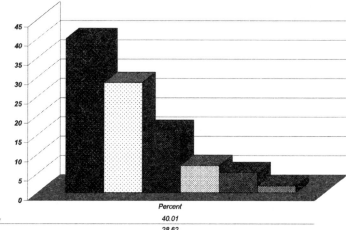

	Percent
■ Improved Public Service	40.01
▢ Agrarian Reform	28.62
■ Profits shared with employees	16.22
▨ Increased Taxation on the Rich	7.10
■ Reduction of Population Growth	5.30
▨ Privatization	1.80

Figure 7.7   Social Policy Priorities According to the Elites (%)

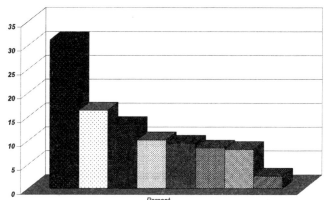

	Percent
■ Agrarian Reform	31.1
▢ Improved Efficiency of Public Services	16.4
■ Control Population Growth	13.4
▨ Deregulation of the Economy	10.2
■ Progressive Taxation	9.5
▨ Expand Social Expenditures	8.5
▨ Profit Sharing with Employees	8.2
▨ Taxation of Wealth	2.6

Although the elites and the people both agree with the contention that the government should fulfil needs and attenuate inequality and even agree on the two public initiative priorities to meet such needs, would they be in agreement regarding the efficacy of such social policies? As observed in the previous section, the elites tend to believe that the success of these policies is inherently linked to the country's economic growth. It should also be noted that the belief in the trickle-down effect of economic growth is very widespread among the populace as the key to reducing inequality. However, it is among those who identify themselves as belonging to the upper class that there is near unanimity that economic growth is a necessary condition to reduce inequality.

To summarize, I would say that a comparison of my research findings regarding the perception of the elites and those of Brazilian society show convergences and divergences between the perceptions, beliefs and values of the elite and the Brazilian people. One of the main points of consensus concerns the unequivocal attribution of responsibility to the government to deal with poverty and inequality. The belief that the state is responsible for doing something to reduce inequalities and meet social needs is generalized. There is also a strong convergence between the two categories concerning the political priorities to fulfil these tasks: improving the supply of government services and promoting agrarian reform. In the case of the national survey, we did not have information available that would permit us to ascertain the underlying motivations for this preference.

With respect to the differences in perception, perhaps the most significant aspect is the attitude towards education. As indicated above, while for the elites education constitutes the ideal manner for assuring equal opportunities, for the Brazilian people at large, this belief does not have the same appeal. In any event, as already pointed out, even where converging perceptions were identified, the intensity of the perceptions of the two universes surveyed must still be compared. To proceed with this attempt to establish if it is possible to speak of a broadly shared cultural code regarding inequality in Brazil, or if it would be more appropriate to conclude that there are parallel subcultures, new analyses and comparisons will be needed. The information gathered regarding the political culture of the elites and the Brazilian population is far from exhausted and this chapter should be seen merely as a preliminary exercise. The causes, consequences, and implications of inequality in Brazil from the point of view of the elites and the Brazilian people require further analytical efforts in order to help us formulate more efficient social policies.

Prospects for Change?

What are the current prospects for reversing long-established patterns of distribution? Would it be possible to expand the area of consensus between Brazilians and their elites as regards the changes to be adopted? Does the generalized recognition that Brazil has shameful levels of inequality constitute a positive sign for social reform? In fact, this recognition has existed for years though it has not contributed significantly to altering the status quo. Nowadays, although many consider the landslide victory of the Workers' Party in the presidential election of 2002 as a clear sign that the nation wants to settle its social debt, there are also signs that the changes different social sectors have in mind will not easily converge. It is probably the awareness of this fact that has led the new government to concentrate all of its efforts on an intense campaign to promote social mobilization around the fight against poverty.

In the official party line of the government the emphasis on stamping out inequality has been increasingly replaced by stressing the eradication of poverty. Despite its high profile image, the 'Zero Hunger' campaign, which is the social programme that epitomizes the new trend, seems to lean more toward philanthropy than to notions of equal rights. The strategy may possibly contribute to creating a more favourable environment for acceptance of institutional mechanisms required to enforce effective redistribution. If it proves successful in mobilizing feelings of solidarity, these may in turn contribute to foster the conditions for political and economic reform. The same old democratic mechanisms that made it possible to replace one political elite with another, which has galvanized people's hopes for change, will be critical for fighting inequality. Most of all, it will be new ways of perceiving what social rights truly represent that will make it possible to reduce inequality. To enforce effective reforms in distribution, a new common perception of justice will be crucial. To appreciate that citizenship rights restricted to a few constitute privileges rather than rights will be a critical aspect of social reform.

Naturally, a panacea of political cultural change is impossible to attain, nor are there cut-and-dried formulae to change the situation. However, perceptions, images, projects, and strategies are the stuff politics is made of. The way people and elites see poverty and inequality constantly interacts with ongoing political choice and the success of the latter depends on a fruitful dialogue with the former.

Acknowledgements

I am indebted to FINEP/CNPq/MCT, which funded my research activities into elite perceptions of inequality through its PRONEX programme. I am also grateful to IUPERJ and FAPERJ for granting access to the national survey on perceptions of inequality. I would also like to thank Carlos Hasenbalg and Celi Scalon for their generosity in sharing the results of the national survey with me.

Notes

1 See Richard Munch, 'The production and reproduction of inequality: a theoretical cultural analysis', in Richard Munch and Neil J. Smelser, eds, *Theory of Culture*, Berkeley: University of California Press, 1992.
2 Oscar Lewis, *Five Families; Case Studies in the Culture of Poverty*, New York: Basic Books, 1959. And from the same author, *La Vida: A Puerto Rican Family in the Culture of Poverty*, New York: Random House, 1966.
3 Exceptions here are Sidney Verba and Gary Orren, *Equality in America: The View from the Top*, Cambridge, MA: Harvard University Press, 1985, and Sidney Verba et al., *Elites and the Idea of Equality*, Cambridge, MA: Harvard University Press, 1987.
4 Louis Dumont, *Homo aequalis; genèse et épanouissement de l'idéologie économique*, Paris: Gallimard, 1977; and Louis Dumont, *Essays sur l'individualisme: une perspective anthropologique sur l'idéologie moderne*, Paris: Éditions du Seuil, 1983.
5 Reis, Elisa P., 'Sobre a Cidadania', in *Processos e Escolhas, Estudos de Sociologia Política*, Rio de Janeiro: Contracapa, 1998, pp. 27–41.
6 Amartya Sen, *Inequality Reexamined*, Cambridge, MA: Harvard University Press, 1992.
7 Douglas Rae, *Equalities* (2nd edn), Cambridge, MA: Harvard University Press, 1989, pp. 185–221.
8 www.ipea.gov.br/ipeadata.
9 Ricardo Paes de Barros, Ricardo Henriques and Rosane Mendonça (2000), 'The unacceptable stability: inequality and poverty in Brazil', in Ricardo Henriques, ed., *Desigualdade e Pobreza no Brasil*, Rio de Janeiro: IPEA, 2000, pp. 21–47.

10 Rodolfo Rodolfo, 'Mensuração da desigualdade e da pobreza no Brasil', in Ricardo Henriques, ed., *Desigualdade e pobreza no Brasil*, Rio de Janeiro: IPEA, 2000, pp. 81–107.

11 Ricardo Henriques, *Raça e Gênero no sistema de ensino: os limites das políticas universalistas na educação*, Brasília: UNESCO, 2002.

12 A detailed description of the elite survey is provided in Maria Regina S. de Lima and Zairo B. Cheibub, 'Elites Estrategicas e Dilemas do Desenvolvimento', Rio de Janeiro: IUPERJ, 1994.

13 The 'Elite Perceptions of Poverty and Inequality' project investigated the views of the elites from South Africa, Bangladesh, Brazil, the Philippines and Haiti. For a general description of the project, see Abram De Swaan, James Manor, Else Oyen and Elisa P. Reis, 'Elites' perceptions of the poor: reflections for a comparative project', *Current Sociology*, 48 (1), 2000, pp. 43–58. The results of the project appear in Elisa P. Reis and Mick Moore, eds, *Elite Perceptions of Poverty and Inequality*, London: Zed Books, 2005.

14 This view is different from that disseminated among the elites of Bangladesh, which put their faith in education, mainly through the formation of social capital, as a means to create power (*social empowerment*). See Elisa P. Reis, 'Percepções da Elite sobre a Pobreza', *Revista Brasileira de Ciências Sociais*, 15 (42), 2000: pp. 143–52.

15 Sidney Verba et al., 1987, commenting on p. 263 on the attitude of the Japanese, Swedish, and American elites in favor of a greater appropriation of resources for the poorest people, but against reducing the distance between themselves and the lower echelons, observe that this outlook represents a constant among elites in general.

16 Abram De Swaan, *In Care of the State*, Cambridge: Polity Press, 1988. The author develops the thesis according to which social policy initiatives in Europe and the USA originated in the development of a perception among the elite of the advantages of collectivism and nationalization of measures to offset the negative external aspects of poverty.

17 The national survey integrated the activities of the Instituto Virtual O Estado Social da Nação, chaired by Carlos Hasenbalg, with funds provided by the Fundação de Amparo à Pesquisa do Estado do Rio de Janeiro (FAPERJ). The research project is part of the collaboration of the Instituto Universitário de Pesquisas do Rio de Janeiro (IUPERJ) with the International Social Survey Programme (ISSP).

18 See, for example, Francisco Javier Noya, 'El Valor de la Ambivalencia. Las Actitudes ante la Meritocracia, la Igualdad y el Estado de Bienestar en España en Perspectiva Comparada', *Revista Española de Investigaciones Sociológicas*, 86, April–June 1996: 185–221. Based on the data analysed by Noya, it can be suggested that Brazilians distance themselves from the view most current in Western European countries, approaching the 'deviation' found by the author in Spain. As it shows, the preference of the Spaniards for government initiatives is much closer to the pattern of responses typical of post-socialist countries of Eastern Europe rather than of Western Europe. Using data of the 1994 ISSS survey on inequality, as well as other sources of information, Noya calls attention to the authoritarian political tradition as a possible explanation for the similarity of the view of the Spaniards and that current among post-socialist societies. Without a doubt, we could invoke the Brazilian political past or our cultural tradition to explain the similarity of this perception with that found by other authors in societies that do not have a solid liberal-democratic tradition. But searching for the historical genesis of the perception of Brazilians regarding inequality is not my intention at this juncture: I am basically interested in mapping out these views here as an aid to understanding the limits and potentialities for formulating and implementing specific distributive policies.

8

Globalization and Inequality in Rural China

Huang Ping

Introduction

If globalization is not an entirely new phenomenon, since the expansion of the market and capitalist society has been proceeding for several centuries, it is nevertheless a new problem for the nation-state system, which is an outcome of modernity and the very container of modernity.

It is an even greater challenge to China, for China, as an old and new country, is still *en route* to 'national modernization', in terms of the transformation and transition from an elderly empire to a young modern nation-state, and from a planned economy to a market economy.

The transnational, or transregional, flows of capital, technology, information, and, above all, people, are constituting challenges to the nation-state system in general, a system under which everything is organized by and within the nation-state system: with the result that there are national economies, national cultures, national identities, even national sciences, and so on. It is a problem for developing countries in particular, which are forced to catch up with the advanced nation-states but have not finished nation-building and state-building yet, at the very moment that the nation-state system is already challenged.

Examples can be seen from the rise of the 'new rich' in these countries, who are not necessarily the middle class, which constitutes the base for elections and taxes, for the 'new rich' are more transnational agents.

Under such circumstances, Chinese issues are considered as global ones. For instance, along with the massive rural–urban migration, the question of 'Who will feed China?' becomes a hot topic.

A hotter topic is perhaps the 'China Threat' discourse, at least among its Asian neighbours, including Japan.

But can China, through its transformation towards a 'modern nation-state', indeed gain benefits from the globalization, as some optimistic observers have predicted, both within and outside China?

Let us return to the problem of 'Who will feed China?'[1] One of the most significant constraints for China has been the unbalanced ratio between a fast-growing population and an increasingly limited availability of arable land, from the eighteenth century onwards, and almost all conflicts, rebellions, revolutions, and reforms have been intricately connected to these constraints.

Modern Chinese history shows that, regardless of their ideological banner, whoever resolves, or even simply alleviates, reduces, or postpones a reckoning with these constraints, will triumph. Dr Sun Yat-sen, Chiang Kai-Shek, Mao, and Deng – each had to tackle this problem.

During the Mao period, China tried to increase its agricultural production, especially food production by a capitalist land reform, and then by socialist collectivization – the commune system was set up to ensure food security. An unintended consequence was, ironically, the opposite, for the food supply suffered such shortages that, for almost two decades, both rural and urban China had to endure the consequences.

When Deng was in power again in the late 1970s, both the authorities and researchers believed that China at last found the key: a peaceful transition from the commune to the principle of 'household responsibility', an institutional innovation by farmers, and later from a collectivized rural economy to the re-allocation of arable land equally to each individual and therefore back to the household-based peasant economy.

However, alongside the rural reform, the long-existing problem of agricultural involution became noticeable. Due to a set of institutional arrangements, rural 'surplus labour' in southern China, especially along the Yangzi Delta, developed rural industries locally (known as Town and Village Enterprises, or TVEs), which were later recognized as the second great innovation created by the farmers.

TVEs were well known for their capacity to absorb a rural surplus. On average, during the 1980s, almost 10 million rural became employees of the TVEs every year. From the mid-1980s on, however, problems for the rural economy, rural community, and rural people became troubling, with less capital and technology input, lack of irrigation, and other kinds of services, a decline of education and the health care system, and heavier financial burdens for both rural people and local governments.

Fortunately there were several thousands of small agricultural experimental stations or research institutes at local county or township levels, established during Mao's time, which now became the main source for new seeds and applied technology. Contrary to the claims of official documents, the development of Chinese agriculture, especially food production, in the late 1980s resulted rather more from such applied or appropriate technologies than from the 'household responsibility' system.

The mid-1980s were important for China, not only because this was the time that the authorities launched the urban reform, which is sharply different from the rural reform in terms of its top-down approach, but also because this was the moment that the government opened three markets for the first time: real estate, stock, and foreign direct investment (FDI). Since it was widely believed that the rural problem was no longer a major issue, more attention was paid, and greater budgets allocated, to the urban sphere.

Alongside the three markets, agriculture and TVEs both suffered. Agricultural production continued to increase, which, as I have stated, was largely because of better applied technology, though at a slower pace and with a lot of difficulties such as a lack of market information. However, a drop in the rate of increase of farmers' income, the phenomenon dubbed 'the more food produced, the less income received', became common throughout China.

When FDI and joint ventures began to have their special development zones or sites in southern coastal China, TVEs became less attractive, as there were greater difficulties with skilled labour, capital, and new technology, and there were higher costs to be paid.

In the mid-1980s, farmers in all the central parts of the country tried hard to understand and to follow the market but, without any subsidies or even information service, almost every time they planted something, it was imported from overseas. There were some years in which farmers were trapped into the endless game of planting-cutting-down-planting-cutting-down, which was one of the key reasons they finally decided to give up and leave for urban areas for non-farm activities.

This was also the time that China had both high unemployment and high inflation in urban areas, which made ordinary Chinese people uncertain and uneasy, as it was long time since they had experienced such a convergence of difficulties.

The rural and urban problems mentioned above in 1986–88 were the main social causes of the chaos of 1989, a context which even now is not adequately analysed by China-watchers, who always pay too much attention to events at the top of society.

Unfortunately, once again, in order to attend to the dissatisfaction of the urban and elite sectors after 4 June, it was the rural people who paid the price. In 1990–92 the price for grain production was reduced continuously, and, as a result, the rural population have earned less and less from agriculture, especially from farming.

All of this was the background to the massive rural–urban migration, which seemed to suddenly become a headache for the urban authorities and residents. In 1993, during the Spring Festival, all the big cities were brimming with young people from rural China.

That was also the background to Leslie Brown's paper 'Who will feed China?', and to the beginning of the shift of my research from focusing on rural poverty to the problem of rural–urban migration.

Having said all this, I would like to ask: if Leslie Brown's conclusions are debatable, is the question he asks none the less worth asking? When young farmers leave their land, will their parents be able to take care of the limited arable land? What about their wives and children? Will China be able to release its huge rural surplus to urban and coastal areas for non-farming activities, especially for industrialization and urbanization? Will the migrants be simply the rural surplus or will they also be the main labour force? How many might there be? Eighty million in the second half of the 1990s, 120 million today, then within the next five to ten years might there be up to 200–300 million? Where will they go, to the big cities, the Special Economic Zones, the SEZs? Will they be able to find jobs, even if they are just temporary, seasonal, low paid, with no welfare or protection? Or are they more likely to become the new urban poor, going from landless to jobless and finally to homeless, and forming a new urban underclass? In terms of the size of the now surplus and later landless population from rural areas, which market will absorb them? ←

For more than fifteen years, those who have been working in FDI or overseas Chinese enterprises and joint ventures have not increased their salaries. As a result of the 1997 Asian crisis, lots of them lost their jobs. Many young females have been forced to turn to prostitution.

In the meantime, the State-Owned Entreprises (SOEs) have made huge lay-offs as a consequence of the governmental programme of privatization. The whole governmental agenda for marketization can be briefly summarized as assuming: lay-offs = higher efficiency = more tax-payers (rather than debtors) = enhanced capability of the state = more social welfare and social security provided by the state or local governments. ←

The most radical programme was launched in 1997, and aimed to complete SOE reform privatization for the sake of high efficiency, social security, and social welfare reform based on the principle of he-who-pays-benefits, plus the marketization of agricultural production, from a household base to a nationwide market, prolongation of the contract of arable land with rural households, and privatization of the TVEs.

On the other hand, the rural situation has been worsening since 1997, except in the coastal regions. The income of the rural population has been dropping for five years, which makes the situation very different from that in the 1980s, during which it was mainly 'surplus labour' which flowed from agriculture either into local industries or into urban areas for extra cash income or off-farm activities.

This time, on the contrary, more rural youth, whether considered as surplus or not, is following the migration tide, or joining the floating population. In the meantime in urban areas both SOEs and other enterprises have either made huge lay-offs or needed less labour.

According to the World Bank, by the end of 1999, there were over 100 million rural people in China who had less than one dollar a day in terms of purchasing power parity. The Asian Development Bank recently estimated that more than half of the total population in China, that is, more than 650 million people, have less than two dollars a day. Official data also showed that since 1997 16 million workers have lost their jobs from SOEs as a consequence of the SOE reform.

After some decades of system alternatives, socialist or not, China was in an embarrassing situation after the end of the Cold War (and of the USSR). Do you want to join in the global club or not? For the ruling elites, who have tried many options, now it seems that there is only one path to follow, the common road towards development. This is the basis for the globalism discourse, and also the rationale for the enthusiasm for the WTO, the Olympics, and so forth. All become the symbols of modernization and integration into the global arena.

Within a vision imagination of globalization, the whole process was considered as a win–win game. If there were some unfortunate consequences of development, they were considered either as the price you had to pay, or as a necessary stage you had to go through. Unemployment, the gap between the poor and the rich, regional disparities, and even corruption and pollution, were all, to a certain extent, justified. If there are losers, it is simply because they are not able to cope: they just do not have what it takes to win the competition. That is the law of the jungle.

One of the real challenges and dilemmas for the globalization discourse is how to deal with the question of the mobility of the world's population. Should the rural populations of China, India, and other developing countries enjoy the same opportunities to become free-floating populations? These populations are not a few thousand strong, nor a few million strong, but comprise at least several hundreds of millions of people. Should they also be able to partake in the free-floating opportunities provided by globalization? But where should they go and how should they get there?

The discussions and debates on the problem of globalization are continuing, and many are really original and fruitful, but if we cannot work out a system that can resolve the issue of the huge 'rural surplus' population in the developing world, these marginal but mobile populations will be left to walk down the 'universal road' to nowhere.

Recent Changes

During the final two decades of the twentieth century, the process of urbanization in China speeded up. A huge number of towns and cities expanded and the urban population with permanent residence status increased from 191.4 million (19.4 per cent of the total population) in 1980 to 301.9 million (26.4 per cent) in 1990, and up to 455.9 million (36.9 per cent) in 2000.

Dramatic changes have taken place since 1997. On the one hand, the living standards in bigger cities in China at least exceeds the level defined as 'comparatively well-off'[2] both by international standards – for instance, PPP – and in terms of ordinary people's observations or experiences. These cities are now competing in the race to 'realize modernization ahead of schedule'. On the other hand, the market prices for farmers to sell their agricultural products have dropped by over 30 per cent, and a slow growth rate of per capita income from agricultural production has been recorded in consecutive years.

In mid-western China, most of the grain-producing areas have seen decreases of annual income from agricultural production, despite increases in production output.[3] In contrast to the dazzling race among metropolises to 'catch the train to the World',[4] rural communities have deteriorated both quantitatively and qualitatively. Numerous village authorities are in heavy debt. Social order, infrastructure construction, irrigation projects, public health, and basic education – all have experienced decline.

As a consequence, not only farmers in big agricultural provinces such as Sichuan, Anhui, and Hunan, but also those in areas widely considered as 'conservative' and 'backward' such as Gansu, Guizhou, and Shaanxi, joined the 'rural labour migrants'.[5] These labourers are not necessarily always the 'surplus labourers'.[6] A paradoxical phenomenon has indeed developed in which the very limited cultivatable land in rural China[7] is increasingly deserted by the 'rural labour migrants' and their entire families.

It is estimated that the number of rural–urban migrants increased from merely 2 million in the mid-1980s to 70 million in the mid-1990s, and, in spite of high unemployment in urban areas and the lay-offs in the SOEs in particular, the number of rural migrant labourers leaped up to 90–120 million in 2002, according to researchers and official resources from the State Statistics Bureau (SSB) and the top authorities.[8]

Since 1997, partly due to the Asian Crisis and partly to the restructuring of the industrial system in China, often these rural labour migrants cannot even find temporary jobs with low pay, and have few welfare benefits and social security services.

Moreover, given the present levels of agricultural productivity and market demand, traditional agricultural production needs only about 150 million full-time farmers. That means at least another 180 million of the 329.83 million-strong total workforce currently in the rural areas – which does not include the labourers who will reach the age of 16–18 in this period – can be considered as a potential 'surplus labour force'. If we recognize the number of dependents who may also join these migrants, the total number of rural people who come to urban areas will be much higher.

From Food Shortage to the Three-Dimensional Rural Issue

For centuries, China was burdened by a shortage of food supplies. Famines always loomed large. Since the establishment of the Household Responsibility System in rural areas, most researchers assumed that farmers had finally received a systematic guarantee for the energy they expended in agricultural production, and that rural problems would at last disappear, or, at most, be only technical: for example, whether fertilizers and chemicals could be delivered to farmers in time, whether the prices for them were reasonable, how to promote advanced science and applied technologies, and so on. Later on would come the need to attend the issues of 'teaching' farmers how to adapt to market economy, how to rationally calculate cost and interests, how to become better off. More recently, the questions of how to raise their income level, how to reduce taxes and fees on them, and how to restructure the economic systems, and so forth, have come to the fore.

In recent years academic journals and the mass media have begun to discuss how to raise levels of agricultural production, to reduce the farmers' burden, and to adjust the industrial structure in rural areas, and these debates have become well known and attracted ever greater audiences. But, it is precisely during this recent period that 'the rural issue in the three dimensions', of rural economies, rural communities, and rural people,[9] has further deteriorated. Some top policy-makers have even asserted that the 'unstable foundations[10] will cause tragic earthquakes'.

The Rural–Urban Gap

One example is the rural–urban gap. Largely thanks to the rural reforms of the late 1970s, the rural–urban gap and regional disparity narrowed in the early and mid-1980s, but it began widening again from the early 1990s, and especially the mid-late 1990s (see Tables 8.1 and 8.2). The gap can also been seen from the perspective of the regional disparities between south-eastern, central, and western (north-western and south-western) regions (tables 8.3 and 8.4).

Table 8.1 Income Inequality in Rural China and Urban China (Gini coefficients)

Year	Gini coefficient in rural areas	Gini coefficient in urban areas
1978	0.212	0.16
1979	0.237	0.16
1980	0.238	0.15
1981	0.239	0.15
1982	0.232	0.15
1983	0.246	0.15
1984	0.258	0.16
1985	0.264	0.19
1986	0.288	0.19
1987	0.292	0.20
1988	0.301	0.23
1989	0.300	0.23
1990	0.310	0.23
1991	0.307	0.24
1992	0.314	0.25
1993	0.320	0.27

1994	0.330	0.30
1995	0.341	0.28
1996	0.323	0.28
1997	0.330	0.29
1998	0.327	0.30
1999	0.336	0.295
2000	0.354	0.32

Sources: *China Statistical Yearbook 2001*, SSB, China Statistics Press, Beijing, 2001.

Note: Some researchers argue that the actual Gini coefficient during 1985–90 in rural China may be lower than the data provided by the SSB (See Ravallion and Chen, 1999, *Oxford Bulletin of Economics and Statistics*, 61 (1), 1999, Blackwell Publishers, pp. 33–56.)

Table 8.2 Per Capita Annual Income and in its Use among Urban and Rural Households (Engel coefficients)[a]

Year	Per capital annual net income of rural households (yuan)		Per capital annual disposable income of urban households (yuan)		Engel coefficient of rural households (%)	Engel coefficient of urban households (%)
	Value (yuan)	Index	Value (yuan)	Index		
1978	133.6	100.0	343.4	100.0	67.7	57.5
1979	160.2	119.2	387.0	112.7	64.0	57.2
1980	191.3	139.0	477.6	127.0	61.8	56.9
1981	223.4	160.4	491.9	127.6	59.9	56.7
1982	270.1	192.3	526.6	133.9	60.7	58.7
1983	309.8	219.6	564.0	140.6	59.4	59.2
1984	355.3	249.5	651.2	158.1	59.2	58.0
1985	397.6	268.9	739.1	160.4	57.8	53.3
1986	423.8	277.6	899.6	182.5	56.4	52.4
1987	462.6	292.0	1002.2	186.9	55.8	53.5
1988	544.9	310.7	1181.4	182.5	54.0	51.4
1989	601.5	305.7	1375.7	182.8	54.8	54.4
1990	686.3	311.2	1510.2	198.1	58.8	54.2
1991	708.6	317.4	1700.6	212.4	57.6	53.8
1992	784.0	336.2	2026.6	232.9	57.6	52.9
1993	921.6	346.9	2577.4	255.1	58.1	50.1
1994	1221.0	364.4	3496.2	276.8	58.9	49.9
1995	1577.7	383.7	4283.0	290.3	58.6	49.9
1996	1926.1	418.2	4838.9	301.6	56.3	48.6
1997	2090.1	437.4	5160.3	311.9	55.1	46.4
1998	2162.0	456.2	5425.1	329.9	53.4	44.5
1999	2210.3	473.5	5854.0	360.6	52.6	41.9
2000	2253.4	483.5	6280.0	383.7	49.1	39.2
2001	2366.4	503.8	6859.6	416.3	47.7	37.9

Source: *China Statistical Yearbook 2000*.

Note: a: Percentage of income spent on food.

Table 8.3 Regional Disparity: Per Capita Income of Urban Households (Yuan)

Region	1981	1989	1993	1996	1997	1998	1999
Average	458	1,261	2,337	4,377	5,160	5,425	5,854
Eastern region	476	1,441	3,140	5,371	6,277	6,574	7,146
Central region	397	1,084	2,118	3,576	4,318	4,492	4,837
Western region	468	1,200	2,287	3,733	4,379	4,665	5,302
Ratio of Eastern to Central to Western	1.20 : 1 : 1.18	1.33 : 1 : 1.11	1.48 : 1 : 1.08	1.50 : 1 : 1.04	1.45 : 1 : 1.01	1.46 : 1 : 1.04	1.48 : 1 : 1.10

Source: Calculated from SSB, 1994, 1996 and 2000, SSB, China Statistics Press, Beijing, 2001.

Table 8.4 Regional Disparity: Per Capita Income of Rural Households (Yuan)

	1978	1985	1992	1995	1996	1998	1999
Average	133.6	397.6	784.0	1577.7	1926.1	2162.0	2210.3
Eastern region	164.1	513.0	1156.1	2346.1	2776.4	3154.3	3236.6
Central region	131.5	380.3	711.7	1422.3	1797.7	2054.3	2058.3
Western region	120.0	322.6	619.0	1051.6	1271.1	1476.4	1519.7
Ratio of Eastern to Central to Western	1.25 : 1 : 0.91	1.35 : 1 : 0.85	1.62 : 1 : 0.87	1.65 : 1 : 0.78	1.54 : 1 : 0.71	1.54 : 1 : 0.72	1.57 : 1 : 0.74

Source: Calculated from SSB, 1994, 1996 and 2000.

Figure 8.1 Rural–Urban Population Ratio in the National Census, 1953–2000

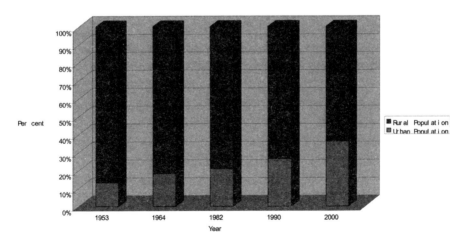

Source: China Statistical Yearbook, 2002.

Figure 8.2 Rural Labour in Agriculture vs. Non-agriculture, 1985–2000

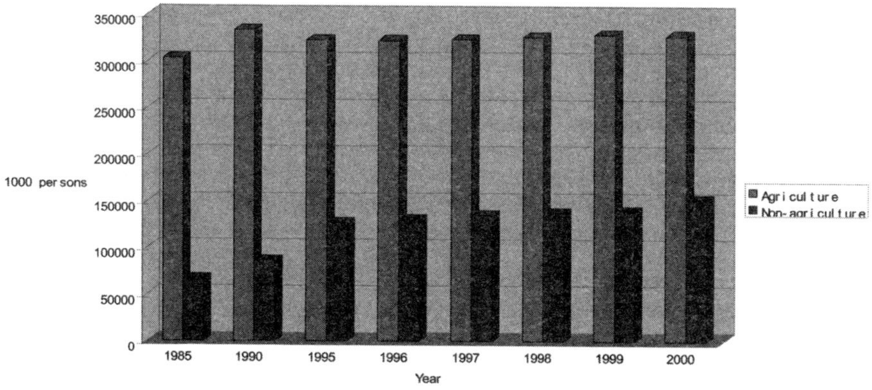

Source: China Statistical Yearbook 2001.

An important cause of rural–urban gap and therefore of rural–urban labour migration is that the income (including in-kind) increase from agriculture, especially grain production, started slowing down from the mid-1990s, whilst daily living expenses rose ever higher (see Figure 8.3). What is more, for four years from 1998 to 2001, farmers' income from grain production kept decreasing, a 2.3 per cent drop for 1998, 4.5 per cent for 1999, 4.7 per cent for 2000, and only in 2001 did it increase a little, but was still 15 yuan less than that in 1999, and 103 yuan less than that in 1997.[11]

It should be pointed out that rural income per capita includes earnings from non-agricultural activities. Of 2,366.4 of the average net income (yuan) in 2001, only 863.6 came from agricultural production (809.5 from planting), while average wage income reached 771; in other words, of the total 2231.5 productive income, that from primary industry took 1,165, and almost half was from non-agricultural activities (see Table 8.5).

The Decline of TVEs and the Increase in Migration

Another cause is that, in recent years, many TVEs are less capable of absorbing rural labourers, largely because of the privatization of the local TVEs, which were forced to make redundancies.

Figure 8.3   Income and Expenditure Structure in Rural Households, 1978–2001 (RMB/per capita)

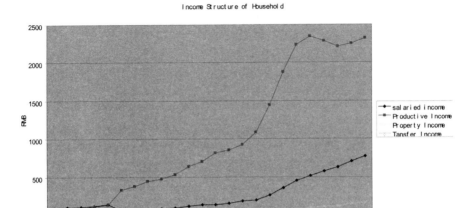

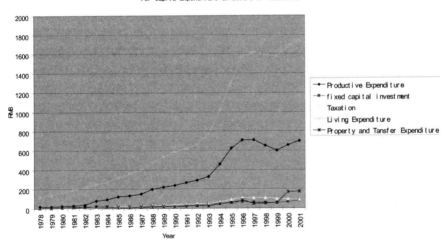

Source: China Household Survey Yearbook 2002.

Table 8.5　Per Capita Annual Net Income of Rural Households

Item	1985	1990	1995	2000	2001
total net income	397.6	686.31	1577.74	2253.42	2366.4
wages I	72.15	138.8	353.7	702.3	771.9
Household income	295.98	518.55	1125.79	1427.27	1459.63
Farming	202.1	344.59	799.44	833.9	863.62
In which planting	191.46	330.11	775.12	783.64	809.56
Productive income	367.69	657.35	1479.49	2129.58	2231.58
Primary industry	298.28	510.86	996.51	1125.34	1165.17
Secondary industry	29.47	70.68	287.24	488.89	532.61
Tertiary industry	39.95	75.81	195.74	515.35	533.8

Source: *China Statistics Year Book*, Beijing: China Statistics Press, 2002.

Rural–urban migration was seasonal or temporary mainly because of the existence of the 'Hukou System' (a system of residence registration, sharply dividing the population into urban and rural, and severely restricting rural–urban migration). A rural Hukou has provided rural residents with a piece of arable land and, perhaps more importantly, with social security, since they cannot take advantage of other types of social services and forms of social welfare, which are designed exclusively for urban residents.[12]

For many young rural labourers, it does not matter whether they belong to the 'surplus labourers' or whether they have proper jobs in the cities, as long as they manage to stay in urban areas, for whatever time period. The urban lifestyle is so attractive that many of the younger generations have actually never done any farm work in their home villages, when they finish – or even when they fail to finish – their primary education or junior mid-school, for they begin to join the other rural migrants. Some claim that even if they cannot find jobs, being in cities is enough. 'Litter collection in an urban area is much better than farming in rural areas', and 'Even if one day we pass away, we prefer being in the cities.'[13] A key to understanding migration is the wide coverage of TV networks, which as an unintended consequence of the governmental programme 'providing free TV sets to the countryside', reaches most remote rural areas. By watching TV programmes, even if it is simply the news, rural youth not only find a new way to kill their spare time, but immediately realize the remarkable contrast between urban and rural life.

Research shows that labour migration from rural to urban areas contributed 16 per cent of total GDP growth over the past 18 years. Migration can be regarded as one of the reasons that the national economy maintains a high rate of GDP growth – 9.2 per cent yearly from 1978 to 1997.[14]

The gap between rural and urban areas has been widening since 1993, when rural–urban migration became a nationwide phenomenon. With their hard work, high savings and frugal consumption, the tens of millions of rural labourers have helped their family members who stayed behind, and filled the gap at the village and household levels, either by sending huge amounts of remittances or loosening the land constraint.

A deeper change has been taking place, largely due to rural–urban migration, namely cross-boundary mobility. Boundaries are broken, or at least narrowed, between the rural and urban, eastern coastal and western central, agricultural; and industrial. It is these rural labourers, by moving to urban areas for seasonal or temporary non-agricultural jobs and by all types of hard work, who have actively changed the situation and narrowed the widening gap.

I would argue that, if we see the reforms in China since the early 1980s as being launched by the farmers when they began the Household Responsibility System, and if it was the farmers again who invented the TVEs which absorbed so many rural labourers locally during the 1980s, then the rural–urban migration can be seen as the bifurcated system of rural and urban living.[15]

A Historical Constraint

The huge rural population and the insufficiency of arable land is one of the most serious constraints for China's development, and also the most profound cause for rural labour migration. Rural–urban migration, at the same time, has contributed much to reduce the pressure. As shown previously, there are about 120 million who managed to migrate themselves to urban areas either within or without their counties by the end of 2000. Some earlier studies show that, with the migration of labourers, per capita arable land increased by more than one-third at both household and village levels.[16]

Some people have doubted or challenged the claim of the inescapability of the historical conditions manifested by overpopulation and insufficient land:[17] is it really true that the amount of land per head in China is much higher than that in Japan? Looking further at the statistics will reveal that the proportion of the agricultural population to cultivatable land in Japan is three times higher than that in China. Less than 5 per cent of the whole population in Japan is engaged in farming, while the percentage in China amounts to nearly 70 per cent. Another example is India, whose population is catching up with that of China but whose total area of land is smaller. However, the proportion of cultivatable land to the whole landmass of India is much higher than in China, and it has much better water resources. Finally, in both Japan and South Korea, the amount of land per head enjoyed by labourers is several times greater than that in China. China is still one of the countries in the world that has the least cultivatable land in proportion to its labour force. In addition, water resources in China are also very scarce and allocated unevenly.

The point is that no matter how important the internal structure and management are in the cases of Japan and the 'Asian Tigers', we cannot simplistically talk about 'Confucian capitalism' in abstraction from their specific historical conditions, especially as regards the geo-political and military conditions and economic-technological aid they received during the Cold War.

'To catch up with the advanced nations' might indeed be politically correct, but we have to consider whether the 'successful experiences' of Japan and the Asian Tigers are comparable to China. There is one neighbouring country, India, which has basically identical features to China: India gained independence during the same period of time as China established the PRC; both have larger populations than they have land; the majority of the populations in both countries are rooted in farming, and so on. Looking carefully, we cannot ignore a basic fact: although India has developed under the parliamentary democracy ever since Independence, its economy has not yet 'taken off'.

It is now unrealistic for countries such as China, India, Indonesia, and Brazil, and so on, to imitate the earlier pattern of development in which undeveloped societies were available for absorbing the 'surplus' workforce and developed societies colonized other territories. Even if the 'surplus labourers' from China and India were willing to go abroad, very few people can actually succeed because of the obstacle of the national frontiers of the receiving countries. In this case it would not be a matter of a few hundreds, or thousands, or millions or tens of millions, but of hundreds of millions!

Unemployment and Underemployment

The question for China is how probable it is that, in the coming two decades and given the slowdown of momentum and limits on resources, economic development measured by GDP will continue to be as fast as over the last two decades. Industrial restructuring in urban areas will also cause additional unemployment and lay-offs. It was estimated that, over the period 2001–05, there would annually be about 23 million young labourers looking for work in urban areas, but the cities could only provide fewer than 8 million job vacancies every year, that is to say, about 15 million would find it difficult to get jobs.[18]

From 1980 to 2000, the Chinese government focused on economic growth measured in particular by GDP and per capita income. 'Development is the number-one priority' has been the consensual social ideology over the last two decades in China. Researchers and government departments have become increasingly concerned with the employment problem in recent years, however. People have recognized that the increase in overall GDP or per capita income is not necessarily linked to an increase in employment. On the contrary, sometimes it is necessary to lay off workers in order to promote productivity and/or efficiency.

By the end of September 2002, the total number of employees in cities and towns decreased (by 3.62 million compared with that of 2001) to 110.053 million. Out of the 75.08 million working in urban state-owned enterprises, SOEs, there was a decline of 4,448 million compared with 2001. Among the 12.535 million in urban collectives, employment decreased by 1.713 million. Supposing China was to be able to maintain an annual economic growth rate of 7 per cent to 8 per cent, the market demand for fresh labourers would be around 8 million.[19] This means there will still be a huge number of unemployed, as many as one quarter of the total workforce. There is no doubt that, over the coming decades, unemployment will be a major social and economic problem among many others that China has to face.

There is an overlapping set of dilemmas in terms of the problem of unemployment over the coming 10–20 years. These are:

- The total labour force vs. structural constraints – there are not merely too many workers, but also many workers who are not necessarily suited to the changing market, as they have less experience and fewer skills. In the meantime some old sectors are declining and new ones do not need so many workers.
- The urban unemployed (including those laid off) vs. rural 'surplus workers' (or the underemployed) – rural 'surplus workers' are now facing a new challenge: competition with the urban unemployed and massive lay-offs from the SOEs, an unintended consequence of the re-structuring of the Chinese economy and of the marketization of the economic system;
- Existing labour forces vs. younger generations (new graduates/young adults) – as noted above, over the coming five years, there are about 23 million workers who need to find jobs in urban areas annually, but the yearly capacity of the urban industries is only 8 million, with the result that almost 15 million face the high possibility of unemployment.[20]

After years of research and effort, researchers and policy-makers have now reached the consensus that one of the priorities for China's development over the coming one to two decades is how to deal with the problem of employment.

As a result, a distinct modification of the early strategy has been made: it has been adjusted from giving overwhelming importance to GDP growth (as from the early 1980s onwards) to a more balanced approach to economic growth (GDP in terms of per capita income) and the multiplication of various types of employment, including part-time, temporary, monthly, weekly, or even daily and hourly work.[21]

Privatization of the Land?

Against such a background, issues of privatization of arable land and large-scale farming become tasks that are easy to talk about but difficult to deal with.

Very soon, there will be greater a outpouring of labourers – 'surplus' or not – in the wake of China entering the WTO and with further weakening of the rural economic and financial situation. Concurrently, in urban areas there will be more laid-off people, making it more difficult for rural labourers to compete for jobs in cities. The widening gap between rural and urban areas in terms of income, education, health, welfare, and social security further encourages such an outpouring. The challenge is: where should China be heading in the coming two decades? How can sustainable growth in both urban and rural areas be maintained?

If we further launch nationwide land privatization in the hope of increasing efficiency through the building of large-scale modern farms, where will the exit routes be for hundreds of millions of rural residents? Should they be forced to repeat the tragedy that took place in many Third World countries where numerous farmers were made landless, then jobless, and eventually homeless and hopeless?

Wen Tiejun and some others have shown that due to natural as well as historical constraints, especially the very limited amount of per capita arable land in China, it is impossible to copy or follow the patterns of Western models of urbanization, including the privatization of land in order to institute large-scale farms.[22] He suggests that in rural China the basic conditions for land privatization do not exist because the government cannot provide social security and social benefits for 800 million rural people in the countryside. My further point would be: for the hundreds of millions who live in rural areas, will the provision of social security and social welfare in the near future prove to be too luxurious?

A dilemma exists between greater work opportunities, and very basic labour rights/protections, including minimum income/welfare/benefits. Many argue that it is too early to establish an overall social security and welfare system for the whole country, they think a more realistic approach is to provide as many job vacancies as possible, even with low salaries and low-level welfare and social security. Some others argue that without basic rights such a situation would be not merely unfair, but also inefficient.[23]

I share the views of some scholars who feel it is to the advantage of China's rural workers that they have a piece of land, which is actually their safety-net, or their social security, which ensures that there will be no urban slums such as those in some other developing societies.[24]

The 'Three-dimensional Rural Problem'

If not the privatization of arable land, then what can be done with the 'three-dimensional rural problem'?

This problem has existed in China for a long time, but it has been getting more serious in recent years, especially since 1997, with a combination of: a) less income from grain production in many rural areas; b) a heaver burden on local finance at county, township as well as village levels, which in turn has led to, c) more fees collected from rural households, especially in agricultural provinces, and d) less governmental input in rural education, health care, and irrigation, but e) greater local conflict among/between villagers and village leaders or local officials.

Some leading researchers feel the solution for the three-dimensional rural problem lies outside the rural areas.[25] One researcher argues that a quicker development of cities and towns, plus further reform of the system, will be the key to resolving 'the three-dimensional rural problem'. 'As long as you hasten the process of urbanization, more off-farm employment opportunities will be ready for rural surplus workers, and "the three-dimensional rural problem" will have a way out. The logic is, the more you push the reform, the quicker the development [of cities].'[26]

But the question persists: with such an increasingly massive growth of rural labour migrants, what might happen in rural society?

There are some factors that restrict rural development in China. One of them is that marginal productivity of agrarian production, especially farming, has been low. Now agricultural production in China stands for about 16 per cent of its GDP, but the rural labour force constitutes 50 per cent of the total workforce. This indicates the low level of agricultural productivity in China. Under conditions of overpopulation and insufficient arable land, marginal productivity cannot be high anyway.

The point is that agricultural production cannot sustain itself, as farmers are no longer content with their low income from agriculture, and in many places funds for agricultural production have to be obtained from non-agricultural activities.

Field research in recent years indicates serious problems of medical care in rural China. While the growth rate of income from agricultural production has slowed down recently, farmers' routine medical expenses have increased rapidly. In many rural areas, medical treatment and prevention are managed separately and there is a tendency to commercialize medication.[27] Many farmers cannot afford to go to clinics, let alone hospitals, which are much more expensive and further away from villages. The need to take care of the sick has dragged many rural families into heavy debt.[28]

A small number of scholars have begun to talk about the possible decline of rural society. Along with rushed urbanization and speedy rural–urban migration, some argue, it is not necessarily true that those who leave their home villages are indeed the 'surplus' labourers: in some cases, they are also likely to be the core labour force in the countryside. A field village study conducted in 1995–96 shows that, in spite of the long-lasting dilemma of limited arable land vs. numerous workers, there is indeed a 'brain drain', for the migrant labour are mostly young males with a higher educational background, and the remaining workers are a combination of 'women, children, and the elderly'. Feminization and the decline of the rural community and agriculture is already taking place in some villages.[29]

Others claim that there is no need to worry, because the total labour force in rural China has been so large that they cannot stay in the countryside, for their own sakes or for the sake of longer term rural development.[30] It is thus not a real challenge, since

- they have choices, and some will not always find that the urban is better than the rural, and when urban areas do not provide job vacancies some will go home;

- when agriculture becomes profitable after structural adjustment, some with higher education will stay or go back; and
- market mechanisms will finally work, which can even out the rural and urban development.

My argument is that, in China, overpopulation and insufficient land have existed for centuries. But this on its own cannot explain why large numbers are leaving the countryside. This 'floating' population has to endure uncertainty in search of off-farm jobs in urban areas, social discrimination, and challenges of psychological adjustment. If rural residents could survive on limited cultivatable land, it would only result in differences between occupations, and rural workers would not have to rush into cities as their only means of life. But if agricultural productivity remains low for too long, farmers will be under more pressure to move out, and it is totally unrealistic to expect them not to go.

Rethinking the Problem

Independent thinkers recognized early on that modern Chinese history proves that the social problems in China in the final analysis are mainly problems of land, agriculture, and the peasantry.[31]

Now more mainstream people – top authorities, academic or policy researchers, some journalists and even fiction writers – have finally recognized that 'farmers are so poor, life in the countryside is so hard, and agriculture is in danger!'

In retrospect, in the decade after the end of the Cold War, almost all of us followed neoliberal nostrums, regardless of what -isms or what -ists we labelled ourselves. No matter how inaccurately we may understand/misunderstand neoliberal economics, basically we all believed that, in the cities, the reduction of the number of state enterprise employees or clearer distinctions of property rights could guarantee efficiency first, and then efficiency would ensure tax payment to the government. Only then would the government be able to allocate funds for education, health, pension, unemployment aid, and other social welfare or social security schemes. Meanwhile, in the countryside, setting up the Household Responsibility System was only a first step that would be followed by an even more important step of redistributing land to every household, and, further, the privatization of arable land. Only after the privatization of the arable land could the expected result – the concentration and mergers of small pieces of land and the modernization of farming – be possible, and only then could farmers become more competitive in a globally marketized economy.

These considerations do not seriously take into account the historically specific context of Chinese societies since the late imperial period. Further, we did not pay enough attention to the fact that even the development of the early industrialized countries in Europe and later Northern America has never been as simple as a 'rational choice'. In addition, the idea of minimizing governmental size and promoting a larger society did not take into account that it is the developed countries in general, and the USA in particular, which are the most powerful nation-states or nation-state groups with the strongest administrative and military forces in the world.

Europe is of course not in total agreement with the Washington Consensus, but its present levels of social welfare, security, legal, and taxation systems would be unimaginable had it not experienced a long history of colonization and exploration of other countries, and the migration of 'surplus labour' to other lands, to mention only a few 'common-sense' factors here. Other factors that have contributed to the prosperity of these countries include persistent social movements of workers, women, students, and peoples with different ethnic backgrounds, and the corresponding policy adjustments in these countries. Even if these factors were all non-existent or not important at all, it would take a long period of time – for Europe at least three hundred years, and for the USA, two hundred – to make the rationale of neoliberal economics prevail.

What then about China? In recent years, Chinese government officials like to use the phrase the 'market economy with Chinese characteristics'. When explaining what the Chinese characteristics were, both Mao and Deng usually referred to the 'enormous population with few land resources'. Of course this is merely 'common sense' again, and can hardly be claimed as a 'scientific discovery'. Sometimes it is too common-sensical to remember![32]

Concluding Remarks

The problems China has been facing in modern history are, in the the final analysis, concerned with rural development. From Dr Sun Yat-sen, through General Chiang Kai-shek, Chairman Mao Zedong, to Mr Deng Xiaoping, all their successes and failures were directly connected to how to deal with this problem. Yet the difference is that in the past it was the problem of the relationship between farmers and the land, and now it turns into one of how to solve the issue of transferring the rural population into non-agricultural communities and how to maintain sustainable agricultural growth and a humane rural livelihood. While in the cities most of us are trying to catch up with an age of high technology and the knowledge economy, few people pay attention to the fact that such kind of economy tends to exclude the raw labour-power that is over-supplied in China. If we simply let these redundant rural labourers 'die to be reborn', that is 'easier said than to be done'. Moreover, how can we promise that they can be 'reborn,' and who gives us the right to let them die first?

If we can solve such rural problems in three dimensions – rural production, the rural community, and rural labourers – in a careful and steady manner, China as well as the whole world will have a more peaceful and safer environment for future development. The key issue here is whether China can succeed in handling the task of transferring hundreds of millions of rural population to other sectors and urban areas in an increasingly globalizing world.

When this chapter was in draft form, China was completing its final step into the WTO. While some people claim that China's entrance is a win–win scenario, there is a realistic possibility of China's agricultural products losing their competitiveness. Optimists would say it is a good opportunity for implementing a restructuring of agriculture and transforming it along the lines of the modern farm model. Again, the real issue here is how and where we could possibly transfer such a large rural population. If such a transfer is possible, do we really think China's future will exactly resemble today's advanced countries? And even if we completely agree that all societies have been travelling the same course (urbanization, industrialization, privatization, globalization) over the last two centuries, this process will still take a long time to finish, during which we will have to experience twists and turns, and pay a great price for its accomplishment.

No doubt, benefiting groups in big cities (they are in fact groups of vested interests, including ourselves) do not want to see any more social revolutions, turmoil, 'peasant rebellions'[33] or 'ruffian movements'. On the other hand, can we simply imitate the process of land privatization or modern farming in the developed countries, letting the surplus population go out to explore new continents or colonize other peoples? If we cannot, we have to think of a 'third way' or 'fourth way', or 'X way'. We have to realize that we do not have to choose either 'black' or 'white,' 'left', or 'right'. We have to ask ourselves why in so-called 'backward areas', such as remote mountain villages, people enjoy not only fresh air and unpolluted water but also mutual trust, communal support, and a strong sense of confidence, while in more developed areas there are security gates, barred windows everywhere, and an unending supply of criminals and terrorists coming out of nowhere![34]

Notes

1 Leslie Brown, Worldwatch Institute, Washington, DC, 1994.
2 Xiao Kang.
3 Statistics show that in 1995, only 1 per cent of farmers did not receive any income in cash. In 2000, by contrast, this figure increased to 46 per cent. Lu Xueyi calculated and concluded that prices of grain products, vegetables, eggs, and fruits fell year by year since 1996. For grain production only, compared to 1996, the profits in 1999 decreased 32 billion yuan. Still, the total decrease of income amounts to 40 billion yuan, and over 160 billion yuan over four years! (Lu Xueyi, 2002; *Nongmin yu nongcun wenti* [On peasants and the countryside], Beijing: Sheke Wenxian Chubanshe.)
4 Jie Gui.
5 Referring in this chapter to those who left their home villages for at least three months annually – to urban areas, including nearby townships, county towns, and small cities within or out of provinces, or other provincial capitals and metropolitans.
6 By the end of 2001, the rural population was 795.63 million and rural labour 490.85 million, or 62.34 per cent and 67.22 per cent of the total population and labour force respectively (*China Statistical Yearbook, 2002*.) Of the total 490.85 million rural labourers, about 329.83 million were working in rural agriculture, while others were either working in local off-farm enterprises or had become 'rural labour migrants'.
7 There are 13.0004 billion hectares of arable farmland across the country and per capita acreage is less than 0.11 hectare (*China Statistical Yearbook*, 2002).

8 Chen Xinwen, 2002, in *www.ccrs.org.cn/big/rhcjncfyld.htm*; also Wen Jiabao, in *People's Daily*, 19 March, 2003; see also *Peasants' Daily*, 3 April 2003.

9 This refers to the rural issues occurring in China nowadays. It is important to note that, in my opinion, this does not mean there are three separate issues, but rather that there is one issue with three dimensions.

10 Mainly referring to a) the drop of income increase for rural people; and b) the financial debt for villages and townships.

11 *China Rural Household Survey Yearbook 2002*, Beijing: SSB.

12 Huang Ping, 1997, *Wei wanchengde xushuo* (unfinished interpretations), Chengdu: Sichuan Renmin Chubanshe.

13 Cf. Lau Kin Chi and Huang Ping, eds, 2003, *China Reflected*, Hong Kong: ARENA Press.

14 Cai Fang, 2001, *Ways and Means: Population Flows in China*, Beijing: Social Sciences Documentation Press.

15 Huang Ping, 1999, 'When young farmers leave the land: what will happen to rural development in China?', Cecilia Lindqvist, ed. in *Globalization and its Impact*, Stockholm: FRN, 56–67.

16 Huang Ping et al: 1997, *Xun Qiu Sheng Cun [In Search of Survival: A Sociological Study of Rural–Urban Migration in Contemporary China]*, Kunming: Yun'nan People's Press. It is important, however, to realize there are scholars who argue that, in spite of a rapid increase of rural labourers in non-agricultural sectors, in terms of both proportion and absolute number, the rural migrants and those who work in TVEs are actually coming mainly from among the new labourers rather than existing ones, who are remaining in rural areas engaged in agriculture, and the total number of the labourers in agriculture has not really decreased (Bai Nansheng, 'The Effect of Labor Migration on Agriculture: An Empirical Study', inRural Labor Flows in China' Berkeley: University of California Press, 2000; also cf. Figure 8.2.)

17 As seen above, China's cultivatable land per head amounts to less than 0.11 hectare. But in more than 300 counties in southern China, the figure is much lower than the average. Although farmers in northern China have larger land areas, they are more often the victims of drought.

18 Huang Ping, 'Social situation in China: 2002–2003', in Run Xin et al., *Analysis and Forecast Social Situation in China: Blue Print, 2002–2003*, Beijing: Chinese Social Sciences Document Press, 2003.

19 Ibid.

20 Ibid.

21 *People's Daily*, 13 September 2002.

22 Wen Tiejun, 2000, 'Sannong wentide shiji fansi' (Reflections on the three rural problems' at the turn of the 20th century); *Dushu*, 12, 2000.

23 Jing Tiankui, 2002, Zhongguo shehui baozhangde linian jichu (Philosophical basis of China's social security system); *Shehui Zhengce Pinglun*, 4 (4): 1–5.

24 Interviews with Cai Fang, Cui Zhuanyi, Wen Tiejun, 2003, in Frank Pieke and Huang Ping, 2003, 'China migration country study', presented at the DIFID Conference 'Migration, Development, and Pro-Poor Policy Choices in Asia', Dhaka, 22–24 June 2003.

25 For instance, Lin Yifu, 2003, 'Dui dangqian Zhongguo nongcun zhengcede jidian yijian' (Some suggestions for policies for contemporary rural China), *Jianbao*, 2003:

29, Centre for Economics Research, Peking University; Lu Xueyi, 2002, *Nongmin yu nongcun wenti* (On peasants and the countryside), Beijing: Sheke Wenxian Chubanshe; Wen Tiejun, 2000, 'Sannong wentide shiji fansi' (Reflections on the three rural problems' at the turn of the 20th century); *Dushu*, 12, 2000.

26 Zhao Shukai, interview, 2003, in Frank Pieke and Huang Ping, 2003, 'China migration country study', presented at the DIFID Conference 'Migration, Development, and Pro-Poor Policy Choices in Asia', Dhaka, 22–24 June 2003.

27 This tendency further aggregates the problem of medical care in rural areas, increasing in the long run the burden on the patient.

28 See Huang Ping, 'Stay Healthy: the Bottom Line for Development', *Horizons*, No. 7, 2002, Zhijiazhuang: Hebei Education Press.

29 Huang Ping et al., 1997, *Xun Qiu Sheng Cun*, Yunnan: People's Press.

30 Interviews of Cai Fang, Cui Chuanyi, 2003, in Frank Pieke and Huang Ping, 'China migration country study', presented at the DIFID Conference 'Migration, Development, and Pro-Poor Policy Choices in Asia', Dhaka, 22–24 June 2003.

31 This quotation comes from a letter to the top leadership by Li Changping, a young rural official who worked in townships for more than 15 years.

32 Here I am talking not about politicians but about ourselves as academic researchers. In my case, I did not read any of Philip Huang's books until a decade ago. He studied in detail the problem of agricultural involution in China caused by overpopulation and insufficient arable land. His research is indeed innovative. He did not simplistically imitate any established paradigms but went deeper into Chinese social history and thus discovered why Chinese peasants did not follow the seemingly obvious 'rational rules' that everyone can easily take for granted. See Phillip Huang, P.C.C., 1985, *The Peasant Economy and Social Change in North China*, Stanford, CA: Stanford University Press; 1990, *The Peasant Family and Rural Development in the Yangtze Delta, 1350–1988*, Stanford, CA: Stanford University Press. Similar research that impressed me very much also includes James C. Scott's *The Moral Economy of the Peasant* (1976, Yale University Press), and Samuel Popkin's *The Rational Peasants* (1979, University of California Press).

33 We should recognize the fact that peasants never staged a rebellion unless they really had no other way to survive.

34 Unfortunately, such places are becoming rare as the process of modernization is sweeping over almost every corner of the world. Decline and desertion are becoming the main features of the vast underdeveloped regions in the world.

9

Classes in the Making? The Russian Social Structure in Transition

Markku Kivinen

The Nomenklatura, Middle Classes and the Working Class

Let me begin by briefly sketching the processes of class relations at different stages of Soviet history.

Early Soviet Union/War Communism and NEP

- The class positions of old propertied classes are destroyed. People in those positions have to find new locations. This is complicated because of active discrimination based on class background.
- Locations of new ruling class are created and occupied by the Soviet intelligentsia and activists with a working-class background.
- There remain many petty-bourgeois intermediate and transitional classes in small enterprises and on farms, as described by Nikolai Bukharin (1924).[1]
- The working class initially disappeared almost completely with the Civil War, but from the early 1920s onwards it began to show signs of growth again, mainly stemming from transfers from the peasantry.

- The labour process remains collective and trade unions continue (intermittently) to defend the interests of workers against management.
- There are still very few new middle-class locations, and they are occupied by bourgeois specialists.

Stalinism

- Recruitment into the nomenklatura from outside the lists is increasingly rare, although the people occupying nomenklatura locations do change with the continuing purges. Privileges attached to locations increase.
- Intermediate groups based on small ownership disappear altogether.
- New middle-class locations (bosses, experts, and engineers) increase very rapidly and are occupied by people with a working-class background. The working class is not given power as a class, but it is integrated via 'affirmative action' politics.[2]
- At the micro-level of the planned economy there develops the ideological and social phenomenon of the 'labour collective', which unites all workers in the enterprise. Trade unions lose their independence. Privileged locations within the working class are created (e.g. Stakhanovites), offering some workers the opportunity to get ahead.
- In rural areas peasants become a target of internal colonization on account of strict quota for the delivery to the state of agricultural products.

Khrushchev's and Brezhnev's Era

- The position of collective peasants improves considerably as investments are poured into agriculture and delivery quota are slackened. Farming on private plots is allowed.
- The growth of the new middle classes continues, but the locations are more and more often occupied by people with a middle-class background. At the same time, however, the privileges attached to middle-class locations are reduced. Increasingly, party activists and members come from a middle-class background.

- Within the working class the position of core labourers is strengthened. Although the demographic identity of the urban working class is increasingly coherent, their way of life remains predominantly rural.

As we can see, the overall pattern of class structuration differs very clearly between different stages in the historical development of the Soviet Union. Forms of subordination and exploitation also differ at different stages. Changes in the classes' demographic identity and way of life also produce different class identities at different stages. The nomenklatura of the 1920s is after all a very different matter from the same social class 50 years on; nor is the 'sacred working class' of the Bolshevik project the same or in the same sort of position. There have been changes with respect to both the 'locations' appearing in the class structure and the 'people' occupying those places.

The official classifications also change, as do the practices connected with them. Sheila Fitzpatrick even argues that the process of revolutionary ascription produced social entities that looked liked classes, and were so described by contemporaries, but might more accurately be described as Soviet *sosloviia*, coming close to the estate categories in the Russian empire.[3] My argument is that all these identities and categorizations were seen in the contexts of a moral space of classes at the centre of which is the sacred working class.

Although Marxism portrayed the bourgeoisie as the main enemy of the working class, the Bolshevik sacred evolved not in relation to one single enemy but within a field of several different class forces, each of which required its own cultural interpretation. In fact it was necessary to construct an entire social space in which different classes had their own virtues and vices.

The proletariat is the single most important factor in the whole social construct; all other social classes differ from the desirable virtues in their own ways. There are many different dimensions:

- proletariat – bourgeoisie (hedonism, calculation);
- proletariat – aristocracy (snobbery and experimentation);
- proletariat – peasantry (carnivalism);
- proletariat – bosses (bureaucratism); and
- proletariat – intelligentsia (individualism, daydreaming).

The proletarian virtues were defined separately for each dimension. The proletariat had the following characteristics: they were honest and straightforward; faithful to the party; committed to large organizations and strong central authority; disciplined; and collectively minded.

The bourgeoisie in general and the kulaks in particular are pleasure-seeking and calculating:

> But the Kulaks
>   had heaps of both butter and flour.
> Kulaks,
>   they weren't no boobies;
> hid and hoarded
>   till a fitter hour
>   their grain
>   and their greasy
> rubles.
> Hunger
>   hits harder,
>   kills surer than bullets.
> You need a steel grip here,
>   not cotton-wool lenience.
> So Lenin sets out
>   to fight the kulaks
>   by food requisition teams –
>   grim expedients.
> How could the very notion
>   of democracy
>   at such a time enter
>   any fool's head?!
> At 'em
>   and none of your mincing hypocrisy.
> Only iron dictatorship
>   to victory led.[4]

The antitheses of the bourgeoisie's vices were proletarian straightforwardness and the choice of the necessary.[5]

The cultural construction of classes is not just a matter of ideology and discourse; it is a real practice of social classification and definition. In the 1920s, for instance, virtually all Soviet institutions exercised some kind of active classification on the basis of class categories.[6] Although the bourgeoisie (which in fact was a mixture of Russian aristocracy and bourgeoisie) had been liquidated as a social class with the disappearance of social positions based on capital and land ownership, there still remained large numbers of people of the wrong origin, so-called 'formers' (*byvshii* is the Russian term, corresponding to the category of *cidevant* from the French Revolution). These people were not eligible for higher education, for party membership, or even for membership of the party's youth organization, Komsomol. If their class background came out in the open, they would lose their vote, and possibly even be evicted or deprived of their ration cards. However, the discrimination was entirely haphazard because the internal passes introduced for purposes of class identification had been discarded in connection with the revolution. In contrast to the situation in India, the 'casteless' in the Soviet Union had no place at all in the traditional classification system.[7] The 'formers', 'kulaks', and 'NEP men' could escape their class position only by moving to a new environment. Indeed, the disclosure of people's real class positions was part and parcel of activists' political practice.

The transition to the Stalinist period proper from the early 1930s onwards was highly contradictory as far as class politics was concerned. On the one hand, internal passes were introduced to indicate the holder's class position. This, according to Sheila Fitzpatrick, clearly ties in with the old Russian classifications based on estates. Indeed, at least as far as peasants were concerned the similarities were quite striking.[8] Not all *kolkhoz* members were even granted a pass, but they had to apply to the *kolkhoz* to get permission to move, just as they had earlier had to turn to the village community. Each Soviet estate also had its own privileges clearly demarcated. On the other hand, class position was beginning gradually to lose its political significance. The struggle against class enemies transformed into a hunt for 'people's enemies'. In Stalin's class analysis, Soviet society was divided into workers, collective peasants, and the intelligentsia. This division was at sharp variance with real socioeconomic trends in development, for it was precisely in Stalin's era that the nomenklatura gained a firmer hold on power and the new middle class emerged as a significant social category.

Although the majority of new entrepreneurs during the NEP period did not have a bourgeois background, they too were regarded with suspicion.[9] If nothing else, it was suspected that all they had in mind was an easy life. NEP men were represented as ruthless exploiters who would walk along with great self-conceit, their well-fed and well-dressed wives on their arms.

The bosses, for their part, represented a different kind of threat. Although Soviet factories had a one-man management system (which Kaganovich described by saying that when the manager does his rounds on the shopfloor, the earth must tremble), even managers could not feel safe. One of the deviations attributed to managers was their bureaucratism. As many managers tried to contain the effects of the demonization of reality at their factories or to reduce the chaos caused by the Stakhanovist movement, the 'beloved leader' himself would intervene.[10] Any specialists who tried to prevent the Stakhanovist movement from below, he said, would have their teeth kicked in. And he was not speaking rhetorically.

In the family, in the workplace, in the party, everywhere the proletariat represented steadfastness, discipline, collectivism. Although labour collectives had been dismantled and although all forms of organized interest defence had been made impossible, collectivity remained rhetorically an important element of Soviet life.

The collectives of the Stalinist era (in which the party played an important leading role) were in fact one interpretation for this fascinating concept that for decades had seemed to offer an important expression for the revolutionary way of life.

In Russian history collectivity has had the following, closely interwoven meanings:

- collectivity related to the rural village community (*obshchina*) and Orthodoxy;

- syndicalist emphasis on workers' experience;
- collective and state ownership;
- direct power of the working class in factories and labour collectives; and
- collective culture, housing, and family forms.

From the October Revolution until 1930, these dimensions of collectivism appeared simultaneously and were closely interwoven in the effort to set up communes. In rural areas peasants pooled their possessions and tried to share both their work and their everyday life in the spirit of mutual assistance and extended family, often inspired by the Orthodox faith. In urban housing communes people shared not only their possessions but everything else, too; their time and space, their joys and worries, friendships, and sometimes even love. Labour collectives tried to operate in a spirit of solidarity and equal incomes.[11] All this came to an abrupt end during the first five-year plan. All that remained (apart from state ownership) were the collectives of workplaces and residential areas, where even very personal matters were still dealt with collectively during Stalin's time. There also remained the rhetoric, which stressed the absolute superiority of collectivity.

As early as the 1920s the main view in the party was that the threat of bourgeois and petty-bourgeois influences was ever-present. Sometimes these influences were seen quite literally, for instance in the ties of workers to the countryside, but any 'deviation' or way of life could become classified as bourgeois or petty-bourgeois.

Individualism was represented not only by the petty bourgeoisie but also by the intelligentsia, which in general was unreliable, wavering, and cowardly. By the mid-1920s the word *intelligent* began to assume negative connotations. During Stalin's reign sentences were directly based on this kind of false class background:

So in what sense was the habitus of the proletariat really the foundation for Bolshevik politics?

First, there did not exist in Russia any set proletarian habitus that Bolshevik politics postulated. In fact since the Civil War the proletariat had more or less completely disappeared as a socioeconomic category. Nevertheless, when the first five-year plan got under way over half of the working class had been in employment before the Revolution and the majority were second-generation workers. However, during the period between 1928 and 1940 the working class increased threefold in size, with the majority of the new recruits coming from the countryside. The cultural formation of the proletariat is closely interwoven with the process of its economic and social formation. There is a constant tension between the real worker and the constructed 'proletariat'.

Second, there are certain sides to the proletarian consciousness that are never made explicit but that are nevertheless utilized for purposes of political mobilization.[12] These include sexism and deep-seated prejudice against mental labour (which is regarded as weak and feminine). The feelings of strength and softness that are related to sexism can be used for instance in making a distinction between really important (hard) economic and political questions and, on the other hand, themes concerning family policy or women's position. The reserved attitude towards mental labour can be used for mobilizing campaigns against the 'bourgeois intelligentsia' or the 'industrial party', for example.

Third, some traditional elements of proletarian consciousness (such as egalitarianism) constitute a significant cultural resource for Stalinist politics. On the other hand the kind of proletarian collectivity which involves resistance and the promotion of one's own interests is made impossible by heavy repression. As the significance of professional and managerial positions increases, egalitarianism is denounced as sectarianism.

It is clear that the official version of working-class power is at variance with the real dominant position of the nomenklatura; political processes develop and unfold out of this tension. In fact the relationship between the working class and bourgeoisie represents one fundamental aspect in a more general strict duality of the Bolshevik culture (Figure 9.1).

If it was the opposition between the bourgeoisie and the working class that gave the impetus to the revolutionary action of workers, the nomenklatura appears as an unintended result of the project and becomes a taboo. As Michael Burawoy has pointed out, it is far more difficult to legitimize

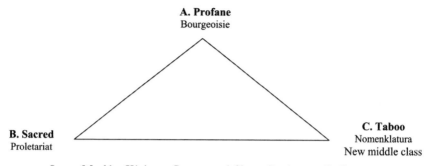

Figure 9.1   The Structure of Russian Culture: Binary Code and Unsuitable Reality

A. Profane
Bourgeoisie

B. Sacred
Proletariat

C. Taboo
Nomenklatura
New middle class

Source: Markku Kivinen, *Progress and Chaos: Russia as a Challenge for Sociological Imagination*, Helsinki, 2002 .[13]

privileges in a system that does not accept inequality.[14] This makes the nomenklatura an absolute taboo in the public sphere (Figure 9.1). At the everyday level the nomenklatura proper, for the absolute majority of people, was only a distant reality: 'they' (*oni*) were out there somewhere.

New elements began to appear in the class structure from the 1930s onwards. When Stalin at that time criticized excessive equality, he was in effect appealing to the new social forces that Stalinist politics itself had produced. These new social forces were precisely the new middle class: professional-managerial groups. These were major groups produced by Stalinist industrialization, education, and bureaucratic expansion; our 'own intelligentsia' as opposed to the 'old bourgeois intelligentsia' with whom all accounts had been settled in the early 1930s.

To some extent the rapprochement with the middle class and the growth of the middle class was a conscious policy on the part of the Stalinist administration. Having said that, there was also a definite measure of spontaneity about these processes that together contributed to the growing significance of middle-class groups.[15]

If proletarian collectivism was associated with public life, private life since the 1930s was increasingly characterized by ambitions of upward social mobility. With the growth of the new middle-class groups the requirements of collectivism began to lose their relevance with regard to the maintenance and development of the system. What was now needed were hard-working, individually committed citizens.

So, Soviet society was not a classless society. Classes existed there both as multi-layered cultural constructs and practices and as socioeconomic realities. There was constant tension between these different levels, which explains the seemingly strange coincidence of class positions gaining official recognition with empirical class analysis becoming impossible. The census of 1926 is the last major effort in this direction. It is only with the dawn of perestroika that empirical studies of the social structure of Soviet society are resumed.

A new, quite dramatic feature that emerged after the Second World War was the exclusion of the working class from the position of central social subject, i.e. the breakdown of the habitus codes described above. What emerged instead was what Vera Dunham has described as a 'great contract'. Successful managerial groups emerged as the main new partners for Stalinist administration.

The Khrushchev period, to some degree, marks a new proletarian turn in Soviet politics; and not only a proletarian turn but even more a turn in the direction of the peasantry. Khrushchev had already put forward some ideas during Stalin's period with the aim of improving the position of the peasantry (proposal on agro-cities in 1949). When Khrushchev came to power he got rid of the strict delivery quotas imposed on *kolkhozes* and a massive agricultural investment programme was launched. Foodstuffs production and consumption soon began to increase quite rapidly.[16] By the early 1960s, the Soviet Union had reached the southern European level of nutrition intake. (All this happened in spite of the failure of both of Khrushchev's major campaigns, the introduction of new land and the farming of maize.) The position of peasants improved markedly, but so too did the standard of living in the urban working class improve, when minimum wages were raised and pension systems were created. By contrast, the professional-managerial groups did not achieve the same sort of clearly privileged position under Khrushchev and Brezhnev that they had during the last years of Stalin's rule.

Both in people's everyday life and in political decision-making there developed a strained relationship between the official code system and the upward mobility of the middle classes (Figure 9.1): upward social mobility in private life; and on the other hand identification, especially through mediating organizations. Burawoy's analysis of socialism's specific legitimacy problem clearly shows this tension.

The Problem of the Middle Classes

In advanced capitalist countries a distinction is customarily made between two different middle classes: the old and the new. The old middle class refers mainly to small entrepreneurs and farmers, the new middle class comprises bosses and experts, i.e. managerial and professional groups. The distinction dates back to Karl Kautsky, who distinguished between the petty bourgeoisie and the *neue Mittelstand*.[17]

In Russia the weakness of the middle class was discussed even before the Revolution. It was pointed out that the bourgeoisie in Russia was fairly small, and the same was said of the professions: doctors, lawyers, engineers, and teachers.[18] Strictly speaking this was not quite true, however, because these professional groups had a strong representation among Russian liberals. Besides, Russia had its intelligentsia, and that certainly was not an insignificant force.

The absence of any analysis of the middle classes is the main problem of traditional class theories of Soviet society and deserves closer attention. Indeed, in general the question of the middle classes is one of the most fundamental issues of sociological analysis.

In state socialist societies there was of course no middle class based on ownership. In some people's democracies there were independent farmers, but their holdings were very small; the majority had no more than ten hectares of land. Russia, by contrast, had neither independent peasants nor an urban petty bourgeoisie. Now, after more than sixty years, these groups are being revived with the process of privatization. The discussion here focuses on the middle class, which in the West is traditionally known as the new middle class, but which in the current situation in Russia is 'old' in the sense that it has inherited its locations from the Soviet era. I will try to show how this is related to the question of professional development and the formation of managerial hierarchies. These processes are quite different in capitalism and in Soviet socialism.

The key strategic solution in my own work[19] is to link up class theory with the sociology of work. In the conceptualization of collective power resources at the level of the labour process, it is essential that we do not content ourselves with the simple juxtaposition of two subjects (as in classical Marxist analyses), but also take into account the power resources possessed by the new middle classes and the related forms of organizing the 'relations in production'. This leads to the discovery that 'mental labour' is no simple concept, but comprises different forms involving different kinds of power resources, strategies, and historical processes. A crucial role in the analysis of the power resources of the new middle classes is played by professionalization. Indeed, it is precisely in relation to 'professional autonomy' that all other forms of mental labour should be characterized.[20]

Although the position and situation of middle classes in the Soviet Union were in many ways dependent on their relationship to the nomenklatura and to the party apparatus, it would be far too simplistic to suggest that these class groups simply served the nomenklatura.[21] We need instead to look more closely at the underlying processes of class relations.

The processes of class relations that lie behind different forms of mental labour can be conceptualized as follows:

- professionalization;
- evolution of managerial hierarchies;
- evolution of scientific-technical occupations;
- separation of clerical work from management and the degradation of its content;
- the development of caring as a specific form of wage labour, its professionalization;
- changes occurring in the position and qualification requirements of skilled workers; and
- the position of small firms in the economic structure and the development of distinctive forms of organization (e.g. paternalism).

To construct an adequate picture of class relations in socialism and post-socialism, we need first of all to ask how these processes differ in socialist and capitalist society. It is only after this question has been addressed that we can move on to the interests and special nature of the middle class.

There is a tendency in Western critical sociology to reduce the mental labour of the middle class to mere barbarism and control, with the traditional values of working-class culture representing the opposite pole. But doesn't the labour of the middle class have any 'civilizing effects'?[22] If the antagonism between the new middle class and the working class is postulated on grounds where the development of the welfare state, health care systems, and school systems are regarded as mere repression, this leads to a politically very clear conclusion. This is the line that Pol Pot pursued in Cambodia.

In present-day Russia, key objectives include the creation of a health care system and a modern and ecologically viable technology, the rebuilding of the education system, and the modernization of transportation and communication.[23] None of these can be accomplished by a radical return to the former working class ways of life. All humane or left-wing reform programmes must accept that professional knowledge and professional practices are inevitable.[24] The time of an all-embracing critique of professions and the middle class in social theory is over.

The position of middle-class groups in the Soviet Union is not, however, distinctive only in terms of their relationship to the working class. The professions also have far more restricted chances to use their own power resources.[25]

First of all, professional organizations did not have the same sort of power to fend off external interventions in the definition of job tasks; second, the labour market did not operate as a pure market mechanism but was always to some extent subordinated to the political allocation of the labour force. No real professional markets existed, and all middle-class people worked in large bureaucracies. Professions had only very limited opportunity to wage a struggle for professionalization in public, which in the West has become more and more important. It was quite clear that professions in the Soviet Union had very limited possibility to control the 'production of producers', i.e. the apparatuses of education and the numbers to be trained. There developed several fields in which much larger numbers of professionals were trained than in the West; this was true, for instance, of medical doctors and engineers. Closely related to this was the feminization of many fields that in the West were clearly male-dominated.

The process that shaped the position of managers and the engineering and technical intelligentsia (and that was certainly not of their own making) was the complete 'politicization' of society. This, however, was no straightforward process void of conflicts and contradictions. In relation to managers and engineers it involved two clearly different interpretations of the relationship between mental and physical labour.

The first, functionalist interpretation has it that the distinction between mental and manual labour is irrevocable. Engineers and managers are seen as representatives of technology and science and the development of the forces of production, and they have every reason to expect special treatment and privileges.

The second interpretation regards these groups as dubious bourgeois intellectuals who are trying in every conceivable way to damage the efforts to build socialism. Closely related to this are the trials, the so-called Shakhty affair, the case of the industry party, and so on. This is also the frame of interpretation in which we find the occasional campaigns that encouraged workers to attack the dubious intelligentsia. This may be defined as a class struggle interpretation in which the scientific-technical intelligentsia represents the dubious class enemy.

There is a constant tension between these interpretations and the strategies of 'politicization' that are grounded in these interpretations. However, they do not follow one another clearly and unambiguously, even though the functionalist interpretation is dominant in the NEP period and the class struggle strategy predominates, especially during the first five-year plan.

However, the critique was aimed specifically at the 'bourgeoisness' of the intelligentsia, not at the positions of managers or the intelligentsia as such. In this sense Stalin's strategy was less radical than Pol Pot's, who tried to get rid of both places and the wrong kind of people at one and the same time.[26] All views on workers' rule in production were rejected from very early on as syndicalist. The one-man management system was complemented by the '*troika*', which represented enterprise management, trade unions, and the leadership of the party organization. Eventually the representation of trade unions was marginalized, leaving a '*dvoika*'. During the early years of Soviet rule the dual power of the party and bourgeois experts was often seen in company managers leaning back on a political career, whereas the chief engineer was a 'bourgeois specialist'. Over time these career structures became increasingly interwoven, however.

The process of industrialization brought a sharp increase in the number of managerial positions and in the number of engineers. Between 1929 and 1934 the number of managers increased almost sixfold. During the same period the number of industrial workers and employees doubled, whereas the number of engineers and technicians increased more than fivefold. The industrialization of the Soviet Union implied a rapid increase in 'mental labour' or 'middle-class positions'.[27]

The whole economy was about bargaining and negotiation between company departments, between enterprises and ministries, between different ministries. Although there were clear differences between managers and the working class in terms of wages, for instance, in key industries (such as metalworking), the wage differentials were several times greater than in less important industries, such as the textile industry.

Although many workers and their children were given the opportunity to advance to management positions and to the technological intelligentsia, the relationship between the working-class and middle-class groups remained highly problematic. Problems were caused at least by relations of authority in the workplace as well as by middle-class privileges.

The relative position of lower white-collar employees in socialism was in many ways much poorer than that of their colleagues in capitalism.[28]

- Their salaries were lower than in any other urban wage-earner group;
- they had no real opportunities for career advancement – although this did not apply to the few men in these positions;
- their level of job satisfaction was exceptionally low;
- they enjoyed far less social prestige in their occupations than skilled workers; and

- unlike skilled craftsmen, white-collar employees in socialism did not generally receive training on the job. Their tasks were considered highly routine and easy to learn. Even with the introduction of computers the relevant debate has not raised the issue of changing qualification requirements in clerical work.

In comparison with white-collar employees, craftsmen and skilled workers were held in fairly high regard in socialism, for both ideological and cultural reasons. This is reflected in wage levels, the prestige attached to the job, and the amount of on-the-job training. The exceptionally privileged status of skilled workers was particularly outstanding. However, there remains some disagreement as to how the cultural difference between the factory and the office has developed in socialism.[29]

A Potential Middle Class?

The basic idea that informs my analysis of the middle classes is that the working class proper consists of those wage workers who have become alienated (in a strong and empirically unambiguous sense) from their work. This refers to such wage workers who have no decision-making authority concerning their work organization, either on investments, tools and equipment, or basic working methods. Second, the working class do not have control of their work in the sense of being able to plan the product of their work or even the performance of the job. Middle-class wage-earners comprise those groups who have had the power resources they need to safeguard their autonomy. Strong middle-class groups comprise professionals, managers, and engineers. Skilled workers, workers in care and reproduction, and certain autonomous groups in clerical jobs have less power resources and features of a middle-class position. A special kind of autonomy is retained in capitalism by employees in small companies as a result of the less advanced technologies and division of labour in these work organizations.

I have tried to demonstrate elsewhere[30] that, as in the West, the question of the alienation and autonomy of labour in the Soviet Union was a crucial distinguishing dimension between the middle class and the working class. On the other hand, I have also tried to show that the middle classes in the Soviet Union had far fewer resources to protect their own positions than is the case in advanced capitalist countries.

Let me now proceed to operationalize the concepts of working class and middle class, from these vantage points, as accurately as possible. Different occupations are classified into certain types of autonomy. For readers who are not familiar with class theory, this sort of detailed operationalization may seem quite cumbersome. There are, however, three points I would like to make in defence. First of all, the operationalization of class theories is a difficult and demanding task because there is such a huge number of occupations and professions in modern society. I believe it took John Goldthorpe and his colleagues a couple of years to establish which occupations can genuinely be operationalized as occupying middle-class positions on the criterion that the real labour process involves decision-making authority and autonomy.[31] Second, although there may be differences in how individual occupations are classified, there is in fact a rather broad consensus of opinion on the basic structure, whether we start out from John Goldthorpe's or Erik Olin Wright's or my own class theory. In particular, there is broad agreement on the position of professional and managerial groups. Not even the critics of class analysis deny the role of professionalization or 'credentialism'.[32] Third, although different kinds of operationalizations lead to somewhat different conclusions about the sizes of class groups, the picture that emerges when we proceed to analyse the structuration of class situation and consciousness is in the end rather similar. The only theories that differ from the mainstream (and that in empirical terms appear more or less untenable[33]) are those that deny the significance of professional and managerial positions and that define the middle class as consisting of such groups as state workers.[34]

My operationalization of the class structure is grounded in the following premises:

The hard core of the new middle classes consists of all types of professional, scientific-technical, managerial or administrative-bureaucratic autonomy, regardless of managerial status. In addition, people in leading positions of office work are included. By contrast, care workers, skilled workers and small enterprise autonomy types as well as those in performance-level autonomous office jobs constitute a contradictory class location in the middle ground between the core of the new middle classes and the working class.[35]

Autonomy has been measured with three different questions concerning product design, performance design, and genuine problem-solving in the work process. These dimensions are combined into a measure of autonomy by weighting the product design and problem-solving components on the basis of rules of deduction borrowed from Wright's original theory of autonomy. The professional and managerial groups included in the core of the middle class are thus groups who possess this kind of real autonomy.[36]

However, I have argued above that on account of their lacking power resources, Russian professionals have had less autonomy than professionals in capitalist countries. To highlight this phenomenon I have formed one new class group, which I call marginal group 2. This group comprises those wage-earners whose occupation would imply a position in the core, but who do not really possess autonomy. Examples include doctors, teachers, lawyers, and engineers with no autonomy. Additionally, I have operationalized a third marginal group, which comprises those wage-earners who have at least some supervisory tasks. In both versions of Erik Olin Wright's theory these people would represent marginal middle-class groups, whereas in my theory, in which the accent is on autonomy, they belong to the middle class.

Table 9.1 illustrates the class structures of Finland, the Baltic countries, and Russia on the basis of this operationalization. The Russian material is for 1996, while the interviews for the other countries were conducted in 1994. Russia, in this case, is represented by St Petersburg, which obviously represents urban Russia only. In the whole country the share of the working class would be much greater and the class positions of the agrarian population would also be quite outstanding.

Table 9.1   Class Structure in St Petersburg, the Baltic Countries and Finland, 1994/96 (%)

	Russia	Estonia	Latvia	Lithuania	Finland
Core of middle classes	15	16	12	12	21
Marginal group 1	6	4	6	2	14
Marginal group 2	36	25	28	29	12
Marginal group 3	6	4	6	5	3
Working class	30	45	40	43	31
Entrepreneurs	6	5	8	9	20
N	(1364)	(724)	(791)	(941)	(878)

Source: Kivinen, *Progress and Chaos: Russia as a Challenge for Sociological Imagination.*

The basic result of the table is quite clear. The core of the middle classes is markedly bigger in Finland than it is in the former Soviet Union. The professional power resources seem to be very important for actual class position even in a situation where the occupational structures between countries seem to be rather identical, as is the case here. This implies, on the other hand, that both the Baltic states and St Petersburg have very large marginally middle-class groups. This concerns especially marginal group 2, which we could call the 'potential middle class'. Many people have professional or managerial occupations without a proper middle-class autonomy or decision-making authority. These people could be seen to comprise a potential middle class because of their habitus and aspirations. In Finland the real power resources have been present. For their more independent power resources the marginal group of skilled workers and care workers (marginal group 1) is clearly bigger in Finland. Indeed, the forced autonomy of the planned economy has consisted mainly of 'task autonomy',[37] offering no real professional substance. Since the analysis is based on the basic features of the work organization that are extremely slow to change, there is every reason to assume that this specificity of class structure has been inherited from the Soviet Union and has nothing to do with the ongoing transition in which the middle classes are faced with completely different kinds of problems. To assess how the interests of the Russian middle class are now taking shape on the basis of the structuration of their class situation, we need to do more concrete analyses.

The Fate of the Middle Classes

Is the middle class the best card that history has given the Russians to play? Many Russian political forces as well as sociologists seem to think so. Almost all political parties seem to be hankering for a middle class, and social scientists are giving their full backing. In this discourse political, moral, and social aspects are intertwined in a spirit that comes pretty close to traditional talk about the 'sacred proletariat'. Let me take an example from a recent article by Grigoriev and Maleva:

> In a normal market economy the middle class is the main tax paying force. The economic living conditions of this class define both the investment activity of the nation, and conditions of the state budget and the realisation of social programmes and, most importantly, social and economic processes in general. What makes the middle class the basis for social stability? Most of all its middle position in the scale, indicating its material situation and property. . . . They want to secure their position and achievements and thus do not want to change the 'rules of the game'.[38]

But the middle class is not seen only as a stabilizing force. It is also a moral *avant garde* and a key to the development of civil society:

> It formulates the moral standards of society (in a sense its ideology) because it dominates in the system of justice, in religious as well as in political organisations. And it also has specific functions: to guarantee high productivity of labour, to produce and mediate knowledge and information; determine the profile and structure of consumption. And last but not least, the middle class as a whole is seen as a guarantee of political freedom.[39]

In the Russian discussion this kind of high-spirited formulation of the 'historical task and function' of the middle class is usually followed by an effort to operationalize the concept by using various criteria (incomes, decision-making capacities, cultural capital, and so on).[40] The size of the 'nucleus' of the middle class in various studies is shown in Table 9.2. In spite of the fact that this size is about the same, a more detailed analysis reveals much discrepancy. However, when we move on to the next step of class analysis – that is, to the analysis of the structuration of class situation – there is a broad consensus of opinion among Russian sociologists. Their main point is that because of its low incomes and insecure employment, the middle class is not able to play its historical role.[41]

Table 9.2 Scales Estimations of the Middle Class

Sources of information	The size of the 'nucleus' of middle class, % of total number of households
Institute of socioeconomic problems of the population of the Russian Academy of Sciences	25.6
Russian longitudinal monitoring inspection of welfare and health of the population	22.8
The All-Russia Centre of Study of Public Opinion	19.7

Source: Grigoryev and Maleva, *Srednii klass v Rossii na rubezhe etapov transformatsii*.

I am inclined to see in this argument an analogy with the traditional Soviet argument about the hegemonic role of the working class. This new argument on the leading function of the middle class is open to several critical remarks. In these considerations only limited attention is paid to the real interests and endeavours of the middle class. As Alvin Gouldner has noted, many social scientific grammars start out from the assumption that the powerful are good and the bad weak. However, Gouldner adds, moral goodness and power do not necessarily go hand in hand. The sacred character of the middle class is taken for granted in contemporary Russian sociology. But what about the moral ambivalence of this new social force?[42] Should we not also in Russia follow Gouldner's point that the new middle class is as profoundly flawed as a new universal class? It is elitist and self-seeking, and uses its special knowledge to advance its own interests and power and to control its own work situation.

The view I have been defending above is that the professional competencies of the middle class play a crucial part in resolving many of the key social problems in present-day Russia. On the other hand, the middle class has its own interests and relations to other classes. One may also ask how much is it really possible to say about the role of the new middle class in general terms, without exploring the nature of the 'general needs' in a particular society. For example, what will be the role of the middle class in formulating the development path of post-industrial Russia? Are there any real prospects for the creation of a European welfare state? And what about agency in the process of constituting the middle class? Is this process the making of the class itself or not?

How, then, has the situation of the middle class changed during the transition – is the middle class now developing into a stronger social force?

Table 9.3 illustrates some of the key features of the situation of Russian class groups in 1996. In almost all respects the situation of entrepreneurs seems to differ quite markedly from that of wage-earners. Entrepreneurs' incomes are developing more favourably and their professional competencies are in better use than previously, but on the other hand large numbers have to do two jobs. It seems that even entrepreneurs often have physically strenuous jobs, but they suffer from mental stress far more often than the working class. There are only comparatively few entrepreneurs who spend all their income on food and housing, whereas in the working class this is the case for the majority. The jobs of people in the core of the new middle classes and in the working class differ quite clearly from one another in terms of control exercised over work, and quite a few in the middle class feel that the chances to put their professional skills to use are also improving. It would seem then that in the case of the middle class, the contradiction between the middle-class work situation and the working-class reproduction situation (low incomes) has been further heightened since the days of socialism. By contrast, the marginal groups seem rather proletarian even in terms of their work situation. The values for all variables lie in between those of the core of the middle class and the working class, although they come closer to the latter almost without exception. Marginal group 3 (which, according to Wright's theory, should be slotted in the middle classes), appears to be showing particularly strong working-class features.

Table 9.3 Selected Features of the Situation of Russian Class Groups, 1996 (% or scale 0–5)

	Entre-preneurs	Core of m/c	Marginal group 1	Marginal group 2	Marginal group 3	Working class
Physically strenuous job	2.1	1.9	2.3	2.0	2.2	2.3
Mentally strenuous job	3.3	3.3	2.8	2.7	2.6	2.1
Professional competence in better use than before	50	41	23	24	13	16
Paid less than before	38	60	55	65	63	65
Superior checks quality of work several times a week	9	20	47	35	46	56
Has two jobs	62	34	28	43	46	39
All incomes spent on food and housing	14	38	49	41	49	52

Source: Kivinen, *Progress and Chaos*.

If Table 9.3 is used to test my class theory, the variables would seem to lend support to it. Autonomy is clearly the main determinant of class situation. On the other hand, the table does draw our attention to two clear and highly significant anomalies. One concerns the weakness of the level of reproduction in middle-class groups; the other is the proportion of people with two jobs. Taking on a second job is of course precisely a reaction to the situation where one's livelihood is fundamentally at risk. Another finding that points in the same direction is that in virtually all class groups, about half have a garden plot that they cultivate. What would be worth studying is the development of new, evolving combinations that undermine or strengthen different class positions. When a professional has to work in a manual job simply to make ends meet, that is a definite case of eroding professional skills. So, if the new work organization unfolding with the process of transition seems to promise better prospects for developing professional skills, the necessity of a second job may adversely affect professional identities. As far as entrepreneurs are concerned, it might be assumed that in many cases they are looking at new kinds of opportunities for upward social mobility.

General satisfaction with life is at a high level among entrepreneurs, whereas the working class has been badly disappointed by the difficulties that have sprung up during the transition period.[43] Entrepreneurs take an active part in political life. On both these dimensions the core of the middle classes lies in the middle ground between entrepreneurs and the working class.

The theory that the new class is picking up the role of the old elite is supported by the fact that the people who now occupy the top positions are largely the same as before. This applies equally to 'new Russians' and to managerial positions in general. On the other hand, the professional middle class in Russia is in many ways historically distinctive. It has grown up as an heir to the Russian intelligentsia, as if it were an unintended consequence of the Bolshevik project. Its structure and situation differ from the corresponding groups in the West.

In terms of their lifestyle and rationality, entrepreneurs and managerial groups differ quite fundamentally from professionals in the core of the new middle classes. Entrepreneurs have developed their own lifestyle, in which the accent is not on high culture but rather on international mass culture and related ways of life: discos, nightclubs, cafés, and restaurants. By contrast, it seems that they lack 'cultural goodwill', which is characteristic of Western middle classes. The lifestyle of the new business elite in Russia is also a curious combination of conspicuous consumption and Russian conformism.[44] They seem to be so addicted to work that they have no interest and no time to consume the money they are earning. They also have essentially Russian feelings of guilt about their own success, as well as fears of outsiders. Professionals, on the other hand, do possess cultural capital, but they lack established professional practices and a stable position.

Traditionally it has been assumed that a special interest for the core of new middle classes is to reinforce the position of their own special type of mental labour.[45] Managers have quite successfully defended their position in company-level politics. In a broader sense, however, the position of professionals remains weak, as do their organizations. There exists no strong public sector that could provide the basis for the reproduction of professionals' position. In fact it is precisely the position of professionals in the public sector that in the West goes a long way towards explaining radical social movements and the success of social democratic parties.[46]

The main collective needs in Russian society today have to do with the kind of post-industrial society that is developing in the country. In spite of its large potential middle class, the Soviet Union remained until the very end a fundamentally industrial society. There are many different kinds of advanced post-industrial societies, but the two basic forms are the American and European versions.[47] In the former, services consist mainly of personal as well as business services; in the latter, the most important category of services are welfare services provided by the public sector.

If Russia relied on the old state apparatus and on the potential middle class, it could opt for the latter path. This could be combined with diverse forms of ownership, systematic efforts to develop the public sector, its infrastructure, education, health care, day care, and so on. However, this would need to be backed up by strong organizations – that is, by the broad organization of civil society into independent professions, trade unions, mass parties, and so on. This, however, is restricted by political action based on special interests attached to old patriarchal labour collectives, and by weakly organized professions. The middle class could even become a decisive force in defining the trends in social development, as Russian sociologists and political parties are suggesting. But, at least for the time being, it remains comparatively weak.

Growing Poverty and Inequality

If the middle class are among the winners in the process of transition, then there inevitably have to be losers as well. What about the poor and the working class? The cornerstone of Soviet welfare was the right to work. Individuals without a job were subject to the charge of 'social parasitism', a conviction that generally involved a sentence in a labour camp. Alongside universal job guarantees, enterprises had a significant welfare role. This involved the provision of significant non-cash benefits: housing, childcare centres, affiliated policlinics, cafeterias providing subsidized meals, and a system of health and recreational facilities. In transition, this is all about to disappear. I further discuss the erosion of the labour collective below.

Despite the official view that poverty was non-existent in the Soviet Union, several estimates suggest that poverty was in fact an established fact of life for about 10–13 per cent of the Russian population during the last decade of the Soviet era.[48] Upon the introduction of a new pension law in 1990, Prime Minister Ryzhkov broke the official silence for the first time by estimating the number of poor people in the USSR at approximately 40 million.[48] Subsequent published data suggested that 12.6 per cent of the Soviet population (36 million people) were below the official poverty line of 78 roubles per month household per capita income. Families with children made up at least half of the poor. The second largest group of poor people consisted of pensioners who lived alone or lacked any other source of income.[49] The third group was the working poor in low-paying occupations. The worst-off were the homeless and recently institutionalized.

The extent of poverty increased dramatically with the beginning of transition (Figure 9.2). Poverty was widespread during the first years of the transition and has remained at the level of 30 per cent ever since, with 1998 marking the lowest point in this respect. By January 1999, average wages were worth about 40 per cent less than in January 1998. While there has been quite remarkable economic growth since late 1999, the scale of economic and social problems facing Russia is greater than virtually anything experienced in the OECD countries.[50]

Figure 9.2   Poverty Rate Series, 1985–99

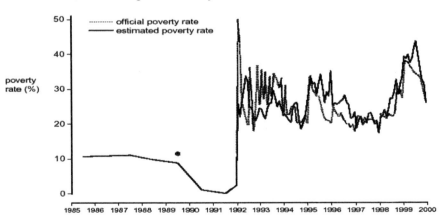

Source: Anthony Shorrocks and Stanislav Kolenikov,
Poverty Trends in Russia during the Transition, Helsinki, 2001.

In Russia today the number of poor people is several times higher than the figures recorded in the USSR. As wages and social transfers failed to keep up with rising prices, the number of families with children falling into the poverty trap started to rise. Pensioners were also hard hit in the same process. However, there were also a growing number of working poor and a rapidly increasing number of households that were affected by unemployment. In February 1999 unemployment, as defined by the ILO, reached the unprecedented level of more than 14 per cent. Economic growth has now seen that figure slowly drop to about 12 per cent. The system of social redistribution has not been able to react to this new dramatic situation. The large majority of benefits favour households with above-average resources. Most of the households receiving these benefits had incomes above subsistence level. Almost half of the households that dropped below the poverty line in 1998 were recorded as having received none of the major transfers. Housing allowances in particular seem to favour the better-off households. All social transfers have a modest equalizing effect on household consumption, as shown by Gini coefficients calculated before and after the inclusion of social transfers.[51] However, nearly all of the differences between *ex-ante* and *ex-post* Gini coefficients were attributable to the effect of pensions.

It is widely believed that the fall in average real incomes accounts for most, if not all, of the rise in poverty during the 1990s. However, as Shorrocks and Kolenikov have shown, other factors have also had a significant impact.[52] This can be seen in Figure 9.3. First of all, one consequence of increasing inequality is that the most vulnerable sections of society have received a smaller share of the shrinking cake. Thus, while average real incomes have declined to 40 per cent of their 1991 level, the real incomes of the bottom quintile of the population have dropped to 21 per cent of the figure in 1991. This disproportionate decline in the real incomes of those most exposed to poverty has also had a substantial effect on the poverty rate.

The problem of assigning factor contributions to the poverty trend has formal similarities with a classic problem in cooperative game theory, which seeks to allocate a certain amount of output among a set of agents. Shorrocks exploits this in order to construct a general decomposition procedure based on the Shapley value, which is a concept in game theory introduced by Lloyd

Shapley (1953).[53] It describes one approach to the fair allocation of gains obtained by cooperation among several actors. The technique involves considering the impact of eliminating each factor in succession, and then averaging these effects over all the possible elimination sequences. A more sophisticated version of the technique allows for a hierarchical structure in which groups of factors are treated as a single entity in the first stage of the decomposition, then each group effect is allocated among its constituents. Shorrocks has proposed an extension to the Shapley value based on Owen.[54] He refers to the general framework as the Shapley–Owen–Shorrocks (or SOS) procedure. The SOS decomposition has two major advantages. First, it is *exact*. In the present context, this means that the sum of the per capita income, inequality, and poverty line effects is equal to the observed change in poverty. Second, it is *symmetrical*, so that the factors are treated in an even-handed manner: in particular, the contributions do not depend on the order in which the factors are considered.

Figure 9.3 suggests that per capita income and inequality made similar contributions to the poverty change over 1985–99, each raising the poverty rate by about 20 per cent. A third factor has been the change in the poverty

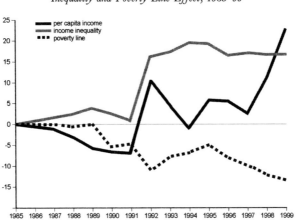

Figure 9.3 Cumulative SOS Contributions of Per Capita Income, Inequality and Poverty Line Effect, 1985–99

Source: Shorrocks and Kolenikov,
'*Poverty Trends in Russia During the Transition*', Helsinki, 2001.

standard. A new methodology adopted in 1991 replaced the minimum material security budget, which functioned as a quasi poverty line in the Soviet era, with new minimum subsistence levels for various household types, based on a methodology used by the World Bank in other countries. In fact the poverty situation was worse in the 1990s than the official statistics suggest. If the poverty standard that prevailed in the pre-reform era had been in place in 1999, then 60 per cent of the Russian population would be counted as poor.[55] It should be noted, however, that the figures for personal income are unreliable because of the growth of informal economic activities.

Informal mechanisms of self-help and help from other people are important survival strategies. Among the most important forms of self-help is growing food, for household consumption or for barter, on a small plot owned or rented by the household. This activity nearly doubled between 1994 and 1998.[56] Social networks and transfers from relatives and friends accounted for a small but not insignificant share of household budgets. Their indirect effect on employment and consumption is much more important than in the West.[57]

The overall picture of declining living standards marks wide variations in individual experiences. Those who were able to start new enterprises or found new jobs acquiring new skills fared better than those who remained attached to jobs in declining sectors such as agriculture, mining, or the military industry. These diverging processes led to a dramatic rise in inequality.

Figure 9.4   Level of Economic Development and Inequality in Incomes Distribution (Gini index)

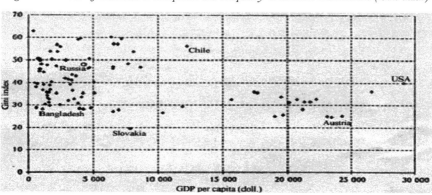

Source: Grigoryev and Maleva, *Srednii klass v Rossi na rubezhe etapov transformatsii.*

Figure 9.4 shows the Gini coefficients and the level of economic development. In terms of GDP per capita, present-day Russia ranks at about the same level as Turkey, Mexico and Brazil.[58] The most recent figures from the World Bank for 1992–97 report a Gini value of 48 per cent, a level traditionally associated with Latin American countries such as Ecuador and Venezuela, or African nations such as Nigeria. However, this figure still falls short of the most extreme inequality recorded for Brazil and South Africa.

Figure 9.5   Changes in Income Inequality in Selected Transition Economies

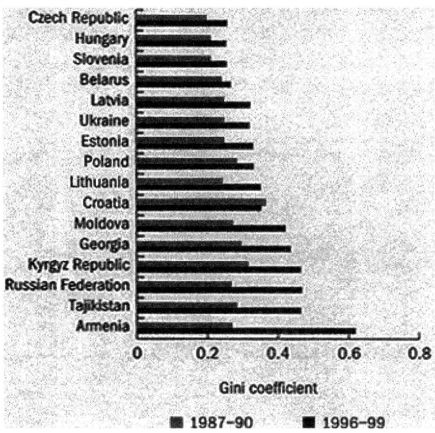

Source: World Bank, *Making Transition Work for Everyone: Poverty and Inequality in Europe and Central Asia*, 2000.

If the world is divided into three categories, most of the transition countries in Central Eastern Europe belong to the relatively small 'middle class' in the world population.[59] This middle class has living conditions between high-income countries (North America and Western Europe) and low-income countries (the vast majority of the world population, China, India, South Asia, African countries). In this classification Russia belongs to the better-off part of the low-income countries. In all CIS countries the changes in income inequality have been much more dramatic than in Central Eastern Europe (Figure 9.5).

The former USSR used to have a relatively high standard of living in terms of such non-monetary aspects as literacy and life expectancy. Health indicators showed a sharp deterioration in the early transition years, but some improvement has been recorded since 1994. Life expectancy for men, for example, declined from 65 years in 1988 to 58 years in 1994, before it recovered to 61 years by 1997, but is going downwards again. Most alarming is the re-emergence of diseases that now rarely appear in developed countries, while suicides, alcoholism, and accidents have also been increasing rapidly. The educational system has also been deteriorating, but it still covers the whole population in Russia, while in some former Soviet republics in Central Asia and Caucasus this is no more the case.[60]

Many Western advisers are now asking how best to target social policies.[61] Direct targeting of social programmes on households with incomes below a certain level (using means-testing) is a common approach in many OECD countries. However, the creation of the necessary informational and administrative infrastructure for these purposes is a major problem in present-day Russia because of unrecorded incomes and the myriad special benefits. Consequently there will be strong pressure to preserve the status quo in the social distribution system.

The Working Class and the Erosion of the Labour Collective

Simon Clarke has made one of the most interesting and original efforts to connect social structure and economic analysis in the Soviet Union and Russia. He attaches less importance to the conceptual categorization of the middle class than to understanding the interests of the working class.[62]

The ideological representation characterizes a Soviet enterprise as a 'labour collective':

> The labour collective includes all those with a right to work in the enterprise, including, for example, women on extended maternity leave or young people in military service, as well as the pensioners of the enterprise. It is the labour collective that produces and reproduces itself through its activity in the enterprise (and it is the labour collective that is the principal claimant to ownership rights in the process of privatisation). This means that the achievements of an enterprise are not measured in money, not simply in tons produced, but in the size, education and skill composition of the labour force, the number of houses built, kindergartens supported, etc., which dominate the iconography of the Soviet enterprise and of the achievements of socialism.[63]

The idea of the enterprise as a labour collective has been a fiction, but it is precisely in the name of the labour collective that management has ruled the enterprise, in the name of the labour collective that it has pressed its interests *vis-à-vis* higher authorities and required that workers are subjected to managerial authority.

The Soviet enterprise was not just a unit of production or an enterprise in the sense in which the term is understood in capitalism. It also provided extensive social and welfare services. Large enterprises had kindergartens, sports and cultural facilities, holiday resorts, and pioneer camps. They organized housing, social assistance, and education. In this sense labour determined the position of the Soviet worker to a much greater extent than in capitalism. Many of these things were accessible only through the 'labour collective'.

Labour collectives have had a significant impact. This is seen in Table 9.4, which illustrates the social benefits provided through the labour collective during the Soviet era and today. The table also shows how the labour collective has been eroded. If Clarke's theory is taken seriously, this must be seen as one of the key processes of class relations in the transitional phase.

Table 9.4 Social Benefits Provided by the Labour Collective 1996/Earlier (10–15 years ago) (%)

	1996	Earlier
Housing	3	13
Child care	2	17
Holidays	16	46
Meals at work	20	19
Clothing	33	37
Travel	18	10
Food	10	28
Other goods	5	20

Source: Markku Kivinen, *Progress and Chaos*.

However, the specific sacred of the workers' movement[64] is not a problem for Clarke, but rather a premise. This means that he does not call into question the nature of this movement as a cultural phenomenon or as a way of life; it is as if the interests and consciousness of the working class, and any hegemonic projects pursued by the working class, could be determined at the level of the mode of production, without any connection to the specific social situation, history, or culture of Russia. This kind of reasoning will make it very tough going if Russia wants to proceed from its present burgeoning trade union endeavours towards a programme of 'democratic socialism'.

Managerial Revolution in Russia

Privatization in Russia got under way during Gorbachev's reign. The purpose of privatization was to replace the means of 'administrative' regulation by 'economic' regulation: to create a new kind of control system rather than to release companies from the shackles of government control. Pavlov's government passed the first all-union privatization law, which made it possible for companies to be collectively or cooperatively owned. Joint-stock companies and even direct private ownership were now possible. Although the law did not set out any specific procedures for privatization, most of the first projects were based on cooperative or rental arrangements. Shares were sold to workers at reduced prices, with the company offering loans. As far the workers were concerned, all this seemed to promise a secure job and an opportunity to break loose from centralized wage control. For managers, it meant that the company became legally independent of state control. At the same time it effectively legalized various financial arrangements for pathological privatization.

Gaidar's government aimed initially at a form of state privatization that was oriented against the industrial nomenklatura. Gaidar was opposed to releasing any property for free, and did not want to relinquish control to the former company managers in the name of the 'labour collective'.[65] Privatization was to create a new 'propertied class' and at the same time generate income to stabilize the national economy.

However, the industrial nomenklatura mobilized strong pressure, both in Parliament and through the old trade unions, for privatization based on labour collectives.[66] Many neo-liberal economists in Russia were persuaded to support this model because there was very little popular resistance and because for them the chief concern was not ownership, but getting the markets up and running.

The privatization programme of July 1992 marked an almost complete surrender to the demands of the industrial nomenklatura.[67] Companies were offered three options of privatization. The decision was to be made by the meeting of the labour collective. According to the first model, workers were entitled to 25 per cent of the company's shares without a vote; in addition they would have the option of buying 10 per cent of the shares at a reduced price. Top management would be allowed to buy a further 5 per cent of the share stock. The rest would remain in the hands of state or local privatization committees, to be sold at a later date by auction. This was the model that privatization committees tended to favour. However, it was also preferred by those liberal democrats and worker activists who were still hoping to break the power of the industrial nomenklatura.

In the second model the company's labour collective, provided it had the backing of two-thirds, would be able to buy 51 per cent of the company's shares at nominal value. This seemed to offer opportunities for both workers and management. The workers would be majority shareholders. In practice, however, managers had control over the information related to the privatization programme and also represented the workers on boards of directors.[68]

Intensive propaganda campaigns and ritual labour collective meetings sealed the 'managerial revolution' in Russia during summer 1992.

The first object of the managers' strategy was to make sure that the company did not go to outsiders. They wanted to make sure that the new administrative bodies of joint-stock companies were as firmly under managerial control as the old labour collectives.[69] Managers have various means at their disposal to control joint-stock companies, particularly in a situation where there is no real trading in stocks. In many firms managers can, by virtue of their position, buy more shares than the workers – but this is only one side of the matter, and by no means the most important one. Managers can get shares from workers by exchanging them for cheap consumer goods, by leaving wages unpaid and in this way create pressure to sell shares, by persuading or forcing resigning or retiring workers to sell their shares. Shares can also be distributed or sold to subsidiaries owned by managers.

Managers can also use the trade union to further the interests of their own branch or region. In fact most of the strikes started by workers in Russia have transformed precisely into these kinds of 'managerial strikes',[70] with the demands of workers backed up by managers' demands concerning credit arrangements, tax benefits, and subsidies.

In general, one of the key elements of the strategy of managers in Russia is quite simply to find a way in which to cope. Coping is here understood not so much in terms of making a profit as in terms of surviving as a production unit and above all as a labour collective.[71] The third element is the orientation to long-term profitability in the new market environment.

The sale of company shares to outside investors should represent the third wave of privatization. This, in principle, could restrict the power of company managers. However, managers have been inclined to form larger conglomerates together with regional and state organizations related to the branch of production and with proto-capitalist commercial firms. The role of the state has been increasing with the growing number of bankruptcies and companies going into liquidation.[72] Professionals are one of the groups excluded from the insider circles. Their fate was effectively sealed by shady banks and investment companies.

As we can see in Table 9.5, the only group significantly affected by privatization, apart from managers, is that of entrepreneurs; for everyone else the process has had very little, if any, real impact. Having said that, it must be noted that one-third of the working class and up to half of the core of the middle classes have acquired some kind of landed property. One-third of the core of the middle classes have also bought a private flat or house.

Table 9.5 Participation of Russian Social Classes in Privatization (%)

	Privatization: significant	Privatized land	Privatized flat	Privatized shares	Considers private firms better
Entrepreneurs	29	50	44	13	68
Core of middle class	10	49	33	8	22
Marginal group 1	6	42	19	21	26
Marginal group 2	9	42	26	14	22
Marginal group 3	2	38	19	11	24
Working class	6	34	18	12	26

Source: Kivinen, *Progress and Chaos*.

All in all, it seems there are three kinds of actors involved in the process of privatization, each of which has its own power resource.[73]

1 Forces aiming to reinforce the state apparatus. Initially the process of privatization was set in motion by Pavlov and Gorbachev, whose aim it was to change the nature of state control. Yeltsin was left with the task of having to try to strengthen that control with economic structures continuing to cave in. Gaidar's fraction is trying to undermine the industrial nomenklatura, but they remain a force to be reckoned with even within the state apparatus. In recent years the power of ministries and local privatization committees has been increasing again in connection with bankruptcies, for instance.

2. Another major group of actors with a crucial impact is represented by company managers, who, at least so far, have taken a keener interest in control rather than dividends – and succeeded quite outstandingly.

3. Workers, who on the one hand have been subjected to attempts of ideological commitment to the ideas of social partnership and

participation, but whose power resources have largely been controlled by managers in both labour collectives, joint-stock companies' administrative bodies and in the trade union movement.

All in all there are clear signs now of a new bourgeoisie growing up out of the old industrial nomenklatura. However, the relationship between ownership and control is clearly in the process of taking shape. In the long term the situation will certainly be affected by the entry of external investors in companies and by the development of (mainly local) capital groupings. On the other hand, the involvement of traditional ministries in the power structures does afford them a special nature.

Among middle-class groups it seems that managers and new entrepreneurs are now strengthening their power resources, whereas the situation of professionals is largely dependent on the fate of the state sector. This implies that the internal breakdown of the wage-earning middle class may become a relevant issue in a different way from that in Western countries. So far there has grown up a strong hegemonic project at the level of the politics of production, with managers – the old industrial nomenklatura – representing the dominant party and even controlling the power resources of the working class.[74] Traditionally the class conflict in the Soviet Union was transformed into a conflict over the distribution of resources within a hierarchic framework of patronage and dependence. This tradition remains strong, and is strengthened even further by companies struggling for their survival. From this point of view interests related to company and region would seem to be more important than class interests.

Trends in Class Relations

Although Russia is currently in a state of profound social disorganization, there remains one objective in Russian society that shows no signs of weakening: the attainment of market economy. However, market economy and capitalism come in many different shapes and forms; there is more than one possible path of development towards capitalism:

We were promised capitalism and that's what we got. Not only the popular masses but also managers of all descriptions had these fancy ideas of chic Parisian shops, while they forgot all about the hungry and unemployed people of Lima and São Paulo, which are much closer to us. The aeroplane has taken off and some of the passengers still think that they will be landing in Paris or Stockholm. But in actual fact the plane is headed for Burkina Faso, because this airline and planes constructed like this do not fly west. Someone may eventually reach their destination and live in Moscow just like in Paris. But that is at the expense of those who live as if they were in Burkina Faso.[75]

A growing industry of research on 'transitional dilemmas' has been unfolding in parallel with the East European and Russian change.[76] In their book *Making Capitalism Without Capitalists*, Gil Eyal, Ivan Szelenyi, and Eleanor Townsley analyse the class formation and elite struggles taking place in post-communist Central Europe. They make a basic distinction between Central Europe and Russia. In the former case, the revolution by the nomenklatura was blocked by an independent intelligentsia. In these countries privatization proceeded more cautiously than in Russia, and typically produced diffused ownership rights.[77] The result was 'capitalism without capitalists': reasonably developed capital and labour markets, functioning mechanisms of stock exchange, and budding capitalist forms of corporate governance, all administered by the intelligentsia in its role as 'cultural bourgeoisie' but without a propertied class. In Russia the nomenklatura managed to convert itself into a propertied class via spontaneous privatization.[78] The result was a powerful propertied class thriving in the context of weak, rudimentary, or even absent, capitalist market institutions – 'capitalists without capitalism'.

The analysis by Eyal et al. of the 'spirit of capitalism', the ethos of the new elite in Central Europe, is concrete and convincing. As far as the social structure of transition is concerned, the analysis concentrates too heavily on the ruling elite and makes comparisons only within transitional societies. I am inclined to argue that the specificity of transitional class structures should be analysed in more concrete terms and put into a more comprehensive comparative perspective.

One generalizing perspective on interest formation in transition is provided by World Bank reports.[79] They also raise the issue of the specific path of Russia. The political economy of reform within a discourse of 'discipline and encouragement' is expressed graphically by tracing the suggested paths of winners and losers of transition. Figure 9.6 depicts the gains and losses in income accruing to different constituencies of reform in a 'typical transitional economy'.

Figure 9.6   Winners and Losers from Reform

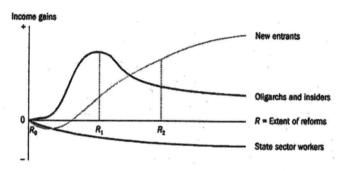

Note: R_0 = no reforms; R_1 = point at which income gains of oligarchs and insiders are maximized; R_2 = level of reforms that allows the winners of reforms beyond R_1 (new entrants) to compensate for or exercise enough political pressure to neutralize the resistance of oligarchs, insiders, and state sector workers.

Source: World Bank, Transition: The First Ten Years:
Analysis and Lessons for Eastern Europe and the Former Soviet Union.

1. State sector workers, employed in state enterprises and lacking the skills to become new entrants in the competitive market, face a sharp decline in income as discipline calls for downsizing the sector, with little hope of any substantial recovery with the intensification of reform.
2. Potential new entrants, workers in state enterprises, and new entrepreneurs with skills to become new entrants in the competitive market have a classic J-curve pattern of income. They face severe adjustment costs at low levels of reform as they exit the state sector. In addition, they realize gains only when enough progress has been made with policy and institutional reforms to promote and support new entry into the competitive market.

3. Oligarchs and insiders begin the transition with substantial *de facto* control rights over state assets and close ties with the political elite inherited from the previous command system. However, because of limited skills to compete in the market economy, they face an inverted U-curve of income gains.

Given these patterns of gains and losses, each group prefers a different combination of reforms. State sector workers prefer the status quo R0 and reject all reforms. Oligarchs and insiders prefer a partial reform and sustain the reform process through R1, the point where their gains are maximized and beyond which further implementation of policies of discipline and encouragement threaten to undermine gains from rent-seeking and tunnelling. And for potential new entrants, the reform process offers sacrifices at the beginning of the process and gains when the reforms are further advanced.

The main argument here is that the policy should prevent the early winners in liberalization and privatization from undermining further reforms that would impose discipline and encourage new entry and competition and thus reduce their rents. The risk is of getting stuck at a low level of reform (R1). As both insiders and state sector workers face declining incomes after R1, these groups have a strong incentive to join forces to oppose further economic reforms.

This analysis sees interests and structures as a mere reflection of economic reform policy and its phases. It is open to question whether state employees really were a major force in slowing down the reform process. Table 9.6 shows that state employment diminished very rapidly in the privatization process. A clear majority of Russian employees are already in the private sector.

Table 9.6   The Sectoral Composition of Employment: Russia 1990–2000 (%)

Employment by sector	1990	1992	1994	1996	1998	2000
Total employment	100	100	100	100	100	100
State and municipal enterprises, etc.	82.6	68.9	44.7	42.0	38.1	37.9
Private enterprises	12.5	19.5	33.0	35.6	43.2	46.1
Social organization, funds	0.8	0.8	0.7	0.6	0.7	0.8
Joint ventures	0.1	0.3	0.5	0.8	1.6	2.7
Mixed ownership	4.0	10.5	21.1	21.0	16.4	12.5

Source: Goskomstat Rossii, *Rossiiskii statisticheskii ezhigodnik*, Moscow, 2001.

It can also be asked to what extent the oligarchs and insiders really are the losers in the reform process. From the primitive accumulation of capital we know that it does not make much difference whether the original money was made by rent-seeking, tunnelling or arbitrage. Rents have fluctuated sharply, which is surely not in the long-term interest of the oligarchs and insiders.[80] It may even be that reform phase two is more and more in their interest.

Most of all, this analysis is too abstract as far as the forms of market economy and capitalism are concerned. The existence of capitalism may have many faces, depending of the strength of class forces. I have pointed out earlier that the classification of societies' development models on the basis of whether or not class relations are polarized is too crude a typology. It is possible to identify many historically real types on the basis of classes' power relations.

A social class may be regarded as strong when:

- the relations of ownership or power resources that lie at the heart of its position are firmly established;
- the basic dimensions of its class situation are well established; and when
- it has strong organizations to fall back on.

This, of course, is a simplification inasmuch as all these conditions do not necessarily apply at one and the same time. However, we can from this vantage point compare Russia with other types of class relations and sketch possible courses of future development.

Table 9.7 illustrates the different types of class relations on the basis of the strength or weakness of social classes. The classes included in this analysis are

Table 9.7 Alternative Models of Class Relations

Bourgeoisie				
	strong	strong	weak	weak
Middle class				
	strong	weak	strong	weak
strong	1	2	3	4
Working class				
weak	5	6	7	8

Source: Kivinen, *Progress and Chaos. Russia as a Challenge for Sociological Imagination.*

the bourgeoisie, the working class, and the new middle class. This, again, is something of a simplification in that peasants have played a crucial role in the class relations of many societies, and of course the urban petty bourgeoisie also has a relevance of its own.

In the analysis in Table 9.7 Western European countries (and Nordic countries in particular) are slotted in cell 1. In these countries relations of ownership are well-established and the core of the new middle classes, both managers and professionals, have certain undisputed privileges compared to the working class. On the other hand the working class also has its own strong organizations, trade unions, and parties through which it exercises an influence as part of civil society. Only a small portion of the societal residue goes directly into private consumption by the propertied class. That is why these societies cannot be regarded as exploiting societies proper.

Russia, then, seems to fall into cell number eight. Relations of ownership in Russia are still in the process of making, and the middle class's power resources remain weak. The working class's organizations are weak, and at the company level the power resources of workers are controlled by managers. No doubt the positions of the new bourgeoisie are already taking shape as the process of privatization is moving into its final stages. But, for the time being, the process of structural change in the economy is still very much ongoing; it is still far too early to talk about profitable industries or about certain prospects. The organizations and interests of the middle class are beginning to take shape, although in many ways and in contradictory and difficult circumstances. Indeed, the success of classes will largely depend on more general hegemonic projects in society, and on their own successes and failures and struggles in formulating strategies.

It is unlikely that we will see Russia move straight from cell number eight to cell number one. But what other options are there?

The class structure of the Soviet Union immediately after the Civil War would in this analysis come under cell 4, where both the bourgeoisie and the middle class are weak and the working class is strong. However, the organizations of independent working-class power were overthrown during Lenin's rule, and under Stalin destroyed for ever. The longer Stalin was in power, the weaker the working class's independent organization and the stronger the middle classes became – quite in contrast to the initial intentions of the Bolshevik project. In a sense this brings us close to a seventh option, as is assumed in theories of a new dominant class. However, the force that really gains in strength is the nomenklatura: not so much the middle class but a new kind of ruling class.

If with the privatization process the nomenklatura develops into a new bourgeoisie, there are still various different ways in which the classes' power relations might take shape. Alternative two would resemble the situation in Germany during the Weimar Republic, where the middle classes were crushed in between a strong bourgeoisie and the working class.[81] There are some such elements to be detected in the position of the professional middle class in Russia. The bourgeoisie is growing stronger and the numerically strong industrial working class must be taken into account, at least to some extent. It is not easy to classify the political forces that are at work in the Russian working class as either left-wing or right-wing;[82] even the Communist Party is now saying that one of its important tasks is to develop Russia's major power role on a national basis. In this sense the model of authoritarian movements is not too remote a possibility. National self-assertion and a fragile middle class sounds like a rather worrying combination.

The worst-case scenario for Russia today is the prospect of it regressing into a developing country. If this were to happen, the class structure in Russia would begin to resemble the situation in countries where the bourgeoisie is so strong that most of the surplus production in society goes to the private consumption of the ruling class. There are plenty of examples in Latin America, Asia, and Africa. These, quite literally, are societies of exploitation. The factor that is pushing things in this direction in Russia is the absence of the rationality of capitalism. If the present way of doing business (which relies primarily on speculation and in which the aim is make as big a profit in as short a space of time as possible) remains predominant, then there is a risk that Russia will begin spinning towards the Third World. On the other hand there are still forces pulling it in the other direction, most particularly the high level of education in the country and its tremendous economic potential.

The fifth alternative resembles the situation in the USA, where the middle class is so strong that even the working class has largely adopted middle-class ways of thinking.[83] The working class is quite weak in terms of its organization, and there are no real left-wing projects. This is not a very likely scenario in Russia, given the weak and unstable position of the middle classes. In the USA this situation has been based on the country occupying a special status at the hub of the world order and an exceptionally high level of affluence. Such middle-class projects, which heavily stress the difference between performance and planning at the level of the labour process and aim to create highly differentiated educational structures, are certainly not unknown in Russia, but this would require that the middle classes set up new institutions supporting this kind of development. In this alternative the interests of the middle class and the working class would really be antagonistic.

If the process of economic transition becomes a drawn-out process and if the restructuring fails, this model will come quite close to alternative seven. In this scenario the old structures at the company level will probably be retained.[84] Managers will retain their control in weak companies and professions will begin to evolve into major forces in modernization. The dissolution of political control no doubt would push things in this direction. At the same time there would be increasing unemployment and organizational fragmentation within the working class.

Alternative three could be based on the working class successfully turning the solidarity of the labour collective into genuine organizational activity and interest defence. Closely related to this could be the endeavour outlined above towards a European post-industrial society and the commitment of the middle class to a modernization project based on the growth of the public welfare state. In this case the translation of the labour collective's nominal ownership into real ownership could provide the foundation for a democratic left-wing alternative based on a pluralism of forms of ownership rather than on a strong propertied class. This kind of social democratic path of development is possible in Russia. The structural foundations are already in place, but the political and cultural obstacles are also certainly real. Above all, a new hegemonic project requires a conscious effort to dismantle the old cultural forms and the institutions based on those forms.

Notes

1 Nikolay Bukharin, *Teoriya istoricheskogo materializma*, Moscow, 1924.
2 Sheila Fitzpatrick, *Education and Social Mobility in the Soviet Union, 1921–1934*, Cambridge, 1979.
3 Sheila Fitzpatrick, 'Ascribing class: the construction of social identity in Soviet Russia', in Sheila Fitzpatrick, ed., *Stalinism: New Directions*, London, 2000.
4 Vladimir Mayakovsky, *Vladimir Ilyich Lenin*, Moscow, 1976, p. 153.
5 Pierre Bourdieu, *Distinction: A Social Critique of the Judgement of Taste*, London and New York, 1984.
6 Fitzpatrick, 'Ascribing class'.
7 Marc Galanter, *Law and the Backward Classes in India*, Berkeley, CA, 1984.
8 See also David Moon, *The Russian Peasantry 1600–1930*, Harlow, 1999.
9 Sheila Fitzpatrick, *The Russian Revolution*, Oxford, 1982, p. 19.
10 Cf. Donald Filtzer, *Soviet Workers and Stalinist Industrialization*, London, 1986, p. 199.
11 Richard Stites, *Revolutionary Dreams*, Oxford and New York, 1989.
12 Ibid., p. 84.
13 See also Juri Lotman and Boris A. Uspenskii, 'Binary models in the dynamics of Russian culture (to the end of the eighteenth century)', in Alexander D. Nakhimovsky and Alice Stone-Nakhimovsky, eds, *The Semiotics of the Russian Cultural History*, London, 1985.
14 Michael Burawoy, *Politics of Production: Factory Regimes under Capitalism and State Socialism*, London, 1985.
15 Vera S. Dunham, *In Stalin's Time: Middle-class Values in Soviet Fiction*, Westford, MA, 1974, pp. 12–14.
16 Alec Nove, *Socialism, Economics and Development*, London, 1986; Pekka Sutela, *Neuvostotalouden vaikeat vuodet*, Jyväskylä, 1987.
17 Karl Kautsky, *Bernstein und das Sozialdemokratische Programm: Eine Antikritik*, Stuttgart, 1899.
18 Harley Baltzer, ed., *Russia's Missing Middle Class: The Professions in Russian History*, New York, 1996.
19 Markku Kivinen, *Parempien piirien ihmisiä*, Jyväskylä, 1987; Markku Kivinen, *The New Middle Classes and the Labour Process: Class Criteria Revisited*, Helsinki, 1989.
20 For more on the relevance of the theory, see Ludmila A. Belyaeva, 'Srednii sloi rossiiskogo obshchestva: problemy obreteniya sotsialnogo statusa', *Sotsiologicheskie issledovaniya*, 10, 1993.
21 Tatyana Zaslavskaya, 'Socialism, perestroika and public opinion', *Sociological Research*, 4, 1992.
22 See for example Barbara Ehrenreich and John Ehrenreich, 'The professional-managerial class', in Pat Walker, ed., *Between Labour and Capital*, Hassocks, 1979.
23 Boris Kagarlitski, *Hajonnut monoliitti*, Helsinki, 1992, pp. 170–1.
24 Michael Kennedy, *Professionals, Power and Solidarity in Poland: A Critical Sociology of Soviet-type Society*, Cambridge, 1991.
25 Cf. Magali S. Larson, *The Rise of Professionalism*, Berkeley, CA, 1977, pp. 47–8; Markku Kivinen, 'Perspektivy razvitiya srednego klassa v Rossii', *Sotsiologicheskii*

zhurnal, 1994, 2; Belyaeva, *Srednii sloi rossiiskogo obschestva: problemy obreteniya sotsialnogo statusa*.

26 Markku Kivinen, ed., *The Kalamari Union: Middle Class in East and West*, Aldershot, 1998.

27 Sheila Fitzpatrick, *Education and Social Mobility in the Soviet Union, 1921–1934*, Cambridge, 1979.

28 V. F. Shernovolenko et al., *Semya i vozproizvodstvo struktury trudovoi zanyatosti*, Kiev 1984; B. G. Russkikh, *Prestizh professii sluzhashchikh-nespetsialistov kak odin iz faktorov upravleniya razvitiem sotsialnoi struktury obshchesta*, Moscow, 1983; Christel Lane, 'The impact of the economic and political system on social stratification and social mobility: Soviet lower white-collar workers in comparative perspective', *Sociology*, 1, 1987.

29 E. g. Frank Parkin, *Class Inequality and Political Order: Social Stratification in Capitalist and Communist Societies*, London, 1971; Lane, 'The Impact of the Economic and Political System on Social Stratification and Social Mobility'; Howard Davis and Richard Scase, *Western Capitalism and State Socialism*, London, 1985.

30 Markku Kivinen, *Progress i khaos. Sotsiologicheskii analiz proshlogo i budushchego Rossii*, Sankt-Peterburg, 2001; Markku Kivinen, *Progress and Chaos: Russia as a Challenge for Sociological Imagination*, Helsinki, 2002.

31 John Goldthorpe, *Social Mobility and Class Structure in Modern Britain*, Oxford, 1980.

32 Jan Pakulski, 'The dying of class or of Marxist class theory', International Sociology, 3, 1993.

33 See Kivinen, *The New Middle Classes and the Labour Process*, pp. 164–97.

34 *Projekt Klassenanalyse*: Materialien zur Klassenstruktur der BRD 1–2, West Berlin, 1973.

35 Cf. Markku Kivinen, *Parempien piirien ihmisiä*, Jyväskylä, 1987, p. 195.

36 Kivinen, *The New Middle Classes and the Labour Process: Class Criteria Revisited*, pp. 295–6.

37 Raimo Blom, Markku Kivinen, Harri Melin, and Erkki Rannik, 'Structuration of Work Situation in Finland and Soviet Estonia', *International Sociology*, 3, 1991.

38 Leonid Grigoriev and Tatyana Maleva, 'Srednii klass v Rossii na rubezhe etapov transformatsii', *Voprosy ekonomiki*, 1, 2001, p. 45.

39 Ibid., p. 46.

40 E.g. M. K. Gorshkov et al., *Srednii klass v sovremennom rossiiskom obshchestve*, Moscow, 1999; Grigoriev and Maleva, 'Srednii klass v Rossii na rubezhe etapov transformatsii'.

41 Grigoriev and Maleva, 'Srednii klass v Rossii na rubezhe etapov transformatsii'.

42 Alvin Gouldner, *The Future of Intellectuals and the Rise of the New Class*, London and Basingstoke, 1979.

43 Kivinen, *Progress and Chaos*, pp. 150–3.

44 Olga Kryshtanovskaya, 'The new business elite', in David Lane, ed., *Russia in Flux: The Political and Social Consequences of Reform*, Aldershot, 1992; Johan Bäckman, 'New Russians and social change', in Markku Kivinen, ed., *The Kalamari Union: Middle Class in East and West*, Aldershot, 1998.

45 Nicholas Abercrombie and John Urry, *Capital, Labour and the Middle Classes*, London, 1983, p. 122.

46 Ibid., pp. 122–32.

47 Wallace Clement and John Myles, *Relations of Ruling: Class and Gender in Postindustrial Societies*, Montreal and Kingston, 1994.

48 Jeanine Braithwaite, 'The old and new poor in Russia', in Jeni Klugman, ed., *Poverty in Russia: Public Policy and Private Responses*, Washington, DC, 1997, pp. 27, 32.

49 Mervyn Matthews, *Poverty in the Soviet Union: The Life-styles of the Underprivileged in Recent Years*, Cambridge, 1986; Alastair McAuley, *Economic Welfare in the Soviet Union*, Madison, WI, 1979.

50 OECD, *The Social Crisis in the Russian Federation*, Paris, 2001.

51 Ibid., p. 35.

52 Anthony Shorrocks and Stanislav Kolenikov, 'Poverty Trends in Russia During the Transition', paper presented at Wider Conference on Debt Relief, Helsinki, 2001. www.wider.unu.edu/conference/conference-2001–1/shorrocks-kolenikov.pdf. See also Branko Milanovic, *Explaining the Increase in Inequality during the Transition*, Washington, DC, 2000.

53 Anthony Shorrocks, *Decomposition Procedures for Distributional Analysis: A Unified Framework based on Shapley Value*, University of Essex, 1999.

54 See Guillermo Owen, 'Values of games with priori unions', in R. Heim and O. Moeschlin, eds, *Essays in Mathematical Economics and Game Theory*, New York, 1977.

55 Shorrocks and Kolenikov, 'Poverty Trends in Russia During the Transition', Helsinki, 2001.

56 OECD, *The Social Crisis in the Russian Federation*, p. 23.

57 Markku Lonkila, *Informal Exchange Relations in Post-Soviet Russia: A Comparative Perspective*, Sociological Research Online, 2, 1997.

58 Timo Piirainen, 'Globaali hyvinvoinnin jakautuminen', in Timo Piirainen and Juho Saari, eds, *Yhteiskunnalliset jaot. 1990-luvun perintö*, Helsinki, 2002.

59 Branko Milanovic and Shlomo Yitzhaki, *Decomposing World Income Distribution: Does the World Have a Middle Class?*, Washington, DC, 2001.

60 For a fuller treatment of demographic, epidemiological, educational, and other indicators, see World Bank, *Making Transition Work for Everyone: Poverty and Inequality in Europe and Central Asia*, Washington, DC, 2000; OECD, *The Social Crisis in the Russian Federation* 2001.

61 World Bank; OECD; ibid.

62 See Simon Clarke, 'The contradictions of "state socialism"', in Simon Clarke et al., *What about the Workers: Workers and the Transition to Capitalism in Russia*, London, 1993; Simon Clarke and Veronika Kabalina, 'Privatisation and the struggle of control of the enterprise in Russia', paper for conference 'Russia in Transition: Elites, Classes and Inequalities, Cambridge: 15–16 December 1994; Simon Clarke, ed., *Management and Industry in Russia: Formal and Informal Relations in the Period of Transition*, Aldershot, 1995; Simon Clarke, ed., *Conflict and Change in the Russian Enterprise*, Aldershot, 1996; Peter Fairbrother, 'A Russian middle class in formation? Social strata and sectional trade unionism in the aviation and coal industries', in Markku Kivinen, ed., *The Kalamari Union: Middle Class in East and West*, Aldershot, 1998.

63 Ibid., p. 25.

64 Kivinen, *Progress and Chaos*.

65 Simon Clarke, 'Privatization and the development of capitalism in Russia', *New Left Review*, 196, 1993.

66 Clarke and Kabalina, 'Privatisation and the struggle of control of the enterprise in Russia'.

67 Ibid.

68 Petr Biziukov, and Simon Clarke, 'Privatization in Russia – the road to a people's capitalism', *Monthly Review*, 6, 1992.

69 Simon Clarke, 'Privatization and the development of capitalism in Russia'.

70 V. Borisov, *Talousuudistus ja lakko työläisten aktiivisuuden muotona esimerkkkinä Donbassin lakko kesäkuussa 1993*, Idäntutkimus, 1995, pp. 32–43; Simon Clarke, ed., *Conflict and Change in the Russian Enterprise*, Aldershot, 1996.

71 Borisov, ibid.

72 Pavel Romanov, 'Rossiiskaya promyshlennost vstupila v epohu bankrotstv', paper presented at the conference 'Restructuring of Management and Industrial Relations in Russia', 4–7 December 1994.

73 Cf. Clarke and Kabalina, 'Privatisation and the struggle of control of the enterprise in Russia'.

74 Jouko Nikula, *From State-Dependency to Genuine Worker Movement? The Working Class in Socialism and Post-Socialism*, Tampere, 1997.

75 Kagarlitski, *Hajonnut monoliitti*, p. 14.

76 For a good introduction and an example of interesting empirical case analyses, see Marja Nissinen, *Latvia's Transition to a Market Economy: Political Determinants of Economic Reform Policy*, London, 1999.

77 Gil Eyal, Ivan Szelenyi and Eleanor Townsley, *Making Capitalism Without Capitalists: Class Formation and Elite Struggles in Post-Communist Central Europe*, London, 1998.

78 Gil Eyal, 'Anti-politics and the spirit of capitalism: dissidents, monetarists, and the Czech transition to capitalism', *Theory and Society*, 2000: 50.

79 World Bank, *Making Transition Work for Everyone: Poverty and Inequality in Europe and Central Asia*, Washington, DC, 2000; World Bank, *Transition. The First Ten Years: Analysis and Lessons for Eastern Europe and the Former Soviet Union*, Washington, DC, 2002.

80 Anders Åslund, 'Why has Russia's economic transformation been so arduous?', paper presented at the Annual World Bank Conference on Development Economics, Washington, DC, 28–30 April 1999.

81 Theodor Geiger, *Die Klassengesellschaft in Schmelztiegel*, Köln, 1949; Hans Speier, *German White-Collar Workers and the Rise of Hitler*, New Haven, CT, 1986.

82 Vesa Oittinen, 'Marxismi-leninismistä valtiopatriotismiin. Venäjän kommunistien aatteellinen kehitys', *Venäjän ja Itä-Euroopan instituutin tiedonantoja ja katsauksia*, 2, 1995.

83 Göran Ahrne and Erik Olin Wright, 'Class and social organisation in the United States and Sweden: a Comparison', *Acta Sociologica*, 3–4, 1983.

84 Simon Clarke, 'Privatization and the development of capitalism in Russia'.

Are Social Classes Really Dead? A French Paradox in Class Dynamics[1]

Louis Chauvel

Contemporary France, as with many other post-industrial countries, is a society where social classes are broadly supposed to be of little interest for the understanding of current social dynamics. For the last two decades, the future of class structure has been less a controversial issue than simply an old-fashioned one, a rarely considered question, and may have become a kind of sociological taboo. But, more or less occluded over the last two decades, the sociological analysis of contemporary class formation and structure offers us a picture that is far more paradoxical than that usually painted in mainstream post-empirical French sociology.

This chapter will describe the French mainstream (official) hypothesis on the death of social class – a hypothesis that is not so different from the American 'decline and fall of social class' literature.[2] The clarification of the notion of 'social class' offers the opportunity of a confrontation between the mainstream hypothesis and empirical evidence pertaining to the dynamics of the last two decades. The mobilization of available data shows a decline of subjective class affiliation, even if the trends of objective egalitarian economic progress over the former 'Golden Age' period of the previous three decades (the so-called *Trente Glorieuses* 1945–75[3]), have been stalling since the mid-

1980s. A profound contradiction thus appears – a paradoxical change in objective and subjective aspects of social classes – and a long-term analysis offers a new hypothesis on the development of contemporary capitalism.

Social Classes: The 1970s Totem has become the Taboo of the Last Two Decades

After the collapse of the French utopian socialist ideology of the post-1968 era, which was a rich period of social critique and of leftist political and ideological creativity, the hypothesis of the end of social classes has become the 'common sense' of French sociology and social-political thinking since the early 1980s. However, the French history of the debate on class began earlier: Raymond Aron[4] was the first French sociologist to stimulate this debate and to import Nisbet's now classic question 'Are social classes dying?'[5] The more recent works by Clark and Lipset[6] and Kingston[7] are clearly a revival of that theory. Aron followed a schema close to Nisbet's. First, the 'tertiarization' (the emergence of the post-industrial economy based on services and the tertiary sector) implies a new society where class boundaries are (as Nisbet says) blurred and even unclear. Second, the development of trade unions' political power and their diffusion in different social milieux means a profound change in the political representation of blue- and white-collar workers, with a stronger democracy where class domination of bourgeoisie declined. Third, with fast economic growth, the affluent society of the 1960s and the trickle-down mechanism of the diffusion of goods from higher to lower classes, the former consumption borders are destabilized: cars, vacuum cleaners, toasters, and so on define a new inter-class standard of consumption where no goods can define strong and long-term social frontiers that could stabilize a clear class identity. With fewer empirical resources than Goldthorpe et al.[8] for their research on the consequence of affluence on the working class, Aron and his followers developed some new arguments, such as the diffusion of property, educational and university expansion, the increase of women's participation in the labour force, and the consequences of heterogamy ('which is the position in terms of class of a household composed of a worker and a schoolteacher?').

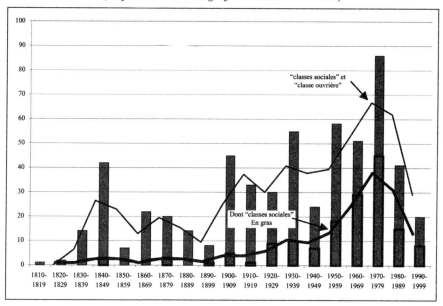

Figure 10.1 Number of Book Titles in the Catalogue of the Bibliothèque Nationale de France (BNF) Containing 'Classes sociales' or 'Classe ouvrière' (20 years Mobile Average of Per Decade Occurrences)

Source: Bibliothèque Nationale de France catalogue.

In fact, Aron's first attempt rapidly collapsed faced with the *Zeitgeist* of the 1970s. Between May 1968 and the early 1980s, with the climax of the victory of socialist François Mitterrand in the presidential elections of 1981, a large movement of utopian social critique shaped a clear atmosphere of (over-) recognition of class, supposed to be the *primum movens* of all social change. As ever, the excess of political activism provokes subsequent backlashes: the same socialists elected in 1981 promoted in 1984 a large reversal in economic policy with the policy of *rigueur*, a mix of wage stagnation (*modération salariale*), of monetarist control of inflation, fostering ultimately an intense acceleration of capital income, of profits and surplus value, at the expense of employed workers.[9] In a fascinating development, most of the former devotees of class analysis and even of the class struggle often became the most vigorous supporters of the idea that classes no longer exist. Most progressive sociologists and leftist social thinkers[10] consider that, today, social class is no longer a useful notion for analysis. More generally, if we consider the occurrence of 'class' in the French sociological PhD thesis titles, a strong decline occurred in the mid-1980s, right at the moment of the ideological transformation accompanying the phase of *rigueur*: an analysis of the BNF catalogue offers similar evidence (see Figure 10.1).

Defining 'Social Classes'

The problem of the 'death of class' debate in France is the capacity of the participants to dissimulate the definition of social class they are using: most conservative sociologists prefer a strong Marxist definition, where a class is a powerfully organized holistic group, marked by an intense class consciousness, mobilized in a violent struggle against other classes, in a society where the *rapports sociaux* (social relations[11]) are characterized by a complex of exploitation and domination. With such a definition, the result is uniformly a clear disappearance of classes in contemporary societies. Conversely, pro-class sociologists prefer loose nominalist (Ricardo-)Weberian definitions of classes, where classes are simply occupational groups of individuals sharing the same position and, also, similar social life chances in markets, since the use of such definitions allows an easy demonstration of the continuing pertinence of class in post-industrial societies. Since the definitions ever remain imprecise, manifest manipulations of the evidence recurrently appear.

Since this chapter is an attempt to assess the dynamics of class in the French context, an empirically based definition of class is proposed here. In fact, this definition is an array of factors of 'classness' (of the intensity of class) and not a rigid definition allowing an assessment in dichotomic terms such as 'Configuration A relates to a class society' and 'Configuration B does not'. Our definition mixes different complementary factors, and we define as social classes social groups that are:

1. objectively structured and defined in economic terms by the unequal shares of the collective production they receive in relation to their position in the economic organization; and

2. organized by three complementary dimensions of class identities:
   - *temporal identity* (2a), permanence of the category, low permeability to intra- and inter-cohort mobility, low heterogamy, and intense social reproduction;
   - *cultural identity* (2b), that is, large sets of common symbolic specific references, shared lifestyles allowing collective inter-recognition, capacity to adopt or reject collectively the same symbolic references; and
   - *collective identity* (2c): capacity to participate in collective action, conflictual acknowledgement in the political sphere of the unity of the class and of its interests.

We should add that the three identity dimensions could be mobilized for any kind of social group: social class, gender, ethnic, regional, religious, and so on. The first economically objective modality of our definition is the only one to be specifically linked to a class delineation.

A broad criticism of this definition is that it is obviously empirical, and not theoretically founded: there is no explicit mention either of exploitation or of domination. There is no mention of a theory of value, or of the question of the relation to any kind of assets. The definition is oriented not by research into the origins of class formations, but by the discovery of empirical symptoms. The usefulness of the definition is that it offers an array of factors for a systematic empirical assessment of 'classness' or the degree of class organization of a macro-occupational group. Undoubtedly, the intensity of exploitation will result in economic gaps and have an impact on the strength of observed inequalities,[12] and symbolic domination will create cultural fractures between social groups that we expect to observe. The main intention is here a diagnosis much more than an explanation of class formation, and this diagnosis is, in France, striking.

The *Trente glorieuses* and *Moyennisation*

We have seen the trajectory of the sociological concern for class issues in France: after a period of post-1968 fascination for analyses in terms of 'social classes',[13] the notion progressively became an old-fashioned one. What about the factual evolution of the French class system in this period? During the *Trente glorieuses* 1945–75 (the French golden age of rapid economic growth and of affluence), a clear trend of objective convergence of class positions was observed.

First, in economic terms, the lower economic positions (white- and blue-collar routine workers) benefited from a strong acceleration of their income: compared to 1913, the average level of living in France is now fivefold greater, while the income of the highest centile has only doubled.[14] Other analyses show the intense trend of equalization (even if that trend was not entirely achieved) observed after the Second World War. If we consider social welfare, there was a clear improvement in workers' living conditions in terms of health, retirement, wage stability, and working conditions, resulting from social bargaining and social struggles. In terms of culture and consumption, a sort of convergence of former working-class specific traits could be observed, notably with the emergence of leisure, holidays, and transportation (ownership of cars), housing (the destruction of old deteriorating tenements, the spreading of new standards, and even access to individual property-holding). Considering education, despite Bourdieu's reproduction theory,[15] the expansion of secondary education for children of all social milieux blurred former social borders.[16]

Many social trends seemed to encourage an optimistic view of social class system dynamics towards a potential convergence.[17] Hence the French theory of *moyennisation*.[18] Indeed, *moyennisation* is almost untranslatable, since the French term of *classes moyennes* and the English 'middle class' are not exact equivalents. In 1970s French sociology, the *classes moyennes* were social strata close to exact average income (higher foremen, technicians, nurses, school-teachers, lower management, social workers, and so on), as in Alain Touraine's definition of the *nouvelle classe moyenne salariée* (the *new employed middle class*).[19] So *moyennisation* could be translated by 'averagization' rather than 'middleization', since in English 'middle class' is a much higher social stratum, a kind of 'comfortable class' intermediate between the proletariat and the higher bourgeoisie, closer to the position of higher professionals, experts, managers, engineers, and so on. *Moyennisation* is much more than a simple numerical expansion of the members of these intermediate strata: it is also claimed to be the emergence of a new class, a *tertius gaudens* between the proletariat and the older bourgeoisie, which creates new *rapports sociaux* (social relations), but also new cultural and consumer traits (rock, barbecue, jeans), and dismantles older configurations of domination.[20] Was the theory fallacious? If we consider the proposition as a diagnosis pertaining to the social trends of the post-war period, *moyennisation* was certainly true: economic, social, and cultural inequalities are now much less marked than in the first half of the twentieth century, and the 1945 to 1975 or 1980 evolution was remarkable. However, if the theory claims to describe contemporary evolutions, or to be a normative prophecy, or even a diagnosis proclaiming that we are right now experiencing an egalitarian system of perfect convergence of all social strata into a single 'average' class, the theory seems to be false, and more and more inappropriate for the understanding of contemporary trends.

Are Social Classes Really Dead: An Objective Restratification?

Let us thus turn to a diagnosis of *moyennisation* in contemporary France: in objective terms, are the social positions of classes more and more egalitarian and the social frontiers between strata really blurred? We propose here some indicators to assess the degree of objective economic structuration of social classes in France. The general result is that the former trend of continuous objective blurring of class structure is no longer operative: indeed, a reversal of the process appears on some levels.

We must remember that, historically, in the French social debate, occupational inequalities and stratifications are to a certain extent officially recognized: ever since their establishment in 1954, the *Catégories socioprofessionnelles* (CSP) have constituted a commonly acknowledged 'class schema', similar to the logic of the Erikson–Goldthorpe–Portocarrero class schema.[21] The advantage of this is that it allows empirically informed discussions about 'classes' without having to pronounce the word 'class'. The CSP schema defines six main occupational groups (more detailed schemata exist), where almost everyone can identify their position.[22] The CSP code is doubly helpful: first, the schema has been reformed only once, in 1982, over the last five decades; second, it is included in any large social survey, and thus offers long-term comparative data on the modification of class structures. The use of this code demonstrates the relativity and even the falseness of many 'death of class theory' arguments.

The very first one, the 'death of class' resulting from the 'death of the working class' (that is: the decline in the proportion of blue-collar workers in the labour force), seems to be less self-evident than often believed. In the French CSP class schema, we can identify *employés* who are structural equivalents in the tertiary (information and services) sector of the economy of the *ouvriers* (blue-collar workers) of the secondary (industrial) sector: *employés* and *ouvriers* have the same level of income, of education, are assigned the same level of responsibility in the occupational hierarchy (routine execution), and can be considered as being two different components of the 'popular class' (*classe populaire*). The analysis of the dynamics of the last three decades offers clear evidence on the so-called 'death of the working class': if *ouvriers* have declined from 40 per cent to 30 per cent of the labour force, *employés* have expanded concomitantly so that for the last 30 years *employés* plus *ouvriers* have constituted a group of about 60 per cent of the total labour force, with no clear trend indicating any decline.

Figure 10.2   Distribution of Occupational Groups in the French Labour Force, 1969–2000 (%)

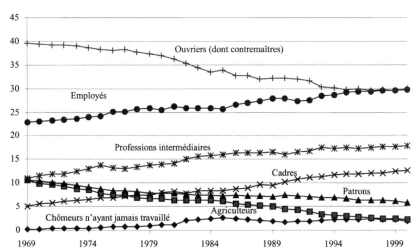

Source: *Enquêtes Emploi* (1969–2000), INSEE, data archive: LASMAS-IDL/IRESCO.
Note: unemployed are classed in their former occupational group.

Another argument on the standardization of the 'lower classes', supposed to be less specific nowadays, is the economic equalization between social classes. This is one of Nisbet's main arguments: affluence and rapid economic growth blur the social class divisions because of the *embourgeoisement* of working-class consumption habits. Let us consider seriously Nisbet's theory: if we do so, economic stagnation should reinforce class divisions because of a restratification due to the growing temporal distance or time-lag between classes.

Over the last decades, static economic inequalities between occupational groups seem to have declined.[23] The *cadres* to *ouvriers* wage ratio was about 1:4 in the 1950s and 1960s, began to weaken from the early 1970s and fell to 1:2.5. In terms of interdecile ratios[24] the evolution is softer, since a part of the fall of the *cadres* to *ouvriers* ratio comes from a strong development during the 1970s of intermediate higher experts and managers with intermediate incomes. The

*Figure 10.3   Annual Average Wage for Full-time Wage-earners,
2000, constants French francs (= 1/6.5) $US*

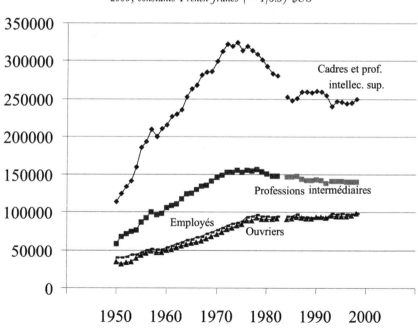

Source: Long term series on wages – INSEE.

interdecile ratio is less reactive, even if it declined substantially. However, behind this static measure of inequality, Nisbet's point of view suggests another indicator, based on dynamic inequalities: how many years do we need, with a given growth rate, to observe the catching up of the *cadres'* level of wages by the *ouvriers?* The catch-up time-lag is a measure of the social distance between employed professionals and workers in terms of standards of living. The idea of the trickle-down economy is based on the anticipation by the lower classes of their own economic future by observation of the economic situation of the higher classes. Evidently, because of a kind of Zeno paradox, the catch-up is never perfect, since, over the time-lag, the income of the higher classes can increase too, but it remains a measure of objectively based hopes of progress. The catch-up time-lag can be calculated over the last five decades.

The results are striking: even if the static measure of inequality shows a weakening class gap (mainly during the 1970s), the dynamic measure of the class gap demonstrates a strong increase with the new period of slow growth. During the fast progression of the *Trente glorieuses*, the catch-up time-lag was about 30 years, since a growth in real terms of about 4 per cent implies a doubling of income in fewer than 18 years. At that point, the time-lag of less

Table 10.1   Catch-up Time-lag, 1955–2000

	Wage ratio cadres/ ouvriers (A)	Full-time wage-earners interdecile ratio	Annual average real growth wage for full-time workers during the last 5 years (%) (B)	Catch-up time-lag (years) [= log(A) log(1 + B/100)]
1955	3.9	3.5	4.8	29.1
1960	3.9	3.8	2.8	49.7
1965	4.0	4.1	3.5	40.0
1970	3.8	3.6	3.7	36.8
1975	3.4	3.4	3.5	35.7
1980	2.9	3.2	1.6	65.1
1985	2.7	3.1	0.3	371.9
1990	2.8	3.2	0.3	353.0
1995	2.6	3.2	0.3	316.2
2000	2.5	3.1	0.6	150.6

Source: Long-term series on wages – INSEE.

Note: in 1955, the cadres' average wage was 3.9 times higher than the workers'. Between 1950 and 1955, the average real growth wage was 4.8%; in 1955, with this rhythm, the catch-up time-lag (= the time after which workers' wage would catch up with the cadres') was 29.1 years.

than a generation meant a realized ideology of progress since, for a young worker, his level of living would catch up the *cadre*'s before his retirement; for an older worker, over time, his children's conditions of life could be expected to improve mechanically, compared to his own.

However, economic stagnation (0.5 per cent is a quasi-stagnation since this level is of the same order of magnitude as *the uncertainty on the measure of inflation*) expanded the time-lag: after 1975, the time-lag jumped to about 300 years, and, while the previous dynamic permitted one to close the gap in less than a generation, ten generations are now needed to obtain the same result. This new dynamic produced, over time, a renewal of stratification (a restratification), since the chronological distance between classes in terms of anticipations of living conditions is much more substantial now than during the *Trente glorieuses*.

In fact, static measures of inequality such as wage and income interdecile ratios show no clear skyrocketing increase of inequality in France, contrary to other developed countries, notably in the Anglo-Saxon world. However, the stability of these inequality ratios hides a much less optimistic view, which clearly appears when we observe the generational dynamics of inequality.[25] At the end of the 1970s, poverty was the curse of elderly people, and was the result of older generations excluded from social progress. Nowadays, poverty is much more developed for those under 35 than for those over 75: the poor are the young and this prefigures a long-term future of poverty. Obviously, conditions are easier for young people who are successful at school and at work, but the gap is widening between this group and less-qualified workers. For those who were young adults after 1975, cohorts born after 1955, the collective project (of equality, solidarity, and wide-ranging social protection measures), which was established after the Second World War and reached its apogee in 1970, is crumbling little by little. A new social pyramid has been re-established with, at its base, a generation subjected to exploitation and social exclusion. Thus the stability of static inequality measures hides a generational dynamics of regression towards greater inequalities.

Another argument is that, today, objective inequalities between classes are only residual, since the ratio of 2.5 between *cadres*' and *ouvriers*' wages is almost nothing, and demonstrates a perfect equalization in standards of living and culture. Such an argument does not resist empirical analysis. Two decades

**Table 10.2   Average Share in the Household Budget and *Cadres/Ouvriers*
Gaps, in 1995**

	(A) % bud. *Ouvriers*	(B) % bud. *Cadres*	absolute gap (C) = (A)-(B)	(D) = (A)/(B) (B = 100)
Tobacco	1.95	0.67	1.28	291
Bread	1.21	0.54	0.67	224
Gasoline	4.38	3.16	1.23	138.6
Delicatessen and cooked meals	2.73	1.80	0.93	151.6
Electricity	2.18	1.39	0.79	156.8
Tools and repairs	1.05	0.60	0.45	175
Meat: beef	1.20	0.73	0.48	164.3
Meat: poultry	0.62	0.30	0.31	206.6
Combustible: bottled gas	0.26	0.06	0.20	433.3
Meat: pork	0.45	0.20	0.26	225
(. . .)				
Weekend expenditures	0.05	0.18	−0.13	27.7
Transport (bus, train, etc.)	0.64	1.12	−0.48	57.1
Reimbursement second home mortgage	0.29	0.62	−0.33	46.7
Car rental	0.03	0.17	−0.14	17.6
Books	0.29	0.83	−0.54	34.9
Gifts to other households	2.11	3.60	−1.49	58.6
Restaurants	1.13	2.29	−1.17	49.3
Household repairs	1.23	3.17	−1.93	38.8
Holiday expenditure	2.02	4.66	−2.64	43.3
Human services and *domesticity*	0.04	0.68	−0.64	5.8

Note: The budget coefficients are the average share in the budget of the items: the workers devote
1.95% of their total expenditures to smoking (A), and cadres only 0.67% (B). The gap can have
two definitions (presented here as ranked ouvriers' consumption, at the top, and cadres below):
first, an absolute difference (C): the ouvriers devote 1.28 points more than cadres to tobacco;
second a relative difference (D): the ouvriers' share of budget for tobacco is 191.7% higher than
for cadres. The absolute gap shows gaps for large items (gasoline, holidays, etc.) but hides gaps
on little items which could have higher symbolic distinctions. This is the purpose of relative gap
(weekend or car rentals). The 20 items are selected (out of 108) considering their significance on
both aspects.
Source: Budget des ménages 1995, enquête obtenue auprès du LASMAS-IDL/IRESCO; ménages
dont la personne de référence est âgée de 18 à 65 ans, de CSP cadre ou ouvrière.

after Bourdieu's *Distinction*,[26] and one century after Halbwach's pioneering
analyses,[27] the *cadres'* and *ouvriers'* standards of living remain remarkably
stratified: economic and cultural resources continue to involve massive inequalities of consumption habits and access to goods. Basic consumption defined by
raw materials, basic food, tobacco, and energy, continue to be over-represented

in the lower classes' consumption, whereas costly or culturally selective consumption elements are still distinctive of the higher classes. Further research shows[28] that, over the last two decades, no clear convergence between the working-class and professional classes' modes of consumption can be observed. Beyond consumption, many authors demonstrate the continued intensity of occupational status and CSP on voting,[29] even if most international theories affirmed the necessary decline of class determination on political behaviour.

In fact, the neo-Nisbetian theorists frequently forget another argument, namely that the *Trente glorieuses* were a period not simply of massive expansion of wage earners' income, but also of *droits sociaux* (social entitlements). Before the 1950s, provision against the main social risks (health, ageing, and so on) were organized at an individual level; in other terms, for the majority, they were not organized and consequently excluded those who could not get access to insurance and asset accumulation. The mutualization (socialization) of risks via mandatory retirement and health and social security contributions proportional to wage earnings shaped a *société salariale* (wage-based society, and welfare),[30] a new society where social rights to retirement were based less on capital inequalities and more on work stratification. Since wage inequalities are based on a 1:3 interdecile ratio while capital inequalities are founded on a 1:70 interdecile ratio, a wage-based society is incomparably more egalitarian than asset-based society. The strobiloïd representation below (from *strobilos*: tap, in Greek[31]) offers a graphic comparison of the two social architectures resulting from wage-based and from asset-based inequalities. The architectonics of a wage-based society is based on a larger middle class (or, better, 'median class') with fewer extremes (fewer rich and fewer poor), while an asset-based society implies large gaps between the different levels of society.

However, it is now time, in France as in any post-industrial country, to analyse the consequences of a reversal of the process toward the 'wage-based society'. If stronger incentives are given to social actors to found their future on savings and capital accumulation, that new society of 'asset-based welfare' emerges, and its the shape is closer to the 1:70 interdecile ratio. The potential result of such a trend is a profound destabilization of the social construction of the *Trente glorieuses* where the 'median class' which tended to emerge in the late 1960s now explodes, caught between climbing and falling fragments.

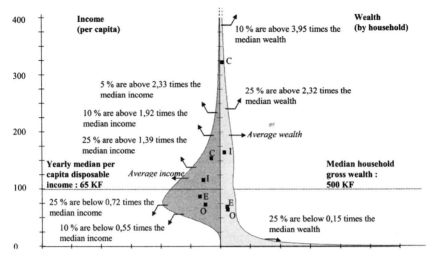

Figure 10.4   Income and Wealth Strobiloïd, 2000
French Francs (=1/6.5 $US) 100 = Median Income 100 = Median Wealth

Note: the strobiloïd is the shape of social pyramid corresponding to the distribution of income (*versus* wealth).[32] At a given level of income, the larger the curve, the more people are positioned around this point. If 100 is the median income (per capita in the household) a large strobiloïd at level 100 shows a large middle class (in the Swedish situation, for instance) at an equal distance between extremes. For wealth, there is clearly no middle class, and the population is stretched between the extreme high level of accumulation and the extreme low point. The points C, I, E, and O shows the median C 'cadres' = higher professionals, managers, etc. I 'professions intermédiaires' = lower professionals and intermediate white-collars, E 'Employés' routine white-collars, and O 'ouvriers' = blue-collar workers. For wealth, these are not the median but average positions.
Source: income: *Budget des ménages* survey 1995 and wealth: *Actifs financiers 1992*, re-evaluation for year 2000 (growth and inflation).

Since social inter-generational immobility continues to divide the opposite social classes, even if the baby-boom generation benefited from more porous social borders and greater social fluidity,[33] the restratification that we perceive in the contemporary trends of evolution of French society could imply for most members of the 'popular class' a social decline that their American counterparts have experienced over the two last decades.

This wide-ranging diagnosis of objective trends that the popular class is facing not only invites a relativization of the *moyennisation* theory (which is no longer operative for the analysis of contemporary French society) but also offers a striking objective falsification (in Popperian terms) of the 'death of class' thesis. But why, then, do we still see no clear class formation in contemporary French society?

A Vanishing of Identitarian Traits
of Contemporary Class Formations?

Despite the objective trends of restratification, class consciousness continues to decline progressively. Even if we doubt the capacity of opinion polls to measure this decay in class-membership consciousness, explicitly confirming one's social class belonging seems to be more and more old-fashioned. However, the decline is not steep: 68 per cent said that they belonged to a class in 1975, 55 per cent in 2002; compared to 1966 (61 per cent), the decline is even slower. This is not extinction but weakening.

Figure 10.5   Respondents Answering that they belong to a Social Class, 1966–2002 (%)

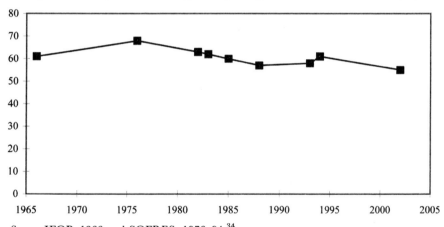

Source: IFOP, 1966 and SOFRES, 1976–94;[34]
completed with 'Panel Electoral Français 2002', Cevipof.

Other sources and interpretations offer clearer diagnoses: the fall in trade union membership, the collapse of the Parti Communiste français (about 21 per cent of votes in the early 1970s, under 5 per cent in 2002), the concomitant decline of working-class local organizations, the decline of communist-based associations promoting collective travel, lifelong education and conferences, and disseminating elements of socialization of all kinds. While the 'popular class's' structuration used to be able to impose strong values, norms, and high levels of political participation, and to structure the 'popular class' in a clear reference group, the new system is blurred. First, the analysis of subjective class membership shows that more and more *ouvriers* and *employés* consider themselves to be members of the 'middle class'. The increasing gap between aspirations (identification to higher reference groups) and the objective social means of their satisfaction (income stagnation, work flexibility, and so on) implies a strong subjective destabilization of the 'popular class', which is less and less a collective actor. The objectively structured working class is also, today, a subjectively atomized grouping of individuals subjected to increasing risks of social alienation. Conversely, the subjective traits and collective consciousness of the upper bourgeoisie seem to be governed by a different dynamic, implying that the bourgeoisie is now the only real class 'in itself and for itself'.[35]

The Class Spiral and the Split Between
Objective and Subjective Aspects

The combination of the trends of objective restratification and subjective destructuration of class consciousness requires a new diagnosis of class dynamics over the last two centuries. In fact, many social analysts have founded their analyses of 'death of class' on the disappearing consciousness of their members. We have underlined here that objective and subjective aspects of social class formation are not collinear: a diagnosis in terms of subjective trends cannot offer any certainty on the real objective evolution. We have now to develop this idea further.

Consider two dimensions: the first (horizontally) is the intensity of objective class traits, such as the intensity of inequality, the strength of class domination and exploitation, and any materialistic subdimension; the second (vertically) is the subjective intensity of class formation, such as consciousness, political mobilization, the strength of the *rapport social*, and so on. The main element is here that these two dimensions are mutually independent, or, better, paradoxically linked. When we cross these two complementary dimensions, a large system of class dynamics appears. Four ideal-typical positions are first

Figure 10.6   The Historical Social Class Spiral

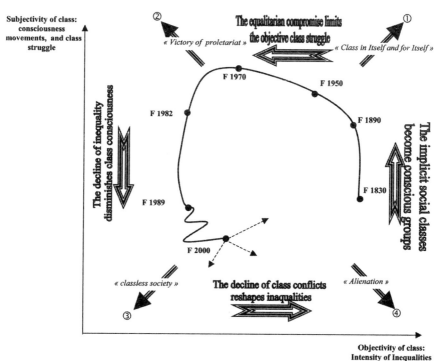

revealed: the upper right-hand position is a situation of a 'class in itself and for itself'(1): both objective and subjective contrasts and oppositions are at their limits; the lower left-hand position ('classless society'(3) is at the opposite pole, a situation of low subjective and objective tensions. A common-sense hypothesis would be that this dyad could sum up the entire social system. We argue that two other positions have been forgotten: strong class conflict can go with lower inequalities, as well as its opposite: some periods of 'victories of the proletariat'(2) go with both lower objective class contrasts and higher class consciousness for the working class. Conversely, strong inequalities can match low social consciousness of the true situation, in a configuration of 'Alienation' (4), as the contemporary American situation suggests.[36]

The most fascinating aspect of this four ideal-types system is that no pole is intrinsically stable. In fact, *social strengths* imply clear tensions that destabilize each pole. The first pole of the 'class in itself and for itself (1) entails social struggles that ultimately impose redistributions and equalization more probably than social appeasement. 'Victory of the proletariat' (2) is difficult to maintain because lower inequalities could produce less social consciousness and interest in social inequalities and much more cultural conflict and symbolic differentiation;[37] otherwise, remaining in (2) would require a strong socialization of newer generations, who might find it difficult to understand the objective substratum of the strong social conflict they are supposed to endorse. The 'classless society' (3) could be a pleasant harbour, but inherent economic tensions could stimulate the desire of the ruling class to expand its power over economic activity, and increase its rates on collective production, and it would be able to do so since the lack of clear structuration of people's consciousness would obstruct collective denunciation of the emerging signs of exploitation. Finally, 'Alienation' (4) cannot be a dead end, since we cannot understand how violent inequalities can emerge without a collective denunciation about to produce the subjective structuration of the victims of the new economic divide. Such a system can be used to summarize French dynamics from 1830[38] to the beginning of the twenty-first century, when the drift from the post-*Trente glorieuses* classless-like society towards working-class alienation became well established. The history of this later period has not been yet written of course, but the clear lack of organization of the new 'popular class' impairs its ability to offer resistance to the higher classes' desire for enrichment. Contemporary France has not advanced down that road as far as the USA, where the counterparts of *ouvriers* and *employés* have been subjected to a strong decline in their income as well as to the deterioration of their collective organizations. For France, the evolution is much more complex, with stronger opposition to this tendency, but the presidential elections of 2002, marked by massive popular abstention and by an upsurge in extreme right-wing populism, indicated powerful signs of alienation.

Conclusion: Dis-socialization

The contemporary problem is the emergence of unconscious objective social classes. The consequences of these unorganized class condition groups on the stability of democracies are highly uncertain: the 2002 French elections showed some of them. When most people experience social situations for which their education did not prepare them, collective forms of destabilization can emerge. An implicit consequence of the confrontation and of the mismatching of objective and subjective aspects in social class dynamics is *dissocialization*: the lack of consistency and even the conflictual relation between the values, ethics, ideologies, and representations that people receive from their social environment and the real situation that people face every day.

This is not simply a question of Mertonian anomie, linked to a growing gap between aspirations and the social possibilities of their satisfaction, but rather a real divergence. Individualism and autonomy offer clear examples of the mismatch:[39] people are presented with stronger incentives to behave as individuals, autonomous, and entirely responsible for their acts. Simultaneously, the economic means that are socially required to act as autonomous individuals are increasingly disappearing for larger social strata. Since the social process that has produced this failure to achieve autonomy is not clear for most people, the victims of the new inequalities cannot give expression to the divide they experience.

Despite collective forms of externalization of this social experience of the mismatch between injunctions to autonomy and the reality of heteronomy, a massive internalization of failure produces a collective atomization of suffering. Young people are more and more socialized in this context of subjective autonomization that only a minority can really live up to, since they have the necessary social and economic resources; the others experience strong tensions that forbid collective recognition of the despair implied by their apparent failure, due to the lack of collective means to satisfy the model of autonomy. A correct form of socialization would encourage the understanding that only a privileged minority can conquer autonomy, and that the others should find the collective resources for their social development. Before a possible new phase of mutual adjustment between required behaviours and social means emerges, a massive dissocialization of the popular class will accelerate the drift towards a subjectively unconscious class system of objectively strongly stratified economic classes. The potential political consequences of such a mismatch are tremendous. With this in mind, let us simply mention a final paradox concerning the complicated fluctuation between a reduction of this mismatch between objective class positions and representations. On the one hand, an intellectual re-examination of class issues is emerging in sociology, with a new sociological agenda for a re-evaluation of social classes as important objects for the analysis of contemporary societies[40] – we can speak of a new and visible intellectual shift towards class issues. Similarly, in the objective sphere of the behaviour of people, one interpretation of the May 2005 French referendum on the European Constitutional Treaty – where the working class and now lower middle class rejected a market-based vision of Europe – is that this was a political mobilization potentially based on social class beginning to re-emerge today.

Notes

1 Two papers (in French) from which this chapter is drawn may be downloaded from the internet: *www.cepremap.ens.fr/~levy/chauvel.rtf* (L. Chauvel, 1999, 'Classes, et générations: l'insuffisance des hypothèses de la théorie de la fin des classes sociales', *Actuel Marx*, 26: 37–52); and *www.ofce.sciences-po.fr/pdf/revue/9–79.pdf* (L. Chauvel 2001, 'Le retour des classes sociales?', *Revue de l'OFCE*, 79: 315–59.)
2 Nisbet, 1959.
3 See Fourastié, 1979.
4 Aron 1969.
5 Nisbet 1959.
6 Clark and Lipset 1991.
7 Kingston 2000.
8 Goldthorpe et al. 1968–69.
9 Todd 1995.
10 Even Touraine or Dubet and Martuchelli 1998.
11 In French, '*rapport social*' is a much stronger expression than 'social relation'; it refers to a violent trial of strength, whereas '*relation sociale*' is a more neutral term.
12 Wright 1979, 1985.
13 During this period, Poulantzas's (1974) book was a high point in French sociological theory.
14 Piketty 2001.
15 Bourdieu and Passeron 1964, 1970.
16 Evidently, Bourdieu's question is the theory of the timeless trend of reproduction, whereas the trend analysis of educational social inequalities attempts an analysis of historical variations in reproduction intensity: these analyses are more complementary than contradictory in their conclusions.
17 Then, the definition of modernity was not really challenging, since the idea of universalistic progress was clearly emerging (Therborn 1995); in terms of inequality analysis, the impact on lower classes of economic stagnation tend to support the view of our post-modernity as rather a *counter*-modernity.

18 Mendras 1988.
19 Touraine 1969.
20 Mendras 1988.
21 Erikson and Goldthorpe 1992.
22 In the French statistical system, these 'socioprofessional categories' CSP are a type of *monopolistic descriptive* tool of occupational stratification (Desrosières et Thévenot 1988). *Cadres* are the higher professionals, managers, and highly qualified experts; *professions intermédiaires* are second-rank professionals; *employés* are routine white-collar and service workers; *ouvriers* are blue-collar workers; *agriculteurs* and *patrons* are the self-employed in agriculture and of other sectors respectively. This nomenclature is widely used by official and private statistical agencies and constitutes a tool broadly adopted by individuals to describe their own social position. A book such as Bihr and Pfefferkorn's (1995), which offers a large panorama of occupational inequalities, is an example of the usefulness of the CSP schema.
23 Chauvel 1997.
24 The interdecile ratio is the ratio between the level of income above which are the richest 10 per cent of the population and the level of income below which are the poorest 10 per cent. The interdecile ratio is the most common means by which to measure inequality.
25 Chauvel 2002.
26 Bourdieu 1979.
27 Halbwachs 1915, 1913.
28 Chauvel 1999.
29 Boy and Mayer 1997; Héran 1997.
30 Aglietta and Brender 1984.
31 Chauvel 1995.
32 See Chauvel 1995.
33 Vallet 1999; also Thélot and Vallet 2000.
34 Michelat and Simon 1996.
35 Pinçon and Pinçon-Charlot 2000.
36 Chauvel 1995, 2001.
37 Pakulski and Waters, 1996.
38 We mention 1830 as a period preceding the *prise de conscience* (emergence of class consciousness) of the working class. Strong class conflicts emerged in the 1848 period and attained their climax during the first half of the twentieth century. Thompson's (1963) question regarding the making of a class is still the most fascinating question for sociology.
39 Castel 1995.
40 Bouffartigue 2004; Choppart and Martin 2004.

References

Aglietta, M., and A. Brender, 1984, *Les Métamorphoses de la société salariale*, Paris: Calmann-Lévy.
Aron, R., 1969, *Les Désillusions du progrès: essai sur la dialectique de la modernité*, Paris: Calmann-Lévy.

Bihr, A., and R. Pfefferkorn, 1995, *Déchiffrer les inégalités*, Paris: Syros.
Bouffartigue, P., (ed.), 2004, *Retour des classes sociales, inégalités, dominations, conflits sociaux*, Paris: Éd. La Dispute, pp. 55–71.
Bourdieu P., 1979: *La Distinction, critique sociale du jugement*, Paris: Editions de Minuit.
Bourdieu, P., and J. C. Passeron, 1964, *Les Héritiers: les étudiants et la culture*, Paris: Editions de Minuit.
—, 1970, *La Reproduction: éléments pour une théorie du système d'enseignement*, Paris: Editions de Minuit.
Boy, D., et N. Mayer, 1997, 'Les "variables lourdes" en sociologie électorale: état des controverses', *Enquête*.
Castel, R., 1995, *Les Métamorphoses de la question sociale: une chronique du salariat*, Paris: Fayard.
Chauvel, L., 1995, 'Inégalités singulières et plurielles: l'évolution de la courbe de répartition des revenus', *Revue de l'OFCE*, 55: 211–40.
— 1997, 'Les inégalités au fil du temps: 1954–1994', in L. Dirn, 'Tendances de la Société Française', *Revue de l'OFCE*, 61: 201–7.
— 1999: 'Du pain et des vacances: la consommation des catégories socioprofessionnelles s'homogénéise-t-elle (encore)?', *Revue française de sociologie*, LX: 79–96.
— 2001, 'Un nouvel âge de la société américaine? Dynamiques et perspectives de la structure sociale aux Etats-Unis (1950–2000)', *Revue de l'OFCE*, 76: 7–51.
— 2002 (2nd edn), *Le Destin des générations, structure sociale et cohortes en France au XXe siècle*, Paris: PUF.
Chopart, J.-N., and Claude Martin (eds), 2004, *Que reste-t-il des classes sociales?* Rennes: Ecole Nationale de la Santé Publique.
Clark T. N., and S. M. Lipset, 1991, 'Are Social Classes Dying?', *International Sociology*, VI: 397–410.
Desrosieres, A., and L. Thevenot, 1988, *Les Catégories socioprofessionnelles*, Paris: La Découverte.
Dubet, F., and D. Martucelli, 1998, *Dans quelle société vivons-nous?*, Paris: Le Seuil.
Erikson, R., and J. H. Goldthorpe, 1992, *The Constant Flux: A Study of Class Mobility in Industrial Societies*, Oxford: Clarendon Press.
Fischer C., M. Hout, S. R. Lucas, M. Sànchez-Jankowski, A. Swidler and K. Voss, 1996, *Inequality by Design: Cracking the Bell Curve Myth*, Princeton, NJ: Princeton University Press.
Fitoussi, J.-P., 1995, *Le Débat interdit*, Paris: Arléa.
Fitoussi, J.-P., and P. Rosanvallon, (eds), 1996, *Le Nouvel Âge des inégalités*, Paris: Le Seuil.
Fourastie, J., 1979, *Les Trente Glorieuses ou la révolution invisible*, Paris: Fayard.
Goldthorpe, J. H., D. Lockwood, F. Bechhofer and J. Platt, 1968–69, *The Affluent Worker*, Cambridge: Cambridge University Press (3 vols).
Halbwachs, M., 1905, 'Remarques sur la position du problème sociologique des classes', *Revue de métaphysique et de morale*, 13: 890–905.
—, 1913, *La Classe ouvrière et les niveaux de vie*, Paris: Félix Alcan.
Heran F., 1997, 'Les intermittences du vote: un bilan de la participation de 1995 à 1997', *INSEE Première*: 546.
Kingston, P.W., 2000, *The Classless Society*, Stanford, CA: Stanford University Press.
Mendras, H., 1988, *La Seconde Révolution française: 1965–1984*, Paris: Gallimard.
Michelat, G., and M. Simon, 1996, '1981–1995: changements de société, changements d'opinion', in Sofres, *L'Etat de l'opinion 1996*, Paris: Le Seuil.

Nisbet, R., 1959, 'The Decline and Fall of Social Class', *Pacific Sociological Review*, 2 (1): 119–29.

Pakulski, J., and M. Waters, 1996, *The Death of Class*, London: Sage.

Piketty T., 2001, 'Les inégalités dans le long terme', in T. Atkinson, M. Glaude, L. Olier and T. Piketty, 'Inégalités économiques', *Rapports du Conseil d'analyse économique*, 33.

— 2001, *Les Hauts Revenus en France au XXe siècle: inégalités et redistributions*, 1901–1998, Paris: Grasset.

Pinçon, M., and M. Pinçon-Charlot, 2000, *Sociologie de la bourgeoisie*, Paris: La Découverte.

Poulantzas N., 1974, *Les Classes sociales dans le capitalisme d'aujourd'hui*, Paris: Le Seuil.

Simmel, G., 1981 (1896–1897), *Sociologie et épistémologie*, Paris: PUF.

Therborn, G., 1995, *European Modernity and Beyond*, London: Sage.

Thelot, C. and L.-A. Vallet, 2000, 'La réduction des inégalités sociales devant l'école depuis le début du siècle', *Économie et Statistique*, 334: 3–32.

Todd, E., 1995, 'Aux origines du malaise politique français: les classes sociales et leur représentation', *Le Débat*, 98–120.

Touraine, A., 1969, *La Société post-industrielle*, Paris: Denoël.

Thompson, E., 1963, *The Making of the English Working Class*, London: Gollancz.

Vallet, L.-A., 1999, 'Quarante années de mobilité sociale en France: l'évolution de la fluidité sociale à la lumière de modèles récents', *Revue française de sociologie*, Vol. 40: 5–64.

Wright, E. O., 1979, *Class Structure and Income Determination*, New York: Academic Press.

— 1985, *Classes*, London: Verso.

List of Contributors

Louis Chauvel is Professor of Sociology at Sciences Politiques Paris and Research Fellow at the Observatoire Français des Conjonctures and Observatoire Sociologique du Changement. His recent publications include *Le Destin des générations, structure sociale et cohortes en France au XXe siècle.*

Michael Hout is Professor of Sociology at the University of California, Berkeley. He is co-author of *Inequality by Design* and *The Facts on Conservative Christians.*

Arne L. Kalleberg is Kenan Distinguished Professor of Sociology and Senior Associate Dean for Social Sciences at the University of North Carolina at Chapel Hill. His most recent books include: *The Mismatched Worker*; *Fighting for Time: Shifting Boundaries of Work and Social Life* (co-edited with Cynthia Fuchs Epstein); and *Inequality: Structures, Dynamics and Mechanisms; Essays in Honor of Aage B. Sorensen* (co-edited with Steven L. Morgan, John Myles, and Rachel A. Rosenfeld). He is currently writing a book on changes in job quality in the United States.

Markku Kivinen is Director of the Aleksanteri Institute, Finnish Center for Russian and East European Studies, University of Helsinki. He has published widely on Russia and on transition in Russia and in the West. His most recent books are *Progress in Chaos* and, co-edited with Katri Pynnönniemi, *Beyond the Garden Ring*: *Dimensions of Russian Regionalism.*

Michèle Lamont is Professor of Sociology and Director of the European Network on Inequality at Harvard University. She has published widely in the fields of cultural sociology, inequality, race and immigration, comparative sociology, the sociology of knowledge, and contemporary sociological theory. Her book, *The Dignity of Working Men: Morality and the Boundaries of Race, Class, and Immigration* won the 2000 C. Wright Mills Award from the Society for the Study of Social Problems.

Huang Ping, Senior Fellow and Professor of Sociology, Chinese Academy of Social Sciences, has been a co-editor (with Wang Hui) of *Dushu* since 1997, and is also an executive member of the International Social Sciences Council, and vice-president of the International Institute of Sociology. Most recent publications include: *Towards a Society with Harmony*; *Globalization and China: Washington Consensus, Beijing Consensus, or What?* (edited with Cui Zhiyuan), and *Challenging Development Discourse*.

Elisa P. Reis is Professor of Political Sociology at the Federal University of Rio de Janeiro, chair of the Research Network on Social Inequality in Brazil, and vice-president of the international Comparative Research on Poverty. She has published extensively in Brazil and abroad. Among her latest publications in English is *Elite Perceptions of Poverty and Inequality* (co-edited with Mick Moore).

Göran Therborn is Director of the Swedish Collegium for Advanced Study in the Social Sciences, and Professor of Sociology at Uppsala University, Sweden. His most recent books are *Between Sex and Power: Family in the World, 1900–2000*, and *Asia and Europe in Globalization* (co-edited with H. Khondker).

Denny Vågerö is professor of medical sociology and the director of CHESS, Centre for Health Equity Studies at Sockholm University and the Karolinska Institutet. He has published widely in both medical and sociological journals on health inequalities, on the health crises in Eastern Europe and on early life factors of importance for adult health. Since 2005 he is a member of the WHO Commission on Social Determinants of Health, the purpose of which is to address health inequalities across the globe.

Peter Weingart holds a chair for Sociology and Sociology of Science at Bielefeld University, Germany. He is also the director of the Institute for Science and Technology Studies and a member of the Berlin-Brandenburg Academy of Sciences. He has published widely in the area of sociology of science and science studies. His latest publications are: *Die Stunde der Wahrheit?*, *Die Wissenschaft der Öffentlichkeit*, and together with S. Maasen (eds), *Democratization of Expertise*.

Index

Africa 6, 21, 22, 23, 24, 26, 36, 49, 69,
    164, 170
Africa, sub-Saharan
  books published 176
  comparative inequality 29, 30, 32, 33
  de-colonization 100
  education spending 171
  ethnic fractionalisation 19
  fertility rates 18
  health and mortality xiv
  illiteracy rates 168
  income inequality 19
  income per capita 75
  life expectancy 21, 73
  patriarchy 23, 25
  per capita GDP 26
  RD 172, 173
  schooling statistics 169, 170
  scientific output 174, 175
  vital inequality xiv, 9, 20
African-American immigrants 93–107
African mobility
  see under social mobility
Alexander, Jeffrey 96
Algeria 109 n18
American mobility
  see under social mobility
Anderson, Benedict 108n
Arab states
  books published 176

  education spending 171
  RD 172, 173
  schooling statistics 168, 169
  scientific output 174, 175
Argentina 31, 33, 147
Armenia 276
Asia 24, 69
  books published 176
  education spending 171
  RD 172, 173
  schooling statistics 168, 169
  scientific output 174, 75
Atkinson, Anthony 2
Auer, Peter 149–50
Australia 23, 143, 146, 148, 169, 170, 175
Austria 27, 141, 143, 175

Bairoch, Paul 38
Baker, D. 71
Balkans, the 23
Baltic republics 79, 80
Bangladesh 9, 15, 25, 175, 219 n13, 219
  n14
Barker, D. 69
Barlösius, E. 3
Barros, Richard Paes de 198
Barth, Fredrik 95
Belarus 71, 79, 80, 81, 276
Belgium 67, 143, 147, 165, 175
Ben-Shlomo, Y. 83

Benin 173
Benson, John 148
Bernhardt, E. 62
Biblarz, T. 124
Blair, Tony 8
Blau, Peter 127, 130
Blumer, Herbert 95
Boenheim, F. 67
Bolivia 29, 31
Botswana 170, 198
Bourdieu, Pierre 2, 8, 9, 13, 25, 126, 300,
  306, 314 n16
Bourguignon, François 3, 10
Brazil 21, 29, 31, 33, 34, 42, 173, 174,
  176, 260
  see inequality in Brazil
Brezhnev, Leonid 248, 256
Brockenhoff, M. xiv
Brown, Leslie 223
Brunner, E. 83
Bukharin, Nikolai 247
Burawoy, Michael 255, 257
Burkina Faso 30, 169
Burström, B. 62
Burundi 30
Bush, George 8
Butler, C. 73

Cambodia 259
Canada 28, 33, 35, 40, 41, 67, 143, 165, 175
capital flows, global 47–8, 50
Caselli, G. 64, 75
Casey, Bernard 154
Castells, Manuel 176–7
Cazes, Sandrine 150
Cebrián, Immaculada 151
Central Africa 32
Central Asia 22, 23, 26
Central Europe 15, 27, 77, 174, 276
centre-periphery problematic 18
Ceylon 47
Chauvel, Louis xvii-xviii, 295–317, 319
Chiang Kai-Shek 221
Chile 29, 31, 90n, 170, 172, 173, 175
China
  capitalism 39
  comparative inequality 32

disposable income 33
economic growth 18
economic growth 38, 47
education spending 171
existential inequality 23
fertility rates 28
Gini coefficient 30
hierarchization 13
high degrees 180
income inequality 39, 42
internal inequality 38
life expectancy 21
low-income country 277
RD 173
scientific output 174, 175
vital inequality 25
women's income 33
world inequality 16
see also inequality and globalization, in
  China
Clark, T. N. 296
Clarke, Simon 277–9
class analysis xviii
  see also class structuration
  see also social classes, death of
class relations xv
class structuration xvii, xviii, 157
  and restructuration, in Russia, 247–94
  fate of the middle classes 266–71
  the managerial revolution 279–83
  the nomenklatura and classes 247–57
  potential middle class 262–6
  poverty and inequality 271–7
  middle classes, problem of 257–62
  trends in class relations 283–90
  working class and the labour
    collective 277–9
  see also social classes, death of
Colombia 29
Congo 5, 49
Cook, Lomax 112 n36
contracting out
  see nonstandard employment relations
Cornia, Giovanni Andrea 2, 49, 74
Costa Rica 30, 32, 172, 198
Croatia 276
Cuba 30, 173

cultural capital 8
cultural membership
    French and American worker's views
        93–118
    French cultures of solidarity 96–102
    American-style collectivity 102–5
Cyprus 170, 173
Czech Republic 27, 28, 33, 78, 85, 276

Delamonica, E. 75
Delerm, Robert 111 n31
Demine, A. 72
Deng, Xiaoping 221, 242
Denmark 84, 143, 148, 169, 175
Desrosières, A. 315 n22
Dikhanov, Yuri 31, 38
Dominican Republic 29, 171
Drever, F. 65
Drori, G. 182
Dumont, Louis 186
Duncan, Otis Dudley 121–2, 127, 130
Dunham, Vera 256
Durkheim, Emile 95, 96
Dworkin, Ronald 8

East Africa 25
East Asia 10, 21, 24, 33, 44, 45
    books published 176
    education spending 171
    illiteracy rates 168
    RD 172, 173
    scientific output 174, 175
Eastern Europe
    communism, collapse 42
    health 62, 77, 78, 85, 86, 88
    industrialization 15
    patriarchy 24, 44, 45
    poverty 26
    turn to capitalism 39
    undernourishment 22
    women's income 33
Ecuador 29, 31, 172, 176, 276
Egypt 21, 172, 173, 174, 176
El Salvador 29, 175
electronic revolution 40
England 35, 64, 66, 84
equality mechanisms 14–16

equality of opportunity
    see inequality of opportunity
Erikson, R. 83
Estonia 27, 76, 79, 86, 276
Ethiopia 25, 30, 32
Europe , xiv
    books published 176
    brain drain to 79
    comparative inequality 27
    development in 242
    education spending 171
    employment relations 155
    gender equality 36
    health inequalities 83
    illiteracy rates 168
    life expectancy 69, 81
    mortality rates 76
    neoliberal policies 82, 234
    patriarchy 23
    post-patriarchy 23
    poverty 26
    racism 24
    reform of medicine 67
    RD 172–3
    schooling statistics 169, 170
    scientific output 174, 175
    temporary work 145, 147
    see also Western Europe; Eastern
        Europe; Central Europe
Europe, health inequalities
    see inequalities of health
Eyal, Gil 284

Featherman, David 124
feminism 24, 46, 50
Field, M. 72
Fiji 168, 172, 176
financial markets, liberalization of 40
Finland 71, 75, 76, 84, 144, 148, 170,
        264, 265
Firebaugh, Glenn 2
Fitoussi, J.-P. 3
Fitzpatrick, Sheila 249, 251
France
    comparative inequality 34
    exclusion 12
    hierarchization 13

income inequality 38
life expectancy 77
mortality statistics 67, 76, 77, 84
nonstandard work 139, 141, 143, 144, 154
scientific output 175
small-scale enterprise 148
university education 126
vital inequality 35
women's income 33
see also cultural membership; social classes, death of
Fraser, Nancy 2

Gaidar, Yegor 280, 282
Galtung, Johan 19
Gambia 30
gender (in)equality xiii, 23, 24, 33, 36, 45, 81,
144, 152–3, 199
see also feminism; sexism; sexual inequality; existential inequality
Gerber, Theodore 132
Germany
  class structuration 289
  comparative inequality 27
  economic inequality 38
  income inequality 41
  mobility 153
  mortality statistics 67
  nonstandard work 139, 141, 143–5, 151   scientific knowledge 165
  scientific output 175
  scientists and engineers 172, 180
  self-employment 148
  vital inequality 35
  women's income 33
Gerschenkron, Alexander 15
Ghana 30, 32
Gisselman, M. 82
Glass, David 121
globalization xiv, 105, 164, 165, 178, 186–7
  see also global outcomes *under* inequalities
  see also inequality and globalization, in China

Goldthorpe, John 263, 296
Goodman, Leo 121
Gorbachev, Mikhail 279, 282
Gouldner, Alvin 267
Great Britain 22, 28, 35, 38, 49
Greece 143
Grigoriev, Leonid 266
Guatemala 29, 173
Gwatkin, D. 75

Haiti 19, 22, 219 n13
Halbwachs, M. 306
Harris-White, B. xvi, xvii
Havel, Vaclav 28
Hegel 7
Henriques, Ricardo 191
Hewett, P. xiv
HIV-AIDS 6, 9, 22, 35, 42, 73, 81, 186
Holland 165
Holmlund, Bertil 145
Honduras 29, 168
Hong Kong 130
Honneth, Axel 2
Hoque, Kim 154
Hout, Michael xv, 119–35, 319
Huang Ping xiv, xvii, 220–46, 320
Hungary 33, 85, 169, 276

Iceland 173
Ieronimo, Nick 148
immigrant integration 94
  and cultural citizenship 94–118
  and human rights 94, 105, 106
immigrants
  ordinary citizens' views 93–118
India 7, 9, 18, 19, 21, 22, 23, 25, 30, 38, 39
  books published 176
  education spending 171
  RD 172
  schooling statistics 170
  scientific output 174, 175
Indonesia 30, 235
inequality
  countries, comparative 27, 29, 32
  economic resource xvi, 8, 25–35, 37

existential xv, 2, 3, 7–8, 8, 9, 10, 22–5, 36, 42, 51
of health and mortality xiv, 2
income 2, 20, 37–41, 41–2, 45
and morality, 1, 4
of opportunity 2, 5, 6, 11, 36
of outcome 5
resource xviii, 3, 8–9, 9, 10, 20, 51
sociological treatment of xiii-xviii
vital xiv, 3, 6–7, 9, 20–22, 35–6, 39, 42, 48, 51
see also inequalities; racial/ethnic inequality; gender (in)equality; sexual inequality; inequality in Brazil; inequality and globalization;
see also under class structuration
inequality in Brazil
facts and perceptions 193–219
Brazilians' perceptions 209–17
elite perceptions 199–208
facts about 197–9
prospects for change? 217–8
social inequality 194–7
inequality and globalization , in China 220–46
a constraint to development 234–6
food shortage onwards 227–8
land privatization? 238–9
recent changes 226–7
rethinking the problem 241–3
rural-urban gap 228–31
'three-dimensional rural problem' 239–41
un- and underemployment 236–7
inequalities, an introduction 1–58
explanations 41–51
global outcomes 42–49
social theory 4–20
arenas, interactions, sources, pathways 9–10
differences and inequalities 4–5
four mechanisms 11–16
inequality of what? 5–9
(in)equality among whom? 16–18
shapes of inequality 18–20
trajectories over time 35–41
income inequality 37–41

world pictures, past and present 20–35
economic resources inequality 25–35
existential inequality 22–25
vital inequality 20–21
see also inequality
inequalities of health, global 61–92
European Health Divide 75–81
global growth and health 72–5
long-term health determinants 65–72
long-term health trends 62–5
social inequalities in health 81–6
inequalities and injustice 4, 5
International Monetary Fund (IMF) 39, 46
internet, the 176, 177
Iran 172
Iraq 73
Ireland 130–1, 143, 144, 149
Irish mobility
see social mobility
Israel 175
Italy 33, 84, 143, 144, 148, 175

Jamaica 35, 171, 172
Japan
family reform 46
job stability 149
land per head 235
management doctrine 15
nationalism 28
part-time work 143, 144, 151
post-patriarchy 23
RD 171, 172, 173
scientific knowledge 165, 177
scientific publications 174, 175, 177
skilled workers 180
trade flows 47
vital inequality 20
women's income 33
Jordan 169, 172
justice, see inequalities and injustice

Kautsky, Karl 257
Kalleberg, Arne xv, 136–62, 319
Kenya xiv, 22
King, Elizabeth 3
Kingston, P.W. 296

Kirkpatrick, Ian 154
Kivinen, Markku xvii, 247–94, 319
Klaus, Vaclav 28
knowledge
  and inequality xvi, 163–90
    determinants and dynamics 177–80
    indicators, knowledge inequality
      166–77
    'indigenous knowledge' 183–6
    overcoming inequalities 180–3
knowledge society, the 165, 187
Kolenikov, Stanislav 273
Korea 28, 47, 130
Khrushchev, Nikita 248, 256
Kuh, D. 83
Kunst, A. 83, 86
Kuwait 168, 170, 175

La Dou, J. 79
Lamont, Michèle 15, 93–118, 320
Latin America
  absolute poverty 26
  books published 176
  capital flows 47
  class structure 289
  comparative inequality 29, 30, 31
  distributive paths 10
  education spending 171
  fertility rates 18
  global internet users 177
  illiteracy rates 168
  income inequality 19, 39, 41
  life expectancy 69
  post-colonial governance 49
  RD 172, 173
  schooling statistics 169, 170
  scientific output 174, 175
  women's income 33
Latvia 79, 276
Leinsalu, M. 86
Lenin, Vladimir 288
Leon, D. 87, 88
Lesotho 30, 169, 171, 174
Lewis, Oscar 194
Lichtenstein 174
life expectancy 61–90
  see also inequality, vital

Lipset, S. M. 296
Lithuania 79, 172, 276
Low Countries, the 26
Luhmann, Niklas 9
Lutz, W. 73
Luxembourg 143, 146
Lu Xueyi 244 n3
Lynch, J. 84

Madagascar 172
Mackenbach, Johan 83, 84–5
Maddison, Angus 44
Malawi 30
Malaysia 168, 172, 173
Maleva, Tatyana 266
Mali 30, 169
Mao Zedong, Chairman 221, 242
Mare effect 126
Malta 170, 176
Marmot, M. 70, 83
Marx, Karl 11
Massey, Douglas 120
Mauss, Marcel 95
McKeown, Thomas 66
McMichael, T. 72
Meslé, F. 77
Mexico 29, 33, 34, 40, 47, 276
Middle East, the 74
Milanovic, Branko 3, 31
Minujin, A. 75
Mitterand, François 297
Moldavia 71, 79, 80, 81
Morgan, W. 17
Morocco 110 n18, 168, 170
mortality
  kinds and statistics 61–90
  see also under inequality; and inequality,
    vital
Moser, K. 73
Mozambique 169, 170
Muslim immigrants 93, 97, 98, 99

Namibia 22, 30, 31, 34, 171
nation-state
  and common good 99
neoliberalism 31, 40, 49, 82, 241, 242,
  280

Nepal 168, 171, 175
Netherlands 143, 144, 154, 156, 175, 176
New Zealand 169, 171, 175
Nicaragua 29, 169
Niger 30, 168, 169
Nigeria 22, 25, 30, 172
Nisbet, R. 303–4
nonstandard employment relations
  cross-national patterns 142–9
    contracting out 147–8
    independent contractors 148–9
    part-time work 142–5
    short-term employment 145–6
    temporary agencies 146–7
  and labour market inequality xv, 136–62
  labour market outcomes 149–56
    careers and mobility 153–5
    growth of bad jobs? 150–2
    job insecurity? 149–50
    job quality 152–3
    triangular employment relations
      155–6
  standard and nonstandard work 137–42
Nordic Countries, the 26, 35
North Africa 23, 25
North America 17, 24, 25, 33, 69, 242,
  277
North Korea 75
Northeast Asia 28
Norway 84, 143, 171, 175
Northwestern Europe 28
Norway 83, 141, 148
Nussbaumer, J. 75

Oceania 23, 24, 69
  books published 176
  education spending 171
  RD 172, 173
  schooling statistics 169, 170
  scientific output 174, 175
Oman 169
Omran, Abdel 63
Owen, Guillermo 27

Pakistan 9, 25, 168, 172
Panama 30
Papua New Guinea 30, 170

Paraguay 30
part-time work
  see under nonstandard employment
    relations
patriarchy 7, 23, 24, 25, 36, 44, 45–6, 50
Patterson, D. 77
Pavlov, Valentin 279, 282
Peru 30, 31
Philippines 169, 171, 219 n13
Pol Pot 259, 260
Poland 26, 33, 77, 175, 276
Portugal 27, 143, 144, 149, 156
poverty, absolute 26
poverty, relative xviii, 27
poverty, rural
  see inequality and globalization, in
    China
Prebisch, Raúl 18

race relations xv
racial/ethnic inequality xiii, xv, 23, 24,
  31, 33, 34,
49, 81, 82, 93–118, 199, 203
  see also existential inequality; racism;
    xenophobia
racism 7, 23, 36, 51, 96, 99
  see also racial/ethnic inequality
Rae, Douglas 195
Raftery, Adrian 124
Ravaillon, Martin 3
Reis, Elisa xvi, 193–219, 320
republicanism, French 94–5, 98, 99, 101,
  105, 106–7
Rogoff, Natalie 121
Rokkan, Stein 19
Romania 171
Russia
  capitalism 39
  communism 35
  comparative inequality 27, 32
  disposable income 33
  EastWest health divide 75–81
  epidemiological transition 64, 71
  Gini coefficient 30
  income shares 34
  internal inequality 38
  life expectancy 76

mobility 131–3
mortality statistics 67, 77
patriarchy 24
scientific output 175
vital inequality 7, 21, 25, 42
women's income 33
see also class structuration
Russian mobility
see social mobility
Ryzkhov, Prime Minister 272
Rwanda xiv, 19, 30, 32, 173

Savidan, P. 3
Scandinavia 24, 27, 36, 70, 82
Scotland 175
Sen, Amartya xiii, 1, 5–6, 7, 64
Sennett, Richard 2
sexual inequality 9, 24
see also gender (in)equality
sexism 23, 36
see also gender (in)equality
Shapley, Lloyd 274
Shkolnikov, V. 86
Shorrocks, Anthony 273
short-term employment
see nonstandard employment relations
Sierra Leone 30, 169, 172
Silesia 67
Simmel, Georg 95
Singapore 130, 170
Slovenia 27, 276
Smith, G. Davey 84
Spain 139, 140, 143, 144, 151, 153, 154, 168
Sobel, Michael E. 121
social classes, death of
a French paradox 295–317
the class spiral 310–12
dis-socialization 312–14
a restratification? 301–9
social classes, definitions 298–9
social classes and French sociology 296–8
the *Trente glorieuses, moyennisation* 299–301
vanishing of identitarian traits 309–10

social mobility
case studies 124–33
African American mobility 127–30
American mobility 124–7
Irish mobility 130–1
Russian mobility 131–3
and economic change 119–33
and social inequality 119–20
structural and exchange mobility 120–23
social perception xvi
see also inequality in Brazil
social structuration xvi
Sorokin, Pitrim 120
South Africa 5, 17, 23, 24, 26, 30, 31, 33, 34, 36
books published 176
illiteracy rates 168
inequality 276
RD 173
science 186
scientific output 174, 175
South America 23
South Asia 19, 20, 21, 23, 25, 35, 45
books published 176
education spending 171
RD 172
scientific output 174, 175
Southeast Asia 23
South Korea 28, 47, 172, 175, 176
Soviet Union (USSR)
comparative inequality 28
epidemiological transition 71
European health divide 75, 77, 78
health inequalities 88
health problems 73
scientific publications 174
vital inequality 7, 21, 22
Spain 84
Sri Lanka 168, 176
Stalin, Joseph 248, 251, 252, 256, 260, 288
Storrie, Donald 145
Sudan 175
Sun, Yat-sen, Dr 221
Swaziland 30

Sweden
  comparative inequality 28
  immigration 17
  income shares 34
  income inequality 41
  health trends 62
  knowledge production 165
  life expectancy 5, 76
  mortality statistics 67, 71, 84
  nonstandard work 141, 143
  origins and destinations 126
  part-time employees 156
  RD 172
  scientific output 175
  self-employment 149
  women's income 33
Switzerland 84, 165, 175, 177
Székely, Miguel 3
Szelenyi, Ivan 284
Szreter, Simon 66

Taiwan 28, 29, 47, 130, 175
Takihistan 33
Thailand 47, 80, 172
Therborn, Göran xiii-xviii, 1–58, 178, 314 n17, 320
Thevenot, L. 315 n22
Thompson, E. 315 n38
Tilly, Charles 1–2
Touraine, Alain 300
Townsley, Eleanor 284
Tribalat, Michèle 111 n29
Trinidad Tobago 169, 170
Tunisia 110 n18, 171
Turkey 23, 168, 172, 276

Uganda xiv
Ukraine 71, 79, 80, 81, 172, 276
United Arab Emirates 171, 176
United Kingdom 21, 27, 28, 33, 39, 41, 77, 143, 175, 176
United Nations Educational, Scientific and Cultural Organisation (UNESCO) 163, 164, 176, 184, 187
United Nations (UN), the 35, 46, 50, 184, 187

United States of America (USA)
  class structuration 289–90
  comparative inequality 28, 32
  disposable income 33
  existential inequality 24, 36
  Gini coefficient 30
  health divide 85
  health inequalities 85
  immigration 17, 24
  income differentials 16
  income inequality 39, 40
  income shares 34
  knowledge production 165, 174, 177, 178, 180
  mortality statistics 67
  national income gap 47
  nonstandard work 139–56
  pluralistic political culture 95, 106–7
  racism and slavery 17, 23, 49
  RD 173
  scientific output 174, 175
  segregation 24
  social mobility 120, 124–30, 133
  women's income 33
  see also cultural membership
Uruguay 30, 32, 168
Uzbekistan 171

Vågerö, Denny xiv, 61–85, 320
Venezuela 30, 276
Verba, Sidney 219 n15
Vietnam 39, 176
Virchow, Rudolf 67–8

Walberg, P. 78
Wales 35, 64, 66
Wallerstein, Immanuel 19, 49
Ward, Michael 31, 38
Weingart, Peter 25, 163–90, 321
Wen Tiejun 238
West Africa 25
Western Europe xiv
  circulatory diseases 69
  epidemiological transition 64
  European health divide 75–81
  health inequalities 61
  income inequality 40

mortality rates 85, 88
religion 7
RD expenditure 171
scientific publications 174
social mobility 119
vital inequality 20
women's income 33
Whitehead, M. 65
whooping cough 55
Wilkinson, R. G. 2
women's income 33
women's life expectancy 24

World Health Organization (WHO) xiv, 35, 71–2, 82, 88, 89, 90n
world systems theory 182
Wright, Erik Olin 263, 264, 268

xenophobia 97, 105

Yeltsin, Boris 282
Yugoslavia 28

Zambia 25, 30, 171
Zimbabwe 25, 30, 31, 171